Governing Metropolitan Areas

DISCARD

Interest and research on regionalism has soared in the last decade. Local governments in metropolitan areas and civic organizations are increasingly engaged in cooperative and collaborative public policy efforts to solve problems that stretch across urban centers and their surrounding suburbs. Yet there remains scant attention in textbooks to the issues that arise in trying to address metropolitan governance. *Governing Metropolitan Areas* describes and analyzes structure to understand the "how" and "why" of regionalism in our global age. The book covers governmental institutions and their evolution to governance, but with a continual focus on institutions. David K. Hamilton provides the necessary comprehensive, in-depth description and analysis of how metropolitan areas and governments within metropolitan areas developed, efforts to restructure and combine local governments, and governance within the polycentric urban region.

This second edition is a major revision to update the research and current thinking on regional governance. While the text still provides background on the historical development and growth of urban areas and governments' efforts to accommodate the growth of metropolitan areas, this edition also focuses on current efforts to provide governance through cooperative and collaborative solutions. It also provides information on how regional governance outside the United States has evolved and how other countries are approaching regional governance.

David K. Hamilton is director of the MPA program at Texas Tech University. Current research interests include democracy and efficiency, patronage and human resource management, comparative regional governance, and local government reform. He is co-editor of *Regional Policies for Metropolitan Livability* (2008) and author of *Governing Metropolitan Areas: Response to Growth and Change* (1999). He has published numerous articles on patronage, human resources, and regional topics in leading journals.

Governing Metropolitan Areas
Growth and Change in a Networked Age

Second edition

David K. Hamilton

Routledge
Taylor & Francis Group

NEW YORK AND LONDON

First published 2014
by Routledge
711 Third Avenue, New York, NY 10017

and by Routledge
2 Park Square, Milton Park, Abingdon, Oxon OX14 4RN

Routledge is an imprint of the Taylor & Francis Group, an informa business

© 2014 Taylor & Francis

Library of Congress Cataloging in Publication Data
Hamilton, David K.
 Governing metropolitan areas : response to growth and change / David Hamilton.—Second edition.
  pages cm
 1. Metropolitan government—United States. I. Title.
 JS422.H285 2014
 320.8'50973–dc23   2013043427

ISBN: 978-0-415-89934-5 (hbk)
ISBN: 978-0-415-89935-2 (pbk)
ISBN: 978-0-203-12187-0 (ebk)

Typeset in Bembo
by RefineCatch Limited, Bungay, Suffolk

Contents

Preface

Since the publication of *Governing Metropolitan areas: Response to Growth and Change* in 1999, interest and research on regionalism has significantly increased. There is increasing focus in the college classroom, among practitioners and in society on policy issues relating to regional governance. Courses on regionalism are increasing in political science, public administration, urban studies and sociology curricula at both the undergraduate and graduate level. Local governments in metropolitan areas and civic organizations are increasingly engaged in cooperative and collaborative public policy efforts. Residents in metropolitan areas are becoming more vocal in demanding solutions to regional governance issues.

Metropolitan areas have taken on new significance as the economic engines of the nation. Local governments in metropolitan areas that previously competed with each other are now cooperating with each other and collaborating with civic and private sector leaders in networks. These networks are vehicles that address regional policy issues and are also used to organize competition with other metropolitan areas in the United States and in other countries for development. We have become a networked society on a global scale. Hence the slight change in the title of this edition of the book to reflect the reality of the networked age.

The 1999 edition of the book was a comprehensive, in-depth description and analysis of how metropolitan areas and governments within metropolitan areas developed, efforts to restructure and combine local governments, and governance within the polycentric urban region. This edition follows the same model as the first edition. It updates the literature since the first edition and adds significant material to reflect the new governing directions. While metropolitan areas were experimenting in the 1990s with the concepts of governance as opposed to government structure reform, in the twenty-first century these concepts have been embraced. Governance in a networked society is a major focus of the book and is reflected in a number of the chapters. In addition, a chapter on regional governance in selected metropolitan areas in other countries has been added to reflect the global age in which metropolitan areas compete across national borders for development.

The updated version continues to be a thorough discussion of the historical development of metropolitan areas and the problems and issues in the governance of metropolitan areas. It expands on the framework that I introduced in the first edition to apply in the study of centralized and decentralized local and regional governing systems. This framework is used to categorize and study the various responses to regional governing pressures. The various responses are then analyzed in depth with the focus on cooperative and collaborative approaches to regional governance. The framework provides a basis to clarify and understand these responses to the regional governing pressures. This edition not only updates the current research and thinking on regional government and governance, it provides mini-case studies and examples to illustrate the concepts.

Two opposing forces, one centralizing and the other decentralizing, have interacted to shape political boundaries in urban areas. At various times in our nation's history, each force has been dominant. During most of the nineteenth century, centralized government responses dominated. For most of the twentieth century, decentralized government responses were dominant. In the twenty-first century a new paradigm has emerged. This is a governance response that is based on a decentralized model but in some instances has a centralizing effect and in other instances continues to be a decentralized response. The shift is now how to address regional policy issues, not how to restructure local government. The governing focus is also more inclusive in bringing together both government and nongovernment leaders who can help address regional problems. These various responses to regional governing pressures are analyzed in the book.

As with the first edition, this book serves a number of purposes. It is a text to be used in upper-division undergraduate and graduate courses in political science, sociology, urban studies, and public administration concerned with urban and regional politics and government. It introduces a framework that is useful in the study of regional governing systems. It is also useful to practitioners and others interested in a comprehensive study of local and regional government and governance. It is helpful in understanding the current governing systems in metropolitan areas. In addition, it covers a subject in depth that is usually approached in a fragmented and piecemeal fashion. Finally, it brings together in one place much of the thinking on the subject of regional government and governance.

David K. Hamilton

Acknowledgment

I wish to thank my wife, Caroline, for her patience and support as I engaged in the research and writing of this edition. She made countless suggestions that have vastly improved the book. I, of course, take full responsibility for any errors in the pages that follow.

1 Growth of Urban America

Our metropolitan cities have assumed such gigantic dimensions that the evils of congested population are more and more forcing themselves on public attention.
—Adna F. Weber, 1901[1]

From Rural to Urban

Despite its vast tracts of farmland and uninhabited areas, America is classified as an urban nation (more than 50 percent of the population living in urban areas). Large cities, suburbs, and small towns dot the country. For most of its short existence, America has been classified as a rural nation. Classifications, however, are subject to definitions. The definition of urban has changed a number of times over the course of America's history. Each change in definition reduced the population necessary to be classed as urban. In 1870 urban centers were defined as any municipality with a population of 8,000 or more. In 1880 that figure was reduced to 4,000. In 1900 an incorporated municipality with a population of 2,500 or more was designated as an urban area. In 1950 the concept of urbanized area was adopted to include people living in unincorporated communities. The 1950 definition has remained virtually unchanged, with urban areas defined as all persons living inside and outside urbanized areas in incorporated or unincorporated places with 2,500 or more inhabitants.[2]

America's short urban history has been one of rapid, often spectacular growth. Prior to the War of Independence, only five communities in the United States had populations of 8,000 or more. Only 20 communities were incorporated with self-governing charters.[3] From only 6 percent urban and 33 urban places of 2,500 or more inhabitants in 1800, America's cities grew so rapidly that by 1860, 20 percent of the population consisted of urban dwellers and there were 392 urban places with 2,500 or more inhabitants. From 1820 to 1860, the total population of the country increased by 226 percent while the urban population increased by almost 800 percent.[4] Although this was a period of westward expansion with land for farming available at little cost, urban areas still attracted the most growth. Farming was a hard and uncertain occupation with many physical risks and financial uncertainties. More secure jobs, without the uncertainties of crop failure, were readily available in the cities.

During the later part of this period, America was industrializing at an astonishing pace, and most non-farm jobs were located in areas that rapidly grew into large urban centers. In 1850 New York's population reached the 500,000 mark and became the third largest city in the world.[5] By 1860 Philadelphia was larger than Berlin, and Chicago had exploded from a scruffy little village of 50 people in 1830 to 60,000 people by 1853.[6] New York continued to grow at a phenomenal rate and doubled its population between 1850 and 1880. There were three additional cities of 500,000 or more at that time, yet only 6.2 percent of the population lived in these larger cities.

Between 1880 and 1920, massive numbers of immigrants and farmers, displaced by mechanization, moved to urban areas. This was the period of the greatest percentage of urban growth in America's history. By 1920 America had moved from a rural to an urban nation as more than 50 percent of the population resided in incorporated places with 2,500 or more inhabitants. Also during this period, America had the largest percentage growth in its largest cities. By 1920 there were three cities with over one million population and nine cities with between 500,000 and one million. The percentage of the population living in cities with a population over 500,000 had more than doubled to 15.5 percent.[7]

After 1920, the largest cities continued to grow faster than the nation's population as a whole. Immigrants and people from rural areas continued to crowd into cities looking for jobs. The rural, black population movement to the cities added substantial growth. Between 1940 and 1970, five million blacks left the South to find work in northern and western cities.[8] Fueled by the steady stream of African Americans, urbanization continued, and the percentage of the population living in urban places increased by 1960 to 70 percent. The migrants provided willing workers for the numerous factory jobs and increased the demands on city resources. As urban areas grew, the complexity of providing services also grew. Social and welfare services became a bigger burden on city budgets. Problems with housing and segregation became major issues, and the political and social separation between the central cities and the suburbs became more pronounced.

Since 1960s, urbanization has slowed but continues to inch up. It was just slightly over 75 percent urban by the 1990 census and is listed as just under 81 percent in the 2010 census.[9] The top three urbanized areas have stayed the same since 1950. Note that these are urbanized areas, not cities. Table 1.1 shows the top ten urbanized areas as of the 2010 census. The fastest growing urbanized areas between 2000 and 2010 were in the South and

Table 1.1 Most Populous Urbanized Areas 2010

Urbanized Area	Population	Land Area (square miles)	Density
New York–Newark, NY–NJ–CT	18,351,295	3,450.2	5,318.9
Los Angeles–Long Beach–Anaheim, CA	12,150,996	1,736.0	6,999.3
Chicago, IL–IN	8,608,208	2,442.7	3,524.0
Miami, FL	5,502,379	1,238.6	4,442.4
Philadelphia, PA–NJ–DE–MD	5,441,567	1,981.4	2,746.4
Dallas–Fort Worth–Arlington, TX	5,121,892	1,779.1	2,878.9
Houston, TX	4,944,332	1,660.0	2,978.5
Washington, DC–VA–MD	4,586,770	1,321.7	3,470.3
Atlanta, GA	4,515,419	2,645.4	1,706.9
Boston, MA–NH–RI	4,181,019	1,873.5	2,231.7

Source: 2010 Census Urban Area Facts. http://www.census.gov/geo/www/ua/uafacts.html [Accessed May 2, 2012].

West. Among urbanized areas with populations of one million or more, the Charlotte, N.C.-S.C. area grew at the fastest rate, increasing by 64.6 percent, followed by the Austin, Texas area at 51.1 percent, and Las Vegas-Henderson, Nevada at 43.5 percent. The Charlotte and Austin areas also had the highest rates of land area change, increasing by 70.5 percent and 64.4 percent, respectively.

Of the nation's four census regions, the 2010 census revealed that the West is surprisingly the most urban, with 89.8 percent of its population residing within urban areas, followed by the Northeast, at 85.0 percent. This is surprising because of the perception that the West has substantial wide open spaces and farm areas with people scattered across the landscape. The Midwest and South have lower percentages of urban population than the nation as a whole, with rates of 75.9 and 75.8 respectively. Of the 50 states, California was the most urban, with nearly 95 percent of its population residing within urban areas. New Jersey followed closely with 94.7 percent of its population residing in urban areas; New Jersey has 92.2 percent of its population within urbanized areas of 50,000 or more. The states with the largest urban populations were California (35,373,606), Texas (21,298,039), and Florida (17,139,844). Maine and Vermont were the most rural states, with 61.3 and 61.1 percent of their populations residing in rural areas. States with the largest rural populations were Texas (3,847,522), North Carolina (3,233,727), and Pennsylvania (2,711,092).[10]

While the nation's urbanized areas continued to attract population growing at a 12.1 percent rate from 2000 to 2010, outpacing the nation's overall growth rate of 9.7 percent for the same period, the central cities grew much more slowly. However, nine of the ten most populous cities in 2010

Table 1.2 Population Change for the Ten Most Populous Cities in the United States

Place	Population 2000	Population 2010	Percent Change
New York City, NY	8,008,278	8,175,133	2.1
Los Angeles, CA	3,694,820	3,792,621	2.6
Chicago, IL	2,896,016	2,695,598	−6.9
Houston, TX	1,953,631	2,099,451	7.5
Philadelphia, PA	1,517,550	1,526,006	0.6
Phoenix, AZ	1,321,045	1,445,632	9.4
San Antonio, TX	1,144,646	1,327,407	16.1
San Diego, CA	1,223,400	1,307,402	6.9
Dallas, TX	1,188,580	1,197,816	0.8
San Jose, CA	894,943	945,942	5.7

Source: U.S. Census Bureau, 2010 Census and Census 2000

gained population over the last decade. Chicago, which grew between 1990 and 2000, was the only one of these cities to decline in population. Led by New York, Los Angeles, and Chicago, the six most populous cities kept their same ranks as in 2000. Fourth-ranked Houston surpassed the two million mark during the decade. Of the cities ranked from seventh through tenth, San Antonio moved ahead of San Diego and Dallas. Detroit dropped out of the top ten and was replaced by San Jose, California. See Table 1.2 for the 10 most populous cities. The table also shows the fastest growing cities. All but one is in the Southwest and West and mainly in the states of Texas, California, and Arizona. It is also interesting to note that Texas and California house the majority of the ten largest cities.

The highest percentage of the nation's population living in cities of 500,000 or more was reached in 1950 at 17.6 percent. Since that time, the percentage has gradually declined, even though the number of cities has increased. It reached a low of 12.1 percent by 1990 but has since rebounded to 12.9 percent. Even while the percentage of the population living in cities over 5,000,000 declined, between 1950 and 1970, the number of cities in this category increased from 18 to 26. However, between 1970 and 1990, the number of cities in this category decreased by three. This occurred even though the number of cities with over one million population increased from five to eight. Reflecting the out migration from the older, larger central cities to the suburbs, Denver, Kansas City, Pittsburgh, and St. Louis, major urban centers of the late nineteenth and early twentieth centuries, lost population and fell to under 500,000 by 1980, New Orleans's population dipped below 500,000 by 1990, and Cleveland's population was reduced to 493,000 by 1994. Regional population shifts reflected job opportunities in the South and West as San Jose, California, became the newest member of the "over 500,000 club" by 1980, Seattle and El Paso attained a population of over 500,000 by the 1990 census, and Nashville-Davidson County and Austin grew to over 500,000 by 1994.[11]

However, the continual movement to urbanized areas continued and many cities that were under 500,000 in the 1990 census grew through the population shifts and the large immigrant influx. From 1990 to 2010 large cities mainly in the South and West but also in the Midwest grew, and a new peak of 29 cities over 500,000 population was reached by 2000 and 33 by 2010.[12] The large numbers of foreign immigrants to the cities also contributed to their growth. Generally, older large cities based on industrial-era manufacturing are either losing population or are growing quite slowly, whereas newer cities with economies based on new technology, parti-cularly those located in the West and South, are experiencing phenomenal growth. These figures reflect a continued concentration of population into urban areas. Table 1.3 shows the growth of cities and percent of US population from 1950 to 2010.

Table 1.3 Growth of U.S. Cities over 500,000 Population

	1950	1960	1970	1980	1990	2000	2010
Cities over 1 Million	5	5	6[a]	6	8[b]	9[c]	9
Cities 500,000 to 1 Million	13	16	20	16	15	20	24
% Population in Cities 500,000 or More	17.6	15.9	15.6	12.5	12.1	12.7	12.9
% Population in Cities over 1 Million	11.5	9.8	9.2	7.7	8.0	8.1	7.6[d]
% Population in Cities 500,000 to 1 Million	6.1	6.1	6.4	4.8	4.1	4.6	5.2[d]

Sources: U.S. Bureau of the Census, *Historical Statistics of the United States: Colonial Times to 1970*, part 1 (Washington, DC: U.S. Government Printing Office, 1975), pp. 43–46; U.S. Bureau of the Census, *Statistical Abstract of the United States 1997 and 2012* (Washington, DC: U.S. Government Printing Office, 1997), pp. 43–46; Info Please, htrtp://www.usinfoplease.com/ipa [Accessed May 11, 2012].

Notes:
[a] Houston became the sixth largest city.
[b] Dallas and San Diego became the seventh and eighth largest cities.
[c] The population in Phoenix and San Antonio climbed to over 1 million, but Detroit fell to 951,000.
[d] Makes total to 12.9 because of rounding.

Defining Metropolitan

The federal government's definition overstates the extent of urbanization or the urban condition of the United States, because a town of 2,500 has little in common with a city of 100,000. Just as there are major differences between a town of 2,500 and a city of 100,000, there are major differences between an isolated city of 100,000 and a city of 100,000 that is part of a large urban complex consisting of many municipalities. The term *metropolitan* is used to designate urban agglomerations composed of at least one large city and several smaller cities and towns joined together by geography and economics. While it took the nation over 100 years to move from mostly rural to mostly urban, it has taken only a few decades to move from mostly urban to mostly metropolitan. The change has had as dramatic an impact on the nation as the move from rural to urban.

The first systematic attempt to collect data on the metropolitan population was in the 1910 census with metropolitan districts defined for cities with populations of 200,000 or more and contiguous minor civil divisions which met certain rules of proximity and population density. In 1949 metropolitan areas were redefined as any county containing a city or twin cities with a combined population of at least 50,000. Contiguous counties were included if they were socially and economically integrated with the central county. They were named standard metropolitan areas. The term was changed to standard metropolitan statistical area (SMSA) in 1959 and to metropolitan statistical area (MSA) in 1983. In accordance with the definition for the 1980 and 1990 censuses there were two types of areas: (1) Metropolitan Statistical Areas and (2) Consolidated Metropolitan Statistical Areas that consisted of more than one Primary Metropolitan Statistical Area. The terms "Consolidated Metropolitan Statistical Area" and "Primary Metropolitan Statistical Area" are now obsolete. Under the 2000 standards, "Metropolitan Statistical Area" and "Micropolitan Statistical Area" are the terms used for the basic set of county-based areas. In addition, the term "Metropolitan Division" refers to a county or group of counties within a Metropolitan Statistical Area that has a population core of at least 2.5 million. While a Metropolitan Division is a subdivision of a larger Metropolitan Statistical Area, it often functions as a distinct social, economic, and cultural area within the larger region. For comparison purposes, a Metropolitan Division would generally be analogous to the old Primary Metropolitan Statistical Area.

The Office of Management and Budget (OMB), which defines and designates which urbanized areas are metropolitan, has introduced the term "Core-Based Statistical Areas" (CBSA) to define and delineate metropolitan and micropolitan statistical areas. A CBSA is a geographic entity associated with at least one core of 10,000 or more population, plus adjacent territory that has a high degree of social and economic integration with the core as measured by commuting ties. The standards designate and delineate two categories of CBSAs: metropolitan statistical areas and micropolitan statistical areas. A metropolitan statistical area is a core-based statistical area associated with at least one urbanized area that has a population of at least 50,000. The metropolitan statistical area comprises the central county or counties containing the core, plus adjacent outlying counties having a high degree of social and economic integration with the central county or counties as measured through commuting. A micropolitan statistical area is a core-based statistical area associated with at least one urban cluster that has a population of at least 10,000, but less than 50,000. The micropolitan statistical area comprises the central county or counties containing the core, plus adjacent outlying counties having a high degree of social and economic integration with the central county or counties as measured through commuting patterns. A metropolitan division is defined as above. Cities and towns are used in New England instead of counties. OMB has also introduced the term "Combined Statistical Area." This designation is to recognize ties between contiguous metropolitan and/or micropolitan statistical areas, but the ties are not significant or intense enough to combine them into one CBSA.[13]

Figure 1.1 shows a map of the state of Texas that shows the various statistical subdivisions. Figure 1.2 shows the metropolitan and micropolitan statistical census designated areas in the United States. The micropolitan areas are lighter and the metropolitan areas are the darker areas.

The definition of metropolitan area is significant because it categorizes and defines these areas for statistical data gathering, analyzing, information dissemination, and grant distribution by federal government agencies. There are at least two problems with this definition in terms of revealing the real extent of the urban condition. First, the entire county is included in the definition. There are a number of large counties included in metropolitan-designated areas, particularly in the West, that have substantial rural population. To mitigate this problem, the Census Bureau added other terms for which it publishes data. An urban cluster is a statistical geographic entity consisting of densely settled census tracts and blocks and adjacent densely settled territory that together contain at least 2,500 people. For purposes of delineating core-based statistical areas, only those urban clusters of 10,000 or more population are considered. An urbanized area is a statistical geographic entity consisting of densely settled census tracts and blocks and adjacent densely settled territory that together contain at least 50,000 people.[14]

Notice that these terms do not connote incorporated places. This designation provides a way to differentiate highly developed territory from rural and less densely populated areas. Even with this refinement, however, it is not realistic to compare all or part of a MSA with many municipalities and millions of inhabitants to one with one or two municipalities and 200,000 residents. The vast differences in the complexities of addressing governance issues and providing public services that have an impact beyond political boundaries make such comparisons meaningless.

The second problem is that changes in the definition of metropolitan areas result in data that are not comparable over time. For example,

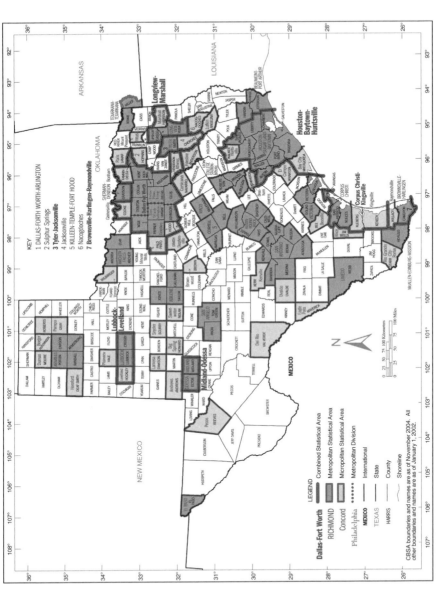

Figure 1.1 State of Texas Designated Statistical Areas, 2004

Source: http://www2.census.gov/geo/maps/metroarea/stcbsa_pg/Nov2004/cbsa2004_TX.pdf [Accessed November 10, 2013].

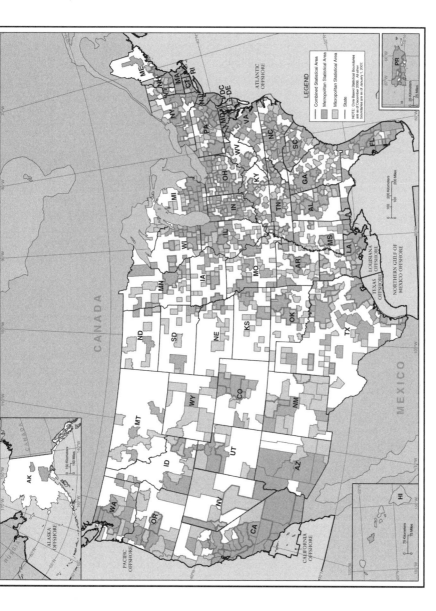

Figure 1.2 Metropolitan and Micropolitan Designated Areas in the United States, 2007

Source: http://www.census.gov/econ/census07/pdf/maps/united_states/natl_cbsa.pdf [Accessed May 15, 2013].

metropolitan division is not compatible with the former PMSA, and micro-politan does not equate to any previous definition. This tends to negate any advantage that may have been derived in developing a definition to differen-tiate larger from smaller metropolitan areas. With the changes, the numbers of metropolitan areas have fluctuated widely. There also have been changes in what is included in the definition producing uncertainty in the data and non-comparable data with previous censuses. This makes it impossible to accurately reflect historical trends using current definitions. The Census Bureau has attempted to adjust for this to some extent by giving comparable figures in some tables from old definitions, but this is confusing and sporadic. Given the wide fluctuations, one questions the overall usefulness of the various designations. One must, therefore, be cautious in interpreting data. Despite the problems, there is at least consistency among federal agencies in gathering and reporting data resulting in a wealth of information, much more than for nonmetropolitan areas. Finally, cities in metropolitan areas are advantaged because they receive relatively more community development funds than nonmetropolitan cities.

From Urban to Metropolitan

Although it took the United States 130 years to progress from a rural to an urban nation, it was only 40 years from the Census Bureau's first effort to define metropolitan in 1910 and 30 years from its designation as an urban nation to the time when over 50 percent of the population lived in areas designated as metropolitan. Table 1.4 shows the growth from urban to metropolitan. Even though the percentage of people living in cities of 500,000 or over declined between 1950 and 1990 before rebounding slightly (see Table 1.3), the percentage of people living in metropolitan areas has continued to increase, indicating the outmigration of people from the central cities to the suburbs and the continued movement of people from farms and farming communities to urban areas. As indicated above, census-designated metropolitan areas are county-based areas. Some counties included in metro-politan designated areas cover substantial territory, particularly western counties. For example, the Riverside-San Bernardino-Ontario metropolitan area covers a good part of southern California almost from the coast to the border with Nevada.

As Figures 1.1 and 1.2 show, large sections of the country are designated as metropolitan and micropolitan. As areas grow in population and meet the criteria, the entire county is included in the statistical designation. Statistics include rural population living in counties designated as metropolitan. Indeed, the percentage of metropolitan population classified as rural increases as the number of metropolitan areas increase. For example, 12 percent of the population designated as metropolitan was actually rural in 1970, which percent increased in 1990 to 13.7.[15] In 1970, 30 percent of the U.S. rural

Table 1.4 U.S. Population Growth from Urban to Metropolitan

Year	Population % Urban	Population % Metro	Number of Metro Areas
1940	56.5	47.8	140[a]
1950	64.0	56.1	168[b]
1960	69.9	62.9	212[b]
1970	73.6	68.6	243[b]
1980	73.7	74.8	318[b]
1990	75.2[d]	79.5	324[c]
2000	79	80.3	362
2010	80.7	83.7	366

Sources: U.S. Bureau of the Census, *The Growth of Metropolitan Districts in the United States: 1900–1940* (Washington, DC: U.S. Government Printing Office, 1947), pp. 5–11; U.S. Bureau of the Census, *Historical Statistics of the United States: Colonial Times to 1970*, part 1 (Washington, DC: U.S. Government Printing Office, 1975), p. 11; U.S. Bureau of the Census, *Statistical Abstract of the United States* (Washington, DC: U.S. Government Printing Office, 1953 and 1995), pp. 20, 43. U.S. Census Bureau. American Factfinder. http://factfinder2.census.gov/faces/tableservices/jsf/pages [Accessed May 15, 2012].

Notes:
[a] Metropolitan districts as defined by the Census Bureau in 1940.
[b] Metropolitan areas as defined by the Census Bureau in 1950, 1960, 1970, and 1980 as SMSAs.
[c] Metropolitan areas defined by the Census Bureau as MSAs and PMSAs. The number does not include MSAs and PMSAs in Puerto Rico. The number is as of July 1, 1994.
[d] With the change of definition of urban for the 2000 census to include all urban population whether living in incorporated places or not, the percent urban in 1990 would have been 78.

population was included in metropolitan areas and in 1990 the numbers increased to 42.9 percent.[16] Table 1.4 shows how we continue to crowd into metropolitan areas. It indicates that metropolitan areas are the economic engines of the nation. Despite the obvious inconsistency of including rural in metropolitan, it is clear that 83.7 percent of the population in America lives in metropolitan areas and has fairly easy access to the urban amenities offered by the MAs. Moreover, while enjoying the amenities of urban life, the rural population in an MA experiences to a lesser degree the disadvantages of urban life, such as crime, pollution, and other problems of density.

As the population grows, it continues to shift to the South and the West. In the last few decades, just as the major growth in large central cities occurred in the South and West, so did the major metropolitan growth. The 2010 census showed that metro areas grew almost twice as fast as micro areas, 10.8 percent compared to 5.9 percent. Population growth of at least twice the national rate occurred in many metro and micro areas, such as some areas in parts of California, Nevada, Arizona, Texas, Florida, and the Carolinas. All ten of the most populous metro areas in 2010 grew over the decade, with Houston, Atlanta, and Dallas-Fort Worth (26.1 percent, 24.0 percent, and 23.4 percent, respectively) the fastest-growing among them. Among all 366 metro areas, Palm Coast, FL, was the fastest-growing between 2000 and

Table 1.5 Population Change in Metropolitan Areas[a]

	U.S.
1950 Central City Population % of MA	58.5
1960 Central City Population % of MA	51.4
1970 Central City Population % of MA	45.8
1980 Central City Population % of MA	40.9
1990 Central City Population % of MA	39.5
2000 Central City Population % of MA	33.5

Sources: U.S. Bureau of the Census, *Historical Statistics of the United States: Colonial Times to 1970*, part 1 (Washington, DC: U.S. Government Printing Office, 1975), p. 39; U.S. Bureau of the Census, *1990 Census of Population and Housing Supplementary Reports* (Washington, DC: U.S. Government Printing Office, 1993), Table 1. 2000 census. American factfinder. http://factfinder2.census.gov/faces/tableservices [Accessed May, 20, 2012].

Note:
[a] 2010 census data not available at the time of writing.

2010 (up 92.0 percent), followed by St. George, UT, (up 52.9 percent), followed by three other areas with population growth rates over 40.0 percent: Las Vegas, Raleigh, and Cape Coral-Ft. Myers, FL.[17]

Table 1.5 shows the percentage population shifts between the central cities and the suburbs from 1950 to 2000. In 1950 the central cities clearly dominated the MA as almost 70 percent of the metropolitan population lived in central cities. By 2000 the central cities no longer dominated the MA as the share of central city population to the total MA population slipped below one third. At the time of writing, the 2010 census figures were not available, but from the growth of population in central cities that took place between 2000 and 2010, this decline might be stabilizing. Moreover, as more places are added to the list of metropolitan areas, they tend to be more recently settled areas with central cities containing a larger share of the population of these MSAs, which counteracts the trend of movement of population from older large central cities to the suburbs.

Characteristics of a Typical Metropolitan Area

There is no such thing as a typical metropolitan area in America. Metropolitan areas vary by the number of government units and by the number of residents. Most metropolitan areas, however, contain a large and growing number of governmental units with the major growth occurring in special-purpose governments. The Census Bureau reports that the number of general-purpose municipal governments in the United States grew from 18,000 in 1962 to 19,492 in 2007, a growth of 7.2 percent.[18] Growing much faster than general-purpose municipalities, special-purpose authorities and districts increased from 18,323 in 1962 to 37,381 in 2007, not counting

Table 1.6 Additions of Municipalities and Special Districts Inside and Outside
Metropolitan Areas

	% Change 1977–82	% Change 1987–92	% Change 1977–92
Municipal Additions Inside MAs	1.4	0.8	8.0
Municipal Additions Outside MAs	1.0	0.2	1.6
Special District Additions Inside MAs	10.2	7.8	38.0
Special District Additions Outside MAs	10.1	7.0	36.7

Source: Compiled by the author from: U.S. Bureau of the Census, *Census of Governments*, vol. 1 (Washington, DC: U.S. Government Printing Office, 1977, 1982, 1992).

school districts, for a growth of 104 percent. Many of the governments are located within metropolitan areas. Available data on addition of all govern-ments indicate that the addition of governmental units inside metropolitan areas is greater than outside metropolitan areas.

Table 1.6 shows the difference in addition of municipalities and special districts between 1977 and 1992. Some of the differential could be the addi-tion of a number of metropolitan areas. However, addition of metropolitan areas would not explain the total differential. For all three time periods investigated, there was a greater percentage increase in creation of general-purpose governments and special districts inside than outside metropolitan areas. It would seem logical that the increase of metropolitan population and changes in delivery of services could be readily accommodated within the existing government structure through annexation and adjusting boundaries and services of special districts. The data indicate, however, that this is not the case; fragmentation of governments in metropolitan areas continues and grows at a faster rate than in nonmetropolitan areas.

Table 1.7 provides some idea of the complexities of governing in this highly fragmented government system. Over 40 percent of the general purpose local governments are now in metropolitan areas. With little over one-third of the counties, metropolitan areas house almost 50 percent of the municipal governments. The large numbers of local governments result in an extensive overlay of governments. Numerous special districts, each providing its own function and with its own separate boundaries, overlap other special districts and general-purpose governments. Municipalities in metropolitan areas are often developed border to border, and the only way to tell when one travels from one municipality to another is by the street signs.

The extent of local government fragmentation varies among metropolitan areas. The average MA has over 100 local governments. Of these, 40 are special districts, 24 are municipalities, 19 are independent school districts, 16 are townships, and 2 are counties. Chicago is the most fragmented MA, with almost 1,200 governments having taxing authority, 574 general-purpose governments, and 623 special districts including independent school

Table 1.7 Number of General Purpose Local Governments in Metropolitan Areas, by Type

	Total in U.S.		Number in MAs		% Total in Metro Areas	
	1992	*2007*	*1992*	*2007*	*1992*	*2007*
General Purpose Local Governments	38,975	39,044	33,004	16,151	38.8	41.7
Municipalities	19,279	19,492	7,590	9,279	39.4	47.6
Townships	16,656	16,519	5,067	5,802	30.4	35.1
Counties	3,043	3,033	740	1,087	24.3	35.8

Source: U.S. Bureau of the Census, *1992 Census of Governments: Government Organization*, vol. 1 (Washington, DC: U.S. Government Printing Office, 1994), p. 39, 2007 Census of Government, Census Bureau Report on Metropolitan Populations, http://www.census.gov/govs/cog/govorgtabl355.html [Accessed May 23, 2012].

districts (362 if independent school districts are excluded). This compares to the Anchorage and Honolulu MSAs, each with one taxing body. There are 19 MAs with no special districts (81 if independent school districts are excluded). Even though the Chicago area has the most local governments, Allegheny County, the central county of the Pittsburgh MSA, has the largest number of governments compared to the size of the population. It has 2.23 governments per 10,000 population compared to St. Louis County, Missouri, with 1.55, and Cook County of the Chicago MA with 0.98.[19]

Comparing just general purpose governments, Table 1.8 indicates the 10 most fragmented metropolitan statistical areas. New York leads with 590 units, which includes 23 counties, 188 towns or townships and 379 municipalities. Chicago is not far behind. The table also shows the population rank. Notice that there is no rhyme or reason to the number of governments in a metropolitan area. It is not dependent on geographical size or number of residents. There is no magic number of governments needed in an MA for it to function effectively. It is strictly a matter of local preference and historical development. The fact that the Chicago MA is dotted with more municipal governments than Honolulu and Anchorage is not evidence that the local government needs of Chicago MA residents are being better provided for. Likewise, the variation in the number of special districts is an indication that services across the MA can be provided with few or no special districts.

Not only do most urban areas have a multiplicity of governments, they exhibit a substantial unevenness in levels of prosperity across the urban landscape. There are pockets of affluence and growth and areas of poverty and decline. The disparities between the areas of affluence and the areas of poverty tend to be moving farther apart. Government fragmentation exacerbates the disparities through political boundaries that separate areas

Table 1.8 Metropolitan Statistical Areas with the Most General Purpose
Governmental Units: 2000

Metro Area	Pop	Total Pop	Governmental Units				
	Rank	000	Rank	Total	Counties	Townships	Municipalities
New York	1	18,323	1	590	23	188	379
Chicago	3	9,099	2	574	14	212	348
Pittsburgh	20	2,431	3	466	7	202	257
St. Louis	18	2,699	4	401	16	107	278
Philadelphia	4	5,687	5	388	11	210	167
Minneapolis	16	2,969	6	345	13	137	195
Kansas City	26	1,836	7	282	15	93	174
Cincinnati	24	2,010	8	259	15	97	147
Columbus	31	1,613	9	231	8	135	88
Detroit	9	4,453	10	217	6	100	111

Source: U.S. Census Bureau, Table 2a. Population in Metropolitan and Micropolitan
Statistical Areas and Their Geographic Components in Alphabetical Order and Numerical
and Percent Change for the United States and Puerto Rico: 1990 and 2000, http://
www.census.gov/population/www/cen2000/briefs/phc-t29/index.html [Accessed January
27, 2012].

with resources from areas with needs. Generally, suburbs are more affluent
than the central cities, but pockets of deep poverty are evident in both the
central city and the suburbs. Poor people in cities are more than four times
as likely to live in concentrated poverty as their suburban counterparts
(census tracts with 40 percent or more of the residents with incomes below
the official poverty level).[20] Residential segregation of minorities is glaring
in its visibility in metropolitan areas, and the concentration of minorities
in central cities has increased over the years. Unemployment rates are
significantly higher in the central cities than in their suburbs. Employment
opportunities are shifting from the central cities to the suburbs in increasing
numbers. There is a significant relationship between political fragmentation
and the degree of job decentralization. In metropolitan areas with many
political units, firms are more likely to locate far from the city center.[21] (See
Chapter 2 for a more thorough discussion of poverty, unemployment, and
racial segregation in metropolitan areas.)

Local Government Organization in America

The basic system of local government established in the late eighteenth and
early nineteenth centuries involved counties, municipalities, and, in some
states, townships. In addition, special-purpose districts, most notably school
districts, were authorized. Each class of local government was assigned
functions largely unique to it with little or no overlapping of functions with

other units of local government. In New England, counties were not established and townships and municipalities were the basic functioning units of general-purpose government.

Counties provided certain state administrative functions such as conducting elections, recording and preserving legal documents, and providing state judicial services. They also provided minimal municipal services in unincorporated rural areas such as building and maintaining roads, and keeping the peace. Townships, where they existed, were artificial subdivisions assigned minimal duties by the state. These were responsibilities otherwise provided by the county, such as real estate tax assessment, road maintenance functions, and certain kinds of assistance to the poor.

Municipalities were the basic self-governing units. They were established by petition to the state when enough people were living together in close proximity to form a viable community for self-governing purposes. These municipalities performed local services to meet the needs of the community such as fire protection, law enforcement, public works, and sanitation. Each municipality was largely self-sufficient in its economic, social, and governmental activities. The hinterland around the municipality was usually rural, undeveloped land, and the nearest municipality often was miles away.

School districts were generally the only special districts overlying the municipalities. These special districts were established to bring a single focus and revenue source to a critical local public function. It was also deemed important to free them from the politics of other local governments. School districts were kept small because the means of transportation–horse or foot–limited travel. Occasionally, communities established other nonschool special districts. For example, a nonschool special district was operating in Philadelphia in 1790, but there were few of these.[22]

Every state developed its own local government traditions. Generally, the original colonies served as a model for other states as they developed. The example of Illinois illustrates how local government developed. From its ratification as a state in 1818 until 1850, Illinois followed the Virginia model. The entire state was subdivided into counties. These counties provided services and served as the administrative arm of the state in carrying out state functions. In 1850, at the insistence of the large influx of northeastern settlers who were familiar with township government, the state added townships as an option. These governing bodies sorted out their duties and, with little overlap, carried out the basic functions of taxation, law enforcement, building roads, running schools, holding elections, and so on. For example, schools were organized at the township or municipal level, elections at the county level, and each government had road and taxation responsibilities.

Every Illinois municipal incorporation until 1870 was granted by special act of the legislature upon petition by residents from the geographical area seeking incorporation. The incorporation provided self-governing powers within state laws and allowed residents to develop and determine types and levels of local government services. After the 1870 constitutional convention, incorporations were granted pursuant to a general incorporation law; the legislature was not required to act on each incorporation request. The general incorporation law allowed Illinois three forms of incorporated government: the city, the village, and the township. The city was an urban settlement, the village a rural settlement. Townships were a combination of rural and urban settlements. The incorporated township was generally not satisfactory, as three were annexed to Chicago by majority vote of the township residents by 1900.[23]

America's System Compared to Other Countries

Even though the United States' cultural and political heritage stems from England, it evolved much differently. Sociologist Roland Liebert argues that the self-governing powers of the colonial cities and their relative autonomy and independence were not unlike those of English cities of the time.[24] After America won its independence, it continued to borrow heavily from English thought and traditions as the nation developed. The nation also borrowed heavily elsewhere, particularly from French political philosophy. In all cases, however, America tailored European thought and culture so that the political systems and traditions that evolved took on a distinctly American form. Local government developed in a decentralized federal system that stressed the rights of the individual and the value of small-scale governments with substantial authority. Thus, local government in America has been much more independent and autonomous than local governments in other countries.

The political structure and cultural traditions in the United States have resulted in a substantially different government system than in Canada or Great Britain. In Great Britain's unitary system, authority over local government is centralized in the national government. Efficiency is the major value that has dominated local government debate in Great Britain. These arguments were important in the reform of the London government in the 1960s and local government reforms in the rest of the country in the 1970s. The result of the reform was fewer and larger governments. While the number of local governments in America continues to increase, the number in the United Kingdom has decreased. For instance, between 1972 and 1987 the number of local governments increased in the United States by 33 percent while decreasing in the United Kingdom by 71 percent.[25] In Canada, efficiency has also been a major consideration in local government debate, and structural changes have been made in efforts to enhance efficiency.

America was the isolated exception in major industrialized countries as European countries were also caught up in the efficiency movement. Countries such as Sweden, Denmark, and Germany substantially restructured their local governments. In each case, the restructuring was imposed by the central or provincial government and involved the consolidation of municipalities. Dramatic changes occurred in Sweden, where the number of municipalities was reduced from around 2,500 in 1950 to less than 300 by 1980.[26] Germany reduced the number of local governments from 24,444 in 1965 to 3,417 in 1982. In one German state the number of local governments was reduced from 2,690 in 1967 to 426 by 1980 through a series of statutory and voluntary actions. Before the municipal reforms, more than 70 percent of German municipalities had fewer than 1,000 residents. Most municipal administrations now have populations of over 10,000.[27]

In contrast, the efficiency arguments and optimum size of government debates of the 1960s had little impact on restructuring general-purpose local governments in the United States. Thus, the cultural and political traditions in the United States resulted in a local government system that averages 12,000 people for each local government while England, America's cultural and governmental progenitor, has an average population of 120,000 for each unit of local government.[28] Both Great Britain and Canada continue to adjust their local government structure, ostensibly to improve efficiency. They introduced two-tier governments in their larger urban areas in the 1960s and 1970s. Then in the 1990s, they eliminated most of the two-tier systems in favor of a unitary structure. The elimination of the upper tier continues in Great Britain, while it appears to have ceased in Canada. Great Britain eliminated upper-tier governments in seven regions in 2009 and eliminated 35 local governments in the process.[29] (See Chapter 11 for a more in-depth discussion on regional governance outside the United States.)

Influences in the Development of the Local Government System

Control and Self-Governance

To better understand responses to growth in urban areas, it is helpful to consider the motivations for the establishment of the numerous local governments. The antecedents to the current local government structure go back to colonial times. A major purpose for colonial local government was to control what happened inside the town borders. Sociologist Roland Liebert maintains that colonial towns were "internally autonomous, inclusive, and self-governing urban centers."[30] They had broad powers to regulate commerce and urban development. This power included authority to establish and promote markets, license crafts, require trade to be conducted in the urban center, control ports, and so forth. The hope of the British authorities was to provide maximum autonomy for towns, with the intent that the powers would be used to coordinate and stimulate commerce which would benefit British business interests.

Self-government to control what occurred in the community was extremely important in colonial times and became even more important with the suburban movement. Many suburbs incorporated to maintain the exclusive nature of their communities. In the late 1800s, a number of suburban municipalities incorporated strictly to ban the establishment of saloons and the sale of liquor. For instance, Arlington Heights, Illinois, incorporated in 1887 to keep the town dry; Evanston resisted annexation to Chicago at least partially because its citizens wanted to keep liquor establishments out of the community.[31] In the twentieth century, many communities incorporated to establish barriers to exclude minorities. (Incorporation to avoid annexation is further discussed in Chapter 2.)

Service Provision

Another major reason for establishing local governments is to provide services. Until about the middle of the nineteenth century, most urban areas were small, and there was not much pressure for collective provision of services. In colonial and frontier communities, such functions as water supply, waste disposal, and fire protection were attended to by households themselves or by private companies. Few streets were paved. The police force typically consisted of the night watch with a standby citizen militia that handled more serious threats to public order. Communities took some responsibility for the poor, the physically impaired, orphans, and widows, but the care usually was minimal and provided without elaborate formal structure. Generally, such public concerns were addressed through individual or collective private action. Government established the legal framework for private behavior but provided few services.[32]

The local government, however, had the power and responsibility to provide functions as they became public. Indeed, Liebert argues that early cities were like city-states in their self-governing powers. They provided basically all the governmental functions within their borders because there were no other governmental units at the time providing local services. He claims that the history of U.S. cities has not been one of devolution of powers and functions on local governments but just the opposite. Starting from a position of autonomy and self-control over functions, municipalities have lost control to regional or state agencies. There has been a gradual centralization of functions as society urbanized and became more complex.

As commerce grew and expanded, local control and protection were not enough because contracts in one place often were not recognized in another. The state had to establish uniform regulations, and the county became the locus of administration. By the time of the Revolutionary War, most judicial functions including the maintenance of legal records and the administration of elections had become state functions, with counties acting as the administrative agencies of the state. In some instances, narrowly construed police courts and specialized trial courts were kept within the city jurisdiction.[33] In areas where there was a strong tradition of local government, where the function had been previously performed by the local jurisdiction, and where the city was large enough to have political clout, the local government often retained some authority over functions that otherwise went to the state or county level. For example, the southern colonies did not have strong traditions of local self-government, giving the county a much stronger local government role than in the northern colonies. Also, major cities outside the colonies with extensive control over patterns of commerce and trade tended to successfully resist county control and its administrative overlay. The result was often either a city–county consolidation, such as occurred in New Orleans and San Francisco, or a city–county separation, such as occurred in St. Louis.

In most instances, residents looked first to local governments to provide public services as the services became necessary or feasible with population growth and technological advances. Social, health, and safety issues fueled considerable local government service expansion. Dense urban populations and industrial activity required more extensive physical infrastructure. Paved streets and bridges were more efficiently built and maintained by the local government. The pollution or exhaustion of nearby groundwater supplies required the construction of dams, aqueducts, and water lines which–for reasons of cost, planning, and public health–favored government operation or regulation. Rising volumes of residential and industrial waste required the construction of sewers, establishment of sanitation and public health codes, and regulation of plumbing. Fire suppression gradually became a government function because the failure to suppress a fire in any structure posed a danger to entire neighborhoods or the whole city. Police forces expanded to manage congestion and to contend with the unrest that resulted from widening class, economic, and ethnic differences. State and local governments sometimes initiated or supported such economic ventures as canals, railroads, highways, and port facilities that no private firm or consortium of private interests was willing or able to undertake on its own.[34]

Government assumption of new or private functions accelerated with technological advances and the pressures resulting from urbanization. For example, municipal water systems started to be provided in the 1830s and municipal lighting and railway systems in the late 1800s.[35] Once the service became a public responsibility, it was not always provided by the municipal government. Often, a special district was created to provide the service. An example of this is the provision of public education. Initially, education was provided privately or through a system of neighborhood voluntary schools. By the mid-nineteenth century the concept of compulsory education under the auspices of the government had been accepted throughout the country. The professional educators also advocated the establishment of nonpolitical districts as the best system of delivering this service.This became the accepted method of delivery and was generally adopted except in those northeastern cities that had already established a voluntary neighborhood school system under the jurisdiction of the city. These cities retained control of education.[36] Education was the first government function to make extensive use of special districts, establishing a model for the delivery of new functions as they became feasible. Existing functions with an already established pattern of service delivery were generally not subject to special district provision. The basic control and police functions are examples of established functions not subject to special district provision.

In unincorporated areas, municipal-type functions either were not provided or only minimally provided by the state through its administrative subdivisions of the county and township. Therefore, it was not unusual for residents in unincorporated areas with service concerns to seek either incorporation or annexation to a nearby municipality. Developers also encouraged and supported incorporation, annexation, or, alternatively, the establishment of special districts to obtain services to their property. Municipal services enhanced the value of their development and drew homebuyers from the city who were accustomed to, or were seeking, a certain level of services.There were a variety of different options provided by developers in unincorporated areas. Some simply laid out streets. Others built houses with the necessary connections for indoor lighting and plumbing. Obviously, the value of their development was enhanced by train access for commuters into the city or the location of business in the area to provide jobs for the residents.

Indeed, in the late nineteenth century, provision of services became a major reason for incorporation. Developers needed an organized municipality to provide services to make their subdivisions more attractive. They would install the infrastructure in the subdivision but needed to hook into water and sewer systems. Organized governments were needed to maintain the roads the developers built and to provide educational services. Counties and townships were not authorized to provide a complete array of municipal services. Suburban residents demanded services not simply for reasons of comfort; their health and safety required it. As population increased in outlying areas, problems associated with the central city appeared in the suburban subdivisions. Crime and civil disturbances, increased threats of disease due to inadequate water or sewer systems multiplied, and streets and sidewalks became impassable in rainy or snowy weather. Residents turned to government and either incorporated or sought annexation in order to receive the needed services.

Residents in unincorporated areas were generally willing to incorporate or be annexed to the city and pay the additional taxes associated with the costs of basic municipal services. Indeed, annexation to the large city was often sought either to receive the services or to obtain them more cheaply than could be provided by a small community because of scale economies. When basic services benefitting from scale economies started to be provided through regional districts and authorities, however, there was less incentive to join the large city. In fact, the high tax rates in the city often were a disincentive. Smaller municipalities could provide basic services to their residents using a combination of local government and district or authority provision and keep a relatively low tax rate. More recently, contracting out to other local governments or to the private sector has been used to take advantage of economies of scale.

City Taxes

Taxes and the social and political problems of the city were incentives for many communities to incorporate in order to escape annexation. Many residents moved outside the city to avoid paying for city services they could not afford. Keating, referring to early settlements outside Chicago, writes that those who moved into many suburban developments willingly gave up the city's luxuries and comforts for lower living costs. One Swedish immigrant in a suburban development stated: "When I came here, I did not expect to have city improvements. When they did come after annexation they came slowly and were considered as a matter of course."[37]

Higher city taxes often resulted from the higher expenditures due to the central city's growing concentration of poor people. This was increasingly evident with local government's involvement in the Great Society programs of the 1960s. These federally-subsidized redistributive programs vastly increased the array of social and welfare services available through local governments. Since most federal grant programs required some sort of local fiscal effort, the result was massive state and local tax increases. This increase was not uniform throughout the metropolitan area. The cities with high-cost citizens had the most social programs and, therefore, the greater portion of city budgets devoted to these social programs. As services increased, tax considerations became a more important motivator to incorporate to avoid annexation to the central city.[38]

Philosophical and Social Influences

Philosophical and social influences generally favored small, independent governments. The philosophical champion of America's local government system was Thomas Jefferson. His concern for direct democracy and individual participation provided a theoretical basis for early American municipal government. He advocated a system of small local governments where every citizen could attend municipal meetings and be an active participant in governance. Jefferson championed the New England town as the perfect manifestation of the sovereignty of the individual. Allocation of local government functions also followed the Jeffersonian ideal. He felt that each local government should be independent and autonomous. The local government would perform the bulk of government functions with units of government farther removed becoming progressively less involved.[39]

In addition to philosophical support for small towns, there has been a strong anti-city bias in American intellectual thought. Anti-urbanism in America even pre-dates the development of large cities. Jefferson, obviously looking at the large cities of Europe, wrote that large cities were "pestilential to the morals, the health, and the liberties of man." Henry David Thoreau, Henry James, and other writers of the nineteenth century wrote about the evils, unhealthiness, pollution, and ugliness of the cities. They extolled the virtues of rural life.[40] One urbanist observed:

The most important roots of anti-urbanism lie in the large commercial cities - New York, Philadelphia, Boston - of the eighteenth century that forged the links between themselves, an expanding countryside, and other nations. The anti-urban story is about the introduction in these cities of values and practices antithetical to those held and followed by people living in rural areas. The commercial world substituted cash transactions between strangers for personal relationships. A complex division of labor and businesses formed to facilitate trade based upon agriculture and the natural resources of the countryside. Rural values were quite the opposite: bartering, interpersonal respect, and self-sufficiency dominated. That rural farmers would subsequently feel alienated from and exploited by cities comes as no surprise, and it is only a short journey from that feeling to a broader condemnation.[41]

Anti-city rhetoric also had strong religious overtones. The evangelical movement in England that started in the early 1700s as a renewed emphasis on personal salvation took on an anti-city bias in the latter part of the 1700s with its focus on the role of the family and women. In this movement the city—with its worldly temptations—became the chief enemy of the family. Because women were the guardians and nurturers of religious values in the home, they were not to be exposed to the evils of the city. The evangelical movement, therefore, called for the separation of work and living space and the removal of the family from the city to a new form of suburban living.[42] Social and traditional values also encourage a small, autonomous system of local governments. The German sociologist Max Weber stated there was a special bonding and sense of community when citizens could be autonomous and exercise power over their governmental affairs. Take away their autonomy over governmental powers in the community, and the communal nature and sense of identity within the community begin to dissipate.[43] The German sociologist Ferdinand Tönnies used the term *Gemeinschaft* to express this sense of identification with community. *Gemeinschaft*-like relationships are based on natural desires that include sentiment, tradition, and common bonds as governing forces. These types of relationships appear typically in small, self-contained units such as extended families, close-knit religious communities, or rural villages. Tönnies described the large city as the antithesis of *Gemeinschaft*. It is a place where economic, or *Gesellschaft*-type, relationships predominate. These relationships are based on urban, industrial capitalism. They are rational, impersonal, and oriented to financial dealings. *Gesellschaft* is characterized by little or no emotional identification with the community, affective neutrality, legalism, and segmental conceptions of other members of the community.[44]

According to the concept of *Gemeinschaft,* human beings are attracted to a community of people with whom they have something in common. They desire to be part of a close-knit group of people with similar values and characteristics with whom they can develop emotional ties and have intimate face-to-face relationships. Moreover, this community of people, or *Gemeinschaft*, has spatial as well as social dimensions. Members of the extended family or those with similar religious, ethnic, socioeconomic, or racial identification, often seek to live in close proximity to one another. This spatial dimension is expressed in the urban setting as small neighborhoods or independent, exclusive communities of people with shared interests. These groups seek to control and perpetuate their own kind of community and resist any change that would jeopardize the exclusivity of their *Gemeinschaft*.[45]

Economic Considerations in Growth of Metropolitan Areas

Despite the sociological forces fostering small, decentralized, self-contained communities, economic forces brought people in ever-increasing numbers together in urban areas. Industrialization brought about the factory system, replacing the small-scale industry that previously existed. Pre-industrial means of production did not require large numbers of workers because places of production were small, often located in the family home as cottage industry, or in small factories next to fast-moving streams. The production was usually consumed locally. As trade increased, merchants would contract work to several families located in the area. Although the cities were the centers of commerce, trade, government, and finance, the actual work of production was scattered about the countryside. Historian Robert Fishman gives an example of the cotton industry in Manchester, England:

> Manchester had been traditionally a center for textile merchants who supplied home workers in the agricultural districts of Lancashire with materials for spinning and weaving and then collected the yarn or cloth, finished it, and sold it. The new popularity of cotton goods in the mid

eighteenth century vastly increased the volume of business for these merchants; and the mechanization of spinning put Manchester at the heart of the world's first industrialized region. Yet, the factory system did not come to Manchester until the 1790s, when the steam engine made it possible to move the factories from their original power source–fast running rural streams–into the cities.[46]

With industrialization, large machines were able to do what previously had been done by hand or in small factories. Steam power made it possible to establish factories in the cities where the support facilities had always been located. Bringing together factories and support facilities concentrated economic opportunities in the cities, thus attracting more and more people. As more people were drawn to the city in search of jobs, more jobs were created to service the needs of the expanding population. The result was a massive urbanization brought about by industrialization. Before industrialization, London was the largest city in the world in 1800, with slightly less than one million inhabitants; Paris reached one million by 1850.[47]

In America in 1840, only New York and Philadelphia had as many as 125,000 residents. The typical urban worker was employed in a business with fewer than a dozen people. By 1890, however, the United States had become the leading industrialized nation in the world, with factories employing hundreds and sometimes thousands of workers. New York was closing in on London for largest city honors, with 2.5 million inhabitants. Chicago and Philadelphia each contained approximately one million people. The cities of Minneapolis, Denver, Seattle, San Francisco, and Atlanta, which hardly existed in 1840, had become major regional metropolises.[48]

With industrialization came technological advancements that made it possible for factories to expand, skyscrapers to be built, and new industries to develop. All these advancements brought more people to the cities. New technology also made it possible to decentralize within the metropolitan area. The streetcar and, later, the automobile allowed workers to live farther away from the work site. Communications advances made it possible for businesses to locate different functions in separate facilities. Components of a business were able to locate for competitive or financial advantages. A downtown headquarters location might be chosen to be close to sources of financing, and production facilities might be placed in the South to take advantage of low-wage employees, or in the suburbs for access to less expensive land to utilize advances in manufacturing technology that require more horizontal space.

Moreover, the economic conditions that once favored the development of high-density, central cities moderated. Economic activity in many older cities was often related to proximity to a natural resource that provided the site with a comparative advantage over other locations. Often this was a river or a body of water that facilitated the transportation of commerce and then led to other economic advantages that encouraged clustering of the labor force. Today, economic activity is often associated more with concentrations of capital and human skills than with natural resource endowments. Both capital and labor are significantly more mobile than natural resources. Economic activity no longer needs to be concentrated at a central place. Instead, development has become multimodal, with pockets of economic activity located throughout a metropolitan region. This has permitted specialized economic centers to emerge in proximity to each other but spread over a larger geographic area.[49] With the decentralization of population and economic activity, cities and suburban communities grew until their borders touched, and suburban municipalities multiplied until they ringed the central city, often two, three, or four layers deep. The originally established system of local government where a community's boundaries contained most of the residential and economic development of the area was no longer the norm.

Political Considerations in Growth of Metropolitan Areas

Professor Anthony Orum contends that political institutions in America initially are slow to respond to and accommodate rapid growth. Indeed, governments in pregrowth cities usually rely extensively on volunteer and part-time personnel to provide municipal services. During the growth stage, the political institutions begin to develop, but they lag behind the economic development of the area. As entrepreneurs attract new economic development and population to fill the jobs, political institutions become more important in governing the affairs of the developing city. The growing tax base and service needs propel the city to professionalize its workforce and expand its bureaucracy to meet the growing needs of the city. As the city matures, the government becomes more active in controlling city affairs. It assumes the major role in promoting the growth and economic health of the city and seeks to expand its dominance by annexing suburban growth. City services expand beyond basic governmental services to provide for the diverse social needs of its population. It is during this period that socioeconomic differences between the city and suburbs become distinct, and barriers develop between the city and the suburbs. The suburbs resist all efforts at annexation or other efforts to involve them in the affairs of the city. It is in this stage that central cities experience decline even while their suburbs continue to prosper.

Professor Orum describes the industrial city of Milwaukee as an example of a major city's decline:

> There are both extra-local and local forces that precipitate the decline. The first stage ... began during the course of the Great Depression ... Labor strikes divided the city deeply, setting employer and worker against one another. Individual enterprises began to depart the city,

seeking to secure higher profits in places where there were neither labor unions nor high local taxes. Moreover, municipal government became reshaped in important respects. Certain needs . . . such as health care and other such benefits, now were shifted to both county and federal governments. The net effect was to leave local government as primarily responsible for securing order in the city, rather than also providing for the welfare of local residents. By 1950 . . . the city began to decay both in visible material ways and in terms of its own institutions. Downtown properties became old and worn-out. As properties declined, so, too, did the revenues that municipal government could secure, thereby setting into motion a long period of dwindling resources. More and more local enterprises also began to leave the city, seeking to secure profits more easily elsewhere.[50]

Orum suggests that postindustrial cities will not necessarily suffer the decline experienced by industrial-era cities. Besides having an economic foundation of high-tech and service enterprises that more readily adapts to changing economic conditions, postindustrial cities are generally geographically larger and are not surrounded by incorporated suburbs. They are thus more dominant and better able to respond to population and economic growth in the region than older, more spatially restricted cities. Finally, political relationships between the central city and the suburbs in newer cities are generally not as divisive as in older industrial cities.[51]

Framework for the Study of Regionalism

As can be seen from the above discussion, the local government system was established in a pre-industrial time, to meet the needs of a rural environment. As the country urbanized and new technologies became available, the local government system has been under pressure to respond to the needs that result from a more complex urban environment and take advantage of the opportunities that technological advances bring. The purpose of this research is to investigate the question: As urban areas develop and respond to growth and change in the urban environment, how do the responses affect the governing system? Two types of basic political responses to urban develop-ment have influenced the governmental organization of urban areas. One response is to foster a centralized governing system in the pursuit of efficiency. The other response is a political response, which is to attempt to maintain the current decentralized system that was established in the pre-industrial, rural environment and make marginal accommodations to meet the needs of a more technologically advanced urban environment.

Decentralization responses are categorized as those responses that create or foster a polycentric local government system of small, independent, local governments and numerous regional special districts in metropolitan areas. Centralization responses are those that encourage consolidation of political structures under one or only a few local governments. Another variation of centralization responses is substantial centralized control and coordination over regional functions or extensive cooperation among governments and collaboration with the nongovernmental sector in addressing regional governance issues.

These centralization and decentralization responses were largely complementary during the early years of the development of the United States. Municipalities, when first established, were small and encompassed most, if not all, of the developed area. There may have been nearby communities, but they were independent and somewhat isolated because of the travel difficulties and the rural nature of the country. As the nation became more populated, small municipalities grew into larger cities by increasing their density and expanding their boundaries. For most of the nineteenth century, centralization dominated despite a political and social system that had firmly planted decentralized, rural values in the American psyche. Since the Civil War, these two responses to urban growth have become increasingly competitive instead of complementary. Starting in the late nineteenth century, decentralized values became paramount as evidenced by the proliferation of governments in urban areas and their successful resistance to regional governmental reform.

Some researchers have proposed frameworks and classifications to aid in understanding why some metropolitan areas exhibit more regionalism than others. Professors H.V. Savitch and Ronald Vogel place metropolitan areas on a continuum according to the amount of structural consolidation and the extent of their regional relationships. On one end of the continuum is comprehensive adjustment typified by single-tier city–county consolidation or two-tier metropolitan government. In the middle is mutual adjustment typified by interlocal agreements and public–private partnerships. These arrangements rely on existing agencies or networks of actors to achieve coordination in the area. On the other end of the continuum is a negative response to regional pressures typified by noncooperation, avoidance, and conflict. Savitch and Vogel identify the Jacksonville-Duval County consolidation as an example of a single-tier approach; the Twin Cities, Portland, and Miami as examples of the two-tier approach; Washington, D.C., and Pittsburgh as examples of mutual adjustment; and New York, Los Angeles, and St. Louis as examples of efforts to maintain and perpetuate the decentralized status quo.[52]

A problem with this classification system is that the categories are too broad. It combines both structural consolidation and regional relationships (governance) in the same continuum. There is no differentiation between structure and governance. Partially consolidated or federated areas may exhibit many of the same regional governance problems as decentralized areas. Savitch and Vogel admit to this problem when they wonder how to categorize a two-tier government that through politics and population expansion has become increasingly similar to a conflict-ridden polycentric government structure.[53] For example, one could argue that regional relationships in the Miami area are not much different than in the Los Angeles region even though Miami is classified as a regional two-tier federation at one end of the continuum, and Los Angeles is classified as a non cooperative polycentric system at the other end of the continuum. There are also perception differences as St. Louis, an example of the most conflict-ridden system according to their categorization, has been identified by others as being a model of extensive interregional cooperation.[54]

A framework is proposed that goes beyond a simple structural centralization–decentralization division to look at regionalism and autonomy not only in relation to government structure but relative to a functional or governance system. This is a process framework that incorporates past influences and responses in an attempt to understand present regionalism and predict future directions. It is argued that previous influences and responses establish a general direction that influences and informs present responses to regional initiatives. Although specific past influences may be more or less of a factor in current responses, they should nonetheless be considered. Also, the basic local government structure has experienced very few dramatic changes since the beginning of the twentieth century. Any changes in structure tend to be made at the margin and are evolutionary in nature. Knowledge of the nature and extent of the influences and past responses to regionalism pressures is important in the study and understanding of current responses.

The process model is depicted in Figure 1.3. The condition that starts the process is some change, such as population growth or economic change that affects a substantial part of the region. This change creates or exacerbates one or more problems, such as the effects of sprawl, central city deterioration, congestion, pollution, concentration of poverty, providing municipal services to developing areas, and so on. The interactions of various influences determine the response to the issue. These influences either promote regionalism and cooperation or independence and autonomy. The range of responses is also a function of the legal parameters established by the state. Depending upon the result of the response, the governing system may become more centralized or decentralized. The resulting configuration informs the metropolitan condition which potentially encourages another regional iteration. This, then, becomes a dynamic process with the regional influences vying with anti-regional influences that may at some point lead to another response and effect, and another iteration. Depending upon the metropolitan area, the process may be continual or may take place very seldom.

The responses are those fostering a regional, cooperative governing system and those fostering an independent and autonomous governing

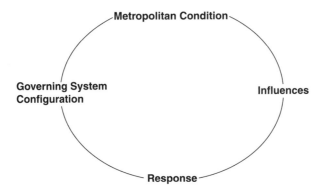

Figure 1.3 The Process of Change in Governing Systems

system. Independent and autonomous responses create or promote a polycentric system of small, independent local governments or numerous regional special districts in metropolitan areas. One variation of regional responses is to promote the establishment of only one or a few political structures. Another variation is substantial centralized control and coordination over regional functions or extensive cooperation among governments and collaboration with the nongovernmental sector in addressing regional governance issues.

Influences on Regional Outcomes

There are a number of factors that influence how metropolitan areas respond to population and economic change. Influences can promote regional approaches, autonomy and independence, or both. As there are a number of conflicting influences at work at any given time, the perceived or actual severity of the impact of the change coupled with the type, interaction, and relative strength of the various influences determine the response. Different metropolitan areas react to influences in different ways. There are a number of potential responses and variables that influence the direction of the response. Influences at various times may promote regionalism and at other times may promote independence. For example, the federal government and many states currently encourage a regional approach in metropolitan areas. Previously, federal and most state policies fostered a polycentric approach to organizing government. Moreover, some influences may promote both regionalism and autonomy at the same time. An example is service provision with some services more efficiently and effectively produced on a regional level and some on a decentralized basis.

Influences in each metropolitan area vary according to a number of factors. Foster identified a number of influences which she called impulses. She postulated that these impulses impact regional responses

Table 1.9 Regional Influences

Influences	Centralizing	Decentralizing
State and Federal Policies	X	X
Active Civic Sector	X	
Business Leaders and Media	X	
Philosophical and Social		X
Self-Determination		X
Developers		X
Service Provision	X	X
Taxes		X
Reform Movement	X	
Economic Development	X	X

either negatively or positively. That is, these influences either promote regionalism or independence and autonomy. Following her pioneering work and based on my own research and additional research of the literature on regionalism, I have identified ten major influences that promote regionalism or autonomy. Table 1.9 lists the major influences and whether they promote regionalism, autonomy or have promoted both at different times.[55]

Government Responses to the Influences

Government structure is narrowly defined for categorization purposes as general-purpose local governments–cities, towns, and municipalities responsible for provision of local government services to residents. The term *governance* is not concerned with government structure per se but with government processes and functions. Governance is a functional and issue-oriented approach to addressing problems of a regional nature. It includes functional arrangements for provision of services, how regional policy issues are addressed, and the extent and processes of regional cooperation. The governance dimension is used to categorize whether the responses to growth pressures in terms of processes, the provision of services, and the addressing of regional issues promote centralization or decentralization. The structural dimension is used to categorize the responses to growth pressures as to whether they promote the establishment of a polycentric or a centralized government system in the metropolitan area. By differentiating governance and government structure, one is able to study the interrelationships between the extent of governmental structure fragmentation and the extent of regional governance in a metropolitan area. It can serve as a mechanism to categorize, study, and relate responses to each other to aid in analyzing and understanding the regionalism movement. The unifying theme is that all efforts to accommodate growth and change in metropolitan areas can be studied in the context of this framework.

The framework, then, consists of two categories of centralization and two categories of decentralization responses. Centralizing responses simplify government structure and governance by reducing duplication and by promoting the establishment of processes to address regional problems. These responses are actions that:

- Absorb adjacent, developed, unincorporated areas into already established, incorporated governments,
- Reduce the numbers of governments,
- Consolidate a number of functions in only a few governments, or
- Promote regional cooperation on a broad scale through mechanisms or processes to address regional issues.

Decentralized structural responses are those that promote a polycentric system of government with political control in metropolitan areas vested in a multiplicity of small general-purpose governments. Decentralized governance responses are limited accommodations to protect and allow this polycentric system of small general-purpose governments to retain their independence and autonomy. Decentralized responses would include centralizing certain functions in regional single-purpose districts as necessary to take advantage of economies of scale, if this did not jeopardize the basic autonomy of the local governments. Lifestyle functions that differentiate communities would be reserved for the individual municipality, while basic services would be subject to centralization. Decentralization responses, therefore, seek to maintain the status quo, with adjustments only as necessary to provide basic services on a regional basis.

The categories and the particular ways metropolitan areas have responded to growth pressures are indicated in Table 1.10.

Decentralized government structure responses. The initial basic response to growth pressures is suburban development. As suburbs develop, there are pressures on the state government to provide mechanisms whereby these communities can become self-governing. One decentralized response is the authorization of different forms of general-purpose local governments. Through this response, small communities can obtain self-governing powers essentially similar to those of larger cities and do not need to become part of the city to obtain municipal services. Structural decentralization responses may also entail the passage of general incorporation legislation that provides communities with relatively easy incorporation requirements and removes incorporation from the politics of the state legislature.

Centralized government structure responses. The major response is annexation by the city as growth occurs beyond its borders. When annexation is no longer feasible, the structural response recommended by reformers

Table 1.10 Response to Metropolitan Growth and Change

	Government Structure	*Governance*
Centralization Responses	Annexation and merger City–county consolidation Multi-tier metropolitan government	Urban county Consolidation of functions Regional governance processes Regional tax sharing Multipurpose metropolitan districts Regional coordinating agencies Federal and state grants and policies encouraging regionalism
Decentralization Responses	New forms of general-purpose local governments in suburbs Easy incorporation laws Local resident voting requirements	Single-purpose districts Interlocal agreements Privatization of functions Federal and state grants and policies supporting fragmentation Regional councils with no authority Collaboration with NGOs and cooperation with other governments Neighborhood government in central cities

is city–county consolidation or a two-tier metropolitan form of government. City–county consolidation or metropolitan government was the major advocated response from the early twentieth century through the 1960s for industrial-era growth cities. It was also a response in the 1990s for a few postindustrial growth areas, although annexation was still the major structural response.

Decentralized governance responses. The major concern of the responses in this category is the delivery of services. Responses vary depending upon the state and federal policies. Decentralized governance responses are promoted by state and federal grants and policies supporting decentralization. Responses in this category are usually designed to reduce costs to individual municipalities in the delivery of basic services, such as roads, sewers, water, and so on, by transferring these functions to a regional entity. This could include interlocal agreements between governments for the provision of services, privatization of services, cooperation among governments or the establishment of regional single-purpose districts. The establishment of regional councils without authority to mandate regional solutions is another manifestation of responses in this category. Decentralized governance responses became the dominant form of response in the post-World War II period.

Centralized governance responses. Centralized governance responses involve major changes in service delivery and metropolitan governance without affecting political boundaries. Responses in this category include multi-purpose metropolitan regional districts, agencies to coordinate regional services, regional tax revenue sharing, and development of the urban county. Cooperation among local governments and public–private collaboration could be in both centralized and decentralized governance responses depending on the extent of the cooperation and collaboration. If it leads to extensive, institutionalized cooperation and collaboration in solving policy issues and providing extensive services, it would be characterized as centralized governance responses. Otherwise, it would be categorized as decentralized responses. State and federal policies encouraging regionalism have a major impact on responses in this category. Relatively few metropolitan areas have experimented with centralized governance responses. Various responses in this group, however, have gained increased support among regionalists, particularly since the 1990s as a general solution for metropolitan governance problems.[56]

Besides the influences described earlier in this chapter, the responses to growth, as embodied in the four categories, have been heavily influenced by politicians, academics, and community activists. Those who would reform the system advocate the centralized responses, while others support the decentralized system with many independent municipal governments voluntarily networking with one another and making accommodations as necessary to provide regional services. In most metropolitan areas the decentralized governance approach predominates, although there is substantial variety in the extent of decentralization and centralization. Responses to population and economic pressures determine the configuration of governance in the region. The result of the chosen response, given the particular issues, either fosters or encourages centralization or it makes it possible to maintain an independent, decentralized government system.

Responses to population and economic change vary by metropolitan area and by the period that the major growth occurs. Responses during the industrial period tended to be different from responses during the post-industrial period. Growth areas in the postindustrial period developed under different federal and state policies and different technological conditions. These growing areas were able to simultaneously pursue a number of options that were not available to the urban areas of the nineteenth century. Different variables and conditions that are factors in the responses to population growth and change include (1) the number of general-purpose governments in the area, (2) the dominance of the central city, (3) state and federal policies supporting centralization and decentralization, and (4) the involvement in community affairs of the private and civic infrastructure as the area experiences growth. Moreover, past experiences of older metropolitan areas provide examples informing responses. Most urban growth areas, as they grow and develop, have experiences with a number of responses in each category. For example, most metropolitan areas have central cities that have been involved in annexation programs; many have made attempts at major structural reform such as city–county consolidations or some form of metropolitan government; special districts and regional councils have been established to provide specific regional services and comply with federal regulations on the distribution of funds; and there is increasing interest in cooperation among governments and collaboration with the nongovernmental sector to address regional issues.

Approach of the Book to the Study of Regional Governing Systems

For the remainder of the study, changes in regional relationships are referred to as reform. This is in keeping with the general use of this term in the local government literature. Reform generally has a connotation of improving a condition. In the context of this study, reform is defined as a value-neutral term. That is, it is applied in this study of regionalism, not to imply that the change or attempted change is better than what was before, but simply as a way to easily identify a change effort. The terms *regional, metropolitan,* and *area-wide* are used interchangeably to refer to an urbanized geographical area with a central city or cities and the suburbs tied together economically. Within the context of this study, regionalism is the way in which metropolitan areas respond to growth, configure local government structure, and address governance of the region.

The remainder of the book approaches the study of regional governing systems as follows: Chapter 2 provides a current perspective on many of the policy issues that create regional pressures. Subsequent chapters analyze the various responses and ways that local governance is provided in metropolitan areas. In Chapter 3 the suburbanization movement, a decentralized structural response to growth, and annexation, the initial structural response to suburbanization, are analyzed. Chapter 4 considers centralized government structural reform through the city–county con-solidation and metropolitan government movements. State and federal policies influencing the configuration of metropolitan areas are covered in Chapter 5. This chapter analyzes how state and federal policies affected and are still impacting the structural configuration and responses to growth in metropolitan areas.

Institutional accommodation to provide governance in polycentric metropolitan areas is the subject of Chapters 6 and 7. The subject of Chapter 6 is institutional arrangements to provide services in decentralized areas. The major accommodation to provide regional services is the special district approach. This chapter also analyzes the academic debate surrounding decentralization, particularly public choice theory, which is the major support for decentralized government. Finally, the neighborhood movement, an even more decentralized governance movement, is analyzed in this chapter.

Chapter 7 continues the discussion on providing services in decentralized metropolitan areas. It analyzes the intergovernmental cooperation movement and contracting of services. This chapter covers interlocal agreements, the Lakewood plan, and regional councils. In Chapter 8 the county, long championed by those advocating more centralized government, is discussed. The county home rule movement, or lack thereof, is a major focus of this chapter. Although the county has not been a major focus in the regional governance movement, it is recognized and championed as a potential force in regionalism. Few counties have reached the point where they are major providers of municipal-type services. In this sense, it is more akin to decentralized governance accommodation than it is to centralized government response.

Chapter 9 covers unique approaches to regional governance. The approaches are institutional entities that are somewhat similar to regional special districts discussed in Chapter 6 but provide a stronger regional governance impact. There are few regions that have these hybrid entities. Three case studies of regions with these hybrid entities are analyzed in this chapter. Each one is uniquely different, but each one provides a stronger regional governance presence than the standard regional special district. Another unique approach to regionalism covered in this chapter is fiscal regionalism. This is an approach used in a few metropolitan areas to share revenue among governments in the region for such purposes as reducing fiscal disparities among municipalities, economic development, and supporting regional assets.

In Chapter 10 collaborative regional governance is examined. Collaborative governance goes beyond cooperative governance to include the involvement of nongovernmental entities. This chapter deals with the involvement of the private and nonprofit sectors in governing the region. This approach to regionalism rests on the assumption that major forces other than political leaders and public administrators have a major influence on government public policy and implementation. Urban regime analysis is a major theory supporting this approach to regional governance. This collaborative governance concept has been called "new regionalism." This chapter discusses the elements that facilitate effective collaborative regional governance. Case studies of collaboration in selected metropolitan areas are provided and analyzed in the chapter.

Chapter 11 provides a brief look at regional governance in selected areas outside the United States. Regional governance is not just an issue in the United States. The major countries where regionalism is examined are in Europe and Canada. The focus on European countries is because these countries had a major influence on government structure in other countries during the Colonial period. Much of the influence remains, although local customs have mitigated it to varying degrees. Given the globalizing economy, it is important to understand how other countries have responded to regional governance pressures in the competition with other regions for economic development. Finally, Chapter 12 looks into the crystal ball and considers the future of regionalism in a global society. In our globalizing world, traditional governance is giving way to new forms and methods. Regional governance is here to stay. The form regionalism takes will differ according to a number of factors that are discussed in the chapter.

Notes

1. Adna F. Weber, "Growth of the Cities of the United States: 1890–1990," *Municipal Affairs*, 5 (June 1901): 375, quoted in Robert A. Beauregard, *Voices of Decline: The Postwar Fate of US Cities* (Cambridge, MA: Blackwell Publishers, 1993), p. 65.
2. George Thomas Kurian, *Dataphedia of the United States 1790–2000* (Lanham, MD: Bernan Press, 1994), p. 3.
3. Alexander B. Callow Jr., (ed.), *American Urban History: An Interpretative Reader with Commentaries* (New York: Oxford University Press, 1982), p. 65.
4. Samuel Humes IV, *Local Governance and National Power: A Worldwide Comparison of Tradition and Change in Local Government* (London: Harvester Wheatsheaf, 1991), p. 123.
5. U.S. Bureau of the Census, *Historical Statistics of the United States: Colonial Times to 1970*, Part 1 (Washington, DC: U.S. Government Printing Office, 1975), p. 11; Callow, *American Urban History*, p. 65.
6. Callow, *American Urban History*, p. 65.
7. U.S. Bureau of the Census, *Historical Statistics of the United States: Colonial Times to 1970*, p. 11.
8. Jan Crawford Greenburg, "A New South Lures Blacks from North," *Chicago Tribune*, Aug. 1, 1996, sec. 1, p. 1.
9. 2010 *Census Urban Area Facts*. http://www.census.gov/geo/www/ua/uafacts.html [Accessed May 2, 2012].
10. Ibid.
11. U.S. Bureau of the Census, *Statistical Abstract of the United States: 1981*, 101st ed. (Washington, DC: U.S. Government Printing Office, 1981), pp. 21–23; U.S. Bureau of the Census, *Statistical Abstract of the United States: 1991*, 111th ed. (Washington, DC: U.S. Government Printing Office, 1991), pp. 34–36.
12. *The 2012 Statistical Abstract Population* http://www.census.gov/compendia/statab/cats/population.html [Accessed May 3, 2012].
13. *Federal Register*, Monday, June 28, 2010, Part IV Office of Management and Budget 2010 Standards for Delineating Metropolitan and Micropolitan Statistical Areas. http://www.whitehouse.gov/sitestwo/default/files/omb/assets/fedreg_2010/06282010_metro_standards-Complete.pdf [Accessed May 10, 2012].
14. Ibid.
15. U.S. Bureau of the Census, *Historical Statistics of the United States: Colonial Times to 1970*, p. 6.
16. U.S. Bureau of the Census, *1990 Census of Population*, Metropolitan Areas, sec. 1 (Washington, DC: U.S. Government Printing Office, 1990), table 1.

17. Paul Mackun and Steven Wilson, *Population Distribution and Change: 2000 to 2010 Census Briefs* (Washington, DC: U.S. Bureau of the Census, March 2011).
18. U.S. Bureau of the Census, *Census of Governments*, vol. 1 (Washington, DC: U.S. Government Printing Office, 1987, 1992), pp. vi, 109.
19. Michael A. Nelson, "Decentralization of the Subnational Public Sector: An Empirical Analysis of the Determinants of Local Government Structure in Metropolitan Areas in the U.S.," *Southern Economic Journal*, 57 (October) (1990) 445; Advisory Commission on Intergovernmental Relations, *Metropolitan Organization: The Allegheny County Case* (Washington, DC: U.S. Government Printing Office, 1992), p. 5.
20. *The Re-Emergence of Concentrated Poverty: Metropolitan Trends in the 2000s*, Brookings Institution, Nov. 3, 2011, http://www.brookings.edu/research/papers/2011/11/03-poverty-kneebone-nadeau-berube [Accessed May 30, 2012].
21. Edward L. Glaeser, Matthew Kahn, and Chenghuan Chu, *Job Sprawl: Employment Location in U.S. Metropolitan Areas* (Washington, DC: The Brookings Institution, Center on Urban & Metropolitan Policy, July 2001), http://www.brookings.edu/es/urban/publications/glaeserjobsprawl.pdf [Accessed May 30, 2012].
22. John C. Bollens and Henry J. Schmandt, *The Metropolis: Its People, Politics, and Economic Life*, 3rd ed. (New York: Harper and Row, 1975), p. 49.
23. Chicago was incorporated in 1833, reincorporated in 1837 as a city, overlaid with three townships in 1850, reincorporated in 1875 under the general incorporation law, and it abolished its townships in 1905. Ann Durkin Keating, *Building Chicago: Suburban Developers and the Creation of a Divided Metropolis* (Columbus, OH: Ohio State University Press, 1988), pp. 199–203.
24. Roland J. Liebert, *Disintegration and Political Action: The Changing Functions of City Governments in America* (New York: Academic Press, 1976), p. 39.
25. L. J. Sharpe, "The Future of Metropolitan Government," in L. J. Sharpe, (ed.), *The Government of World Cities: The Future of the Metro Model* (Chichester, England: John Wiley and Sons, 1995), p. 12.
26. Nelson, "Decentralization of the Subnational Public Sector," p. 443.
27. Humes, *Local Governance and National Power*, p. 59.
28. H. Wolman and M. Goldsmith, *Urban Politics and Policy* (Cambridge, MA: Blackwell, 1992), pp. 9–10.
29. *Local government structure*. http://www.direct.gov.uk/en/governmentcitizensandrights/ukgovernment/localgovernment/dg_073310 [Accessed May 30, 2012].
30. Liebert, *Disintegration and Political Action*, p. 38.
31. Keating, *Building Chicago*, p. 90. Also see Louis P. Cain, "To Annex or Not? A Tale of Two Towns," *Explorations in Economic History*, 20 (January) (1983): 69–70.
32. R. Scott Fosler and Renee A. Berger, "Public-Private Partnership: An Overview," in R. Scott Fosler and Renee A. Berger, (eds.), *Public-Private Partnership in American Cities: Seven Case Studies* (Lexington, MA: D. C. Heath, 1982), p. 2.
33. Liebert, *Disintegration and Political Action*, pp. 41–44.
34. Fosler and Berger, "Public-Private Partnership," p. 2.
35. Nancy Burns, *The Formation of American Local Governments: Private Values in Public Institutions* (New York: Oxford University Press, 1994), pp. 47–48.
36. Liebert, *Disintegration and Political Action*, pp. 45–46.
37. Keating, *Building Chicago*, p. 61.
38. Burns, *The Formation of American Local Governments*, p. 62.
39. Gregory Weiher, *The Fractured Metropolis: Political Fragmentation and Metropolitan Segregation* (Albany: State University of New York Press, 1991), p. 2; Harold

Wolman, "Local Government Institutions and Democratic Governance," in David Judge, Gerry Stoker, and Harold Wolman, (eds.), *Theories of Urban Politics* (Thousand Oaks, CA: Sage Publications, 1995), p. 136.

40. Kenneth T. Jackson, *Crabgrass Frontier: The Suburbanization of the United States* (New York: Oxford University Press, 1985), pp. 68–69.

41. Beauregard, *Voices of Decline*, p. 14.

42. Robert Fishman, *Bourgeois Utopias: The Rise and Fall of Suburbia* (New York: Basic Books, 1987), pp. 32–53.

43. Max Weber, *The City* (Glance, IL: Free Press, 1958), pp. 87–96.

44. Larry Lyon, *The Community in Urban Society* (Chicago, IL: Dorsey Press, 1987), p. 7.

45. Philip Kasinitz, (ed.), *Metropolis: Center and Symbol of Our Times* (New York: New York University Press, 1995), pp. 163–167.

46. Fishman, *Bourgeois Utopias*, p. 78.

47. Ibid., pp. 18, 107.

48. Jackson, *Crabgrass Frontier*, p. 47.

49. Richard Matoon, "Issues in Governance Structure for Metropolitan Areas," Paper presented at Midwestern Metropolitan Areas: Performance and Policy workshop sponsored by the Federal Reserve Bank of Chicago, Nov. 28, 1995, p. 3.

50. Anthony M. Orum, *City-Building in America* (Boulder, CO: Westview Press, 1995), pp. 195–196.

51. Ibid., p. 198.

52. H. V. Savitch and Ronald K. Vogel, "Introduction: Regional Patterns in a Post-City Age," in H. V. Savitch and Ronald K. Vogel, (eds.), *Regional Politics: America in a Post-City Age*, Urban Affairs Annual Reviews (Thousand Oaks, CA: Sage Publications, 1996), p. 13.

53. Ibid.

54. R. Parks and R. Oakerson, "Comparative Metropolitan Organization: Service Production and Governance Structures in St. Louis, MO, and Allegheny County, PA," *Publius*, 23 (Winter) (1993), 19–30.

55. Foster, Kathryn A., "Regional Impulses," *Journal of Urban Affairs*, 19 (4) (1997), pp. 375–403.

56. See, for example, Anthony Downs, *New Visions for Metropolitan America* (Washington, DC: Brookings Institution, 1994); Neal Peirce, *Citistates* (Washington, DC: Seven Locks Press, 1993); David Rusk, *Cities Without Suburbs* (Baltimore, MO: Johns Hopkins University Press, 1993); Allan D. Wallis, "Governance and the Civic Infrastructure of Metropolitan Regions," *National Civic Review*, 82 (Spring) (1993): 125–137; and Allan D. Wallis, "The Third Wave: Current Trends in Regional Governance," *National Civic Review*, 83 (Summer/Fall) (1994): 290–310.

2 Public Policy Issues and Regional Governance

We will neglect our cities to our peril, for in neglecting them we neglect the nation.
—John F. Kennedy, statement to Congress, January 30, 1962

Not long ago we became accustomed to the constant rhetorical drumbeat of the crisis of our cities . . . but I believe that we have made sufficient progress in recent years that fears of doom are no longer justified.
—Richard M. Nixon, State of the Union Address, 1973[1]

The Regional Governance Problem

The traditional local governing structure of most countries does not contemplate a metropolitan-scale government. As was shown in Chapter 1, the local government system was established to meet the needs of more rural, isolated communities. Communities provided limited services and were quite autonomous and independent. As countries industrialized, they also urbanized. Urbanization brought increased demand for community services. Technological changes also provided additional opportunities and demands for new and improved local governmental services. As countries urbanized and development spilled over traditional local government borders, metropolitan regions emerged with new governing challenges and issues. Most traditional governing systems are not well-equipped to handle regional governance issues.

Regardless of the configuration of the governing system, the regional level has become a much more important governing focus. With globalization and the increasing importance of metropolitan regions as engines for economic growth, there is increasing pressure on local governance systems to meet the challenges imposed by regional economies and public policy issues that transcend local political boundaries. Additional regional pressures include the ever louder demand for quality local government services by an increasingly urban and discriminating population, technological advances, and the increasing complexity of services. These factors tend to focus local governance issues at a regional scale. Public policy decisions made by one municipality have impacts on neighboring municipalities, and municipalities are less able individually to effectively address governance issues within their own borders. A number of issues, such as transportation, land use, employment, affordable housing, crime, segregation, inform the discussion of the place of the region within the governance system.

The metropolitan region is an amorphous area with unique governing challenges. It is not static but continually changes. People living in metropolitan regions expect seamless services regardless of the community they are in as they travel, work, shop, and play in the metropolitan area. However ill-defined and conceptualized the metropolitan region is, it is demanding attention because of the policy issues and problems that are not and cannot be contained or addressed by individual local governments within a metropolitan mosaic of governments. There is increased awareness that problems that were at one time thought to be contained in the central cities, are migrating to the suburbs. They are becoming more visible and are increasingly perceived as a threat to the well-being of the entire metropolitan area. People are becoming more involved in volunteer activities to try to improve the lot of others. People from both the central city and the suburbs are quietly donating their time through religious and nonprofit organizations to assist in improving conditions in central city neighborhoods. They are engaged in activities ranging from cleaning up neighborhoods to building homes and rehabilitating apartment buildings, to providing food and clothing to those in need. Metropolitan problems are also given wide coverage by the media. Moreover, a number of books have been published on urban issues, many of which call for regional approaches to solve the problems facing metropolitan areas.[2]

Economic activity has decentralized in metropolitan areas to the point that central cities are no longer the focal point of employment. This is creating centrifugal forces driving decentralization and autonomy. Many suburban areas have developed into "edge cities" that compete with the central cities and other areas within the region for economic growth. Suburbs have become self-contained and no longer need central cities; they can survive and prosper regardless of what happens inside central cities.[3] People living and working in the suburbs no longer have a strong connection to the central city. One writer describes a typical suburban New York City family with both husband and wife working in the suburbs. They do all their shopping, and have access to college, state-of-the-art medical care, and legal advice, without going into the city, and they have friends who have not been to the city in 10 years.[4]

A more regional orientation is also the result of lifestyle changes. In the suburbs people are less connected to their neighborhoods or residential communities. Mobility is fostering the development of metropolitan citizens, people who do not have close ties to any one single community. Both parents (or the single parent) often work outside their residential community.

Primary associations are no longer community-based in neighbors, community churches, and block clubs. These associations have, for the most part, been replaced by professional associations or relationships with co-workers. Fewer people are attending church, or they are attending churches that are not tied to the residential community. Moreover, in many instances, fear of crime in the neighborhood keeps people from reaching out to others. With parents working and involved in their children's activities, often outside the community, there is less identification or involvement with the community. Moreover, people shop outside their communities, move frequently within the metropolitan area, and generally exhibit little or no allegiance to their community or interest in its governance. (A major exception occurs when they perceive a threat to their property values, in which case those owning property tend to become very involved in the community.) This greater mobility creates an expectation of uniformity in basic local services regardless of where people travel in the metropolitan area. It also breaks down traditional loyalties to communities because people are involved in activities and concerns that are not connected to their local communities.[5]

However, it could also be argued that the fragmented nature of the decentralized system, with its myriad of general purpose governments and special purpose districts, results in little or no attachment or identification with a particular community. Instead, the general identification is with the larger city, such as Chicago, even though the place of residence may be a small suburb of the metropolis. Within the large metropolis the community identity is usually not to the place of residence, but it varies according to the interest or particular activity of the individual. Because people in fragmented metropolitan areas do not reside, work, shop, worship, attend school, etc. within the boundaries of one municipality, there is no strong attachment to a particular municipality. Whereas life's activities help to foster civic life and involvement in the community, in a metropolitan area, life's activities are spread over a number of neighboring municipalities and governments.

The sense of community in metropolitan areas varies with the adjective preceding community—for example, religious community, employment community, and school community. Indeed, proponents of a centralized, more geographically inclusive local government argue that a centralized system encompasses most of life's activities and thus fosters a greater sense of community. Fragmented local governing systems not only fragment the sense of community but create confusion and accountability issues that result in a diffusion of participation. Absent a strong sense of community of residence, citizens might perceive their local government as more of a provider of municipal services than as a center of community activity.

The increasing resistance to routinely raising taxes also adds to a more regional orientation. Besides resisting tax increases, voters are demanding greater accountability and efficiency from local governments. This is forcing municipalities to consider alternative service delivery options instead of continuing the traditional methods of independently delivering services. The movement was chronicled and popularized by two local government practitioners, David Osborne and Ted Gaebler. The movement spread to the national government with efforts to improve the ways that services were delivered. Efforts continue at the national level and in some local and state governments to improve efficiency, effectiveness, and accountability.[6] The reinventing government movement message was and continues to be that government can improve services by completely rethinking the way it operates. A main agenda item from this movement is that local governments can be more efficient and economical in providing quality services through regional cooperation and outsourcing services.

Metropolitan area residents are becoming increasingly aware that many of the problems facing urban areas do indeed cross political boundaries and require regional solutions. Such issues as environmental concerns, traffic congestion, blighted neighborhoods, loss of open space, and inner-city problems appearing in the suburbs are prompting renewed interest in regionalism. Suburban residents, many of whom fled the central cities to escape central city problems, are facing many of the same problems they thought they had left behind. This is evidenced by a survey of 220 government, civic, and business leaders in the northwest Chicago suburbs. They listed gangs and traffic congestion as leading problems. Substance abuse, dysfunctional families, and property taxes were other major concerns. These last three were not even listed nine years earlier when a similar survey was taken.[7] Table 2.1 indicates these leaders' responses to the survey. It is interesting that many problems which, in the opinion of suburban leaders, have worsened in the last five years are problems that in the past were generally attributed to the central cities. There is also a growing realization among the suburban leaders that these issues transcend municipal boundaries and require a regional approach to effectively address them.

Even though residents are concerned with issues that they perceive transcend community boundaries, surveys show that they do not necessarily favor regional mechanisms to deal with the issues. In one survey conducted in Orange County, California, a suburban area of Los Angeles, less than one-third of the respondents supported regional government. Even though their concerns about traffic and development issues had increased from 33 to 48 percent for traffic congestion and 13 to 20 percent for growth issues in the prior three years, they were not willing to support a regional authority to manage these problems. While almost 70 percent considered these issues regional problems, only 15 percent were willing to support a regional authority for these functions. Moreover, little more than one-third were

Table 2.1 Survey of Community Leaders in Chicago's Northwest Suburbs on Major Problems and Whether They Have Worsened or Improved Over the Previous Five Years[a]

Problem	Very Serious (%)	Not Very Serious (%)	Worsened (%)	Improved (%)
Traffic Congestion	69	2	86	1
Gangs	54	6	86	3
Substance Abuse	48	2	58	2
Dysfunctional Families	46	3	56	0
Property Taxes	44	12	60	9
Public Transportation	40	12	34	13
Crime	38	11	71	3
Political Influence	37	18	21	35
Affordable Housing	34	12	48	5
Business Workforce Needs	33	11	42	6

Source: Adapted from Steve Warmbir, "Gangs, Substance Abuse Top Suburban Leaders' List of Concerns," *Arlington Heights (Ill.) Daily Herald*, Nov. 29, 1995, sec. 1, pp. 1, 5.

Note:
[a] The survey was not a scientific survey, but represents the opinions of 220 leaders of the northwest suburbs of Chicago.

willing to give more authority to county government to solve these problems. By a 2-to-1 margin, residents wanted to maintain the current system of city and county government.[8]

Even though Orange County residents were not ready for regional government, residents of the San Jose, California area revealed strong support for regional approaches to solutions of problems. A recent survey indicated that over 90 percent supported regional cooperation to solve air pollution, traffic congestion, and affordable housing problems. Over 65 percent of the respondents also said they would support a candidate for political office who supported regional government, while over 56 percent supported trading some political independence for regional cooperation and giving a regional agency veto power over development.[9] The difference in the two surveys may be that the perception of the problems in San Jose is so bad that residents are willing to give up some local independence to solve them. During the decade prior to the survey, the San Jose area had experienced a 25 percent population increase, placing tremendous demands on housing, transportation, and public services. There had been a marked deterioration in the general quality of life in the area as evidenced by inadequate water supply, increased traffic congestion, and environmental decay. Area local governments were having difficulty in satisfactorily addressing these growing problems.[10]

While most local governments continue to welcome and solicit development, many are becoming more selective. They want the development to be compatible with the community and to evolve at a pace that enables the community to provide services. While growth measures may be effective within a local government jurisdiction, they have no cumulative effect on reducing either the residential or nonresidential construction in the region for at least two reasons. First, most of the issues local governments attempt to regulate through growth control measures are regional in scope. However, local growth control measures have no authority outside the community boundaries. Thus, residents living in a growth control community will continue to experience traffic congestion, environmental decay, and other effects of sprawl outside their community. Second, sprawl and higher-density land use will continue in the region despite growth control measures because developers will simply move to adjacent communities.[11] Economist Anthony Downs argues that growth-related problems in metropolitan areas must be addressed on a regional basis if the region hopes to solve these problems.[12]

The next sections describe many of the issues that have increasingly had negative effects on metropolitan area residents. As they become more mobile and commute around the metropolitan area to recreate, work, and shop in different parts of the region, they encounter problems that can only be addressed on a regional basis and therefore are creating pressures for regional solutions. These issues have been evident for many years, but they have not been resolved and the perception among residents and community leaders is that they have become worse, and the metropolitan residents are demanding that they be addressed. Most of these issues and problems are interrelated but are organized in the chapter in separate sections to facilitate an in-depth analysis.

Sprawl

Sprawl is characterized by low density (usually fewer than 7,000 persons per square mile), a leapfrog pattern of development, reliance on the automobile as the chief mode of transportation, and zoning of land for incompatible uses.[13] Sprawl is blamed for the majority of metropolitan problems, including traffic congestion, social decay, pollution, loss of irreplaceable open space, and additional taxes. Sprawl is not just the result of private market forces; there are a number of contributing factors. It is the result of actions by developers, individual buyers, businesses, and governments. Under the decentralized land use regulation system that presently exists in most areas of the country, each community establishes zoning and building codes, and issues building and subdivision permits independently and without regard to the impact of their decisions on neighboring communities or the region as a whole. Indeed, due to the fact that development enhances a community's tax base, development is encouraged by most local governments on the fringes of metropolitan areas. Municipalities, seeking growth to expand their tax base, have often made hasty decisions in granting permits that have resulted in poorly constructed housing, congestion, pollution, and health risks from inadequate sewer and water provision. Governments are often forced to upgrade infrastructure or to clean up environmental pollution at substantial cost from ill-conceived decisions encouraging rapid development.

Homebuyers pay for some of the costs of sprawl to the extent that local governments require the developer to provide infrastructure or make a payment to the local government to help defray costs associated with the development. These may include such costs as sidewalks, lateral sewers, and impact fees for schools, roads, and sewers. Impact fees often do not cover the full costs to the community from sprawl. It is difficult to accurately measure the true costs on the community from the addition of another house in terms of the need for wider roads, additional school buildings, fire and police facilities, and so on.

Most impact fees are based on average-cost pricing of services, which means that all users pay the same impact fees. However, the marginal costs of services to the new development are less the closer the house is to the existing services or facilities. The result is that those who live farther away, generally the wealthier, are subsidized by those who live closer to the source of the service. The impact fees on a new home located ten miles from a sewage treatment plant tend to be the same as those levied on homes two miles away even though the actual costs of providing the services to those farther away may be much higher. There is some movement toward a form of marginal-cost pricing with variable impact fees based on geographical location, but charging different fees is more difficult to defend both politically and in the courts. The community, even with impact fees, usually subsidizes the infrastructure costs of sprawl.[14]

Sprawl creates congestion, tax, and infrastructure problems. The communities where sprawl is occurring must put in infrastructure to provide services to new businesses and residents. The infrastructure in communities losing the population and businesses is less efficiently utilized. Because most of the existing infrastructure and services still have to be maintained in the declining community and increased in the growing community, the increase in per capita costs usually requires an increase in the tax rate in both communities. As taxes are raised in the older, more mature communities, residents and businesses continue leaving for lower-tax communities. The lower-tax communities, in all likelihood, must raise their taxes to provide the additional services required by the newcomers. The impact in the older community is often a spiral of decline resulting in a concentration of poor people, blight, and a deteriorated tax base.[15]

Sprawl can have severe consequences on the inner city. Sprawl has served to exacerbate the fiscal problems of many of our core cities. With the flight of a large portion of affluent citizens to the rapidly expanding suburbs, metropolitan economic decentralization, and the development of "edge cities," core cities have often found it difficult to adequately fund their operating budgets. Core cities, due to ever-increasing sprawl, are particularly vulnerable to disinvestment, which has resulted in the departure of many commercial entities from their downtown business districts. As an example of core city disinvestment, one study reported that there were nearly 4,000 abandoned shopping centers in the core cities of the United States in 2002.[16]

David Rusk[17] has noted that when the per capita income of city residents falls below 70 percent of its suburban counterparts, the region, in most instances, has reached a point where core city and suburban economic disparities become so severe that the city, in a broad sense, no longer is a place to invest or create jobs. Core cities experiencing a declining population and disinvestment are confronted with increasing social problems, blight, and fiscal pressures. In the Minneapolis-St. Paul area, for instance, people moving from the inner city and older, inner suburbs to communities on the edge of the metropolitan area necessitated the closing of 132 schools in the inner city and inner suburbs and the building of 41 new schools in the growth communities. This is clearly an inefficient use of infrastructure.[18] Sprawl also often results in abandonment of houses and property as people move to the suburbs. The result of abandoned houses and lots is deteriorated neighborhoods. Kansas City estimates that it has between 4,000 and 5,000 abandoned lots scattered across the city with some concentrated in poorer sections of the city because of sprawl.[19]

New infrastructure in growth areas is often financed by tax revenue from throughout the region. This is particularly true if the infrastructure is constructed by a region-wide special district. In the Twin Cities area, $1 billion in new sewer capacity was financed by debt service fees that were uniform across the region even though the bulk was spent on sewers in the southwestern suburbs. One study showed that inner-city residents in the Twin Cities subsidized the sewer expansion at the rate of $10 to $19 per household while residents in the southwestern suburbs were the beneficiaries of a subsidy between $10 and $136 per household.[20]

Sprawl results in ever-expanding metropolitan areas with accompanying traffic and environmental problems. The growth of population in metropolitan areas has little relationship to the use of land. Between 1960 and 1990 population increased from 95 million to 140 million (47 percent) while urbanized land increased from 25,000 square miles to 51,000 square miles (107 percent). This trend continued in the boom years of the 1990s as the urban areas expanded at about twice the rate that the population grew. The sprawl pattern of development slowed down considerably during the Great Recession of 2007 to 2009. Cities have experienced a resurgence with regentrification, higher use of public transportation, and smaller houses. Preferences for mass transit and smaller homes are not only a result of the Great Recession. Some of these trends began before the recession. Compared to the amount of farmland lost during the boom years of the 1900s, between 2002 and 2007 the annual amount of farmland lost to sprawl was down almost a third.[21]

Public health officials blame American's rising obesity on sprawl patterns of development. Sprawl is not designed for biking or walking but for the automobile. Sidewalks are sometimes built and sometimes not. When they are built, they often end without going anywhere. Crossing busy roads or multilane highways on foot can be hazardous. People in suburbs tend to drive everywhere: to the park, to school, to shop, to work, to the health club to exercise. They argue that we have built an environment that contributes to obesity.[22]

Those who defend sprawl point out that it results from the lifestyle most Americans prefer. The American dream of a detached house on a lot, an automobile, a job in a low-rise workplace with free and ample parking, an environment free from signs of poverty, and community control of land use fosters sprawl.[23] While acknowledging that sprawl does result in some inconveniences and higher transportation costs per household, some argue that sprawl serves, through the market, to enhance the overall quality of the lives of many of our metropolitan citizens. For instance, Nelson Wikstrom argues that sprawl, on balance, has proved to be beneficial for most urban dwellers, providing them with much cleaner, greener, and safer neighborhoods in which to dwell, and more affluence, privacy, mobility, and choice.[24]

Many property owners, builders, and developers regard government interference in land use decision as un-American. Sentiments expressed at one public hearing on growth management proposals capture this philosophy:

- As an American, I strongly believe in our citizens' rights to pursue life, liberty, and property;
- Centralized planning did not work in Russia, Cuba, North Korea or anywhere else they've attempted it;
- Are we going to mandate where they're going to live?
- Our Constitution tells us about the preservation of private property rights;
- The land should be controlled by the individual who has paid for the land and pays the taxes on the land and should be able to do with that property what he wants to do.[25]

In addition to what is a clear public preference to live in the suburbs, there are additional social benefits that offset the added financial costs of sprawl. The results of one study showed that on average those living in sprawling communities spend 30 percent less time commuting to work than their counterparts residing in the least sprawling areas. Moreover, home ownership is much greater in more sprawling metropolitan areas (70 percent), than in the more compact metropolitan areas (57 percent). Further, households in the more sprawling metropolitan areas, benefitting from the lower prices offered by larger grocery stores and "big box" retailers, spend less money on food than their counterparts dwelling in more compact metropolitan areas.[26] Even though transportation costs are higher in a sprawl pattern of development, the other factors are indicative of a higher quality of life.

Critics opposed to government intervention to control or direct growth and limit sprawl suggest that the market is working, and that relocation decisions by firms and households do the job of achieving balance and keeping commuting times within tolerable limits without costly planning interventions. University of Southern California urban planners Peter Gordon, Harry Richardson, and Myung-Jin Jun suggest that the appropriate role for planning agencies and local jurisdictions should be to facilitate the decentralization of jobs by relaxing zoning restrictions that limit commercial land uses in residential communities. Further, they suggest that government "should help in land assembly to provide economic infrastructure, and discourage growth control initiatives."[27]

Central cities are unlikely to be restored by eliminating sprawl because of the myriad other factors involved in the decline of the central city. Unless mass transit is a viable, acceptable alternative, eliminating sprawl will not eliminate air pollution or traffic congestion. Although sprawl is blamed for eliminating valuable agricultural land, only a minuscule amount of land is devoted to urban uses. The entire U.S. population consumes substantially less than 3.5 percent of the land in the country, excluding Alaska.[28] A large amount of the land in the country, however, is not usable for agriculture. One study contends that the most productive agricultural land is close to urban areas. According to this study, 85 percent of the nation's fruit and vegetables and nearly 80 percent of its dairy products are produced in counties subject to urban growth pressures.[29]

Despite the contention of critics, there is mounting support to reduce the negative effects of sprawl development. A report on sprawl co-sponsored by the Bank of America states that California "can no longer afford the luxury of sprawl" which "has shifted from an engine … of growth to a force that now threatens to inhibit growth and degrade the quality of our life." Richard Moe, president of the National Trust for Historic Preservation, states that sprawl is "corroding the very sense of community that binds us together as a people and as a nation." He asserts that sprawl leaves inner-city dwellers "victimized by economic segregation, stagnant property values and declining public services." He notes that children growing up in sprawling subdivisions are "often characterized by a lack of faith in the future and a diminished sense of community."[30]

Transportation

An issue that is increasingly perceived as requiring a regional solution is transportation. Anyone who has driven on the roads in the same metropolitan area over a number of years can attest to an increase in traffic. Anthony Downs gave expression to the frustration of most metropolitan commuters with his book, *Stuck in Traffic*, in 1992.[31] Twelve years later he revisited the topic and found that little had changed and that Americans are *Still Stuck in Traffic*.[32] We have not built capacity fast enough to keep up with the increased number of vehicles on our metropolitan roadways.[33]

Due to the sprawl pattern of development, America is uniquely dependent on the automobile as the main mode of transportation. Traffic congestion and increased time spent in the automobile are considered major social costs of sprawl, as is also the increasing isolation of sectors of the populace who are unable to drive or access alternative forms of transit. In the United States, 84 percent of total trips are by automobile, compared to 74 percent in Canada and 40 percent in Western Europe. Only 3 percent of all urban trips in the United States utilize public transit, while the percentage is four or five times that much in Canada and Western Europe.[34] Dependence on the automobile and distances between activities are increasing as the metropolitan areas continue to decentralize. From 1983 to 1990 the average household vehicle trip in the United States increased from 7.9 miles to 9 miles and the average commute to work from 8.6 miles to 10.9 miles. Average vehicle miles traveled rose 29 percent.[35]

Despite the sprawl and traffic congestion that seem to get worse each year, the average commute to work continues to climb. In 2010, it was 25.3 minutes. Over 35 percent traveled more than 30 minutes to work, which was an increase of 33 percent over the 2009 numbers, an indication that the commute times are increasing rapidly. The longest commute was in the New York metropolitan area at an average of 34.6 minutes. The average longest commute times are in large metropolitan areas. For example, the Washington, DC region had an average commute time of 33.4 and Chicago of 30.8. Approximately 5 percent of the workers used public transportation, and 77 percent drove alone. In the suburbs 81.5 percent of the workers drove alone. The number of workers driving to work tripled between 1960 and 2009 from 41 to 120 million. In only five metropolitan areas is the use of public transportation greater than 10 percent.[36]

Efforts to mitigate congestion include building additional expressways and improvements in existing roads. A number of companies have instituted flex time, which allows workers to travel at times other than during the normal rush hour and allows workers to work some days at home or from a work site closer to home. In any event, whereas downtown employment once dominated, over 40 percent of all commute trips are now suburb-to-suburb. The result is that major highways leading from suburb to suburb are regularly congested. In the San Francisco Bay area, 212 miles of the 812-mile suburban freeway system are regularly congested during rush hours.[37] In addition to the suburb-to-suburb work commute patterns, there are household trips for other purposes such as shopping, recreation, and chauffeuring children to school and activities. Indeed, three-quarters of car trips are not related to work.[38] These household trips significantly add to suburban congestion and air and noise pollution.

Governments cannot build roads fast enough to keep up with the increase in automobile use, and public transportation is not a viable option in a low-density environment with both workplace and residences spread out. The Chicago region is an illustrative example. Between 1980 and 1990, vehicle miles traveled outpaced new roads in the region sixfold. Highway construction increased the number of miles by 5 percent while the number of miles traveled increased by 33 percent; public transit ridership decreased by almost a third during the same time. Despite a large increase in the workforce in the region and one of the best public transportation systems in the country, ridership continues to decline. For example, fewer Chicago-region employees used the public transportation system in 2009 than in 2008. One reason for the decline is that the system is oriented to take workers downtown, and jobs are increasingly dispersed throughout the suburbs. An example is the relocation of Sears's headquarters from the Sears Tower in Chicago's central business district to suburban Hoffman Estates. Prior to its relocation, 92 percent of Sears's workers used public transportation. Since its relocation, public transportation is used by only 5 percent of the workforce.[39]

The major purpose of mass transit is to reduce automobile congestion by moving people around the urban area from home to work efficiently and expeditiously at a cost both the commuter and the government can afford. With the dispersal of jobs and the sprawl pattern of development, these goals are impossible to meet. Expansion and improvement of public transportation have not been successful in reducing traffic congestion. In fact, ridership of workers commuting to work on mass transit is down. In 2009, 6.9 million commuted to work using public transportation, a reduction from 2008 when 7.2 million workers used public transportation. In Los Angeles, about 6 percent of workers commuted by public transportation. The New York metro area had over 30 percent commuters. San Francisco metro area was a distant second at 14.6 percent.[40]

Many transit systems have built or expanded light rail systems at substantial cost with only minor success in getting people to abandon their automobiles in favor of public transportation. The result is that the costs of mass transit have soared without making a noticeable impact on traffic congestion. With the new and expanded service, overall ridership on public transportation is at its highest level even though commute to work riders is down. Even though some areas that have built or expanded light rail systems have met or exceeded their ridership projections, the percentage of people using mass transit is miniscule. However, there are positive signs. Public transportation ridership is up dramatically since 2004. Ridership has increased 12 percent over that period, double the growth of the population. During this same period, automobile miles traveled have not grown. Since 1995, transit ridership has grown by nearly 3 billion trips. Reasons for this increase include better service, construction of new services in many cities, continued and constant investment in public transportation, and renewed interest in central city living.[41]

Many cities have added and expanded light rail systems taking advantage of the available heavy federal subsidies. Cities like Los Angeles and Denver are adding new lines to their rail networks, making high-quality transit available to more people. Other cities have built new rail systems from the ground up and dramatically increased their transit ridership. Transit ridership in Salt Lake City is 55 percent higher than in 2000; in Phoenix, ridership is 71% higher; and in Charlotte, ridership has increased 80 percent since 2000. There are now 35 light rail systems in operation. The federal government provides a substantial subsidy to the costs of building rail systems. For instance, the St. Louis system, which opened in 1993, cost $351 million, of which $345.6 million was provided by the federal government. The local matching funds needed to obtain the federal grant were not provided in cash but in the asset value of the donated railroad rights-of-way and facilities. The federal government provided 41 percent of all capital funding in 2010. In addition to the heavy capital costs, the cost of operation of a light rail system is much higher than buses measured in cost per vehicle mile traveled. In 2010 the cost to operate bus systems per vehicle mile traveled was $9.00 compared to $16.35 for a light rail system. However, when measured in cost per passenger mile traveled, light rail systems compare more favorably to bus systems because passengers travel farther with light rail than with buses. The cost figures for 2010 were $0.69 for light rail and $0.90 for buses per passenger mile traveled.[42]

Critics contend that an overall regional approach is necessary in order to make mass transit, and particularly rail systems, viable. The transit systems must be integrated with an overall land use development plan. Without a plan to increase density and discourage automobile use, mass transit will continue to lose ridership and require huge government subsidies. Critics argue that Portland's system is working because it is one component of an overall regional comprehensive plan. The goal in the three-county urbanized Portland area is to make a majority of new jobs and housing within a five-minute walk of a transit line. The downtown is oriented to public transit, not the automobile. Portland's strategy in light rail development is that public transit cannot be justified solely as a means to move people but as a way to strengthen downtown and as part of a regional growth strategy.[43]

Congestion may be the price Americans pay for their quality of life. Congestion, however, erodes quality of life as well. Mobility affords Americans more choices as to where they want to live and expands opportunities for work. If the quality of life includes a house in a reasonable park-like setting in the suburbs with some space and privacy from neighbors and separation from the noise and pollution of the city, an automobile is necessary to connect people from their enjoyment of this lifestyle to their place of work. The result is congestion and sprawl. Health problems are exacerbated by the pollution caused by the automobile. In addition, time spent in commuting and traffic jams contributes to stress with consequent health issues, such as higher blood pressure, heart disease, and back problems not to mention the bizarre, anti-social behavior of people involved in traffic in "road rage" incidents.[44]

Problems of Competition for Economic Development

A number of studies have been published that purport to show that politically unified metropolitan regions compete more effectively for economic growth than politically fragmented areas, and that the prosperity of the suburbs, measured in terms of income, is dependent to a large degree on the economic viability of the central city.[45] Technology and trade and monetary policies have facilitated the globalization of the economy making it possible for production of goods and services to be located almost anywhere in the world. Indeed, we live in an increasingly globalizing economic world with multinational firms doing business around the world. Firms are no longer tied to a country or specific place within the country to the extent that they once were. Economic production is centered in metropolitan regions, not within individual units but throughout the metropolitan area. Metropolitan areas have become the engines of a nation's economy. They are increasingly competing directly with each other within nation states and across international boundaries for development, making the nation-state less important in the economic sphere.

The political fragmentation of metropolitan areas and the heavy reliance on property taxes create a competitive, not a cooperative atmosphere. Municipalities compete with each other for economic development. When development is attracted to a community, neighboring communities do not share in the tax revenue but may share in many of the negative aspects of the development such as traffic congestion, pollution, and increased crime. One example was the battle between three suburban municipalities in the Chicago region over the rights to prime unincorporated land where two interstate highways bisect and two major interchanges are located. This battle has evoked court suits and charges of racism and greediness. It has also created animosities among the municipalities contending for the property. In another example, Oakbrook, a suburban Chicago municipality, refused to allow a 31-story tower development because it did not meet its building regulations. The development, however, was approved by the neighboring Oakbrook Terrace. It was built on property on the border between the two municipalities. Oakbrook refused to widen a road located along one side of the building even though the developer was willing to pay for it. The reason given by Oakbrook was that it would receive no tax benefits but would experience increased traffic congestion.[46]

Municipalities desire either to attract new development to enhance the tax base or keep it out to maintain the character of the community. More municipalities are interested in attracting rather than excluding development. Providing tax breaks to businesses, as an incentive to locate, is a common practice. Communities compete to outbid each other to attract development. This produces under-taxation or over-subsidization of new business within metropolitan areas that would not otherwise occur. It potentially reduces the competitiveness of the metropolitan area as a whole in national and global terms by wasting resources on developments which would have occurred in the region anyway.

The economic development policies of local governments seldom attract new jobs to an urban area. They may be effective in specific location decisions of firms that have already decided to locate in the general area, or they may be effective in attracting firms from one location in an urban area to another location in the same urban area.[47] The competition between municipalities in urban areas for development, therefore, results in a beggar-thy-neighbor practice. Thus, if a government can attract a firm to locate on its borders from another municipality in the urban area, it has enhanced its property values while the other municipality has potentially lost property value. If the losing municipality cannot attract additional development to replace the lost firm, a downward spiral may commence resulting in blight and urban decay.

In the competitive environment for development to enhance the tax base, it is not uncommon for businesses to be attracted to relocate from one municipality to another within the metropolitan area. However, the incentives offered might result in the attracting community not realizing any additional revenue for years. In one example of an incentive package, Coralville, Iowa attracted a department store to move five miles from Iowa City with an incentive package that included building a larger building, discount the store's property taxes and $650,000 to cover any penalties related to the store's move from Iowa City. One estimate of the value of the incentives was $18 million. City officials in Coralville claim that the incentives were necessary to attract an anchor store that will attract stores and restaurants to the new retail development. Of course, Iowa City officials are bitter and are concerned with the impact on the mall that the store is leaving.[48]

Given the studies that suggest that the central city and suburbs are interdependent and rise and fall together in terms of economic growth, intra-area competition for economic development may, in fact, be more a negative-sum game than a zero-sum game where both the winners and the losers actually lose. When municipalities compete with each other for development, the only winner is the firm that plays one municipality against another for the best deal. Moreover, if people move to be closer to jobs, they may move to a neighboring community instead of the community where the job is located. Residential development can increase the tax burden in a municipality by raising the demand for services. Therefore, economic development in one community can create higher tax rates for neighboring communities. Because of the negative effects of competition, some communities have made efforts to cooperate with each other.[49]

Because economic flows are not restricted by municipal boundaries, the municipalities in the region would be able to make better use of resources and expertise by working together to attract and retain development rather than competing with each other. A region-wide approach would maximize the region's assets in competing for development, and all municipalities would benefit from development in any part of the region. Lightbody[50] asserts that in an age of globalization the regions that will be able to compete best at the economic development game are those that are most united. Those that are able to marshal governance, business, civic, labor, and other nongovernmental organizations (NGOs) under a leadership able to bring the various disparate forces together to address regional governance issues and present a unified economic development program agenda together, will be most successful.

With economic activity becoming more "footloose," there are many factors that determine where companies locate. Richard Florida advances the thesis that "creative" people drive economic development and are attracted to an area by its amenities. According to Florida, quality of life is an important consideration in where these "creative" people, who bring or foster economic development, choose to live.[51] Although some amenities are impacted by local government policies, many are beyond the scope of individual local governments to influence. However, individual government policies can have an impact on the economic development of an area. Research shows that after a manufacturing firm has chosen a region, location within that region can be affected by individual local government policies.[52]

Environmental Concerns

Americans, until the 1970s, were not overly concerned with pollution and the environment. Americans saw environmental protection as primarily a state and local responsibility. The land, and the quality of air and water, was traditionally viewed as economic resources for states and cities to exploit. For the most part, state and local governments paid little attention to environmental protection and pollution. Beginning in the early 1970s, increased public concern about the environment pressured the government to assume a greater role in its protection. The focus of early environmental activists was for the federal government to assume a major policy leadership role. Many environmental groups argued that state and local governments could not be trusted to protect their own environmental resources because they were too focused on promoting local development.

As metropolitan areas expand and consume more land, the public is becoming increasingly concerned with environmental issues. Public pressure to preserve the environment escalates as the quality of life in urban areas deteriorates. The nationwide increase in concern for environmental issues is reflected in surveys of public officials in the Chicago region. They list environmental concerns near the top of the major problems facing the metropolitan area.[53] Since most environmental issues transcend municipal boundaries, there is increasing awareness that protecting the environment requires a regional, coordinated approach. To be truly victorious in the battle against pollution, there must be a coordinated and cooperative effort at the regional level. Yet most municipal governments do not have legal jurisdiction over the full range of their water resources or over the facilities in their jurisdictions producing air pollution. Managing environmental problems is a challenge for metropolitan areas. In addition, preservation of open space is becoming a much more critical issue in metropolitan areas. Large tracts of open space can only be preserved through a region-wide effort.

A major environmental concern with the sprawl pattern of development is increased air pollution. Indeed, sprawl is blamed for the majority of environmental metropolitan problems, including pollution from traffic and loss of irreplaceable open space.[54] Growth control measures have no impact on mitigating pollution unless they are regional in scope. Moreover, individual municipalities usually cannot regulate non-point pollution, such as car exhaust, because such regulation often falls within the purview of state or county governments. Municipal governments use land use controls for their own parochial purposes.[55] This fragmentation of interests often hinders comprehensive regional planning resulting in uncoordinated development in metropolitan areas. This sprawl development pattern reflects the high degree of autonomy granted to municipalities in our intergovernmental system.[56] Improving and protecting urban environments requires strengthening the governance of metropolitan areas. It requires cooperation among local governments and also the involvement of many other actors from both the public and private sectors.

Inequality across the Metropolitan Area

During the second half of the twentieth century, urbanists identified a variety of socioeconomic and infrastructure problems with central cities in the United States. Some of these were of a lifestyle nature, involving race relations, crime, poverty, health, and education. In addition to these widely acknowledged social problems, other central city challenges involve infrastructure including water and sewer systems, roads and highways, mass transportation, and parks and recreational areas. It has been argued that these central city problems serve in varying degrees to undermine the quality of life enjoyed by others in the metropolitan area, not solely central city residents.[57] Numerous publications have appeared over the years depicting the central city crisis and suggesting solutions. Most prescriptions involve infusion of funds from the federal and state governments.

Since the scholarly debates of a half-century ago concerning the severity of our urban problems, the United States has evolved into a more decidedly metropolitan society. The problems that seemed to be only in the central cities have migrated to the suburbs. The inner-ring suburbs, those bordering on the central cities, are experiencing most of the problems that central cities have experienced. Indeed, these suburbs might even be worse off as the central cities have more political clout and also have more resources to apply to the problems. Many inner-ring suburbs have problems generating the revenue to provide even basic services. For example, 59 Chicago suburban municipalities have a lower tax base per household than Chicago. Declining suburbs are depressing localities that lack the public spaces, universities, cultural institutions, nightlife, and downtowns that, despite their problems, still make central cities exciting places.[58]

During the decade of the 1990s, and the early 2000s, many central cities were rejuvenated with new housing and economic development. Regentrification occurred in many cities, a number of downtowns were redeveloped and historical buildings and districts were rejuvenated. Central cities appear to be making a comeback from the gloom and doom scenarios of the "crisis" that the scholars of the 1950s, 1960s, and 1970s depicted. Despite the turnaround, central cities still exhibit many problems that have a regional impact. Indeed, central cities are generally still the major players in the region. The next sections provide a synopsis of some of the regional policy issues in which the central city plays a major role.

Impact of Central Cities on Regional Economic Development

Reversing the economic plight of the central city is a major focus of the proposed responses to economic deconcentration in metropolitan areas. The implication is that regional governance policies to improve the central city are beneficial to the entire metropolitan area. This assumption needs to be closely examined. Critics of regionalism contend that government policies should not hinder but should support market-based decisions. They argue, for example, that government policies to encourage the return of certain kinds of manufacturing to central city locations may be an inappropriate use of government resources given transportation limitations and a workforce without the appropriate skills. These critics suggest that decentralization may, in fact, be more efficient and that central cities may have lost their traditional economic advantage. If firms move out of the central city to become more efficient through lower production or transportation costs, government policies to stop or reverse this would, indeed, create inefficient businesses and the region would eventually decline from an inability to compete in the increasingly global marketplace. If, however, deconcentration is caused by perceived negative externalities such as social problems in the central city, it may reflect an inefficient distribution of resources. If this is the case, decentralization would not result in an optimal reconfiguration of regional resources but rather a type of sorting process in which people and firms relocate to areas that serve their individual needs but do not necessarily promote the interests of the region. Anecdotal evidence indicates that deconcentration is driven more as a flight from blight than from an optimal reconfiguration of resources to maximize efficiency in the regional economy.[59]

The major economic advantage central cities have offered for business location is agglomeration economies. The rationale behind agglomeration economies is that firms cluster in close proximity to each other for mutually enhancing purposes. These purposes include face-to-face communications to facilitate business and improved access to business support services. Spatial efficiencies are realized through agglomeration. Business support services, such as specialized law firms, marketing support services, financial services, and computer support services, locate to provide support to corporate offices. High-density location facilitates the exchange of information through face-to-face contacts that is important in rapidly changing fields and builds trust and understanding that promotes business development.

Critics suggest that the central cities' agglomeration economies are no longer dominant or even necessary. They argue that technology has replaced the need for face-to-face interaction. Even if dense face-to-face interactions are still important in modern economies, the suburbs are developing their own concentrations of employment and economies of agglomeration that compete successfully with central cities. Office space has dispersed from the central cities into suburban clusters called edge cities[60] and more recently into a more highly dispersed configuration called edgeless cities.[61] The evidence of the office space dispersion is that in most metropolitan areas there is more office space located outside the central city than in the central city. Chicago and New York are the only major metropolitan areas with more than 50 percent of the office space still in the downtown. Atlanta has 66 percent and Detroit has 79 percent of its office space outside of their downtowns.[62]

There is still substantial scholarly and empirical support for the value of central cities. A number of scholars have conducted studies that purport to show that the suburbs are still dependent on the central cities and that agglomeration economies of the central cities are still important to the economic viability of the region. Two studies comparing firms that moved out of New York City with firms that remained, concluded that the firms in the city outperformed those that left. One study tracked the stock valuation of 22 firms that moved their headquarters out of New York to the suburbs with 36 that remained in the city. Both groups were composed of major companies near the top of the Fortune 500 list. Although the sample selection was nonscientific, the study showed over an 11-year period that the companies that stayed in New York had an average stock valuation of over two and a half times the average for the companies that moved out. Another study compared the profitability of firms that moved from New York to the suburbs to the profitability of other firms in their industry over a three-year period. The majority that moved had profitability lower than average for companies in their industry.[63]

Because there are many factors in a firm's performance, it is impossible to attribute the inferior performance of a business to its suburban location. The studies imply, however, that the central city continues to have certain agglomeration economies that are not readily available elsewhere in the metropolitan area. Despite the studies and the critics that say suburban headquarters are not as viable as downtown locations, firms continue to move to, and surprisingly thrive in, the suburbs. Firms that provide services to corporations are finding they no longer need a Manhattan address to remain viable.[64]

Although jobs in central cities continue to decentralize, central cities continue to provide substantial employment opportunities. The CBD (central business district) of the central city is still a major center of employment in the metropolitan area. In one study of a sample of 40 metropolitan areas scattered across the nation with a minimum of 100,000 population, using 2002 data, the central cities still had 39 percent of all jobs in the metropolitan area. Moreover, the central cities contributed 41 percent of the annual payroll. The study also looked at the location in metropolitan areas of so-called "creative" industries that have been touted as critical for economic viability and growth. The creative industries included were information, professional, scientific and technical services, and the arts, entertainment, and recreational industries. The study found that almost 44 percent of the employment in these industries was in the central cities along with almost 49 percent of the payroll.[65]

Studies on economic development show a significant relationship between central city/suburban per capita income disparities and job growth in metropolitan areas. Sixty years ago, all central cities had about the same median family incomes as their metro areas. Over the ensuing years, all but a handful of central cities that were not surrounded by suburbs had substantial declines in their median incomes compared to their suburbs. Old central cities experienced the greatest declines. By 2010 older industrial era central cities such as Detroit, Milwaukee, and Cleveland fell below their metropolitan areas in per capita incomes at 52, 56, and 58 percent respectively. Other cities not recognized as industrial era cities lost parity with their suburban areas if they were not able to capture the suburban growth. These included cities such as Houston, which had a median family income equal to 97 percent of its suburbs in 1950 and only 75 percent in 2010. Syracuse went from 100 percent parity to 60 percent, Harrisburg, PA went from 101 to 52 percent, and Richmond, VA declined from 97 to 69 percent.[66]

However, the situation is not as dire for all central cities as one would assume from the above. In the 2000s some older central cities have rebounded and have narrowed the central city/suburban income gap. For example, in the District of Columbia, urban household income increased from 75 percent of regional household income in 2000 to 82 percent in 2009. This pattern was common in the largest northern regions, such as Boston (74 percent in 2000, 83 percent in 2009), New York (from 76 percent to 78 percent) and even some population-losing cities such as Chicago (77 percent to 81 percent) and Pittsburgh (77 percent to 80 percent).[67]

As an example of the interdependence between the city and the suburbs relative to economic growth, one study of 56 metropolitan areas found that, as central city-suburban income differences narrowed, the rate of employment growth improved. The researchers found that metropolitan areas with central city per capita income less than 50 percent that of the suburbs, lost jobs. However, there was a positive employment growth rate of 2 percent in those areas where central city per capita income was between 55.3 and 66.7 percent of suburban per capita income. Moreover, the positive growth rate was almost 6 percent for those areas where the central city per capita income was between 78.4 and 90 percent of suburban per capita income. There are some exceptions to these general findings because a few metropolitan areas with large per capita income disparities had positive growth rates. Also, the study does not purport to show causality, as there are other factors, besides central city–suburban per capita income disparities, that affect employment growth or decline. Despite the increasing suburbanization of jobs and population, indications are that those metropolitan areas that do better in job growth have less income disparities between the central city and the suburbs.[68]

Another indication of the interdependencies of the central city and the suburbs is the amount of central city income that is earned by suburban workers and the fact that central city jobs tend to pay more than suburban jobs. In one study the researchers found that over 70 percent of the earnings from jobs in Washington, DC, went to suburban residents. In Baltimore suburban workers claimed almost 60 percent of the total central city job earnings. In Denver, Philadelphia, St. Louis, San Francisco, and New Orleans, the amount of central city job earnings claimed by suburban workers was over 45 percent.[69] The evidence suggests that a city and its suburbs are not two distinct economies but a single regional economy. The fortunes of city and suburb are highly intertwined: The fate of the regional economy will dictate the fortunes of both. Moreover, the sum of efforts within a metropolitan region yields a unique synergy, which its local parts cannot achieve separately. Central city decline affects the attractiveness of the region as a whole.

Concentration of Minorities in Central Cities

In the 1950s the country's 15 million African Americans were substantially rural and southern, although a tremendous migration into northern and southern cities had been underway since the Great Depression. Similarly, most of the country's Hispanics were scattered in rural areas and small cities located largely throughout the Southwest. Asian Americans, always an urban people in the U.S., were heavily concentrated in West Coast cities. In 1950 America's population was about 86 to 87 percent white and 13 to 14 percent minority. Sixty years later America is 27.6 percent minority, with over 80 percent of all minorities living in metropolitan areas. Residential segregation of minorities is glaring in its visibility in metropolitan areas, and the concentration of minorities in central cities has increased over the years.

One study using 2000 census data for all primary metropolitan statistical areas (roughly equal to Metropolitan Divisions) over 100,000 found that over half of the regions have dissimilarity scores between blacks and whites exceeding 60, with 100 equaling complete segregation. About 20 percent of the regions had dissimilarity scores exceeding 70. The regions did much better at integration of Hispanics with an average dissimilarity score of less than 40. For example, in Chicago the percentage of African Americans went from 14 percent to 36 percent between 1950 and 1970. By 2010, 55 percent of the population of Chicago was African American. In Los Angeles the concentration of the minority population increased substantially between 1980 and 1990, from 39 percent to 63 percent. In 2010 the minority population stood at 71 percent. This increase was largely due to the large influx of Hispanics and the exodus of the white population.[70]

Central cities house a disproportionate share of the metropolitan minority population with over 52 percent of blacks and 21 percent of whites residing in central-city neighborhoods. Suburbs are disproportionately white, where 57 percent of whites but just 36 percent of blacks reside. Segregation, particularly between blacks and whites, persists at high levels, and Hispanic/white segregation has increased in recent years. The typical white resident of metropolitan areas resides in a neighborhood that is 80 percent white, 7 percent black, 8 percent Hispanic and 4 percent Asian. A typical black person lives in a neighborhood that is 33 percent white, 51 percent black, 11 percent Hispanic and 3 percent Asian. And a typical Hispanic resident lives in a community that is 36 percent white, 11 percent black, 45 percent Hispanic and 6 percent Asian.[71]

The suburbs for many years effectively kept out African Americans through exclusionary zoning such as requiring large lots, not adequately providing for multifamily zoning, and enacting other policies. Political scientist Nancy Burns presents convincing research that suburbanites formed municipalities in the 1950s and 1960s at least partially to exclude African Americans. She states: "The evidence suggests, then, that the operative concern here was race, and not simply the presence of low-income populations. The founders' goal, it seems, was the exclusion of African Americans."[72] Another study of segregation in the Kansas City metropolitan area found that class differences as measured by occupational status, educational level, or income level did not explain the segregation of the races. The conclusion of the study was that race is a "more significant factor than class in explaining the high level of residential segregation between blacks and whites."[73]

Table 2.2 shows the metropolitan areas with the highest concentration of the black population in the central city. If the black population were evenly distributed, the city would have the same percentage of the black population in the city as it has to the total metropolitan population. The data in Table 2.2 show that the Detroit, Philadelphia, and Chicago metropolitan areas are particularly effective at keeping the black population in the central city. Moreover, in metropolitan areas where African Americans have moved out of the city, they tend to be concentrated in only a few suburbs. In Chicago's suburbs, for example, two-thirds of all suburban African Americans live in only 18 of the region's 348 suburban municipalities. In 13 of these 18 municipalities, the population is over 50 percent African American.[74]

Concentration of minorities in the central cities in and of itself is not the problem. The problem is that it isolates the minorities from the economic opportunities available in other parts of the metropolitan area. Segregation

Table 2.2 Metro Areas with Highest Percentage Black Population in Central Cities 2010[a]

Metro Area	% in City	% Total Metro Area Population In City	% in Suburbs
New York	61	43	39
Detroit	60	17	40
San Diego	56	42	44
Chicago	54	28	46
Philadelphia	53	25	47

Source: Sonya Rastogi, D. Tallese Johnson, Elizabeth M. Hoeffel and Malcolm P. Drewery, Jr., *The Black Population: 2010 September. 2011 Census Briefs.* Washington, DC: US Department of Commerce, Census Bureau. 2012 Statistical Abstract.

Note:
[a] These figures are for the black only population. They exclude black in combination with other races.

also creates barriers between the races and makes it more difficult to establish avenues of communication and eventual integration of the minorities into the larger metropolitan community. It fosters extreme pockets of poverty where crime, blight, and despair are rampant. Youth growing up in these areas have no role models and little hope of attaining a better life. They feel that because of prejudice they are unable to participate in the economic prosperity evident in the metropolitan area. Rebellion and riots against actual and perceived injustices have occurred with loss of life and property and are likely to reoccur unless measures are taken to remove the barriers so minorities can enjoy the same opportunities afforded others in society. All races should have equal opportunity to pursue the ideals stated in the Declaration of Independence–"Life, Liberty and the Pursuit of Happiness." The following sections further explicate the interconnectedness between segregation and central city problems.

Unemployment and Central City Deterioration

Employment steadily decentralized between 1998 and 2006: 95 out of 98 metro areas saw a decrease in the share of jobs located within three miles of downtown. Although the number of jobs in the top 98 metro areas increased overall during this time period, the outermost parts of these metro areas saw employment increase by 17 percent, compared to a gain of less than 1 percent in the urban core. When overlaid onto existing patterns of residential segregation, employment decentralization can result in different levels of geographic access to employment opportunities for different demographic groups. Metro areas with higher rates of employment decentralization exhibit greater rates of "spatial mismatch" between the relative locations of jobs and black residents. In a study of selected large metro areas, the researchers found that even as low-income and minority populations suburbanize, job growth is fastest in higher-income suburbs, perpetuating patterns of spatial mismatch within suburbia. High levels of employment decentralization may thus impede efforts to connect historically under-employed workers to job opportunities.[75]

As employment decentralized along with suburbanization, the decline in manufacturing jobs and jobs requiring a less educated workforce hit central cities particularly hard. In 1969 manufacturing jobs constituted 23 percent of the total jobs in metropolitan areas. Between 1969 and 2000, the number declined by 12 percent. In the period between 2001 and 2009, at the height of the Great Recession, there was even a bigger drop in the number of manufacturing jobs (27 percent). In 2009, the percentage of manufacturing jobs to total jobs in metropolitan areas stood at just 7 percent.[76] Over 50 percent of retail trade, construction and manufacturing jobs and over 40 percent of transportation and warehousing jobs are located more than ten miles from the central business district. Metro areas with a specialization in the manufacturing industry had higher than average levels of job decentralization. Large metro areas in this category—like Detroit or Chicago—on average have less than 16 percent of jobs in the urban core with 56 percent of employment more than 10 miles away from downtown. Smaller manufacturing metro areas—including Youngstown and Poughkeepsie—locate almost 30 percent of jobs in the outer ring.[77]

Job sprawl exacerbates certain dimensions of racial inequality. Greater job sprawl is associated with higher spatial mismatch for blacks to jobs. The relationship between these measures also holds for Latinos but to a lesser extent. Overall, metropolitan job sprawl is nearly twice as important a factor affecting spatial mismatch for blacks as for Latinos. Detroit, for example, has one of the highest levels of job sprawl among the 102 largest metropolitan areas, and blacks are extremely physically isolated from jobs. Metropolitan areas characterized by higher job sprawl also exhibit more severe racial segregation between blacks and whites. Metropolitan areas with both high mismatch and job sprawl include large cities such as Detroit, Chicago, Los Angeles, Philadelphia, Atlanta and Newark. In high job sprawl areas, about 67 percent of blacks would have to move to achieve geographic parity with the residential distribution of whites.[78]

As employment continues to decentralize from the central city, there are increasing problems of job accessibility for inner-city residents who, because of race or income, are excluded from the suburban housing market. There is high unemployment among central city residents, particularly in African American neighborhoods. A study of commuting patterns in the Pittsburgh area found that over 90 percent of the workers lived within five miles of the work site. The researchers found low-income workers (laborers, domestic, and service workers), as a rule, have an even shorter commute than others in higher-status occupations. The study found that almost 60 percent of low-income workers live within one mile of the work site and almost 90 percent live within three miles.[79] The suburbs are quite remote to inner-city workers. Distances appear to be a major barrier for the willing low-income workers in the central city for firms located in the suburbs with low-skilled job openings. Indeed, there is a growing amount of anecdotal evidence that suburban employers in many large metropolitan areas are experiencing shortages of low-skilled workers.[80]

Given distances and discrimination barriers, available suburban jobs are not easily accessible to inner-city workers. For those inner-city workers who are heavily dependent on public transportation, the journey to a suburban job can be arduous. Public transportation is traditionally designed to bring the suburban commuter to the central city job. As many suburban job sites are either not accessible or only infrequently accessible by public transportation, the commute to a low-wage job in the suburbs for workers without automobiles can require an inordinate amount of time in changing buses.

A commute to one close-in suburban job from Chicago required two hours and four bus or train changes.[81]

Removing spatial barriers to the job site may not improve the unemployment statistics for inner-city minorities. There is evidence that black workers face increased employment discrimination at suburban work sites. One study found that suburban employers had far larger ratios of black applicants to black hires than city employers. Decisions by white-owned firms to locate in the suburbs may be for more than purely economic reasons. It may also be related to a desire to be located in an area with a white-dominant workforce. Racial animosities were clearly evident in the refusal of suburban employers in the Detroit suburbs to become involved in a van service to provide transportation for low-wage city workers to suburban jobs. Most employers that refused to participate indicated that they had moved to the suburbs in the first place to avoid hiring African American workers.[82] The lengthy commute, the fear of a hostile work environment, and the low wages discourage many central city workers from seeking a job in the suburbs.

The Detroit area is an excellent example of the debilitating effects on central cities when businesses relocate. Highland Park, a city completely surrounded by Detroit, once housed Henry Ford's Crystal Palace–the world's showplace for mass production. It was called the "city of trees" and possessed beautiful neighborhoods and vibrant institutions. The community's schools were so good that suburban students flocked to attend. Over the years the community deteriorated as businesses moved out. Chrysler Corporation, long headquartered in Highland Park, relocated to Auburn Hills. The city's finances deteriorated to the point that in 2001, the state appointed an emergency financial manager. With fewer than 12,000 residents, its population has dwindled to half the level it was during its boom years. Suburban Auburn Hills has now become the Highland Park of earlier times. Job growth has been steady and at some periods phenomenal. Auburn Hills is home to major corporations and businesses including Chrysler, Volkswagen/Audi North American Headquarters, Oakland University, BorgWarner, Guardian Industries, RGIS, Great Lakes Crossing shopping mall, as well as the home of the National Basketball Association's Detroit Pistons. The contrast between Highland Park and Auburn Hills shows how economic restructuring is redirecting the flow of capital away from Detroit's central city and into the northwest Oakland County suburbs.[83]

In 1960 Detroit held 50 percent of the region's assessed valuation; Oakland County's share was 14 percent. By 1980, the city's share had plummeted to 18 percent while Oakland County's share had grown to 38 percent.[84] Detroit is, at this writing, in bankruptcy proceedings. With a population of 1.8 million in the 1950s, Detroit's slow decline started with residents migrating to the suburbs in the 1960s and accelerated when automakers relocated to the suburbs. Its population is now 713,777, a 60 percent drop from its peak.

The city's tax base has been diminished to the point that it struggles to provide even basic city services including police protection and fire services. In March of 2013 the state appointed an emergency manager and on July 18, 2013, the city filed the largest municipal bankruptcy in U.S. history.[85]

The dispersion of employment to the suburbs and the barriers to accessing suburban jobs by central city residents results in a high unemployment rate in the central city. Unemployment rates are significantly higher in the central cities than in their suburbs. During periods in the 1980s, central cities such as Detroit, Baltimore, and St. Louis experienced unemployment rates almost double the average rate in their suburbs. Statistics for April 2012, as the United States slowly comes out of the Great Recession, show the median unemployment rate for the 50 largest cities at 9.2 percent with a high of 19.9 percent for Detroit and a low of 5.1 percent for Omaha, Nebraska. The unemployment rate for the Detroit metro area was 8.7 percent, less than half of that for the city and for Omaha, it was 4.1 percent.[86] Table 2.3 shows the variation in the unemployment rate in 16 urban areas for 2010 (the latest available data at the time of this writing). In all but San Antonio, San Francisco, and Phoenix, the central city had a higher unemployment rate than its suburbs. The unemployment rate in Detroit was almost twice

Table 2.3 Unemployment Rate for Selected Urban Areas, 2010[a]

Region	Metropolitan Area	Central City
New York	8.2	8.5
Philadelphia	8.8	13.5
San Francisco	10.1	7.5
Baltimore	8.0	15.2
St. Louis	9.9	17.7
Chicago	9.5	11.0
Detroit	12.4	24.1
Houston	8.7	9.8
Cleveland	8.2	13.6
Dallas	7.1	9.7
Indianapolis	7.3	10.5
Los Angeles	11.1	12.9
Milwaukee	9.5	12.0
Phoenix	8.6	7.9
San Antonio	6.4	6.1
San Diego	7.7	7.9

Source: Bureau of Labor Statistics, *Geographic Profile of Employment and Unemployment 2010, Table 31,* www.bls.glov/gps [Accessed June 11, 2012].

Note:
[a] U.S. unemployment rate: 9.6 percent.

the rate in the suburbs. It is interesting to note that the metropolitan unemployment rate was consistently below the national unemployment rate while the older industrial cities were consistently above the national unemployment rate.

Newer growth areas and cities that encompassed major percentages of the metropolitan area had lower unemployment rates and had rates similar to the suburbs. Within the central cities unemployment is concentrated in the minority population. For example, unemployment in Chicago was 20.3 percent for the black population, 12.9 percent for the Hispanic population and only 9.5 percent for the white population. According to sociologist William Wilson, the dispersion of jobs from the central city and, probably more important, prejudice are major factors in the development of an urban underclass population in the inner-city. Wilson defines the underclass as

> that heterogeneous grouping of families and individuals who lack training and skills and either experience long-term unemployment or are not part of the labor force, individuals who engage in street criminal activity and other aberrant behavior, and families who experience long-term spells of poverty and/or welfare dependency.[87]

Poverty

Poverty continues to be concentrated in the central cities. Within metropolitan areas, the incidence of poverty in central city areas is considerably higher than in suburban areas—20.0 percent versus 11.3 percent, respectively, in 2011. A typical pattern is for poverty rates to be highest in center city areas, with poverty rates dropping off in suburban areas, and then rising with increasing distance from an urban core. The suburban area poverty rate fell from 2010 (11.9 percent) to 2011 (11.3 percent), but poverty rates in center city and nonmetropolitan areas remained statistically unchanged.[88]

In a study by Wende Mix at Buffalo State College using 2008 census estimates, she found that in all but one city of the ten U.S. cities with the highest poverty rates, the city poverty rate was significantly higher than the surrounding urban and metro area poverty rates. There was no statistical difference between the city and the metropolitan area for El Paso because the city encompassed a large portion of the metropolitan area. El Paso's metropolitan poverty rate was more than double the poverty rate for the metropolitan areas surrounding eight of the ten cities with the highest poverty rates. This is an indication of the differential of the poverty rate between the city and suburbs. Table 2.4 indicates the poverty estimates for the ten highest cities and their corresponding metropolitan areas.[89]

Three-fourths of all people living in extreme poverty areas in 1990 (census tracts with 40 percent or more of the residents with incomes below the official poverty level) were in central cities.[90] However, population in

Table 2.4 Cities with Highest Poverty Rates Compared to their Metropolitan Areas (2007)

City	City Poverty Rate %	Metropolitan Poverty Rate %
Detroit	33.8	13.9
Cleveland	29.5	12.7
Buffalo	28.7	13.5
El Paso	27.4	28.7
Memphis	26.2	18.8
Miami	25.5	12.8
Milwaukee	24.4	12.7
Newark	23.9	12.2
Philadelphia	23.8	11.5
Cincinnati	23.5	11.1

Source: The Geography of Urban Poverty, www.buffalostate.edu/geography/documents/paper.pdf [Accessed May 30, 2012].

extreme-poverty neighborhoods rose more than twice as fast in suburbs as in cities from 2000 to 2009. This population in extreme-poverty increased by 41 percent in suburbs, compared to 17 percent in cities. However, poor people in cities remain more than four times as likely to live in concentrated poverty as their suburban counterparts. The concentration of poverty is getting worse. After declining in the 1990s, the population in extreme-poverty neighborhoods rose by one-third from 2000 to 2009 to 10.5 percent but still well below the 14.1 percent rate in 1990.[91]

Although central cities have more than their fair share of poverty, it is not just concentrated in the central cities. Suburban poverty and inequality among suburbs has grown. Charles Stockdale and Douglas A. McIntyre[92] reported on the ten suburbs with the highest poverty rates in 2008 and compared them to their central cities. The suburban poverty rate was still below that of the central city in half of the cities studied. Moreover, the geographical boundary of the central city in most of the areas with a higher suburban rate encompassed the majority of the metropolitan areas. In other words, there are few separate municipalities in these metropolitan areas. Table 2.5 shows the results of the study.

The disparity between the central city and the suburbs continues to show that the city houses more than its fair share of poor people. Lewis and Hamilton computed the ratio of poverty between the city and the suburb using 2000 census data and reported that a city resident is almost twice as likely to be poor as a suburban resident. The greatest extremes are in Milwaukee, Wisconsin, Reading and York, Pennsylvania and Topeka, Kansas, where a resident of the central city is about five times more likely than a

Table 2.5 2008 Poverty Rates in the Ten Most Impoverished Suburban Areas Compared to their Central Cities

Metropolitan Area	Suburban Rate %	Central City Rate %
McAllen, TX	36.7	28.3
El Paso, TX	31	24.3
Bakersfield, CA	24.2	16.7
Fresno, CA	18.8	25.5
Lakeland, FL	15.8	13.3
Modesto, CA	14.6	13.5
Little Rock, AR	14.2	18.6
Jackson, MS	14	26.9
Augusta-Richmond, GA	14	24.1
Albuquerque, NM	13.6	15

Source: Charles Stockdale and Douglas A. McIntyre, Poverty's Not Just for Cities: America's 10 Poorest Suburbs, The *Wall Street Journal*, http://www.dailyfinance.com/2011/08/16/povertys-not-just-for-cities-americas-10-poorest-suburbs. [Accessed May 30, 2012].

suburban resident to be in poverty.[93] Indeed, the actual percentage of poor people living in the suburbs in large metropolitan areas is higher at 53 percent than in the central cities. Of course, a greater percentage of residents in these metropolitan areas also live in the suburbs.[94] Poverty in many inner-ring or first suburbs increased dramatically between 1980 and 2000. In one study of a sample of 3,428 suburbs, 217 or 13 percent of the inner-ring suburbs were classified as suburbs in crisis. Over 12 percent of the inner-ring suburbs in the South and the West are classified as high poverty (over 20 percent of the population in poverty). For the South, the increase is threefold from 1980. Ford Heights, a Chicago suburb, has a 49 percent poverty rate. Gladeview, a Miami suburb, had over 50 percent poverty rate in 2000.[95]

There is also a strong relationship between poverty and the minority population. For example, of the 1,267,149 people below the poverty level in the Chicago metropolitan area in 2010, only 344,973 were non-minorities. Of the total in poverty, 36 percent were black and 30 percent were Hispanic. If you are black living in the Chicago metro area, you have a 29 percent chance of being poor. This is compared to 20 percent for Hispanics and 6.7 percent chance for the white population. However, in Chicago, the chances of being in poverty are high, if you are black or Hispanic, an indication of the concentration of poverty in the central city. Of the black population in Chicago, 33.6 percent are living below the poverty line, while 23.2 percent of the Hispanic population is below the poverty line.[96]

Concentrations of poor require additional government expenditures in increased welfare, health, police, and other services. To the extent that these costs are not financed by federal and state aid, they must be borne by the city's tax revenue, putting an unequal burden on central city taxpayers relative to taxpayers in the remainder of the metropolitan area. In addition, heavy concentrations of poverty result in property deterioration, reducing property tax revenue. Thus, the additional taxes required in the central city to support poverty-related services and the increased costs associated with blighted neighborhoods, dysfunctional families, drugs, and crime must increasingly be borne by a declining property tax base. The result is that taxes increase or services decrease. This encourages a population exodus of middle-class taxpayers to the suburbs to avoid the higher taxes and the deterioration of the neighborhoods. This exodus leads to further neighborhood deterioration.

Violent Crime in Central Cities

There is a correlation between violent crime and dysfunctional, impoverished neighborhoods.[97] Galster and Santiago concluded from a review of the literature that high concentrations of poverty lead to weaker social cohesion and lack of informal social controls and norms, lack of positive role models, increased crime, single parent and dysfunctional families, lack of institutional resources and public services, spatial mismatch with jobs, and exacerbated racial and class differences.[98]

A study in Philadelphia showed that for every percentage point increase in the neighborhood poverty rate, the major crime rate increased by 0.8 percent. A study in Columbus, Ohio, showed that in a neighborhood where the poverty rate is under 20 percent, the violent crime rate is around 7 per 1,000, whereas in neighborhoods where the poverty rate is over 40 percent, the crime rate is 23 per 1,000.[99] With the highest concentrations of poverty in the central cities, crime rates continue to be much higher than in the suburbs. Even though suburbs with increasing concentrations of poor African Americans or immigrants do experience some increases in crime, almost 62 percent of the crimes of violence per 1,000 population and almost 60 percent of the property crimes per 1,000 households were committed in central cities in 2004. This ratio has increased as the central cities accounted for 59 percent of the violent crimes and 57 percent of the property crimes in 1996.[100]

Anthony Downs writes about crime in the central city as follows:

> Inner-city residents are afraid to venture onto their streets and sidewalks. Many families will not allow their children to walk to school unescorted. Homes and stores are routinely burglarized or robbed at gunpoint. In many cities, gunshot wounds are the leading cause of death among black males age 14 to 24. In some inner-city neighborhoods, more than half of all young men are either in jail, on parole, or awaiting trial. These conditions grotesquely mock the personal freedoms a democratic

society supposedly guarantees. If people cannot walk outside their homes without fear of robbery, attack, or injury, they are not free. This extreme insecurity in inner-city neighborhoods results to a large extent from the concentration of low-income household's there.[101]

The rate of violent crime in the United States in 1990 was double the rate in 1970 and the highest recorded rate in the century.[102] However, since that time, crime rates have declined. For example, between 1994 and 1995, violent crime declined 12 percent nationwide, the largest yearly decline in more than 20 years. There are still substantial differences between crime rates in the central cities and the suburbs. For example, in 2006, the most recent available data on crime statistics between the cities and the suburbs, the violent crime rate in the central cities was 29.7 per 1,000 persons age 12 or older, a slight uptick from 2005 compared to the suburban rate of 18.9 per 1,000. However, the suburban rate increased one full point over 2005.[103]

The perception of crime is usually greater than its actual occurrence. The media feed these perceptions with extensive coverage of crime. One study in the Twin Cities found that people's fears of being a victim of crime in the central city were, in many instances, more than six times their true likelihood of becoming a victim. The media help to reinforce negative suburban perceptions of crime in the central cities. Barriers of regionalism increase when suburbanites feel safe in their suburban communities.[104] However, if suburbanites fear that central city crime is spilling over into the suburbs, this could result in pressures for regional cooperation, at least in the area of police services.

Saving our Central Cities

While there is evidence that some of our core cities are staging an economic comeback, many of our central cities continue to be beset by serious economic, fiscal, and social problems. It is rather imperative, for a number of important reasons that we "go about the business" of ensuring and enhancing the vitality of our core cities. The central city serves to identify a metropolitan area, constituting a larger set of mental associations. In this regard, the central city, the "flagship" of its region, serves as a larger, or regional, community image, or symbol, and provides a means of identity for outsiders. Another reason for ensuring the vitality of our core cities arises from their importance as vital centers of business activity and commerce. As indicated above, the economic vitality of the central city has a strong effect on the economic vitality of the region. Moreover, the agglomeration economies that central cities contribute to the region are still important in the global economy for reducing the costs of transportation, increasing access to skilled and specialized labor, and fostering innovation. One survey of 5,000 large firms found that central city firms provided 92 percent of the professional services contracted for in the region. Suburbia does not yet comprise an economically autonomous "outer city" or "edge city". Finally, enhancing the overall economic vitality of our core cities will create employment opportunities for city residents who are often the most disadvantaged residents of the region in obtaining jobs.[105] Former New York City Mayor David N. Dinkins expressed the need to save and revitalize our central cities:

> Cities . . . serve as our commercial and intellectual market-places, where economics and philosophy, entertainment and art, science and technology, ideas and emotions, flourish and enrich the American experience. Like a mighty engine, urban America pulls all of America into the future . . . As our cities go, so goes America and our unique civilization.[106]

Henry Cisneros, former Secretary of the U.S. Department of Housing and Urban Development, stated this theme in a television interview:

> I think one of the things America has to address very, very squarely is whether or not we can live with continued vast spatial separations between the poorest of our populations concentrated in public housing in central cities, and the vast differences that exist across urban geography to the suburbs, which are essentially white. What we've got to do is to break up the concentrations by making it possible for people to live in newly-designed, thoughtfully scaled public housing negotiated with outlying communities.[107]

Others suggest that the cities should get "their own house in order" before looking for help from the federal or state governments. Critics of the bailing-out-the-central-cities solution argue that central cities need to decrease their taxes and spending before looking for additional help from federal and state governments. A study by Stephen Moore and Dean Stansel of the 80 largest central cities shows substantial taxing and spending differences between cities classified as healthy and those classified as unhealthy. City taxes are roughly twice as high in unhealthy cities for a family of four, compared to healthy cities. They calculated the average bureaucracy in unhealthy cities to be over twice as large as in healthy cities. City expenditures in healthy cities averaged half as much per capita than in shrinking cities, $1,152 per capita. This study concluded that cities can and should solve their own problems: "Through an aggressive agenda of budget control, tax reduction, privatization, and deregulation, America's cities can rise again in prominence and prosperity."[108]

Economist Anthony Downs refutes these conclusions. Conducting a regression analysis on the same data, he found that the fiscal variables have some impact on city growth or decline (as measured by population change) but nothing like the dominant causality claimed. Downs concludes:

> Cities might very well profit from reducing taxes, cutting bureaucracy, and privatizing some services. But such policies are not sufficient to cope with the problems society has loaded onto cities by concentrating so many poor people in them. The conclusion that declining cities are overfunded in relation to their capabilities rather than underfunded is not supported by Moore and Stansel's study and probably cannot be supported by any other study.[109]

Regional Policy Issues in One Metropolitan Area: Chicago[110]

The Chicago region has 8,600,000 residents today and must plan for 11,000,000 by 2040. During decades of rapid but largely uncoordinated expansion, the region grew in patterns that were not sustainable. New homes cropped up in areas that were difficult to reach by automobile and virtually impossible by public transit. Jobs created were often far from the region's residential centers, keeping commuters tied up in traffic and wasting billions of dollars in lost time and fuel. Patterns of development consumed land at a rapid rate, with serious implications for natural resources—including less open space, potential water shortages, and diminished air quality. Water is increasingly scarce, especially where communities rely on groundwater. Even in communities that get water from Lake Michigan, its use is limited by law. The lack of walkability and the inadequate recreational and open spaces in some communities create unacceptable health disparities. Some areas—often correlated to race and income—lack grocery stores with fresh produce, which negatively impacts the health of the residents in those communities.

The cumulative choices of 284 municipalities and seven counties determine quality of life and economic prosperity across the region. With local autonomy over land use comes the responsibility to consider how those decisions shape a community's livability, including how they affect neighboring communities and the region as a whole. Achieving livability will take proactive planning by local governments that recognize the potential regional impacts of even seemingly small local decisions. The region lacks a comprehensive plan and consistent land use ordinances and regulations. Communities do not cooperate or collaborate with one another to build on lessons learned to develop solutions for common problems, such as housing, transportation, economic development, water, or other issues. The region lacks adequate parks to provide recreation and open space.

Now more than ever, taxpayers expect efficiency and transparency when governments invest their limited resources. To maximize the benefits that residents of the region expect, government agencies across the region need to coordinate decisions and investments strategically. Current tax policy too often unintentionally encourages choices that undermine the long-term interests of the region and its communities. Sales tax revenues are an incentive for municipalities to seek out retail development that creates fewer high-wage jobs and economic benefits compared to office or industrial development. The current sales tax system pushes communities into intense competition to attract retail businesses that generate sales. Such developments, including "big box" stores and auto dealerships, offer fewer economic benefits compared to the high-wage jobs and economic impacts of office developments and industry. An over-reliance on sales taxes can also leave municipalities short of funds when retail sales slump in economic downturns.

Property taxes vary greatly from community to community. Property taxes can create confusion for taxpayers and local governments alike. For example, assessment levels often differ by county. Special exemptions apply to some property types but not others, and state-imposed local tax caps set arbitrary limitations on annual local tax levies—all of which can create instability and unpredictability. Dependence on the property tax for public education creates wide disparities in school funding throughout the region. Some areas within the region have a much larger economic base of property and retail sales than others, which gives them a greater tax capacity. Extreme divergences make it hard for many local governments to provide essential services and attract new residents and businesses. Even worse, this gap has increased over time, as municipalities with strong revenues have kept property tax rates lower while also providing high-quality services and infrastructure.

In addition to sharing information, the region needs to work together to provide more coordinated delivery of services and remove the barriers that prevent coordination of programs at the local, regional, state, and federal levels. Working together, governments can be more effective, which will help make communities more economically competitive and more livable for all residents. One community, or even a single level of government, cannot solve the most pressing problems alone. Accounts of wasteful and duplicative government spending, whether real or perceived, are common. The unintended consequences of outdated policies and bureaucracies include higher government costs and less accountability. With over 1,200 different units of government providing services to residents, businesses, and visitors of the seven county regions, increasing efficiency depends on better coordination, communication, and where appropriate, consolidation of services.

Historically, the Chicago region's transportation system has been a foundation of the region's success. But the system's infrastructure was built decades ago, with inadequate ongoing investment to keep it up to date. To sustain the region's economy and quality of life, residents must be able to travel quickly and easily around the region so they can choose from a wide variety of jobs and communities in which to live. At present, many residents have no choice but to drive because the communities were designed primarily for car travel. Often residents live long distances from where they work because jobs and housing in their region are far apart. The region's congestion is already among the nation's highest. The region's residents spend 1.8 million hours every day in congested traffic with the annual cost of the congestion estimated at $7.3 billion. The region has 66 percent of the state's population but only receives 45 percent of the state's road funds. Public transportation keeps cars off the roads, reduces congestion for everyone who drives, and improves air quality for all.

Takeaway

The policy issues besetting metropolitan areas call for regional governance solutions. Central city problems negatively impact the region and require a regional solution. Because of the general perception that these problems are getting worse, there is a renewed interest in regional solutions. As long as the problems were contained in isolated areas of the region not generally visible in the suburbs, there was little pressure for regional solutions. However, problems once largely contained in the central cities have come to the suburbs. In addition, sprawl-related problems have negative consequences throughout the metropolitan area. Transportation gridlock, crime, pollution, and loss of open space require regional solutions. As metropolitan residents perceive that conditions are getting worse and their quality of life is deteriorating, they demand solutions that require regional governance. There is also increasing awareness that the central city is an important part of the region and that improving the quality of life for the residents of the inner city improves the quality of life for residents of the entire metropolitan area.

Notes

1. Quoted in Robert A. Beauregard, *Voices of Decline: The Postwar Fate of US Cities* (Cambridge, MA: Blackwell Publishers, 1993), p. 197.
2. See, for example, Henry G. Cisneros, (ed.), *Interwoven Destinies: Cities and the Nation* (New York: W. W. Norton, 1993); Anthony Downs, *New Visions for Metropolitan America* (Washington, DC: Brookings Institution, 1994); Neal R. Peirce, *Citistates: How Urban America Can Prosper in a Competitive World* (Washington, DC: Seven Locks Press, 1993); David Rusk, *Cities Without Suburbs* (Washington, DC: Woodrow Wilson Center Press, 1993).
3. Joel Garreau, *Edge City: Life on the New Frontier* (New York: Doubleday, 1991).
4. Robert Fishman, "Megalopolis Unbound," *The Wilson Quarterly*, 14 (Winter 1990): 40.
5. Martin Easteal, "The Structuring of Local Government: A Blessing or a Bane? A Look at Britain's Proposed Reorganization," in Howard R. Balanoff, (ed.),

Annual Editions: Public Administration, 4th ed. (Guilford, CT: Dushkin/Brown and Benchmark, 1996), pp. 234–35.

6. David Osborne and Ted Gaebler, *Reinventing Government* (Reading, MA: Addison-Wesley, 1992). For information on the national government's efforts at reinventing government, see Albert Gore, *Report of the National Performance Review: Creating a Government that Works Better and Costs Less* (Washington, DC: U.S. Government Printing Office, 1993).

7. Steve Warmbir, "Gangs, Substance Abuse Top Leaders' List of Concerns," *Arlington Heights (Ill.) Daily Herald*, Nov. 29, 1995, sec. 1, p. 1, 5.

8. Mark Baldassare, "Attitudes: On Regional Solutions and Structures," in Joseph F. DiMento and LeRoy Graymer, (eds.), *Confronting Regional Challenges Approaches to LULUs, Growth, and Other Vexing Governance Problems* (Cambridge, MA: Lincoln Institute of Land Policy, 1991), pp. 109–118.

9. Larry N. Gerston and Peter J. Haas, "Political Support for Regional Government in the 1990s Growing in the Suburbs," *Urban Affairs Quarterly*, 29 (September 1993): 154–161.

10. Ibid., p. 156.

11. Madelyn Glickfeld and Ned Levine, *Regional Growth . . . Local Reaction: The Enactment and Effects of Local Growth Control and Management Measures in California* (Cambridge, MA: Lincoln Institute of Land Policy, 1992), pp. 79–81.

12. Anthony Downs, *New Visions for Metropolitan America* (Washington, DC: The Brookings Institution, 1994) pp. 27–30.

13. T. J. Becker, "All Over the Map," *Chicago Tribune*, Jan. 21, 1996, sec. D, p.1.

14. Kevin Kasowski, "The Costs of Sprawl, Revisited," *PAS Memo*, American Planning Association, February 1993, pp. 1–3.

15. Deborah C. Stone, "Does Business Development Raise Taxes? A Commentary," *Public Investment* (Chicago, IL: American Planning Association, March 1995), p. 3.

16. Nelson, Wikstrom, "Central City Policy Issues in Regional Context," in David Hamilton and Patricia S. Atkins, (eds.), *Urban and Regional Policies for Metropolitan Livability* (Armonk, NY: M.E. Sharpe, 2008), pp. 24–52.

17. David Rusk, *Cities without Suburbs: A Census 2010 Perspective*, 4th ed. (Washington, DC: Woodrow Wilson Center Press, 2013), pp. 105–111.

18. Lincoln Institute of Land Policy, *Alternatives to Sprawl* (Cambridge, MA: Author, 1995), p. 22.

19. Mary Sanchez, "What to do with Vacant Lots, the Unwanted Offspring of Urban Sprawl," *The Kansas City Star*, October 9, 2013, http://www.kansascity.com/2013/10/09/4542365/what-to-do-with-vacant-lots-the.html [Accessed October 13, 2013].

20. Lincoln Institute of Land Policy, *Alternatives to Sprawl*, p. 22.

21. "New Research on Population, Suburban Sprawl and Smart Growth," *Sierra Club*, http://www.sierraclub.org/sprawl/whitepaper.asp; Shaila Dewan, "Is Suburban Sprawl on its way back?" *New York Times*, September 14, 2013. http://www.nytimes.com/2013/09/15/sunday-review/is-suburban-sprawl-on-its-way-back.html?_r=0 [Accessed October 14, 2013].

22. Lester Graham, "Sprawling Cities, Sprawling Waistlines," *Community News and Views*, Michigan State University Urban and Regional Planning, 16 (1) (2004): 9.

23. Downs, *New Visions for Metropolitan America*, p. 6.

24. Wikstrom, "Central City Policy Issues in Regional Context," pp. 24–52.

25. Graham, 2004. "The Right to Sprawl," p 6.

26. Wikstrom, "Central City Policy Issues in Regional Context," pp. 24–52.

27. Quoted in Harold Henderson, "Cityscape: Who Planned This Mess?" *Reader* (Chicago), Mar. 12, 1993, sec. 1, pp. 10, 28–29.

28. Becker, "All Over the Map," sec. D, p. 1.
29. Michael T. Peddle, "The Costs and Effects of Growth Management on the Urban Fringe," paper presented at the annual meeting of the Urban Affairs Association, Toronto, April 15–17, 1997.
30. Quoted in Lincoln Institute of Land Policy, *Alternatives to Sprawl*, p. 11.
31. Anthony Downs, *Stuck in Traffic: Coping with Peak-Hour Traffic Congestion* (Washington, DC: Brookings Institution Press, 1992).
32. Anthony Downs, *Still Stuck in Traffic: Coping with Peak-Hour Traffic Congestion* (Washington, DC: Brookings Institution Press, 2004).
33. David Hamilton, Laurie Hokkanen and Curtis Wood, "Are We still Stuck in Traffic? Transportation in Metropolitan Areas," in David Hamilton and Patricia S. Atkins, (eds.), *Urban and Regional Policies for Metropolitan Livability* (Armonk, NY: M.E. Sharpe, 2008), pp. 266–295.
34. Ibid.
35. Downs, *New Visions for Metropolitan America*, p. 8.
36. Brian McKenzie and Melanie Rapino. *Commuting in the United States: 2009*, American Community Survey Reports, ACS-15. http://www.cenusu.gov [Accessed September 15, 2011].
37. Peter Calthorpe, *The Next American Metropolis: Ecology, Community, and the American Dream* (New York: Princeton Architectural Press, 1993), p. 19.
38. Henderson, "Cityscape: Who Planned This Mess?" sec. 1, p. 28.
39. Deborah C. Stone, "Does Business Development Raise Taxes? A Commentary," *Public Investment* (Chicago: American Planning Association, March, 1995), p. 3; Brian S. McKenzie, Public Transportation Usage among U.S. Workers: 2008 and 2009. *American Community Survey Brief, October 2010,* http://www.census.gov/hhes/commuting/ [Accessed June 14, 2012].
40. Mckenzie, Public Transportation Usage among U. S. Workers: 2008–2009.
41. *2012 Public Transportation Fact Book,* 63rd edition. (Washington, DC: American Public Transportation Association, Sept. 2012), p. 15.
42. Ibid., pp. 28–32; Hamilton, Hokkanen, and Wood, "Are We still Stuck in Traffic? Transportation in Metropolitan Areas," p. 276.
43. Harold Henderson, "Light Rail, Heavy Costs," in Howard R. Balanoff, (ed.), *Annual Editions: Public Administration*, 4th ed. (Guilford, CT: Dushkin/Brown and Benchmark, 1996), pp. 168–169.
44. Hamilton, Hokkanen, and Wood, "Are We still Stuck in Traffic? Transportation in Metropolitan Areas," p. 287.
45. Larry C. Ledebur and William R. Barnes, *City Distress, Metropolitan Disparities, and Economic Growth* (Washington, DC: National League of Cities, 1992); David Rusk, *Cities without Suburbs: A Census 2010 Perspective*, 4th ed. (Washington, DC: Woodrow Wilson Center Press, 2013); and H. V. Savitch, D. Collins, D. Sanders, J. P. Markham, "Ties That Bind: Central Cities, Suburbs, and the New Metropolitan Region," *Economic Development Quarterly*, 7 (November 1993): 341–357.
46. Laura Goering, "Land Wars Are Shaping Up in Tax-Hungry Southwest Suburbs," *Chicago Tribune*, May 22, 1993, sec. 2, p. 3.
47. Harold Wolman and Michael Goldsmith, *Urban Politics and Policy: A Comparative Approach* (Cambridge, MA: Blackwell Publishers, 1992), p. 219.
48. Ryan J. Foley, "In Quest for Jobs, some Cities will Raid Neighbors," *The Avalanche Journal*, February 22, 2012, sec A5.
49. New approaches in cooperation to promote economic growth are discussed in subsequent chapters.
50. J. Lightbody, *City Politics: Canada* (Peterborough, ON: Broadview Press, 2006).
51. Richard Florida, *The Rise of the Creative Class* (New York: Basic Books, 2002).

52. M. Schneider and D. Kim, "The Effects of Local Conditions on Economic Growth, 1977–1990: The Changing Location of High-technology Activities," *Urban Affairs Review*, 32 (2, 1996): 131–157.

53. Joyce O'Keefe, *Regional Issues in the Chicago Metropolitan Area* (Chicago, IL: Metropolitan Planning Council, Jan. 15, 1991), p. 2.

54. David Hamilton and Christopher Stream, "Regional Environmental Policy," in David Hamilton and Patricia S. Atkins, (eds.), *Urban and Regional Policies for Metropolitan Livability* (Armonk, NY: M. E. Sharpe, 2008). p. 330.

55. Dennis R. Judd and Todd Swanstrom, *City Politics: Private Power and Public Policy*, 8th ed. (New York: Harper Collins, 2011).

56. Dennis R. Judd, "Cities, Political Representation, and the Dynamics of American Federalism," in Bryan D. Jones, (ed.), *The New American Politics: Reflections on Political Change and the Clinton Administration.* (Boulder, CO: Westview Press, 1995), pp. 212–231.

57. Wikstrom, "Central City Policy Issues in Regional Context," pp. 24–52.

58. Ibid., p 45.

59. Richard Mattoon, "Issues in Governance Structure for Metropolitan Areas," paper presented at Midwestern Metropolitan Areas: Performance and Policy Workshop sponsored by the Federal Reserve Bank of Chicago, Nov. 28, 1995, p. 6.

60. Garreau, *Edge City: Life on the New Frontier.*

61. Robert E. Lang and Arthur C. Nelson, *Megapolitan America*, http://places.designobserver.com/entryproint.html [Accessed November 14, 2011].

62. Igal Chamey, "Re-examining Suburban Dispersal: Evidence from Suburban Toronto," *Journal of Urban Affairs*, 27 (5) (2005): 467–484.

63. William H. Whyte, *City Rediscovering the Center* (New York: Doubleday, 1988), pp. 294–295.

64. Peter O. Muller, "The Suburban Transformation of the Globalizing American City," in David Wilson, (ed.), *Globalization and the Changing U.S. City*, The Annals of the American Academy of Political and Social Science 551 (Thousand Oaks, CA: Sage Publications, May 1997), p. 53.

65. Rick Kolenda and Cathy Yang Liu, "Are Central Cities more Creative? The Intra-metropolitan Geography of Creative Industries," *Journal of Urban Affairs*, 34 (5) (2012): 487–511.

66. David Rusk, *Cities without Suburbs: A Census 2010 Perspective* (Washington, DC: Woodrow Wilson Center Press, 2013), pp. 47–48.

67. Michael Lewyn, "The City/Suburb Income Gap- Bigger or Smaller?" April 22, 2011. http://www.planetizen.com/node/49081 [Accessed October 15, 2013].

68. Larry C. Ledebur and William R. Barnes, *City Distress, Metropolitan Disparities, and Economic Growth* (Washington, DC: National League of Cities, 1992), p. 3.

69. Elliott D. Sclar and Walter Hook, "The Importance of Cities to the National Economy," in Henry G. Cisneros, (ed.), *Interwoven Destinies: Cities and the Nation* (New York: W. W. Norton, 1993), p. 50.

70. James H. Lewis and David Hamilton, "Poverty and Urban Regions," in David Hamilton and Patricia S. Atkins, (eds.), *Urban and Regional Policies for Metropolitan Livability* (Armonk, NY: M.E. Sharpe, 2008), pp. 232–265.

71. Gregory D. Squires and Charis E. Kubrin, "Privileged Places: Race, Opportunity and Uneven Development in Urban America," *Shelterforce Online*, Issue #147, Feb. 20, 2012, http://nhi.org/online/issues/147/privilegedplaces.html06 [Accessed June 12, 2012].

72. Nancy Burns, *The Formation of American Local Governments: Private Values in Public Institutions* (New York: Oxford University Press, 1994), p. 91.

73. Joe T. Darden, "The Significance of Race and Class in Residential Segregation," *Journal of Urban Affairs*, 8 (Winter) (1986): 54–55.

74. Elmer W. Johnson, "The Dispersed and Segregated Metropolis," paper prepared for Preparing Metropolitan Chicago for the 21st Century, forum sponsored by The Commercial Club of Chicago, Sept. 10, 1996, p. 10.
75. Elizabeth Kneebone, *Job Sprawl Revisited: The Changing Geography of Metro-politan Employment*, The Metropolitan Policy Program (Washington, DC: The Brookings Institution, 2009), http://www.brookings.edu/~/media/research/files/reports/2009/4/06%20job%20sprawl%20kneebone/20090406_job sprawl_kneebone.pdf [Accessed October 16, 2013].
76. Rusk, *Cities without Suburbs: A Census 2010 Perspective*, pp. 55–56.
77. Kneebone, *Job Sprawl Revisited*.
78. Michael A. Stoll, *Job Sprawl and the Spatial Mismatch between Blacks and Jobs,* The Metropolitan Policy Program (Washington, DC: The Brookings Institution, Feb. 2005), http://www.brookings.edu/~/media/research/files/reports/2005/2/metropolitanpolicy%20stoll/20050214_jobsprawl.pdf [Accessed October 15, 2013].
79. Allen J. Scott, *Metropolis: From the Division of Labor to Urban Form* (Los Angeles, CA: University of California Press, 1988), pp. 121–122.
80. Myron Orfield, *Metro Politics: A Regional Agenda for Community and Stability* (Washington, DC: Brookings Institution, 1997), p. 7; Keith Ihlanfeldt, "The Spatial Mismatch Between Jobs and Residential Locations Within Urban Areas," *Cityscape: A Journal of Policy Development and Research*, 1 (August) (1994): 220.
81. "Reverse-Commute Schedules Discourage Work in Suburbs," *Chicago Sun-Times*, Oct. 30, 1979, p. 19.
82. Susan C. Turner, "Barriers to a Better Break: Employer Discrimination and Spatial Mismatch in Metropolitan Detroit," *Journal of Urban Affairs*, 19 (2) (1997): 123–41; Ihlanfeldt, "The Spatial Mismatch Between Jobs and Residential Locations Within Urban Areas," p. 222.
83. Highland Park, Michigan, *Wikipedia,* http://en.wikipedia.org/wiki/Auburn_Hills [Accessed October 15, 2013].
84. Richard Child Hill, "Industrial Restructuring, State Intervention, and Uneven Development in the United States and Japan," in John R. Logan and Todd Swanstrom, (eds.), *Beyond the City Limits: Urban Policy and Economic Restructuring in Comparative Perspective* (Philadelphia, PA: Temple University Press, 1990), p. 77.
85. "Michigan Leaders Defend Detroit Bankruptcy Filing, put Blame for Woes on City," FoxNews.com, July 22, 2013 [Accessed October 15, 2013].
86. U.S. Dept of Labor Bureau of Labor Statistics, *Local Area Unemployment Statistics For 50 Largest Cities and for Metropolitan Areas*, April 2012, http://www.bls.gov/lau/lacilg11.htm [Accessed May 30, 2012].
87. William Julius Wilson, *The Truly Disadvantaged: The Inner City, the Underclass, and Public Policy* (Chicago, IL: University of Chicago Press, 1987), p. 8, quoted in Ihlanfeldt, "The Spatial Mismatch Between Jobs and Residential Locations Within Urban Areas," p. 233.
88. Thomas Gabe, "Poverty in the United States: 2011," Congressional Research Services, September 27, 2012, http://www.fas.org/sgp/crs/misc/RL33069.pdf [Accessed October 15, 2013].
89. Wende Mix, *The Geography of Urban Poverty 2008*, Department of Geography & Planning, Buffalo State College, www.buffalostate.edu/geography/documents/paper.pdf [Accessed May 30, 2012].
90. Downs, *New Visions for Metropolitan America*, pp. 71–75.
91. *The Re-Emergence of Concentrated Poverty: Metropolitan Trends in the 2000s*, Nov. 3, 2011, Brookings Institution, http://www.brookings.edu/research/papers/2011/11/03-poverty-kneebone-nadeau-berube [Accessed May, 30, 2012].

92. Charles Stockdale and Douglas A. McIntyre, "Poverty's Not Just for Cities: America's 10 Poorest Suburbs," *Daily Finance*, August 6, 2011, http://www.dailyfinance.com/2011/08/16/povertys-not-just-for-cities-americas-10-poorest-suburbs [Accessed May 30, 2012].

93. Lewis and Hamilton, "Poverty and Urban Regions," pp. 240–241.

94. Margaret Weir, "Creating Justice for the Poor in the New Metropolis," in Clarissa Rile Hayward and Todd Swanstrom, (eds.), *Justice and the American Metropolis* (Minneapolis, MN: University of Minnesota Press, 2011), pp: 237–257.

95. Bernadette Hanlon, *Once the American Dream: Inner-ring Suburbs of the Metropolitan United States* (Philadelphia: Temple University Press, 2010), pp. 74–76, 94–95.

96. US Census Bureau, American Community Survey. http://factfinder2.census.gov/faces/tableservices/jsf/pages/productview.xhtml [Accessed June 12, 2012].

97. Violent crime is defined as rape, murder, armed robbery, and aggravated assault.

98. George C. Galster and A. M. Santiago, "What's the 'Hood Got to do with it? Parental Perceptions about how Neighborhood Mechanisms Affect their Children," *Journal of Urban Affairs*, 28 (3) (2006): 201–226.

99. Douglas S. Massey, "Concentrating Poverty Breeds Violence," *Population Today*, 24 (June/July) (1996): 5.

100. Lewis and Hamilton, "Poverty and Urban Regions," pp. 232–266.

101. Downs, *New Visions for Metropolitan America,* pp. 79–80.

102. Ibid., p. 79.

103. Michael Rand and Shannan Catalano, "Criminal Victimization, 2006," *Bureau of Justice Statistics Bulletin*, http://www.bjs.gov/index.cfm?ty=pbdetail&iid=2173 [Accessed June 14, 2012].

104. Orfield, *Metro Politics*, p. 24.

105. Wikstrom, "Central City Policy Issues in Regional Context," p. 42.

106. Quoted in Charles P. Cozic, "Introduction," in Charles P. Cozic, (ed.), *America's Cities: Opposing Viewpoints* (San Diego, CA: Greenhaven Press, 1993), p. 14.

107. Quoted in Carl F. Horowitz, "Will American Inner Cities Dismantle Suburban Boundaries?" *The Journal of Social, Political, and Economic Studies*, 19 (spring) (1994): 49.

108. Stephen Moore and Dean Stansel, "The Myth of America's Underfunded Cities," in Charles P. Cozic, (ed.), *America's Cities: Opposing Viewpoints* (San Diego, CA: Greenhaven Press, 1993): 29.

109. Downs, *New Visions for Metropolitan America*, p. 78.

110. Excerpted from *2040 Comprehensive Regional Plan* (Chicago, IL: Chicago Metropolitan Agency for Planning. October 7, 2010).

3 Suburbanization and Annexation

Suburbanites want independence from government . . . and they pretty much want to be left alone . . . They've always been paying for Chicago; they've been doing it forever . . . The day of the free ride is over.
—Pate Philip, Republican leader of the Illinois Senate, 1993[1]

As urban areas grew, development took place outside the borders of cities. People living in these areas received minimal services from the county or township because they were in unincorporated territory. To obtain self-governing powers and more extensive services, people living in unincorporated areas had two options: join another incorporated municipality through annexation or seek to establish themselves as a separate government by obtaining a charter of incorporation from the state. Cities could expand their boundaries and absorb new growth through annexation of unincorporated territory and through mergers with communities that were already incorporated. In the literature, annexation is often used as a generic term to refer to both annexations and mergers. Annexation is used similarly in this chapter. Occasionally, an annexation resulted in the addition of a sizable amount of land. In most instances, however, annexation is generally of an ad hoc, piecemeal nature. A series of small ad hoc territorial acquisitions over the years can add up to a sizable addition. Indeed, the annexation approach to expansion was not incidental. In fact, it was the main source of a city's territorial growth in the nineteenth century and is still the major source of growth for cities today.

For most of the nineteenth century it was expected that the development on the fringes of the city would someday become part of the growing city. After the Civil War, pockets of resistance emerged in the developing fringe areas to the idea of becoming part of the central city. This resistance became so widespread that by the early twentieth century, it was opposed in most older, established urban areas of the Northeast and Midwest. By the mid-twentieth century, annexation was generally opposed by suburbanites throughout the country. Methods to resist annexation included municipal incorporation and the establishment of suburban municipal government associations to fight encroachment by the central city. These associations were generally successful in lobbying state legislatures on behalf of measures to require the consent of the population being annexed.

The Suburbanization Movement

The urban area was geographically quite small until nineteenth-century industrialization and new technology provided the opportunity and the means for expansion. With industrialization and new technology, larger factories were built and more workers were employed. Advances in transportation technology made more workers available for the larger factories because they could travel greater distances to work. With transportation improvements, the urban area divided into geographically differentiated residential, commercial, and industrial zones. Previous to these revolutionary changes in transportation, territorial differentiation was limited with employment, shopping, and services in close proximity–generally accessible by foot from the surrounding residential area. Horse-drawn conveyances were generally reserved for the upper classes. Economic activity was on a small scale because of the limited transportation options. Communities prior to the transportation revolution were generally self-contained areas providing for the employment, social, shopping, and service needs of the residents.[2] People generally lived no farther than a one-to-two-mile walk from their place of employment and even closer to shopping and services. As transportation improved with the introduction of streetcars, trolley lines, and then the automobile, workers could live farther away, and, as more workers and new technology became available, factories were able to expand.

The geographical expansion of urban areas was more than just a response to industrialization and new transportation technology. The suburban movement was also driven by land developers and philosophical, social, and religious values. According to historian Robert Fishman, religion played a major role in the suburbanization of urban areas. This was an evangelical movement, a religious revival to separate home from work–to shelter wives and family from the vices associated with the city and to make the home a private place of retreat from the evils fostered by the *Gesellschaft*. The sanctity of the nuclear family and the woman's role as the nurturer and preserver of religious values through the family became the center of the evangelical movement in the late eighteenth and early nineteenth centuries. Catharine Beecher, a major spokesperson for the movement in America, wrote in her influential *Treatise on Domestic Economy* in 1841 that the role of women as homemakers was their greatest work. She wrote that women, as homemakers, must deflect the temptations of urban life and that the home was the best place for preserving and nurturing Christian morality.[3]

Religion had not previously championed the nuclear family. Indeed, the family previous to the evangelical movement had been an open and extended family unit. Its role was as much, if not more, an economic as an emotional unit, useful as a means of organizing work and providing workers for the family business.[4] Business and living, more often than not, took place in the same building. What started as an evangelical religious movement to separate home from work soon became a means of class separation, as only the upper and upper-middle classes could afford the move to the suburbs. It was not until after the mid-twentieth century that large numbers of the lower class could enjoy the benefits of the suburbs.

The role of the private developer was another major factor in the suburban movement. There was substantial money to be made from land development. The developer played a major role in the suburbanization movement starting as early as the 1820s in Manchester, England. Farmland on the periphery was cheaper than land in the urban core. This farmland became much more valuable when subdivided and developed for suburban housing.[5] Furthermore, the property in the core of the city became more valuable as the region grew. Therefore, those merchants who moved to the periphery and transformed their combination house/workplace in the core to a workplace, benefited not only by the increased work space from the transformation but also from the increased value to the property in the core. Moreover, if the merchant bought undeveloped farmland and developed it for himself plus sold plots to others, he profited from the increased value of the developed property.

Those moving to the suburbs in the nineteenth century tended to gather in communities or subdivisions near others with similar interests or backgrounds. There was, thus, a sorting in the suburbs by religion, economic class, work, and ethnicity so that each suburb became a homogeneous community. Historian Ann Keating maintains that this pattern of homogeneous suburban communities was fostered by nineteenth-century developers who sought ways of making their subdivisions marketable to specific groups of purchasers who made similar demands for improvements and amenities. The developers subdivided the land and put in streets, water, and sewers and then marketed the lots for building. They put in infrastructure that would attract particular groups. The size of lots, the locale, and other amenities were important factors in determining the type of purchasers.[6] Some people moved from the central city to seek a more rural, quieter lifestyle. Others left the city to escape the political machines and the central city bureaucracy that had grown to the point that citizens felt powerless toward central city government.[7] Still others moved out, particularly after the mid-twentieth century, because of the influx of blacks and poor people.

As described in Chapter 1, the philosophical and social influences in the development of the local government system also contributed to the suburbanization movement. Anti-city bias of philosophers and writers in the nineteenth century, such as Herbert Spencer, Henry David Thoreau, and Henry James, encouraged people to move out of the cities. In addition, the Jeffersonian ideal of direct democracy and individual participation afforded by small communities influenced the movement. Although America became an urban nation because of economic and technological forces, its social, cultural, and intellectual heritage fostered the desire for small, independent, exclusive communities. Within urban areas people tend to identify with their neighborhood before they identify with the larger city. Their comfort level is in the small neighborhoods. The large sprawling city is a forbidding, but necessary, place where one ventures for work or business. People moved out of the cities not only to seek a better environment in which to raise their families, but also to be in a better position to have their own exclusive community.[8] Moreover, the desire for a more private lifestyle influenced the suburbanization movement. A house on a big lot in the suburbs where a person could retreat and not have to interact with others was appealing both to apartment dwellers and people living in row houses in the city. Thus, within the urban milieu people sought to live in small communities where they could maintain their privacy and feel comfortable within their own small *Gemeinschaft*.

Suburban Government

With the suburban movement, the basic government structure remained but evolved in various permutations. Additional layers were added to accommodate changing technology and to meet the needs of the residents. Neither the county nor the townships had the power to provide the sorts of services available through the incorporated municipality. Because of this, many developers, especially the early ones, made whatever improvements they considered necessary in order to market the land without the aid of local government services. Some developers provided more substantial service improvements, including water and sewer connections. A few continued to provide these services without the aid of local government. A local improvement association, organized by Joseph Sears, made major improvements in Kenilworth, a suburb of Chicago, without any initial help from local government. In Pullman, Illinois, the Pullman train car company, which built the town, assumed many of the functions usually provided by a city corporation. The company furnished the residences with the basic amenities of water, gas, and electric lights.[9] Most developers, however, turned to local government for aid in providing services that would make their subdivisions attractive as suburban settlements. The immediate problem with petitioning local governments outside the city for these services was that these governments often did not possess the powers to provide them. Even if the townships and counties could have supplied the services, their many rural residents were opposed to the tax increases necessary to provide improved services to suburban communities within their midst.

As metropolitan areas grew, different forms of government emerged from the pressures to provide services. In the developing areas of the Northeast and Midwest, the response to suburban pressures for improved services and self-determination was to allow small rural settlements and suburban subdivisions to incorporate as villages. (The Boston area was a major exception to suburban subdivisions incorporating as villages.) Prior to the mid-nineteenth century, only large urban areas were allowed to incorporate as cities. Village incorporation was a new concept. Incorporated villages in outlying areas were granted most of the same powers as cities but on a much smaller scale. By the mid-nineteenth century, most state legislatures across the country, strongly influenced by precedents in New York, granted a village charter to virtually any community that requested one, allowing and even encouraging this new application of what had once been a rarely granted privilege.[10]

Another alternative for local government service delivery, applied mainly in the South and West, was to authorize the county to provide increased services to urbanizing areas outside the city's jurisdiction. The larger county units provided greater geographical bases for service provision. Fewer suburban forms emerged in these areas. A third alternative, used in many states in the Northeast and Midwest, was to allow townships to incorporate. However important the township was in the developing urban areas of the Northeast and Midwest, it played virtually no role in metropolitan areas in the South and West. Historian Ann Keating writes:

> For instance, California did not use the township except as a judicial unit. Nor did townships exist as intermediate forms for cities like Los Angeles and San Francisco to annex as they grew. Instead, the county was the basic unit of local government in California. There, as in some other western and southern states, a chartered county form evolved that was employed in urban areas where more functions were demanded of local government.[11]

Character of the Suburbs

Although the initial character of the area was determined by the developer, the homogeneity of the settlement did not disappear when the original developer faded from the scene. Once a dominant religion and ethnicity were established, others of the same ethnicity and religious persuasion tended to be attracted to the development. Residents preferred exclusive communities.[12] Thus, once the subdivision pattern was set, it was maintained and fostered by residents and the governments they established. This pattern of differentiation and sorting that started in the nineteenth century carried over into the segregated, homogeneous suburban communities of the twentieth century.

As cities grew in the nineteenth century and the suburban movement took hold, a clear differentiation by class and separation of work and living space occurred. Whereas the early cities were inclusive, mixing rich and poor and work and living space, with suburbanization, the wealthy and middle classes moved out of the center areas of the city to the periphery and built exclusive developments. Exclusiveness and class distinctions were maintained by the higher cost of living in the suburbs. The detached, expansive suburban houses were more expensive as contrasted to the row houses and tenements surrounding the factories and businesses in the central city. The expensive homes and the cost of transportation to work were barriers effectively excluding the working poor from the outlying areas. Restrictive deed covenants also maintained the character and exclusiveness of the suburb. Deed covenants prohibited division of lots for smaller houses or their use for multifamily dwellings. Moreover, a typical covenant set a minimum value for a house, prohibited any commercial or industrial use, and frequently barred Jews and blacks.[13] With the twentieth-century migration of blacks from the rural South to the urban areas of the North, racial deed restrictions became more common.

When race-restrictive covenants were outlawed in 1948 by the U.S. Supreme Court, the broad powers granted to incorporated municipalities to maintain economic and social order took on added importance. Local government zoning powers became much more important as a means for controlling who could reside in the municipality. The zoning powers legally could not exclude identifiable groups but could restrict lower-income groups through minimum lot sizes and restrictions on multifamily housing. These restrictions have served well to maintain the exclusiveness of municipalities. Professor Nancy Burns examined a number of incorporations in the 1960s in counties with large minority populations. In all cases she found the minority population in suburban areas that incorporated was minuscule to nonexistent even 20 years later.[14] Since colonial times, incorporation has been an effective mechanism in controlling the development and use of land and determining who would be allowed to reside within the municipality's boundaries.

The suburban movement fostered a more private, individualistic lifestyle. While most city open space is public and is not controlled by individuals, it is just the opposite in the suburbs. The private space allows maximum individual control and provides a privacy buffer between residents. In order to be effective at exclusion through the zoning powers, people have to be able to control their community borders. This is only achievable through the powers granted by the state through incorporation. Therefore, it was not enough just to move to the suburbs. The *Gemeinschaft* had to be able to maintain its exclusiveness. It did this through restrictive deed covenants and through its zoning power to control who or what was allowed to settle in the community.

By the late 1800s, the suburb had become the lifestyle of choice for those who could afford it. The suburban lifestyle was championed as bringing together the best of both urban and rural living: preserving rural values and enabling residents to enjoy the economic advantages available in the city while retaining the amenities of country life. The utopian Ebenezer Howard wrote that suburban living was the "perfect" combination of the advantages of the most energetic and active town life with all the beauty and delight of the country. Landscape Architect Frederick Law Olmsted said the suburbs were "the most attractive, the most refined, and the most soundly wholesome form of domestic life man has yet attained."[15]

The suburban movement following World War II differed from earlier suburban movements in that it was a mass movement extensively involving the working classes that were generally excluded from earlier suburbanization. This movement was ignited by the general demobilization, the pent-up demand for housing by the returning GIs, accessible and affordable transportation, and federal government policies that encouraged suburban development.[16] Suburbanization in this period was not an escape from the evils of the city but a need to find an acceptable, affordable house in a conducive environment with a reasonable commute to work. Indeed, the central city remained the orientation for the majority of the suburban dwellers and dominated the region. Work, recreation, friends, relatives, and major shopping were in the city. The ties between the suburbanites and the central city remained strong.

An unprecedented expansion in the number of births in the immediate postwar period also spurred suburbanization. The residential choices of the new families were the link between suburbanization and the baby boom. Parents wanted outdoor play space, good schools, and pleasant surroundings for their families. The suburbs provided the kind of nurturing environment the parents desired for their growing families.[17] The long commute to work and the isolation from the stimulation and excitement of city life were the necessary sacrifices to provide the desired environment for raising children.

The most recent significant impact on the suburbs has been the large influx of Hispanic and other foreign-born immigrants to the suburbs. The last decade of the twentieth century witnessed the largest influx of immigrants than any other decade in the nation's history. A major portion of the immigrants were Hispanics both legal and illegal. Whereas previous immigrant movements were largely to central cities, in the most recent movement, four out of ten immigrants moved directly to the suburbs. The perception that the suburbs are middle-class, white communities has been forever dispelled by this large influx of Hispanic immigrants. Suburban diversity has become to a large extent a reflection of central city neighborhoods often segregated by race, ethnicity, and economic class.[18]

Impact of Suburbanization on the Metropolitan Area

One result of suburbanization was a substantial change in the most populous cities. Obviously, those cities able to capture a good share of the suburban growth through annexation or consolidation were able to grow while those that could not usually stagnated or declined. The cities with the largest land area tended to be the most populous cities. Prior to the rapid suburbanization after World War II, the large cities were also very densely settled. Many cities with small land area but high population density were among the most populated cities in the United States. For example, in 1940 Newark, New Jersey, with less than 24 square miles, numbered 18 among the most populous cities. Only 6 cities out of the top 25 in 1940 contained more than 100 square miles, and five of those were the top five cities. The median population density of the top 25 cities in 1940 was over 11,000 people per square mile.

With the rapid population decentralization that occurred in the last half of the twentieth century, those cities that could annex unincorporated land or had undeveloped land within their boundaries grew while those cities surrounded by incorporated municipalities stagnated or lost population. As Table 3.1 shows, a substantial change occurred in the top cities between 1940 and 2000, with each of the top 12 cities in 2000 containing over 100 square miles of land and all but six of the top 25 cities having over 100 square miles of territory. Only Boston and San Francisco had less than 50 square miles, and they dropped in the rankings from 1940, with Boston going from ninth to twenty-first. Table 3.1 indicates substantial declines in the population density for the top 25 cities between 1940 and 2000. However, the decline in density reached its nadir in 1990. In almost every city on the list the population density inched up between 1990 and 2000 indicating both a heavy immigrant influx and a regentrification of the inner cities.

The impact of suburbanization also changed the population and employment dynamics in urban areas. Central cities no longer dominated the urban region in population or employment. The impact of suburbanization was more pronounced on older central cities than on newer-growth cities or cities that expanded their boundaries to capture the growth on the periphery. Table 3.2 shows the changes in the population distribution from 1940 to 2010 between the central city and the suburbs for the ten largest cities in 1940. The table also includes Houston and Indianapolis, two cities that substantially expanded their borders–Indianapolis through a city–county consolidation and Houston through aggressive annexation. Although the table shows substantial growth in the suburbs, some of this growth has been through redefinition of the metropolitan area to encompass more land area. Although the geographical area is not consistent through the years, the table shows the population distribution between the central city and the suburbs

Table 3.1 Land Area and Population Density for the Twenty-five Most Populated Cities in 1940 and 2000

1940 Rank	City	Sq. Miles	Pop. Per Sq. Mile	2000 Rank	City	Sq. Miles	Pop. Per Sq. Mile
1	New York	299.0	24,933	1	New York	303.0	26403
2	Chicago	206.7	16,434	2	Los Angeles	469.1	7,877
3	Philadelphia	127.2	15,183	3	Chicago	227.1	12,750
4	Detroit	137.9	11,773	4	Houston	579.4	3,372
5	Los Angeles	448.3	3,356	5	Philadelphia	135.1	11,234
6	Cleveland	73.1	12,016	6	Phoenix	474.9	2,782
7	Baltimore	78.7	10,916	7	San Diego	324.3	3,772
8	St. Louis	61.0	13,378	8	Dallas	342.5	3,470
9	Boston	46.1	16,721	9	San Antonio	407.5	2,809
10	Pittsburgh	52.1	12,892	10	Detroit	138.7	6,855
11	Washington, DC	61.4	10,800	11	San Jose	174.8	5,118
12	San Francisco	44.6	14,227	12	Indianapolis	366.5	2,161
13	Milwaukee	43.4	13,536	13	San Francisco	46.7	16,634
14	Buffalo, NY	39.4	14,617	14	Hempstead Town, NY	120.0	6,301
15	New Orleans	199.4	2,480	15	Jacksonville, FL	757.7	971
16	Minneapolis	53.8	9,153	16	Columbus, OH	210.3	3,384
17	Cincinnati, OH	72.4	6,293	17	Austin, TX	251.5	2,610
18	Newark, NJ	23.6	18,215	18	Baltimore	80.8	8,058
19	Kansas City, MO	58.6	6,812	19	Memphis, TN	279.3	2,327
20	Indianapolis	53.6	7,220	20	Milwaukee	96.1	6,214

(Continued)

Table 3.1 (Continued)

1940 Rank	City	Sq. Miles	Pop. Per Sq. Mile	2000 Rank	City	Sq. Miles	Pop. Per Sq. Mile
21	Houston	72.8	5,282	21	Boston	48.4	12,166
22	Seattle	68.5	5,337	22	Washington, DC	61.4	9,316
23	Rochester, NY	34.8	9,338	23	Nashville, TN	502.3	1,135
24	Denver	57.9	5,568	24	El Paso	249.1	2,263
25	Louisville, KY	37.9	8,419	25	Seattle	83.9	6,717

Sources: U.S. Bureau of the Census, Population: The Growth of Metropolitan Districts in the United States: 1900–1940 (Washington, DC: U.S. Government Printing Office, 1947), pp. 27–32; U.S. Bureau of the Census, 2000 Census of Population and Housing Summary Table GCT-PH1-R http://factfinder2census.gov/faces/tableservices [Accessed June 20, 2012].

Table 3.2 City and Suburbs Population Change for the Ten Largest Cities in 1940 Plus Houston and Indianapolis

City	1940	1950	1970	1990	2010
New York	7,454,995	7,891,957	7,894,862	7,322,564	8,175,133
Suburbs	1,252,671	1,663,986	3,677,037	4,141,141[a]	10,811,976
Chicago	3,396,808	3,620,962	3,366,957	2,783,726	2,695,598
Suburbs	1,102,318	1,556,906	3,611,990	4,549,200[a]	6,765,507
Philadelphia	1,931,334	2,071,605	1,948,206	1,585,577	1,526,006
Suburbs	967,310	1,599,443	2,869,305	3,271,304[b]	4,439,337
Detroit	1,623,452	1,849,568	1,511,482	1,027,974	713,777
Suburbs	672,415	1,166,629	2,688,449	3,354,325[b]	3,582,473
Los Angeles	1,504,227	1,970,358	2,816,061	3,485,398	3,792,621
Suburbs	1,400,319	2,181,329[b]	4,216,014[b]	5,377,766[b]	9,036,196
Cleveland	878,336	914,808	750,903	505,616	396,815
Suburbs	336,607	617,766	1,313,291	1,325,506[b]	1,680,425
Baltimore	859,100	949,708	905,759	736,014	620,961
Suburbs	187,592	507,473	1,164,911	1,646,158[b]	2,089,528
St. Louis	816,048	856,796	622,236	396,685	319,294
Suburbs	551,929	898,538	1,740,781	2,074,414	2,493,621
Boston	770,816	801,444	641,071	574,283	617,594
Suburbs	1,579,698	1,612,924	2,112,629	2,296,386[b]	3,934,808
Pittsburgh	671,659	676,806	520,117	396,879	305,704
Suburbs	1,322,401	1,536,430	1,881,128	1,686,826[b]	2,050,581
Indianapolis	386,972	427,173	743,155	731,327	820,445
Suburbs	68,385	299,949	366,727	578,495	935,796
Houston	384,514	596,163	1,321,394	1,630,553	2,099,451
Suburbs	125,883	339,376	753,637	1,671,384[b]	3,847,349

Sources: U.S. Bureau of the Census, *Population: The Growth of Metropolitan Districts in the United States: 1900–1940* (Washington, DC: U.S. Government Printing Office, 1947), pp. 27–32; U.S. Bureau of the Census, *1990 Census of Population: General Population Characteristics of Metropolitan Areas* (Washington, DC: U.S. Government Printing Office, 1992), sec. 1, pp. 1–29; U.S. Bureau of the Census, *1970 Census of Population: Characteristics of Population*, vol. 1 (Washington, DC: U.S. Government Printing Office, 1992), pp. 180–186; 2010 Census of Population and Housing Demographic Data Profile Table DP-1; www.americanfactfinder.com [Accessed June 21, 2012].

Notes:
[a] Population is for the metropolitan area in the state outside the central city.
[b] Population is in the PMSA or its equivalent outside the major central city.

in the economic area. In every case the central city's dominance has declined over the years as the metropolitan area expanded. It also shows the out-migration of population from the central city except for Los Angeles, Indianapolis, and Houston until after the 1990 census. The 2010 census shows resurgence in growth in some central cities but a continuing decline in most of the older industrial era cities. However, the suburban growth remains strong reflecting the continuing decentralization from the central city, but also the continuing concentration in America's metropolitan areas. The table shows the clear dominance of the suburbs, whereas in 1940 the central cities were dominant.

The exodus to the suburbs did not just involve people. As discussed in Chapter 2, manufacturing jobs, commercial facilities, professional services, and office jobs followed the people out of the central cities to the suburbs. By the early 1960s central cities had experienced sizable losses in employment as suburban employment expanded. In the metropolitan areas with populations greater than one million, the central cities lost over 500,000 jobs while their suburbs were gaining more than 1.5 million jobs between 1954 and 1963. During the 1960s the economic decline of the central cities in most established sectors of economic activity became quite clear.[19]

Suburbs became less and less dependent upon the central city in the postwar years. Urban planner David Birch noted in 1975 that the suburbs were becoming places of self-generating urban growth, and the dominance of the central city's central business district (CBD) as the chief activity center in the region was disintegrating. Many functions formerly found only in the central city CBD moved to the suburbs. He noted that some suburbs were developing complete economic bases of their own and were no longer dependent on the central city for goods and services. He wrote that the economic centers in the suburbs were increasingly oriented to serving markets outside their own metropolitan area. Through networks of highways, air routes, cables, satellites, and computers, suburbs were establishing national and even global economic linkages.[20] Joel Garreau terms these economically independent suburban cities *edge cities*. These suburban cities with complex economies and CBDs increasingly rival the central city CBD. They have high-rise office buildings and provide the same economic services that are found in the central city.[21]

The development of edge cities made possible the decentralization of corporate headquarters that are highly dependent on frequent contacts with associates and clients. In 1994, 47 percent of the Fortune 500 companies were headquartered in the suburbs compared to 11 percent in 1969 and 34 percent in 1978. For example, Manhattan had 29 Fortune 500 companies in 1994 compared to 138 in 1968 and 73 in 1980. Although some left the area, many Manhattan firms relocated to the New York suburbs, which boasted 52 headquarters for Fortune 500 companies in 1994.[22] Other metropolitan areas have experienced similar decentralization of major corporations from the central city. For example, in 2010 the Atlanta metropolitan area had 12 Fortune 500 companies with seven of these located in the suburbs. Chicago had eight Fortune 500 companies while the suburbs had 20.[23] As corporate headquarters move to the suburbs, so also do firms providing corporate support services including highly specialized legal, financial, banking, data-processing, accounting, management, and other specialized business services. Moreover, many professionals have left large downtown firms to start their own firms in the suburbs.

Office space outside central cities has increased dramatically to meet the demand. The boom in suburban office development occurred largely in the 1980s, during which time over half (58 percent) of the suburban office space that exists today was built. In the first half of the 1980s, the square footage of office inventory in the ten largest central city CBD markets increased 25 percent, while the corresponding suburban markets registered more than three times that gain. While the pace of office construction slowed in the 1990s, the overall trend toward suburbanization continued. By 1999, 42 percent of commercial office space nationally was located in suburban areas.[24]

As communications technology became more sophisticated, it provided increased relocation options for back-office functions not requiring frequent personal contacts with clients or associates. Many firms have decentralized these functions to lower-cost areas in the suburbs or even in other cities. For example, American Express has relocated back-office jobs from New York to Salt Lake City, Fort Lauderdale, and Phoenix; Citibank has located back-office jobs to Tampa and Sioux Falls; and some New York-based life insurance companies have established processing centers in Ireland.[25] Even many federal government agencies have decentralized processing of forms from the downtown office buildings to the suburbs.

Decentralized business location patterns are not uniform across the suburbs. In fact, business activity has recentralized in the suburbs in distinct clusters and corridors. The location advantages associated with agglomeration economies is evident in suburban development. A few magnet areas in the suburbs attract growth. In this way, firms obtain the amenities of a suburban location but retain the conveniences and business advantages generally associated with the city's central business district. (See Chapter 2 for a more thorough discussion of the comparative advantages of the central business district of the central city.) Moreover, developers attempt to maximize the returns on their investment by developing business space in relatively high densities in the most accessible suburban locations. Easy access to transportation is a major consideration in the development of business centers and corridors.[26]

In addition to the adverse economic impact on the central city, suburbanization resulted in extreme residential segregation of African

Americans. Between 1950 and 1970 more than 12 million whites moved out of the central cities and five million African Americans moved in. As African Americans won more political equality, whites sought to establish racially exclusive suburbs. According to a study by Nancy Burns, "racial motivations had overwhelming power in the formation of U.S. cities in the 1950s and 1960s."[27] The Voting Rights Act of 1965 not only removed impediments to registration and voting for African Americans but put constraints on the formation of municipalities to preserve exclusionary white enclaves. Section 5 of the Act provided that no changes in election laws or municipal boundaries could be made without prior clearance from the federal government. This section applied to nine states and portions of 13 other states that in the past had enacted barriers to exclude African American political participation. The Act increased incentives to form racially exclusive municipalities but also made it more difficult to do so by increasing the monitoring of both motivations for, and effects of, the creation of new governments.[28] (The impact of racial segregation is also discussed in Chapter 2.)

As a new generation grew up in the suburbs, the children did not have the close ties their parents had to the central city. When their parents first moved out of the central city, they went back to the central city on a regular basis for jobs, to visit friends and relatives, for major shopping, for recreation, and so on. Over the years, as amenities and job opportunities grew in the suburbs, the connection to the central city lessened. The suburban orientation changed dramatically from what it had been in the 1950s. The generation that grew up in the suburbs had no emotional connection to the city. Moreover, jobs, shopping, and recreation came to the suburbs negating the need for regular travel into the central city. Suburban living is the dominant lifestyle in America and is emulated and sought after as a sign of affluence and success.

Many suburbanites seldom go into the city except for a cultural or sports activity. Even in these events, the city is starting to lose its dominance. Some professional sports teams have relocated to the suburbs, and the number of suburban facilities offering theater, concerts, and art displays is increasing. For example, since the mid-1970s, at least 14 theaters or performing arts centers operated by communities, colleges, or private groups have opened facilities in the Chicago suburbs offering a variety of cultural and theatrical productions from classical music to touring theatrical productions. Major shows, once only available in the city, are now regularly offered in the suburbs.[29] In addition to having everything they need in the suburbs, suburbanites avoid the central city because of the social, racial, and cultural differences between the city and the majority of the suburbs. Moreover, many suburbanites shun the city because of its high crime rate, and there is no compelling need for them to drive into the city with its congested and unfamiliar areas. In contrast, the suburbs have a pattern that is familiar and comfortable to suburbanites, and they can find their way around without undue fear of crime and excess traffic congestion.[30]

Another major impact of the suburbanization movement is the increasing political isolation of the central city. Political party representation from the metropolitan area indicates this political isolation. Although members of both political parties serve in Congress and in the state legislatures, the central cities are heavily Democratic while the suburbs tend to be heavily Republican. Recent elections shifted political power in many states to suburban Republicans. To the extent that suburban Republican legislators can coalesce around a particular issue, they can control the political agenda for the metropolitan area.

Annexation in the Nineteenth Century

As cities grew, they sought to expand their borders to acquire the peripheral development. Some of the same factors that encouraged incorporation were at work in city expansion. However, there were other factors as indicated below:

- Big city boosterism fueled competition between cities to be larger and better than others, led largely by the city's major businesses and politicians.
- Better services were generally provided in the larger cities.
- It was generally felt that the capital expenses to provide the necessary city services could be provided more cheaply by a large city through economies of scale.
- In many states consolidation occurred by legislative fiat, in other states by majority vote of all voters. For example, residents of the area had no vote in the reconfiguration of New York City's boundaries in 1898. Although voters in the city of Allegheny rejected the merger with Pittsburgh in 1907, it proceeded because of the overall majority vote.
- It was generally assumed that the large city would eventually extend its borders to cover the urban region.[31]

Although some cities grew in the nineteenth century by large annexations, most cities grew by a series of small acquisitions. However, a substantial cumulative effect in many metropolitan areas occurred. For example, Los Angeles expanded in a ten-year period between 1915 to 1925 to nearly four times its original size from 108 to 415 square miles through an aggressive ad hoc annexation policy.[32] Detroit grew constantly between 1880 and 1918 adding areas as they became settled so that vigorous, independent cities could not develop.[33] Pittsburgh added approximately 21 square miles and six settlements in the East End in 1867, four square miles and 11 communities from the South Side in 1872, and Allegheny with its eight square miles of land and a population of 150,000 in 1907.[34]

People in the annexed areas often bitterly opposed the annexation, but their opposition was usually ignored. Examples of forced annexations in the nineteenth century are numerous. In 1854 the consolidation of Philadelphia with its county was approved not by suburbanites, who in fact sent delegation after delegation to oppose it, but rather by lawmakers in Harrisburg. Local referendums were not held on the San Francisco Consolidation Act of 1865 or on any one of the frequent annexations to Chicago and Baltimore prior to the 1880s. Lawmakers added to both St. Louis and Boston three times before 1860, but the local electorate in each city rejected annexation measures submitted in 1853. A vote to reconsolidate the three municipalities of New Orleans met a popular defeat in 1850, only to be forced by special legislation in 1852. The Louisiana state legislature also gave Carrolton to the Crescent City in 1867 without seeking the approval of the aroused residents.[35]

However, not all annexations in the nineteenth century were opposed by the residents of the community being annexed. Numerous examples indicate voter approval. A favorable vote by the residents in the area targeted for annexation was undoubtedly due to the local government failing to meet the needs of its residents. In fact, in many suburbs voters chose to unite with the central city in the late 1800s to receive the superior city services. Fear of disease from inadequate sewer and water systems prompted many favorable votes. In Memphis, Tennessee, fears of a reoccurrence of the yellow fever epidemic that killed almost 10 percent of the population in 1878–79 spurred that area's annexation movement. After the yellow fever epidemic, Memphis devoted considerable resources to provide a sewer system for its residents. By 1898, although city residents had a sewer system, about 30,000 people living outside the city had no sewer lines. Threatened with the possibility of another yellow fever epidemic, suburbanites voted overwhelmingly to annex to the city. As a result, Memphis increased its territory by 12 square miles or 322 percent. Within the next three years the city extended its sewer system by 88 miles.[36] Large cities, like Chicago, Los Angeles, Detroit, Cleveland, and Boston, with their impressive public improvements had something valuable to offer. According to Jon Teaford, between 1850 and 1910, suburban voters generally seemed to favor union with the central city with only a small group regretting their loss of autonomy. Teaford writes about the inconveniences and expense associated with many suburbs:

> Throughout the nation, few suburbs could equal the central cities in provision of public services. In 1890 the Long Island municipality of Jamaica was without sewers, while neither Flushing nor College Point had franchises for electric lights. Although many New York suburbs had

a piped supply of water, in suburban Flatbush the water rate per family was $40, in College Point it was $24.50, and in the Staten Island municipalities of New Brighton and Port Richmond households paid $42 for water. In contrast, the rate in New York City was only $15. New York City had sewers, electric lights, and cheap water, and in 1894 Jamaica, Flatbush, College Point, New Brighton, and Port Richmond each voted to abandon the extravagance and deprivation of independence and to join the much-blessed central city.[37]

Decline of Annexation

During the latter part of the nineteenth century, there were many changes and experiments in government forms to accommodate the growth of urban areas. The state legislatures became more permissive toward incorporation, establishing general laws governing incorporation (as opposed to special act legislation) and providing for different classes of incorporated municipalities so that even communities with small populations could incorporate. The movement to local self-determination on annexation decisions and the easier incorporation process did not seem to hinder central city expansion as long as the central city offered superior services. But easier incorporation and local self-determination became obstacles when alternative methods of obtaining services were available. To the extent that some forms of government were not successful in providing adequate services, annexation to the central city was facilitated. However, if the incorporated municipality was successful in providing services, the easier incorporation laws and opportunity for self-determination brought central city annexation to a halt.

As was previously discussed in this chapter, during the nineteenth century in most Northeast and Midwest states, two forms of incorporated government were authorized to provide for the municipal needs of the developing suburbs: the village and the incorporated township. As urban areas developed, annexation provided the major means by which unsuccessful suburban governments were eliminated. The incorporated township in the nineteenth century generally proved not to be an effective form of government to meet urban needs. The requirement to incorporate the entire township resulted in too large an area with too many diverse needs and interests. Both rural and urban areas were included in the incorporated township—the areas closely linked to the city by rail or streetcar and the rural areas with infrequent contacts with the city. The township had a difficult time catering to the needs of a diverse population, a mixture of rural and urban residents who had different expectations regarding services and taxes. Between 1867 and 1875, seven townships in Cook County incorporated. By 1900, only four incorporated townships remained; the others had voted to combine with Chicago.[38]

When suburban governments were successful at providing services, they proved to be a barrier to annexation by the city. The village form generally proved capable in meeting the needs of the developing urban area because the incorporated village was geographically smaller and the residents were more united in their needs and desires. For example, in both New York and Chicago, as the city absorbed incorporated townships and unincorporated suburbs, a number of outlying suburbs incorporated as villages to stave off annexation and to provide for their own self-governance. The end result of these annexations and incorporations was a metropolitan area composed of a central city surrounded by incorporated cities and villages. A similar process took place in the suburbs adjacent to Boston as it grew to metropolitan status. Boston's major difference from New York and Chicago was that village incorporation was not an option in Massachusetts. Many of these outlying townships had a long-established, independent history until the mid-nineteenth century, when commuter railroads and streetcar lines drew them into Boston's suburban orbit. Charlestown, Cambridge, and Roxbury were among the towns that incorporated during the 1840s. These incorporations brought multiple settlements together in a single incorporated government. For instance, the town of Cambridge was composed of at least three settlements: Old Cambridge, Cambridgeport, and East Cambridge. Some of these modified rural governments proved successful at resisting annexation while Boston annexed others.[39]

Smaller townships and townships that incorporated after World War II were generally able to resist annexation by the central city. For example, Wisconsin did not give townships surrounding Milwaukee authority to incorporate until 1955. After the passage of the law, all of the unincorporated townships contiguous to Milwaukee incorporated and have been successful at blocking further annexation by the city. In this instance, the incorporated township proved capable at providing services and in meeting the needs of the residents.[40] Thus, a major factor in the decline of central city annexation was the ability of suburban areas to receive reasonably priced services.

Professionalization of government, county assumption of services, and the increased use of special service districts greatly improved suburban services. By combining a number of suburbs that individually lacked the resources to provide high-quality sewer, water, educational, or law enforcement services, the county or special service district enabled suburbanites to have urban amenities without becoming part of the central city. In 1915, for example, only 45 percent of Chicago's Cook County environs had a public water supply; by 1934, 85 percent of the municipalities within a 50-mile radius of the central business district (Loop) had the service.[41]

In addition, the increasing political power of the suburbs in united opposition to forced annexation countered big-city boosterism and influenced state legislatures to make annexation more difficult. For instance, after

Pittsburgh successfully annexed Allegheny in 1907 despite bitter resistance from the residents of Allegheny, the remaining suburban municipalities formed an organization whose main purpose was to oppose further annexations by Pittsburgh. This organization was successful in convincing the state legislature to change the law to require that further annexations be approved by the voters of the area targeted for annexation. In most instances, with some exceptions in the South and West, state law now requires majority approval of the voters of the suburb being annexed. Indeed, most state legislatures changed from readily approving annexation requests by central cities to stipulating rigorous procedural and substantive requirements. Annexation by special act legislation that was regularly approved in the nineteenth century is now invariably defeated by anti-urban state legislatures. Where annexation is permitted in a state constitution, as in California, the relevant provision seems intended to thwart rather than to promote the process.[42]

Milwaukee is a good example of annexation pressures by the city and suburban resistance. Until 1893, annexation to the city of Milwaukee required specific legislative approval. This was usually granted, as the state legislature was generally supportive of Milwaukee's annexation efforts. In 1893 the state removed itself from the process. The process established by the state legislature required a petition, signed by a majority of the property holders in the community requesting annexation. The Milwaukee City Council could then approve the annexation request. The city aggressively pursued acquisition of adjacent territory during the first half of the twentieth century. It established the Department of Annexation in 1923 to be the focus for annexation efforts. A major enticement to induce outlying areas to join the city was cheap and accessible water and sewer service. Milwaukee also appealed to the sense of civic pride and the improved property values from becoming a part of a great city. Despite these enticements, there was substantial resistance. In an attempt to negate this resistance, the city unsuccessfully tried to change state legislation to allow annexation by the city with no veto power by the area targeted for annexation. The city did have some success until the state allowed the incorporation of townships in 1955. The townships surrounding Milwaukee incorporated, effectively prohibiting further expansion by Milwaukee.[43]

The communities in Westchester County are another example of how suburbs resisted annexation. They responded to annexations by New York City of developed areas in the 1870s and the 1880s by a series of defensive incorporations. In 1874, around the time New York annexed Morrisania, West Farms, and Kingsbridge, there were a number of incorporations. Again, a number of incorporations occurred in the 1890s around the time of the annexation by New York of Wakefield, Williamsbridge, the town of Westchester, and parts of the towns of Eastchester and Pelham. Bronxville, for example, incorporated in 1898 with fewer than 500 residents, and

Scarsdale incorporated in 1914 with White Plains expanding in its direction.[44]

Even though residents in the annexed area resisted, annexation to the larger city was considered a natural political response to growth in urban areas until the late 1800s. After the Civil War outlying areas started to resist annexation. The failed effort of Boston in 1873 to annex Brookline is one of the earliest failures of a central city to expand its boundaries into the suburbs. Brookline had existed as a town since 1705 and by the 1870s was providing, with the exception of municipal water, essentially the same services as Boston. Located only three miles west of downtown Boston, Brookline was Boston's most elegant and celebrated suburb. It grew to a population of 6,700 by 1873 with a substantial commuting population. During the 1860s and early 1870s Boston aggressively annexed communities and by 1873 surrounded Brookline on three sides. There was every expectation that Brookline would be the next acquisition. Instead, the opponents of annexation, led by many of the elite Boston families who owned estates in Brookline, successfully resisted annexation by a vote of 706 to 299. Inspired by Brookline's successful rejection, other suburbs in the area and in other urban areas in the country became more aggressive in opposing annexation. The opposition in the Boston metro area became so fierce that Boston's boundaries have not changed since 1873, with one minor twentieth-century exception.[45]

Louis Cain's study of annexation in Chicago in the late nineteenth and early twentieth century illustrates well the forces involved in voter-approved annexation. It also shows the closing of the window of opportunity for annexation and mergers by the majority of the prominent nineteenth-century central cities. Voters in Hyde Park approved an annexation to Chicago in 1889. The overriding reason was to gain access to the superior city services Chicago offered. Particularly, water service and sewage disposal facilities were inadequately provided to the more rural parts of Hyde Park. Additional incentives were the prospect of better police protection, fire department services, and improved real estate values through the improved services and identification with a major city. Finally, the prospect of the major tax increases necessary to obtain these needed services and the argument that annexation would lead to lower taxes because of scale economics was attractive to the Hyde Park voters. The vote was 62 percent in favor of annexation.[46]

In 1909, 800 Evanston businessmen, who were major executives in businesses located in Chicago, instigated a movement to merge Evanston with Chicago. By this time, the disparity in local government services was not an issue. The Metropolitan Sanitary District, which had been approved by the state legislature in 1889 just prior to the Hyde Park merger to Chicago, was in full operation well before 1909. Evanston had joined in 1903. It also owned its own waterworks, and residents generally enjoyed services as good as those provided in Chicago. Moreover, Evanston residents saw from the Hyde Park experience that lower taxes and improved services did not result from annexation. Finally, Evanston's values regarding alcohol consumption were at polar extremes from Chicago's. The fear of its loss of temperance status undoubtedly helped to sway Evanston voters to overwhelmingly defeat the proposal by 3,481 to 851.[47]

As the Chicago example indicates, the closing of the window of opportunity for agreeable annexation was around the turn of the century for older urban areas. It was about this time that many state legislatures established regional districts for the provision of services requiring large capital investments. Communities no longer needed to become part of the city to receive capital intensive services such as sewer and water systems. Most large older cities such as New York, Chicago, and Boston have essentially retained the same boundaries as they had shortly after the beginning of the twentieth century. Annexation efforts did not cease, but the success ratio declined. In Chicago between 1909 and 1914, besides the defeat of the Evanston proposal, Oak Park rejected annexation with Chicago twice and Cicero voters defeated annexation proposals in four separate elections. All these defeats were by large margins of 2- or 3-to-1. A few small, poor communities were absorbed. Morgan Park merged with Chicago in 1914 because residents were dissatisfied with high taxes and poor services. Three other working-class suburbs joined Chicago by 1930, but they were among the poorest suburban areas. They added little to Chicago's tax base.[48]

Other older central cities experienced similar results. In Cleveland the large, well-to-do suburbs repeatedly resisted annexation while those areas with few assets and extensive liabilities voted to join Cleveland. Before 1910 Cleveland had not lost an annexation referendum battle. Between 1910 and 1940 it won four and lost five, and the problems accompanying the four Cleveland won, did not compensate for the five it lost. In Los Angeles the greatest gains were in the 1910–20 decade. Thereafter, annexation slowed. Many of those areas that joined did little to add to the city's tax base and added significantly to the costs of providing services. Richer suburbs such as Beverly Hills, Santa Monica, Burbank, and Alhambra voted against merger. The problem areas, such as Watts with its grimy collection of cheap bungalows and other municipalities seeking city water with little to bring to a merger, voted for annexation.[49]

Annexation Procedures

Prior to the twentieth century, most states dealt with proposed annexation through special act legislation. By the late 1800s states started enacting laws establishing legislative procedures so special legislation would not be required for each proposed annexation. General laws governing annexation became so widespread that by 1990, only six states (Connecticut, Hawaii, Maine,

New Hampshire, Rhode Island, and Vermont) did not have state annexation laws. The procedures are generally designed to protect the interests of the area being annexed. It should be noted that, in those states still requiring legislative approval, special act legislation is easily killed by a coalition of suburban and rural interests.

Legislation governing annexation procedures usually requires a two-step process: a petition and a referendum. In nine states, including Arizona, Georgia, Ohio, New York, and Pennsylvania, a required percentage of property owners in the annexed area is necessary to initiate the process. In other states it may be initiated either by petition of property owners or by the city seeking to annex. Nineteen states require majority approval of the annexed area; the county governing body must approve in eleven states. Only two states require both majority approval of the voters and approval by the county governing body. Michigan also requires approval by a state boundary commission in addition to approval of voters in the annexed area.[50]

A few states with liberal annexation laws remain–mainly located in the South. Texas had extremely liberal annexation laws and annexed areas with impunity until the late 1990s. In 1963 Texas gave cities extraterritorial powers over a zone of unincorporated land contiguous to its borders. In effect, they were able to regulate subdivision practices in this zone, including approvals over incorporation. Houston was one city that took advantage of the liberal annexation law and aggressively controlled and annexed territory. With its five-mile extraterritorial powers, it could annex without referendum annually up to 10 percent of the land within this area.[51] By annexing highway rights-of-way through the unincorporated suburbs, it expanded this zone. In the 1970s alone, it annexed areas that added over 200,000 residents. However, a major annexation battle ensued when it annexed Kingwood, an upscale city of 50,000 residents, in 1996. Even though Kingwood lost the battle, it resulted in Texas rewriting its annexation statute making it more difficult to annex large areas. In Houston annexation has basically come to an end.[52]

Because annexation laws in all states except Nebraska prohibit municipalities from annexing other incorporated areas without the consent of the territory being annexed, cities in the same state often experience different levels of annexation activity. For example, Cleveland is completely surrounded by incorporated municipalities and has not been able to expand its borders. By contrast, Columbus has annexed aggressively with the goal to become the largest city in Ohio and to never be completely surrounded by incorporated municipalities. After Milwaukee went on an aggressive annexation campaign in the 1950s, the remaining townships surrounding Milwaukee incorporated to stop further annexation. However, Madison was able to slow down the conversion of surrounding townships to municipalities and continued annexing territory long after this option was foreclosed to Milwaukee.[53]

Recent Annexation Activity

When the first phase of suburbanization ended at the time of the Great Depression, the central cities of the Northeast and Midwest were mostly encircled by a tier of suburbs. Due to the difficulty of annexing incorporated areas, cities attempted to annex noncontiguous land beyond the first tier of suburbs. Courts generally rejected this concept. In relative terms little annexation activity occurred from shortly after the turn of the twentieth century until after the end of World War II. The total amount of territory absorbed in the decade of the 1920s was substantially smaller than in the 1890s. By the 1930s only a handful of municipalities completed annexations and most of these were small-scale and largely insignificant. Only a few central cities made sizable annexations between 1900 and 1945, Detroit and Los Angeles being the most prominent.[54] Thus, annexations by older central cities as a means of acquiring territory virtually ceased by World War II.

Because of renewed suburban growth following World War II, a new round of annexation occurred. Most of the activity was in smaller cities outside the Northeast or the Midwest with reform-style governments whose residents socially and economically compared favorably to the residents of the area annexed.[55] Also, substantial annexation activity occurred in suburban areas consisting of suburban municipalities absorbing unincorporated territory.[56] In the South and Southwest, however, some central cities grew substantially through annexation involving largely unincorporated land. For example, between 1950 and 1970 San Diego tripled its territory while Dallas, Memphis, and Houston more than doubled theirs. San Jose jumped from 17 to almost 120 square miles. Oklahoma City grew from 51 to 636 square miles, and Phoenix expanded from 17 to almost 250 square miles. Other cities involved in significant annexations during this time included Charlotte, San Antonio, and Austin.[57]

In the postwar period many municipalities have been involved in annexations. For example, 526 municipalities with over 5,000 population participated in annexations in 1955. Most of these, however, were suburban communities annexing small parcels of unincorporated land. From 1970 through 1977, over 48,000 annexations occurred, adding nearly 7,000 square miles and over 2.5 million people to cities with over 2,500 population. Again, most annexations were small–the average land area involved was only one-seventh of a square mile, and the average population annexed was only 53 people.[58] In the 1980s 1 million fewer people were brought into incorporated areas through annexation than in the 1970s. The largest annexations in the 1980s occurred in Texas, with 313,000 population annexed. The only other states with 100,000 or more population annexed included Alabama, California, Florida, North Carolina, and Oregon. Most annexations were small, the largest being San Antonio with 73,000 population annexed, followed by Portland with 54,000 and Houston with 50,900.[59]

Since the aggressive annexation activity of the postwar years, annexation activity has slowed. In Texas, because of Houston's battle over the Kingwood annexation, aggressive annexation by Texas cities has slowed considerably. Moreover, throughout the Sunbelt, annexation activity has slowed. The major cities have already absorbed the easily annexed territory, and suburban resistance has led state legislatures to rewrite annexation laws to make it more difficult to annex. Only in the West have a number of cities, especially smaller cities, continued to grow by annexation.[60] However, annexation is still a viable means of acquiring territory as evidenced by the United States Census Bureau reporting that over 93,000 annexations occurred in the first decade of the twenty-first century. Thousands of municipal annexations occur each year impacting thousands of acres of land and tens of thousands of people. North Carolina municipalities alone were involved in 14,000 annexations between 1990 and 2009.[61]

Most large, older urbanized areas have little unincorporated land adjacent to the central cities that is subject to annexation. In some metropolitan areas the central county is also largely incorporated. This is the case with Allegheny County, the central county of the Pittsburgh MSA; all land other than park land is incorporated. Cook County, the central county of the Chicago metropolitan area, was only 57 percent incorporated as late as 1959. However, by 1976, after the postwar suburbanization movement, the incorporated land increased to 78 percent. Thereafter, the incorporation process basically came to a halt, as by 1981 the incorporated territory had increased to only 79 percent of the total. Over half of the unincorporated land left in the county is in its forest preserve system and much of the remainder is in golf courses and cemeteries. There are small unincorporated residential areas that either resist annexation or are not wanted by adjacent municipalities because of the marginal addition to the tax base and the substantial added costs of providing services. Additionally, a few industrial or commercial areas resist incorporation. No incentive motivates them to incorporate or seek annexation.[62] They receive basic local government services from the county without paying municipal taxes. The downside, however, is that they do not have self-governance powers and are dependent on other governments for their services. In unincorporated areas no corporate body represents the interests of the residents; they are subject to the service whims of the body providing the services.

For those unincorporated areas that finally seek municipal status in metropolitan counties, it is not a matter of simply joining another municipality or incorporating. Many unincorporated areas are often too small, with limited potential for growth in a county that is largely incorporated, to be viable as independent municipalities. Annexation to another municipality creates problems because it disrupts long-standing service arrangements in the unincorporated area, and neighboring municipalities may not want to annex the additional territory. An example of the issues involved in annexation is a 25-block unincorporated subdivision consisting of 500 residents in suburban Cook County, Illinois. This particular subdivision had resisted annexation overtures from a nearby municipality for years because services were satisfactory, and it had a large tax advantage by remaining unincorporated. However, over the years, concerns were voiced about the level of police protection supplied by the Cook County sheriff and the cost of water supplied by a private water company. Also, the tax differential between the unincorporated area and the municipality narrowed. The subdivision finally decided to seek annexation when the fire protection district that provided fire and paramedic services to the subdivision built a fire station farther from the area than the nearby municipality's fire station. However, the fire protection district objected because the reduced tax base would jeopardize the fire protection district's ability to provide services to the remainder of the unincorporated area. If all the unincorporated territory the district serves was annexed by the contiguous municipalities the district could cease operations. This is not possible, however, as at least one municipality has refused to annex some of the unincorporated area.[63]

Legacy of Central City Annexation Activities

The major enticement for joining the large city in the nineteenth century–to have access to superior municipal services–was no longer an enticement in the twentieth century. For twentieth-century suburbanites there was little incentive to be annexed. Most suburbanites felt that their quality of life would be adversely impacted if they became part of the central city. The rallying cry of the opposition to the annexation of Brookline by Boston in 1873 that Brookline's splendid trees, romantic streets, and velvet lawns would become a dirty neighborhood of a large city and that "[t]he beauty of the town would be destroyed by land speculators who would cut down the hills, remove the groves, and lay out streets everywhere like grid irons across the territory"[64] still resonated with suburbanites.

Anti-city feelings in the suburbs and distrust of central city actions are one legacy of the annexation battles. Even though annexation activity by older central cities has long since ceased, the suburbs are still wary of the central city because of memories of past experiences. In the minds of most suburbanites, the central city still dominates the metropolitan area, and the suburbs must be ever vigilant or the central city will reach out and absorb the suburbs, bringing its crime, congestion, style of politics, huge bureaucracy, and social problems to the suburbs. The strategies used by central cities to extend their boundaries have left suburbs hostile and apprehensive. The wounds opened in the years of active annexation efforts have not healed in most metropolitan areas even though many decades have passed. The result usually has been a total lack of cooperation and an unwillingness to work together on issues affecting the region in many metropolitan areas. Differences in political party representation and the different needs of the central city and suburban populations exacerbate this lack of cooperation.

Historically, the central city has politically and economically dominated the suburbs. The suburbs have had mixed results fighting central city annexation efforts. The annexation of Allegheny by Pittsburgh in 1907 led to a court case that went to the U.S. Supreme Court. The case was fought over the issue of whether Allegheny, whose residents had voted against annexation, could be annexed against their wishes. The Supreme Court reaffirmed the annexation and adopted Dillon's Rule into federal jurisprudence when it said that the rules of procedure established by the state legislature were binding even though they ignored the majority wishes of the voters of Allegheny.[65] Although Dillon's Rule gives the state power to dictate rules and procedures to local governments, the Wisconsin Supreme Court in 1951 invalidated an advantage the state legislature had allowed Milwaukee to exercise in annexing territory since 1898. Before the court ruling, Milwaukee was the only municipality that did not have to post a notice 30 days in advance of circulating an annexation petition among the residents. The ruling gave residents opposing the annexation time to organize their opposition, which helped to end Milwaukee's annexation efforts.[66]

Many states with Republican governors and Republican majorities in the state legislature and growing suburban cohesiveness are wresting power and authority away from the traditionally Democratic central cities. For example, in New York, under the Republican governor's first year in office in 1995, New York City's welfare rolls were trimmed by 103,000, and the governor announced plans to move hundreds of state jobs out of the city into Republican areas. Democrats from New York called it "geographic patronage." In Pennsylvania, the Republican-controlled state government took control of the Delaware River Port Authority from the Philadelphia Democrats. This authority controls a large number of jobs and is involved in economic development projects worth millions in contracts. In Washington, the Democratic state delegation representing Seattle is ideologically out of sync with the rest of the state. Seattle's legislative delegation is increasingly marginalized in major state policy decisions. The state's approval of a new sports stadium for Seattle was obtained because the suburban Republicans favored it. Had it been pushed only by the central city Democrats, the stadium probably would not have been approved. In Michigan, Detroit has little power in the state legislature. According to one observer, "[u]nless the Detroit delegation has a coalition with another area, its wishes have little hope in the state legislature."[67]

A final reason for the conflict between the central city and the suburbs is that people in the suburbs consider their municipalities to be morally superior to the central city. They feel that their governments are better administered, more accountable to the citizens, more economical, and less political than central city governments. Suburbs blame the central city as the main source of crime, corruption, social decay, and physical deterioration in the metropolitan area. They feel the central city has looked to other governments for subsidies long enough and needs to "get its own house in order" before looking to other governments for financial assistance.

Suburbanites' wariness and jealousy are not just directed at the central city. Historically, they have not extensively cooperated among themselves. They have competed with each other for economic development or, alternatively, to keep out economic development. They have squabbled over unincorporated land or road and residential development on their borders. Suburbs, with an extensive tax base, have not cooperated with those who are not as well positioned. In the past it was unusual when suburbs could agree on a common agenda to present to the state legislature or common goals for the future of the region as a whole. There is great diversity in the suburbs and no common theme that binds them together except their almost irrational distrust and fear of the center city.

One of the major reasons for central city annexation of suburban development, as discussed above and in Chapter 2, was to capture new suburban growth for the central city to add to its tax rolls. Central cities were especially interested in adding industrial development and elite residential development or vacant land that could be developed. When central cities were no longer able to acquire additional territory, their tax rolls started to stagnate as parts of the city became blighted. This same phenomenon also occurred to municipalities in the suburbs as they aged and also became landlocked as additional tiers of suburbs developed. As housing stock deteriorates the more affluent move farther out and the less affluent, who are less able to maintain their housing, move in. The cycle of decline continues and often accelerates, requiring government intervention. The first tier or inner-ring suburbs are generally the first to experience this transition to more blighted conditions. These suburbs that resisted being annexed by the central city are often less able to intervene in the cycle of decline than central cities because they have less fiscal capacity to deal with their problems. It is indisputable that these suburbs in crisis would be better able to deal with their problems if they were part of the central city with its larger resource base.

Case of Chicago and its Suburbs[68]

The Chicago region is noted for its political fragmentation and central city/suburban antagonism. With more than 940 local governments with taxing authority, it has the most local governments of any metropolitan area in the nation. The city has dominated the region politically as well as economically for most of its history. Strategies used by Chicago to extend its boundaries and otherwise dominate the suburbs have left many suburbs hostile and apprehensive. In the minds of most suburban leaders, Chicago still dominates the metropolitan area. Until recently, there was a total lack of cooperation and an unwillingness to work together on issues affecting the region. This legacy of distrust as well as differences in political party representation and the different needs of the central city and suburban populations have been difficult to bridge.

A major issue that is causing friction between Chicago and the suburbs is noise pollution. The municipalities around O'Hare Airport want Chicago to institute noise reduction strategies and not add additional runways. In one instance the northwest suburbs were desirous of obtaining water from Lake Michigan in order to provide for the needs of their developing communities. The least costly option was to build a pipeline to hook into Chicago's water system at O'Hare Airport. A number of suburbs opted to build a more expensive pipeline through Evanston to avoid any dependence on the city.

Until recently, Chicago and its needs dominated the agenda of the state legislature. Democrats controlled the legislative body, and the Chicago legislative delegation was tightly united and responsive to the needs of Chicago. Although the suburban legislators generally were Republicans, they were not united in their needs nor united against the needs of Chicago. One observer of the Chicago scene analyzes the Chicago dominance as follows:

> For much of the postwar era, Chicago was able to exercise power in the state legislature by striking bargains with downstate rural Republicans and Democrats, and the suburbs were generally left out of such deals. The difficulties that suburban Republicans had in influencing legislative deal making stemmed in part from their more ideological orientation toward politics. In any event, making deals with Chicago Democrats was not good politics for suburban representatives, because these politicians had long made Chicago corruption a key rallying point. Overt anti-Chicago sentiment served Republican suburban representatives well during their campaigns and later, when building legislative coalitions.
>
> Logrolling allowed the city to acquire the two things it wanted most from state politics: support for local development projects and a broader base for financing many city costs, including social spending. A number of the city's social costs were assumed by the county and the state, and other responsibilities were given to special districts. Chicago's remarkable success at shedding responsibility for social programs was partly a product of the state's propensity for creating special districts and partly a product of the political power and acumen of its longtime mayor.[69]

As a result of redistricting following the 1990 census, the Republicans gained control of the state legislative body in the 1994 election. The majority leaders in both legislative bodies were suburban Republicans. Within weeks of the opening of the 1995 session, the Republicans started exercising their will on the city. Nearly 100 bills were introduced in the state legislature to limit or strip power from various city boards, districts, and offices and shift it to the state or the suburbs.[70] The legislature ignored Mayor Daley's request for special legislation to authorize casino gambling in Chicago but authorized river boat gambling and approved a number of licenses for floating casinos on the Fox River, less than an hour's drive from Chicago.

The state also reacted coolly to Chicago's request for a new regional airport on the South Side and started pushing an alternative site in the far south suburbs. There was also a movement to establish a state airport authority that would operate Chicago's O'Hare Airport and the new airport in the far south suburbs, effectively removing O'Hare from Chicago's control. To thwart this movement, Chicago established a bi-state airport authority with Indiana to keep O'Hare under its control.[71] Relations between the city and the state did not improve until the Democrats took control of the General Assembly and a new Republican governor was elected.

Takeaway

In this chapter the suburbanization movement was presented and analyzed starting with the nineteenth-century evangelical movement, continuing with the massive post-World War II exodus of people and jobs from the central city, it continues to the present. The character of the suburbs, from the beginning, was much different from that of the central city with its small-town, homogenous atmosphere. The suburbs were also very exclusive, restricting racial minorities, certain religious and ethnic groups, and lower-income people. Following World War II, they opened more to lower-income people but were still highly restrictive to racial minorities.

In order to capture development outside its boundaries, the central city used annexation. Initially, central cities were extremely successful in annexing development because of the support of state legislatures and because the central cities offered superior or less expensive municipal services than those available to the suburbs. Annexation was the most successful way cities in the nineteenth and early twentieth centuries grew in territory. However, starting in the late 1800s the suburbs started resisting annexation. As the suburbs' resistance to annexation intensified, state legislatures started making it more difficult to annex. Additionally, the state liberalized incorporation laws, making it easier for communities with small populations to incorporate to better resist annexation. The use of the special district and the development of professional administration to provide municipal services as efficiently (often more so) as the larger city negated a major advantage to joining the central city. Although older central cities in the Northeast and Midwest have had little annexation activity since the early twentieth century, annexation is still a major means of boundary expansion for the newer-growth cities of the South and West.

Suburbanization has changed the population and economic dynamics of the metropolitan area. The central city no longer dominates the metropolitan area to the extent it once did. As people and factories moved to the suburbs, ancillary activities and supportive services followed. Central city population density declined, and cities that could not expand their boundaries declined in population and were replaced in the population hierarchy by newer-growth areas of the South and West that have extensive territory and low population density. One legacy of suburbanization and the political fragmentation of the metropolitan areas has been the segregation of the impoverished and racial minorities in the central city from the housing and job opportunities offered in the suburbs. Moreover, the central city is becoming socially and economically more isolated from the rest of the metropolitan area. Suburbanites have fewer and fewer connections with the central city economically, socially, and culturally. In addition, central cities are increasingly isolated in state politics as the suburban Republicans exert their political muscle to force changes on the Democratic central city. The suburbs' bitter resistance to annexation continues to affect central city-suburban relations many decades after annexation activity has ceased.

Notes

1. Quoted in Margaret Weir, "Central Cities' Loss of Power in State Politics," *Cityscape: A Journal of Policy Development and Research*, 2 (May) (1996): 23.
2. John D. Kasarda, "Urbanization, Community, and the Metropolitan Problem," in Mark Baldassare, (ed.), *Cities and Urban Living* (New York: Columbia University Press, 1983), pp. 46–47.
3. Robert Fishman, *Bourgeois Utopias: The Rise and Fall of Suburbia* (New York: Basic Books, 1987), p. 122.
4. Ibid., pp. 29–34.
5. Ibid., pp. 85–86.
6. Ann Durkin Keating, *Building Chicago: Suburban Developers and the Creation of a Divided Metropolis* (Columbus: Ohio State University Press, 1988), pp. 177–178.
7. John J. Harrigan and Ronald K. Vogel, *Political Change in the Metropolis*, 7th ed. (New York: Longman, 2003), p. 234.
8. Philip Kasinitz, (ed.), *Metropolis: Center and Symbol of Our Times* (New York: New York University Press, 1995), pp. 163–167.
9. Keating, *Building Chicago*, pp. 84–85.
10. Ibid., pp. 84–85.
11. Ibid., pp. 117–118.
12. Ibid., p. 124. See also Fishman, *Bourgeois Utopias*, pp. 85–87.
13. Fishman, *Bourgeois Utopias*, p. 151.

14. Nancy Burns, *The Formation of American Local Governments: Private Values in Public Institutions* (New York: Oxford University Press, 1994), pp. 88–89.
15. Donald Muzzio and Jessica Muzzio, "It's a Wonderful Life? The American Small Town and Suburb in Cinema," paper presented at Urban Affairs Association Annual Meeting, New York City, March 1996, p. 11.
16. For an in-depth discussion of federal government policies that encouraged suburban development, see Chapter 5.
17. Robert A. Beauregard, *Voices of Decline: The Postwar Fate of US Cities* (Cambridge, MA: Blackwell Publishers, 1993), p. 121.
18. Bernadette Hanlon, *Once the American Dream: Inner-Ring Suburbs of the Metropolitan United States* (Philadelphia: Temple University Press, 2010), p. 15; Bernadette Hanlon, John Rennie Short, and Thomas J. Vinino, *Cities and Suburbs: New Metropolitan Realities in the US* (New York: Routledge, 2010) pp. 133–134.
19. Benjamin Kleinberg, *Urban America in Transformation: Perspectives on Urban Policy and Development* (Thousand Oaks, CA: Sage Publications, 1995), p. 37.
20. Peter O. Muller, "The Suburban Transformation of the Globalizing American City," *The Annals of the American Academy of Political and Social Science*, 551 (May) (1997): 45–46.
21. Joel Garreau, *Edge City: Life on the New Frontier* (Garden City, NY: Doubleday, 1991). See especially chapters one and 11.
22. Muller, "The Suburban Transformation of the Globalizing American City," pp. 52–53.
23. Maria Saporta, "Fortune 500 List Overstates Atlanta's Headquarters," June 3, 2011, http://saportareport.com/blog/2011/06/ [Accessed June 21, 2012].
24. Paul G. Lewis, *Shaping Suburbia: How Political Institutions Organize Urban Development* (Pittsburgh: University of Pittsburgh Press, 1996), p. 7; Robert E Lang, *Beyond Edge City: Office Sprawl in South Florida*, Center on Urban and Metropolitan Policy (Washington, DC: The Brookings Institution, March 2003), p. 1, http://www.brookings.edu/es/urban/publications/langmiami.pdf [Accessed October 22, 2013].
25. Paul L. Knox, "Globalization and Urban Economic Change," *The Annals of the American Academy of Political and Social Science*, 551 (May) (1997): 26.
26. Lewis, *Shaping Suburbia*, pp. 8–10.
27. Burns, *The Formation of American Local Governments*, pp. 64, 98.
28. Ibid., p. 65.
29. Howard Reich and Desiree Chen, "Sprawling Culture Scene Puts Suburbs in Starring Role," *Chicago Tribune*, Aug. 5, 1996, sec. 1, p. 1.
30. Tom Valeo, "Who Needs Chicago?" *Arlington Heights (Ill.) Daily Herald*, Aug. 25, 1994, sec. 4, pp. 1–4.
31. Louis P. Cain, "To Annex or Not? A Tale of Two Towns," *Explorations in Economic History*, 20 (January) (1983): 59–65; Kenneth T. Jackson, *Crabgrass Frontier: The Suburbanization of the U.S.* (New York: Oxford University Press, 1985), pp. 144–146.
32. Bernard Ross and Myron A. Levine, *Urban Politics: Cities and Suburbs in a Global Age*, 8th ed. (Armonk, NY: M. E. Sharpe, 2012), p. 236.
33. Jackson, *Crabgrass Frontier*, pp. 142–143.
34. David W. Lonich, "Metropolitanism and the Genesis of Municipal Anxiety in Allegheny County," *Pittsburgh History*, 76 (Fall) (1993): 79–88.
35. Jackson, *Crabgrass Frontier*, p. 148.
36. Jon C. Teaford, *City and Suburb: The Political Fragmentation of Metropolitan America, 1850–1970* (Baltimore: Johns Hopkins University Press, 1979), p. 60.
37. Ibid., p. 59.

38. Keating, *Building Chicago,* pp.115–116, 199–203.
39. Ibid., pp. 116–117.
40. Anthony M. Orum, *City-Building in America* (Boulder, CO: Westview Press, 1995), p. 121.
41. Jackson, *Crabgrass Frontier,* pp. 151–152.
42. Ibid., p. 152.
43. Orum, *City-Building in America*, pp. 76–84, 120–121.   .
44. Jackson, *Crabgrass Frontier,* pp. 151–152.
45. Ronald Dale Karr, "Brookline Rejects Annexation, 1873," in Barbara M. Kelly, (ed.), *Suburbia Re-examined* (Westport, CT: Greenwood Press, 1989), pp. 103–108.
46. Cain, "To Annex or Not?" pp. 59–67. Cain's analysis is similar to a general finding Burns makes relative to people seeking to be annexed by larger municipalities because of the better municipal services. Burns, *The Formation of American Local Governments*, pp. 34–35.
47. Cain, "To Annex or Not?" pp. 69–70.
48. Teaford, *City and Suburb*, pp. 92–93.
49. Ibid., pp. 90–100.
50. Advisory Commission on Intergovernmental Relations, *State Laws Governing Local Government Structure and Administration* (Washington, DC: U.S. Government Printing Office, 1993), pp. 9–11 and table C.
51. Harrigan and Vogel, *Political Change in the Metropolis*, pp. 258–259.
52. Ross and Levine, *Urban Politics,* p. 239.
53. David Rusk, *Cities without Suburbs: A Census 2010 Perspective*, 4th ed. (Washington, DC: Woodrow Wilson Center Press, 2013), p. 25.
54. John C. Bollens and Henry J. Schmandt, *The Metropolis: Its People, Politics, and Economic Life*, 3rd ed. (New York: Harper and Row, 1975), p. 239.
55. Advisory Commission on Intergovernmental Relations, *Substate Regionalism and the Federal System: The Challenge of Local Government Reorganization,* vol. 3 (Washington, DC: U.S. Government Printing Office, 1974), pp. 82–84.
56. Harrigan and Vogel, *Political Change in the Metropolis*, pp. 258–259.
57. Jackson, *Crabgrass Frontier,* p. 139.
58. Advisory Commission on Intergovernmental Relations, *State and Local Roles in the Federal System* (Washington, DC: U.S. Government Printing Office, 1982), p. 419.
59. Joel Miller, "Annexation and Boundary Changes in the 1980s and 1990–91," *Municipal Year Book, 1993* (Washington, DC: International City Management Association, 1993), pp. 100–105.
60. Ross and Levine, *Urban Politics,* p. 239.
61. Russell M. Smith and John T. Willse, "Influences on Municipal Annexation Methodology: An Intrastate Analysis of Annexation Activity in North Carolina, 2000–2010," *State and Local Government Review*, 44 (3) (2012):185, 188.
62. Jerry Crimmins, "Few Plots Left in Cook County for Annexation," *Chicago Tribune*, September 3, 1981, sec. 6, p. 1.
63. Joseph Sjostrom, "Annexations Imperil Suburb Fire Service," *Chicago Tribune,* Jan. 15, 1981, and "Editorial," *Arlington Heights (Ill.) Daily Herald*, Aug. 6, 1982, sec. 1, p. 10.
64. Karr, "Brookline Rejects Annexation, 1873," p. 106.
65. *Hunter v. Pittsburgh.* This case is discussed in Advisory Commission on Intergovernmental Relations, *Metropolitan Organization: The Allegheny County Case* (Washington, DC: U.S. Government Printing Office, 1992), p. 23.
66. Orum, *City-Building in America*, p. 120.

67. C. Mahtesian, "Semi-Vendetta: Cities and the New Republican Order," *Governing: The Magazine of States and Localities*, 9 (6) (1996): 32–33.
68. Much of this section is taken from David Hamilton, "Regionalism in Metropolitan Chicago: A Work in Progress," *National Civic Review*, 91 (1) (2002): pp. 63–80.
69. Margaret Weir, "Central Cities' Loss of Power in State Politics."
70. Mahtesian, "Semi-Vendetta," pp. 28–30.
71. Ibid.

4 Government Centralization Responses

Consolidation and Metropolitan Government

We will ever strive for the ideals and sacred things of the city, both alone and with many: We will increasingly seek to quicken the sense of public duty; we will revere and obey the city's laws; we will transmit this city, not only not less but greater, better and more beautiful than it was transmitted to us.

—Ode of the Athenian city-state

Traditional reform is the major structural approach to regional government. It involves major governmental change in the entire urban area. It generally means a reduction of the number of governments or the addition of a new tier of government resulting in a major change in organizational relationships. There are three ways major structural government reform can occur:

- A municipal government combines with the county and essentially spreads its jurisdiction to cover the county in which it is located (city–county consolidation).
- A major reconfiguration of the metropolitan area takes place, resulting in the establishment of one or more additional tiers of government and a substantial change in the allocation of services between the existing municipal governments and the area wide government.
- A merger with a significant number of municipalities occurs, combining substantial land and population into one government.

City–county consolidation, in its theoretical approach, combines all the incorporated municipalities in the county and the county government into one countywide government. In practical application, however, city–county consolidation usually involves combining the central city and the county–with the combined government extending its jurisdiction over the unincorporated areas of the county. Other incorporated municipalities in the county may or may not be brought into consolidation. In most instances where city–county consolidations have occurred, some suburban incorporated municipalities have maintained their independence. Notable examples include the Jacksonville–Duval County consolidation, in which four small cities remained separate; the Nashville–Davidson County consolidation, which allowed all six incorporated municipalities in the county to remain independent; and the Indianapolis–Marion County consolidation, which left 4 of the 20 suburbs out of the consolidation.[1]

Tiered government is a federation concept whereby the existing municipal governments maintain their political autonomy but relinquish some services and authority to an area-wide government. The most comprehensive form is called a *federated metropolitan government*. This is the establishment of a general-purpose government covering most if not all the metropolitan area, with the political authority to provide area-wide services. Metropolitan government in Toronto, Canada between 1954 and 1998 is a good example of this form of government. Miami, Florida, is the closest example of metropolitan government in the United States. Another type of tiered government occurs when the county is given the authority to provide municipal services throughout the county and not just in unincorporated areas. This form is often called the *urban county*. The transfer of functions from the municipal level to the county level may evolve one function at a time over a period of years, or it may occur as a result of a county reorganization pursuant to voter or legislative action. The urban county is not considered major traditional reform for the purposes of this discussion but is classified as a centralized governance response and is covered in the chapter on county government.

Another form of the tiered approach is the establishment of a metropolitan, multipurpose district to provide or coordinate a number of regional functions. Although there are many special purpose districts providing a service countywide and in some cases region-wide, there are few metropolitan, multipurpose districts. An example is the Greater Portland Metropolitan Service District, which was established in 1978 to provide waste disposal, zoo administration, and other designated services in the three-county Portland, Oregon metropolitan area. Another form of tiered government is the Twin Cities Metropolitan Council that was created in the Minneapolis-St. Paul region in 1967 with power to coordinate and give direction to regional, special-purpose districts. The Twin Cities council also functions as a district, since it has operating authority for regional transportation.[2] This type of metropolitan reform is called the *metropolitan district*.[3] For purposes of this study, metropolitan districts are not structural government change but are discussed in the chapter on centralized governance responses.

A merger between municipalities can be significant when incorporated municipalities with substantial territory are combined, such as the reconfiguration of New York City in 1898. The city expanded from roughly 44 square miles to about 300 square miles and added almost 2 million people through its merger with Brooklyn (the fourth largest city in the United

States at the time), most of Queens, Staten Island, and the area known today as the Bronx. Chicago's acquisition of 133 square miles in 1889 almost quadrupled its territory by merging with Hyde Park and other territory on the far South Side.[4] Although there were a few significant mergers in the nineteenth century, most mergers did not involve much territory or population and were included in the discussion on annexations.

Basis for Centralized Government Reform Movement

As prospects for using annexation to extend the central city boundaries in the Northeast and Midwest in the early twentieth century diminished, reformers turned to other structural solutions. The progressive reform movement, designed to replace politics in local government with business principles, formed the basis for the movement to reorganize government in metropolitan areas. The reformers felt that the general acceptance of the tenets of the municipal progressive reform movement to professionalize local government and adopt good business practices of rationality, economy, and efficiency would be accepted on their merits with respect to metropolitan reorganization.

The leaders of the progressive reform movement were the same people who were involved in the regional reform movement. Although academics were the intellectual force behind the reform movement, there were many other groups involved. These groups usually came from the upper or upper-middle classes. The reform movement never enjoyed widespread support at the grassroots level. According to historians Kenneth T. Jackson and Stanley K. Schultz, the roster of reform enthusiasts and organizations in the late nineteenth century included a collection of ministers, educators, journalists, businessmen, newly emancipated college women, professionals like physicians and lawyers, politicians of a genteel, upper-class stripe, and some labor union leaders.[5] In a study of the makeup of reformers in Pittsburgh in the early 1900s, historian Samuel Hays indicated that their interest in reform stemmed not from their economic class but from their professions. They were usually young professionals, bankers, and businessmen from the new-growth industries who provided the guiding force. They were not as opposed to corruption in government as they were to the structure of government which allowed local and particular interests to dominate.[6] In essence, the reformers sought increased access and control for the business and professional person. Various tenets of the progressive reform movement were easily applied to regional reform. For example, the progressive reform movement advocated replacing ward elections with at-large elections to promote a citywide perspective in policy-making. This concept at the metropolitan level was aimed at promoting a regional, instead of an individual, community's parochial perspective. Another major purpose of the progressive reform movement was the elimination of the power of political machines in the central cities. Combining the city and its suburbs would reduce the political machine's control through the influx of suburban voters. For instance, the mayor of Boston advocated adding suburban middle- and upper-class citizens in 1919 when he complained that fragmentation of the Boston metropolitan area allowed the political machine to dominate Boston by controlling the votes of immigrants.[7] Jackson suggests the dilution of the influence of the Democratic Tammany Hall machine was a compelling reason for the significant expansion of New York City's boundaries in 1898 by the Republican-dominated state legislature and the Republican governor.[8]

Another objective of the progressive reform movement to replace politics in administration with politically neutral, professionally trained administrators was also readily applied to the regionalism movement. Regionalists felt professionals trained, nonpolitical administrators concerned with economy and efficiency, would reduce local government parochialism and help lead the way to regionalism. However, instead of advocating regional reform, professionals have fostered further fragmentation of government through what Professors Harrigan and Vogel term *functional fiefdoms*.[9] In this era of professionalism each government agency actively delineates and seeks to protect and expand its area of functional scope or *organizational domain*. The effect is to keep governments fragmented into an array of professionalized public bureaucracies that stand as separate islands of functional power, often operating beyond the control of the elected officials or the general public.[10] This is especially evident with regional, single-purpose districts and authorities. The result is competition among governments, little or no accountability to the elected officials, little or no interest by the general public, a perpetuation of governmental fragmentation, and functional fragmentation. Professional bureaucrats have become the new *political machines*, according to political scientist Theodore Lowi.[11]

The progressive reform emphasis on professional, nonpolitical administration also had the effect of improving the viability of suburban municipalities. Progressive, reform-supported concepts—such as single-purpose districts and authorities for the nonpolitical, efficient provision of services over a large area—made it possible for suburbs to remain independent of central cities and receive services that otherwise would have been prohibitively costly. In addition, by establishing professional administration, suburban municipalities developed the administrative capacity to handle their own needs effectively and efficiently. Therefore, a result of the progressive reform movement was that suburbs became more independent and resistant to annexation by larger cities.[12]

Regional Structural Reform Recommendations

The main rallying cry of the regionalists was economy and efficiency, which they claimed would result from an area-wide approach to metropolitan problems. This was manifested in recommendations to adopt business organization models and to reduce politics from government to the greatest possible degree. The reformers' heavy emphasis on business organization principles was reflected by the writings of William Anderson, one of the early regional reformers, who in 1925 succinctly summarized the progressive reformers' agenda for regional reform:

- Each major urban area should be organized by only one unit of local government.
- The voters in each major urban area should elect only the most important policy-making officials, and these should be few in number. Citizens become confused by long ballots and frustrated in choosing among candidates for numerous public offices.
- The traditional separation of powers should be eliminated from the internal structure of the single consolidated unit of local government.
- The function of administration, on the other hand, should be separated from that of politics. The work of administration should be performed by specially trained public servants who are adequately compensated and employed on a full-time basis.
- The administration should be organized into an integrated command structure in accordance with the hierarchical principle in which authority tapers upward and culminates in a single chief executive.[13]

Following the lead of early reformers, writers in the 1960s continued to expound on the gospel of reform. For example, political scientist Robert Wood described the problems of the mismatch of needs and resources faced by central cities whose political boundaries do not coincide with economic boundaries.[14] John Bollens and Henry Schmandt, in their book *The Metropolis: Its People, Politics, and Economic Life*, listed the problems caused by proliferation of local governments, including lack of public control and accountability, inability to arrive at metropolitan consensus on area wide matters, conflicting programs by the fragmented governments, and the inability to effectively handle regional problems.[15]

Business groups were also deeply committed to area wide reform. For example, the prestigious Committee for Economic Development (CED) swung its weight behind metropolitan reform. Its major concerns with the fragmented government system were as follows:

- Very few local governmental units are large enough in population, area, or taxable resources to apply modern methods in solving current and future problems. Even the largest cities find major problems insoluble because of the limits on geographic areas, their taxable resources, or their legal powers. Small tax bases severely limit the ability of many jurisdictions to provide a full range of services.

- Overlapping layers of local government are a source of weakness. This overlapping impairs overall local freedom to deal with vital public affairs; the whole becomes less than the sum of its parts. Solving regional problems is difficult, if not impossible, with the fragmented and overlapping layers of government.
- Popular control over government is ineffective and sporadic, and public interest in local politics is low. Confusion from the many-layered system, profusion of elective offices without policy significance, and increasing mobility of the population all contribute to disinterest.
- Antiquated administrative organizations hamper most local governments. Lack of a single executive, either elected or appointed, is a common fault. Functional fragmentation obscures lines of authority. The quality of administration suffers accordingly.[16]

The solution, according to the CED, was to reduce the number of local governments by at least 80 percent and to curtail the number of overlapping layers. Moreover, popular elections should be confined to members of the policy-making body and the chief executive in those governments which prefer a strong-mayor form. In addition, all administrative agencies and personnel in each unit should be responsible to a single elected or appointed chief executive. The election of department heads should be halted.[17] The CED recommendations were strikingly similar to those recommended by the early reformers in the 1920s.

Many other *good government* organizations have identified problems and recommended solutions in the same vein as the CED and the early reformers. The U.S. Advisory Commission on Intergovernmental Relations (ACIR) took a strong position in support of regional reform from its creation until about the mid-1980s. This organization was created in 1959 by Congress as a bipartisan body to monitor the operation of the federal system and make recommendations for improvements. Studies and reports of this body continually identified fragmentation of governments in metropolitan areas as a major problem. The ACIR advocated metropolitan reorganization within the context of that which was politically feasible.[18]

Over the years, reformers have added additional reasons to the administrative economy and efficiency argument in an effort to obtain greater support for the reform movement. In the 1960s and 1970s, they argued that political fragmentation created an aggravating mismatch of needs and resources among municipalities.[19] The solution, again, was an overarching, area wide government to eliminate the mismatch of needs and resources. More recently, reformers have argued that regional reform is essential in order to maintain economic viability and compete with other regions nationally and internationally for economic growth. Neal Peirce, in his book *Citistates: How Urban America Can Prosper in a Competitive World*, maintains that the entire metropolitan region is an economic unit, and more politically unified regions can compete more effectively for economic development than those that are less unified.[20] David Rusk, from his comparison study of eight metropolitan areas that are highly fragmented with eight that are more consolidated, also concluded that the regions that were more politically united were better able to compete for economic growth than the fragmented areas. He found that the politically united areas have realized greater overall growth and development than the more fragmented metropolitan areas. He attributed this to the fact that the fragmented areas have more extreme problems of racial segregation, poverty, dependency, and crime.[21] Regionalists list a number of advantages for regions to unite for economic development purposes:

- A major benefit is the reduction of competition among municipalities for economic development. Municipalities would not waste resources competing with one another, and all could benefit from the additional tax base.
- There would be a more orderly development of the region.
- A region that presents a single set of requirements to the business community rather than a hodgepodge of zoning and building regulations from one community to the next would be more attractive for economic development.
- An area wide economic development agency has more expertise and resources to develop and market prime commercial and industrial land than small communities.
- A spirit of boosterism and community renewal could result from regionalism which would instill greater community pride and a more favorable image to attract business development.[22]

City–County Consolidation

The initial direction of the regional structural reformers was a continuation of the annexation concept of combining outlying areas with the city to preserve the dominance of the central city. The spirit of boosterism and competition among cities to maintain or enhance their status in the size hierarchy influenced this direction.[23] One practical manifestation of preserving central city dominance is city–county consolidation, whereby the city expands its boundaries to coincide with the county, absorbing all unincorporated territory and many, if not all, of the county's functions. The county may still exist to provide services to incorporated municipalities in the county and may continue to provide traditional state-mandated functions countywide, such as tax assessment and collections, courts, and vital records The ideal city–county consolidation would consolidate all incorporated and unincorporated territory into the expanded central city.

Although its impact has not been as extensive in restructuring urban areas as annexation, city–county consolidation has been the most successful form of major structural regional change. There are 39 city-county consolidations, 31 of which have been formed since 1945. All consolidations prior to 1945 were by legislative enactment. Since then, all but one has been approved by referendum. The period from 1962 until 1976 was the time of greatest success with 14 consolidations. There were only two successful consolidations in the 1980s. However, the success rate has increased since then with four in the 1990s and eight in the first decade of the twenty-first century. However, there were many failed referendums. The largest number of failed referendums, according to the National Association of Counties,[24] was in the 1970s with 41 failed efforts. The number of attempts has trailed off since then with 27 attempts in the 1980s, 24 attempts in the 1990s, and 21 attempts in the first decade of the twenty-first century. The number of attempts indicates a continuing interest in city–county consolidations.

Over half of the consolidations since 1968 have been in nonmetropolitan areas. Most consolidations through referendums have involved cities with small populations. Voter-approved consolidations appear to be a regional phenomenon occurring mainly in the South and West, where the county has traditionally been a strong player in the delivery of governmental services. Georgia leads the resurgence of city–county consolidations, with six successful consolidations since the mid-1980s. It also is the state with the most consolidations with seven. Virginia and Alaska are second with five each. A list of city–county consolidations is given in Table 4.1.

As stated previously, most city–county consolidations approved by referendum involve combining county government and unincorporated territory in the county with the city. Incorporated municipalities usually have the option of remaining separate, which they invariably do. Thus, the region may not be totally unified. Moreover, many metropolitan areas encompass more than one county. Therefore, consolidating a central city with its county in increasing numbers of metropolitan areas does not achieve the goal of one government in each metropolitan area.

Nashville-Davidson County and Jacksonville-Duval County are examples of how city–county consolidations are organized and provide services. Both have a strong-mayor system of government with large councils. The council in Nashville provides for 41 members, 6 chosen at large and 35 from single-member districts. The Jacksonville charter calls for a 19-member council, 14 chosen from single-member districts and 5 elected at large. The mayors in both cities are restricted to serving a fixed number of consecutive terms. All of the functions in the new governments were not consolidated. Several county offices were retained as separate, elective offices. In Nashville, only the assessor and two other row officers remain in separate, elective status, while in Jacksonville the sheriff, tax assessor, tax collector, supervisor of

Table 4.1 Consolidated City–County Governments

Year	Jurisdictions	Population Prior	Population After	Approval[a]
1805	New Orleans, New Orleans Parish, LA	NA	17,242	LA
1821	Boston, Suffolk Co., MA	43,298	61,392	LA
1821	Nantucket Town, Nantucket Co., MA	NA	NA	LA
1854	Philadelphia City and Co., PA	121,376	565,529	LA
1856	San Francisco City and Co., CA	34,776	56,802	LA
1874/94/98	New York and 5 Boroughs, NY	2,507,914	3,437,202	LA
1904	Denver City and Co., CO	133,859	213,381	LA
1907	Honolulu City and Co., HI	39,306	52,183	LA
1947	Baton Rouge, E. Baton Rouge Parish, LA	34,719	125,629	REF
1952	Hampton, Elizabeth City Co., VA	5,966	89,258	REF
1952/58	Newport News, Warwick Co., VA	42,358	113,662	REF
1962	Nashville, Davidson Co., TN	154,563	426,029	REF
1962	Virginia Beach, Princess Ann Co., VA	8,091	172,106	REF
1962	Chesapeake, South Norfolk, Norfolk Co., VA	73,647	89,380	REF
1967	Jacksonville, Duval Co., FL	201,030	504,265	REF
1969	Carson City, Ormsby Co., NV	5,163	15,468	REF
1969	Indianapolis, Marion Co., IN	476,258	736,856	LA
1969	Juneau, Greater Juneau Borough, AK	6,050	13,556	REF
1970	Columbus, Muscogee Co., GA	155,028	169,441	REF
1971	Sitka, Greater Sitka Borough, AK	3,370	6,111	REF
1972/74	Suffolk, Nansemond Co., VA	9,858	47,621	REF
1972	Lexington, Fayette Co., KY	108,137	204,165	REF
1975	Anchorage, Greater Anchorage Borough, AK	47,081	174,431	REF
1976	Anaconda, Deer Lodge Co., MT	9,771	12,518	REF

1976	Butte, Silver Bow Co., MT	23,368	37,205	REF
1984	Houma, Terrebonne Parish, LA	32,602	101,600	REF
1988	Lynchburg, Moore Co., TN	668	4,721	REF
1990	Athens, Clark Co., GA	45,734	86,522	REF
1996	Augusta, Richmond Co., GA	44,467	186,956	REF
1996	Lafayette, Lafayette Parish, LA	108,635	161,458	REF
1997	Kansas City, Wyandotte Co., KS	144,260	144,351	REF
2000	Louisville, Jefferson Co., KY	256,231	547,839	REF
2000	Hartsville, Trousdale Co., TN	2,395	7,751	REF
2002	Haines City, Haines Borough, AK	1,811	2,508	REF
2003	Cusseta City, Chattahoochee Co. GA	1,196	11,267	REF
2006[b]	Georgetown, Quitman Co., GA	990	2,513	REF
2007	Tribune, Greeley Co. KS	835	1,234	REF
2008	Preston, Webster Co. GA	453	2,799	REF
2008	Statenville, Echols Co. GA	1,040	4,034	REF

Sources: Donald J. Bogue, *The Population of the United States* (New York: Free Press, 1985), pp. 121–123; U.S. Census Bureau, *City and County Data Book* (Washington, DC: U.S. Government Printing Office, various years); National Civic League, "Inventing Regionalism," draft report (September 1994), p. 12; U.S. Census Bureau, *U.S. Census of Governments*, vol. 1 (Washington, DC: U.S. Government Printing Office, 1992), p. C–1; Blake R. Jeffery, Tanis J. Salant, and Alan L. Boroshok, *County Government Structure* (Washington, DC: National Association of Counties, 1989), p. 121; National Association of Counties, personal correspondence, March 1996, July 1997; correspondence with the Lafayette City-Parish Consolidated Government Planning Department, July 1997; *1997 Commercial Atlas and Marketing Guide*, 129th ed. (Chicago: Rand McNally, 1997), p. 301. Figures for Kansas City and Wyandotte County obtained from the Wyandotte County Clerk, August 1997. Figures for Louisville, Jefferson County obtained from the US Bureau of the Census, American Factfinder, http://factfinder2.census.gov/faces/tableservices/jsf/pages/productview.xhtml [Accessed June 29, 2012]. National Association of Counties, City–County Consolidation proposals, http://www.naco.org [Accessed July 16, 2012].

Notes:

[a] LA = legislative action, REF = referendum

[b] Camden and Camden County, North Carolina consolidated in 2006 but this is not a city–county consolidation because Camden was not previously incorporated.

elections, the members of the civil service commission, and the school board maintain elective status.[25]

For provision of services, Jacksonville and Nashville are divided into two districts: the urban service district, consisting of the former city, and the general services district, consisting of the total area within the consolidation including the city. Residents in the urban service district receive additional services not provided to the remainder of the area. For example, in Nashville urban service residents receive fire and intensive police protection, sewage disposal, water, street lighting, and street cleaning. Urban service district residents pay additional taxes for these services. Other municipal and county services are provided through the general services district. A variation of the urban and general services districts is Unigov, the Indianapolis-Marion County consolidation. Certain functions are provided throughout the consolidated government while others, including police, fire, sanitation, libraries, and public housing, are provided through a series of special service and taxing districts of varying territorial size.[26]

An alternative structural configuration, city–county separation, is the separation of the city from the county. Under this concept, the county basically has no jurisdiction in the city; and the city takes over most, if not all, traditional county functions. City–county separation eliminates any duplication of services between city and county and the subsidization by city residents of services provided by the county outside the city. In addition to Virginia with 41 cities that have separated from their counties under state provisions requiring city–county separation, Baltimore and St. Louis also have separated from their counties. Harrigan indicates that the city–county separation in St. Louis has probably caused more sharp divisions and lack of cooperation between the two bodies than would be the case under a normal city–county structural relationship.[27] In addition, Bollens and Schmandt argue that separating Virginia cities from their counties significantly reduces the tax base of the county. The county's ability to be a viable government is brought into question, particularly if the city aggressively annexes county territory.[28]

Metropolitan Government

When regionalists advocating structural reform realized that the suburbs had no reason to give up their independence and were not willing to do so, they started advocating a federated metropolitan government as an alternative to city–county consolidation. They also realized that city–county consolidation in most large metropolitan areas would not achieve comprehensive government because urban areas generally extended beyond the county borders. Even the Committee for Economic Development, which in 1966 articulated the classic case for consolidation in metropolitan areas (see above), proposed in a new 1970 study that the two-tier solution become the model of reform for American metropolitan areas. Suddenly, it became very popular to argue in a burgeoning literature that those activities transcending local boundaries, such as air and water pollution control, garbage disposal, and regional land use planning should be assigned to metropolitan government. Localized activities such as street lighting, local parks and playgrounds, and garbage collection should be retained by lower-tier governments closer to the people.[29]

British urbanist L. J. Sharpe, looking at the distribution of municipal functions, posits the application of five general principles to determine which functions should be retained at the local level and which ones should be transferred to a regional level. These are externality or fiscal equivalence, economies of scale, the fiscal scale, redistribution, and the central business district (CBD) or service burden principles.

- The externality or fiscal equivalence principle is that local services should, as far as possible, be self-contained so that they are paid for by the citizens who use them. For example, an arterial road maintained by one government in a regional area may be used heavily by residents from other areas. Most infrastructure services generate such a high level of externalities that if this were the only criterion, most functions would qualify for metropolitan-level provision or coordination.

- The economies of scale principle suggests that for capital-intensive services, unit costs are generally lower when the service is provided to a larger population. Water and sewer systems are a good example of functions benefitting from scale economies.

- The fiscal scale principle is that some functions should have a broader taxing area to adequately support the function and to cover the benefit area. Public art galleries, reference libraries, and concert halls are examples of functions benefitting from fiscal economies.

- The redistribution principle states that because of income segregation in urban areas, there is a need to pool resources on a regional basis to ensure uniformity in the provision of certain services throughout the region.

- The central business district (CBD) or service burden principle is similar to the redistribution principle. The CBD is used by people throughout the metropolitan area, providing important institutional and economic services benefitting the region. Services include reference libraries, museums; facilitation of communications for economic benefit to the region; and the burden of traffic management, police, and parking for workers and visitors to the CBD.[30]

A rational application of these criteria would produce something similar to the list of services in Table 4.2. These functions would logically and effectively be provided or coordinated at the metropolitan level.

Table 4.2 Services to be Provided at Regional Level Based on Fiscal Equivalence, Economies of Scale, Fiscal Scale, Redistribution, and Service Burden Principles

Master planning	Trunk sewers and main drainage
Arterial highways	Refuse disposal
Traffic management	Water supply
Public transportation	Police
General utilities	Fire
Recreation areas	Major cultural institutions
Housing	Environmental protection

Source: L. J. Sharpe, "The Future of Metropolitan Government," in L. J. Sharpe, (ed.), *The Government of World Cities: The Future of the Metro Model* (Chichester, England: John Wiley and Sons, 1995), p. 19.

Metropolitan planning is particularly essential to integrate the regional functions and provide for their orderly and coordinated provision relative to land development.

Miami-Dade County Metropolitan Government

Miami-Dade County is the only successful, voter-approved, comprehensive metropolitan government in the United States that is similar to a federation. The major difference between Miami-Dade and a true federation is that it exists strictly within Dade County. Moreover, the reform did not replace the existing county government, although it substantially reorganized its structure. There is also unincorporated land in the county in which the two-tier approach does not operate—all services in these areas are provided by the county. Bollens and Schmandt argue that the initial retention of the county commission system makes this reorganization a comprehensive urban county instead of a two-tier approach.[31] However, it was a significant restructuring and is included here as traditional reform in the sense envisaged by structural reformers.

The Miami-Dade County reorganization went into operation July 1, 1957, following a close referendum. A countywide majority was all that was necessary for the reorganization to be implemented. The reorganization passed by slightly more than 2,000 votes out of 87,000 votes cast. A heavy, supportive majority in Miami won despite opposition from the suburbs.[32] Miami's business and civic leadership provided strong support for the reorganization. Miami's government was plagued with charges of corruption which contributed to a positive vote for consolidation. City police were accused of not enforcing the city's gambling and vice ordinances. In contrast, the county government was relatively well regarded. It was also playing an increasing role in local affairs as a number of municipal services had been transferred to the county over the years.[33]

This reorganization provided for a county manager responsible to a district-elected 11-member board. The board makeup has changed twice since the initial reorganization. The first change was to nine commissioners– all elected at large, eight of whom represented specific geographic districts. The ninth commissioner represented the entire county and was given the title of mayor. In 1993, the county was ordered by the court to establish a 13-member board elected by district. The commission has legislative authority, with executive authority in the appointed county manager.[34] Most county row officers were abolished as elected positions. There was also no change in existing municipalities.

Besides the traditional county functions of tax collection, property appraisal, courts, election, regional parks, and public health, the county was given responsibility for services that in other areas were often provided by special districts or by municipalities. These included public transportation, arterial streets, traffic engineering, housing, community development, airports, seaports, parks and recreational areas, solid-waste disposal, libraries, and regulatory services. Originally, Metro, as the reorganized county was named, took responsibility for zoning and building regulation as well as public works; however, the outcry from the cities was so strong that zoning code control was subsequently returned to them. Metro shares regulatory authority with the cities. It sets basic countywide standards, and any regulations established by the cities must minimally meet these standards. If communities fail to meet these standards, Metro is authorized to take over the function. A countywide uniform traffic code, a uniform subdivision ordinance, a uniform building code, a criminal code, and a dog control ordinance were passed soon after Metro became a reality.[35]

All local government services are provided by the county in unincorporated areas, which are also major population growth areas. Unincorporated areas increased from 35 percent of the population when Metro was adopted, to over half the county's population in 2000. As some areas have incorporated, the population of the unincorporated area declined to 46 percent by 2007.[36] Because there is no local municipality to deal with municipal-related issues in unincorporated areas, the county commissioners are forced to spend a substantial amount of time dealing with issues such as whether "a particular property owner should be given a zoning variance to construct lights on his backyard tennis court." For Miami-Dade County to be a true two-tiered structure, the entire urbanized area of the county would need to be incorporated.

Even though the federated system in its true form was never adopted in the United States, in the 1950s and 1960s it was a popular form of regional government in large cities outside the United States. The retention of lower-level municipalities and the establishment of a regional government was the model used in London and major metropolitan areas throughout England. Other examples where it was instituted include Barcelona, Stockholm,

Copenhagen, Istanbul, and Belgrade. In North America, Toronto is perhaps the best example of a federated system. (See Chapter 11 for a further discussion on regional governance outside the United States.)

Criticisms of Traditional Regional Reform

Those who oppose or question the utility of reform are not just politicians or government administrators afraid of losing their authority. Many social scientists and writers also question the advantage of major government restructuring in urban areas. The major opposition in academic circles is known as the public choice model. Advocates of this model maintain that urban areas are actually better served by the current polycentric system of government. (The public choice model is analyzed in Chapter 6.) Besides this opposition, there are a number of other criticisms that should be noted.

One criticism is that the majority of the residents generally oppose any change to an area-wide form of government. Surveys indicate that metropolitan residents are generally satisfied with their quality of life. For example, of a survey of 1,500 randomly selected residents in the New York City region, 76 percent were either "very satisfied" or "somewhat satisfied" with the quality of their life. Surveys conducted of metropolitan residents in Atlanta, Seattle, and Dallas had similar results with over 60 percent in each of these cities pleased with their quality of life. Only a similar survey of Los Angeles area residents showed that less than half (40 percent) had a positive perception of the quality of their life.[37] Residents who are generally satisfied with their quality of life would tend to be opposed to changes in the government that they perceive is a contributor to their quality of life. However, this opposition may be fleeting. In Toronto, for example, surveys a few short years after it consolidated with its suburbs revealed that citizens were generally pleased with the results of the consolidation despite overwhelmingly opposing it at the time.[38] The survey might also be interpreted to mean that people naturally oppose change from the known to the unknown. This is particularly true if they are satisfied with the status quo. Once the change occurs and services are being provided as well as previously, they appear not to care whether the government providing it is a large area-wide government or a small local government.

A further argument against structural comprehensive reform involves the concern that governments will become too big, remote, and bureaucratic. This is a counterargument to those who maintain that reducing fragmentation of governments will lower per unit costs of delivering services. Those opposed to structural reform also point out that centralization, to the extent that average cost curves are U-shaped, may produce diseconomies of scale. Higher per unit costs may occur when the volume of the service exceeds the capacity of the equipment, when services must be geographically extended, or when the function becomes excessively bureaucratic.

All services and even parts of functions do not have the same cost curve. Therefore, economies of scale will vary by service.[39] While capital-intensive services such as sewage disposal and water supply benefit from scale economies, labor-intensive services such as police, education, and welfare services seem to be more efficient when provided on a more intimate, user-oriented basis.

Some economists contend that a city with a population between 50,000 and 250,000 is the best size to take advantage of economies of scale without being too large to experience diseconomies.[40] These population parameters may show where economies of scale are generally best achieved, but there are a number of other issues involved in service delivery, such as quality and responsiveness. There may also be conflicting goals. For example, it is generally recognized that water supply benefits from economies of scale if the policy is for heavy capital investment and an increase in supply but less so if the emphasis is on conservation.[41] Moreover, large bureaucratic organizations reduce the possibility of co-production. Residents of many suburban communities value the opportunity to serve as volunteer firefighters or police. This provides a psychological benefit to the individuals involved, reduces costs to the community, and solidifies the bonds between volunteers and their communities.

A final criticism of region-wide government is its lack of identity with the public. A metropolitan community, according to political scientist Norton Long, exists only in the minds of planners and metropolitan reformers.[42] People identify with their local communities, but there is no sense of metropolitan community. There is no emotional attachment to a metropolitan entity, particularly one that would be superimposed over a municipality with which residents identify. Even the county in many parts of the country has little or no emotional attachment for residents because it is either considered too remote or too inconsequential to engender any feelings of community identity.

Politics of Traditional Reform

Probably the most significant result of the traditional government reform movement is the lack of success in obtaining voter approval for comprehensive government reorganization. Only a few of the many efforts have been successful. There have been over 80 formal city–county consolidation attempts in Virginia alone, with only five successes.[43] Indeed, voters are more likely to turn down regional government proposals than to approve them. Since the 1960s there have been 131 votes on city–county consolidation. The success rate is 21 percent. However, the success rate seems to be improving as there were 8 successes out of 21 attempts in the 2000s for a 38 percent success rate. A number of areas have made multiple attempts at city–county consolidation proposals[44] Macon, GA, Wilmington, NC, and

Albuquerque, NM have made four unsuccessful attempts to combine with their county. The latest attempt for Albuquerque was in 2004.[45] A large number of regional reform efforts never even reached the voter approval stage. Despite the slim chances for success, efforts at metropolitan reform continue. Macon, GA has been authorized to have a fifth referendum on consolidation. Other cities are also considering or have had failed consolidation votes with their counties in the twenty-first century including Pittsburgh, Topeka, KA, Toledo, OH, Muncie, IN, Fayetteville, TN, Fairbanks AK, and El Paso, TX.[46]

Social scientists have conducted numerous studies to determine why voters generally reject traditional reform proposals.[47] The following sections describe their major findings and the factors involved in the success or failure of metropolitan reform proposals. Each factor, taken separately, probably is not enough to ensure the success or failure of traditional regional reform. The factors are interrelated and work together to bring about the success or failure of the regional reform effort. They are discussed here separately for better understanding of why voters support or reject reform proposals.

Lack of Community Support

Proponents of reform are often not effective at mobilizing community support because they are not representative of all segments of the population, the benefits they espouse are too abstract or long-range to interest most voters, and there is generally a lack of political or grassroots organizations actively supporting the reorganization.[48] Area-wide reform is mainly supported by the community elites. A study of an attempt at regional reform in Allegheny County, PA, showed that reform supporters were not broadly representative of the community. The campaign of those supporting reform appealed only to the interests of the segment of the community they represented. On the other hand, the opposition was broadly based in the community. It was not formally organized but appeared so spontaneously from so many different sectors of the community that it overwhelmed the supporters.[49]

The opponents of reform are generally better at appealing to the emotions of the voters. In the unsuccessful Allegheny County effort, the reform proponents waged an unemotional campaign—a campaign designed to show the advantages of reform, not the problems or excesses of the existing government. The benefits, however, were vague and futuristic, not immediate and tangible. The benefits could not be explained by slogans, but only through knowledge of the charter. The opposition, on the other hand, used emotional issues and slogans, which personalized the charter. Proposed passage of the change became synonymous with a loss of individual benefits. Because it involved "bread and butter" issues, those opposed were more effective in their opposition. Those opposing the change created a definite need for opposition, whereas supporters created no pressing need to support the reform.[50]

Crisis in Government

A perceived government crisis in the minds of the voters is an essential element of a successful change effort. Social scientist Brett Hawkins states that the successful Nashville-Davidson County consolidation was, in part, due to the success of the proponents in identifying the unpopular mayor of Nashville with the status quo and creating the need for voters to support the change in order to "throw out the mayor."[51] In the unsuccessful Allegheny County effort, voters did not perceive a need for a change. Services were being provided, and there were no government scandals or crises to motivate citizens to vote for change. Indeed, a survey in the county just prior to the vote showed that residents had substantial confidence in the existing government. They did not favor a change that was stigmatized by the opposition as controversial and did not have the complete support of the community leadership.[52]

A study of city–county consolidation attempts in Tampa-Hillborough County and Jacksonville-Duval County concluded that a major factor leading to success or failure of area-wide reform was how government responded to problems. The government's ability to respond successfully defuses the issue. However, continual inappropriate responses lead to dissatisfaction with government, which builds to crisis proportions. A government crisis, as perceived by many Jacksonville-Duval residents, was a major factor in its successful consolidation.[53] A crisis, of course, is defined by the voter. In reality, it may range from annoyance at government to extreme inconvenience, but it is generally associated with the inability to satisfactorily provide services. A survey of Nashville voters found that 81 percent of those who were dissatisfied with government services voted for city–county consolidation compared with 53 percent voting for the reform who were satisfied.[54]

Voter Turnout

Another factor in the success or failure of reform efforts is the voter turnout. It was found in an ACIR study of 18 area-wide reform attempts between 1950 and 1961 that only one voter in four bothered to vote—about 50 percent of the usual vote for a presidential election. The study indicates that when more people vote, the chances of achieving area-wide reform are better.[55] Political scientist Vincent Marando, however, disputes this assertion. He indicates that a 61 percent voter turnout in Virginia and a 59.5 percent voter turnout in Georgia resulted in substantial defeats. A 37 percent turnout in another Georgia county resulted in an affirmative vote. He claims the participation rate of proponents and opponents is more important than the number of voters.[56] Research shows that people with positions contrary to the expected outcome are less likely to vote. They feel their vote will make no difference in the outcome. A large turnout may affect an overwhelming defeat or a comfortable victory.[57] The timing of the referendum will affect the turnout of positive or negative voters. A study of the unsuccessful attempt to consolidate Albuquerque and Bernalillo County concluded the failure was largely because of a large turnout of negative voters to defeat a bond issue and vote down flood control expenditures. The negative voters generalized their negativism to the proposed consolidation.[58]

Socioeconomic Factors

Studies of reorganization efforts show the importance of socioeconomic factors in the success or failure of the reform. Reform is more likely in areas that are ethnically homogeneous, of relatively high socioeconomic status, have a one-party system, and have a high degree of business ownership. Areas with a high ethnic population or racial mix with a stable or declining rate of growth are more likely to resist substantial structural reform.[59] Social scientists Richard Bernard and Bradley Rice concluded from a study of reform efforts in 156 cities that areas with relatively high socioeconomic status were more prone to adopt structural reform than those with lower socioeconomic status. For example, a study of a home rule effort in Salt Lake City, showed that those districts which endorsed the charter were middle and upper-middle class. Not a single district in the low-income section had a positive majority.[60] The Miami-Dade County success was attributed, at least in part, to positive socioeconomic factors. These included the small labor movement, the rapid influx of population that had not established an attachment to a particular community, and the lack of a political party system.[61]

A random sample of those voting against and those supporting the unsuccessful Allegheny County charter reform showed a correlation between education and income levels and support for regional reform. Over 78 percent opposed to the change were below the county average education level, and 86 percent were below the median family income. On the other hand, all of those areas from the sample favoring the reform were above the county average in educational attainment and median family income.[62] The importance of education was confirmed in a study of structural change efforts in Pennsylvania. This study found that those municipalities with relatively higher percentages of workers employed in professional and management occupations and greater educational attainment were more likely to vote favorably on reform recommendations.[63]

Race Issues

The racial issue as a factor in the success or defeat of regional reform proposals raises a number of questions. Do suburban white voters oppose mergers with central cities increasingly dominated by blacks, or do they support mergers with central cities to prevent blacks from exercising political control in the central cities? Do central city blacks oppose mergers with suburban whites to retain their growing political strength or support it because of the prospect of increasing the tax base and improving the financial prospects of the central city? With so many other factors involved, it is impossible to be definitive about the impact of race on the success or failure of regional reform proposals. Socioeconomic status may be a more important factor than race. In any event, research shows that both white suburban voters and black central city voters have supported some referendums and opposed others.

In Cleveland, for example, metropolitan reform was supported by the central city before the increase in black political power but rejected in the suburbs. After the minority community gained political strength in the central city, the city rejected metropolitan integration by a substantial margin.[64] In Nashville and Jacksonville, however, racial factors had little or no apparent impact. In Nashville, both whites and nonwhites in the central city voted against the reform by similar percentages. In Jacksonville, blacks supported consolidation even though their percentage of the population declined from 42 percent to 23 percent of the merged city–county. With the majority of the council elected by district, black representation on the council increased from two to five in Nashville and from two to four in Jacksonville.[65]

Central city black leaders are as likely to support as to oppose a regional reform proposal. Black leaders' support is generally contingent upon assurances of representation in the reformed government. In a study of 11 city–county consolidation proposals, black central city leaders supported the consolidation in five and opposed it in six. In all cases in which they were opposed, the effort was defeated. In three of the five cases they supported, the effort was successful. This study suggests black leaders have an impact, particularly in defeating the effort. It is, however, tenuous to conclude that black leaders' opposition alone brought about the defeat.[66]

A favorable minority vote is extremely important in the success of the reform effort. Also, suburban support is usually necessary for success of the reform proposal. Suburban voters supported both the Jacksonville-Duval County and Nashville-Davidson County consolidations. If the suburban vote is negative, there must be a strong positive vote in the central city for the reform to be successful. Such was the case in the Miami reform, where strong central city support overwhelmed the suburban opposition. On the other hand, a strong favorable vote from the suburbs overcame a negative plurality in the city in the Nashville-Davidson consolidation.

Political Leaders and Regional Reform

Substantial evidence suggests that the actions of locally elected officials are the major factor in the success or defeat of reform proposals. Their ability to influence is a function of elected officials' credibility, the socioeconomic status of the voter, and the voter's understanding of the issues. Credibility is dependent upon the general popularity of the official, the ability to deliver jobs, and the strength of the political party. Conversely, unpopular actions of an official often result in a crisis of confidence and a vote in support of reform to oust the official.

The literature is replete with examples of officials' influence. A study of the 1959 defeat of a St. Louis multipurpose district proposal indicates that the opposition of the mayor of St. Louis, who had a good rapport with the business community, was the key factor. The business community, which had supported the plan prior to the mayor's announced opposition, noticeably became less enthusiastic after he announced his opposition. and gave only nominal support.[67] One study of 67 local government reorganization attempts in Pennsylvania found that structural reform referendums had an 82 percent chance of being accepted if local officials were supportive but less than a 45 percent chance of success if they were neutral, opposed, or divided.[68] A study of an attempt to reorganize county government in Allegheny County, Pennsylvania, concluded that the opposition of the county commissioners was the major single factor in the defeat. The charter appeared to have a reasonable chance of success until the chairman of the county commission, a member of the locally strong Democratic Party, commenced active opposition. Shortly thereafter, various members of the community announced opposition or became apathetic. Many of these individuals had close working relationships with the commissioners. Opposition or apathy came from many large business corporations, major business-sponsored civic organizations, veterans groups, and all but one county employee union.[69]

Reorganization attempts have a greater possibility of success if the elected officials who oppose the reorganization have been discredited. This could be because of unpopular decisions by the politicians or general dissatisfaction with government services. An important element in the successful Nashville-Davidson County consolidation was the loss of credibility of Nashville's mayor, who opposed the consolidation. His ability to influence was substantially diminished because he had previously instituted measures which were extremely unpopular with the voters outside the city, including annexing additional land and requiring suburban residents to purchase a permit to park in the city.[70] A survey of Nashville voters showed that

81 percent of those who were dissatisfied with government services voted for government reorganization. Even the majority of those satisfied with government services supported the change (53 percent), likely because of their opposition to the mayor.[71]

Knowledgeable voters tend to support reform while those who are not knowledgeable tend to be status quo-oriented or susceptible to influence by others. Research shows that most voters are uninformed on the specifics of regional reform, which allows credible elected officials to potentially exercise a large amount of influence. For example, a poll taken in Indianapolis shortly before the city–county consolidation found that 80 percent were unfamiliar with the proposal. The remaining 20 percent of presumably well-informed voters were 69 percent in support of the proposal.[72] A conclusion from a study of the Nashville-Davidson consolidation was that voters with a lack of specific knowledge were more subject to influence from perceived credible sources than voters who were knowledgeable about the reform recommendations.[73]

Process of Regional Reform

Referendums

One of the major obstacles to regional reform in the United States is the requirement that voters approve the proposed change. The referendum is seldom used in other countries on government reorganization issues. The local government reorganizations in most countries were implemented by national or state legislative action. For example, there has been no voter approval in the regional structural changes of Toronto or Winnipeg in Canada (see Chapter 11), just as there was no voter approvals of major reorganizations in the United States in the nineteenth century. In contrast, all but one of the proposed reorganizations in America since the mid-twentieth century have been subject to voter approval.[74]

Political scientist Frank Smallwood argues that America's insistence on the referendum process on regional reform proposals is probably less democratic than decisions made by elected leaders. He contends that the referendum has a built-in bias favoring the status quo, and it is more accommodating to the basically disinterested and uninformed voter than those who are intensely interested. As indicated above, most voters are uninformed about the issues of reform and are likely to be less supportive of change unless the change is supported by credible public officials. Smallwood argues that democracy should be as responsive to change as it is to the status quo. Decisions by elected representatives rather than through referendums tend to reduce the status quo bias.[75] He contends that the democratic process for complex regional reform proposals is best served through the representative system of government, which allows for reasoned debate and informed discussion on the merits of the issues. The referendum removes it from this legislative forum and places it in an arena of low voter interest and knowledge, where reasoned debate and informed discussion are replaced by emotional symbols that obfuscate the issues. Because of low voter interest and knowledge, the referendum procedure on regional reform is highly susceptible to distortion. He argues that the overall interests of the public are best served, as far as regional reorganizations are concerned, by a system that allows input by interested individuals but reserves the final decision to elected representatives.

Study Commissions

Another critical element in the regional reform process that has a substantial impact on the success of the effort is the type of commission which proposes the reform.[76] The traditional reform process contemplates the establishment of an appointed blue-ribbon commission composed of a group of concerned and knowledgeable leaders drawn from the business, professional, academic, and nonprofit sectors of the community. These commissions theoretically are above politics and proceed in their deliberations and proposals with the best interests of the region in mind. They conduct their study, report their recommendations, and then disband.

There are two problems with blue-ribbon commissions in ensuring a fair hearing on the reform proposal. First, the commission's mandate is only to study and make recommendations, not to oversee the acceptance process. Unless it is reconstituted to sell the proposal to the voters, further involvement in the reform process ceases after the commission makes its recommendations. This disrupts the continuity between proposals and voter acceptance. One would assume the commission would be in the best position to explain its proposals to the voters. Another problem with blue-ribbon commissions is that they are nonpolitical. Their membership is heavily representative of the professional and business leadership in the community. Blue-ribbon commissions often ignore political realities and make recommendations that are politically unacceptable. Nonpolitical bodies drawn from the business and civic leadership usually have difficulty connecting with, and generating interest and support from, the average citizen. They seek to provide rational answers and engage in reasoned debate—not in the type of sound bites necessary to arouse voter support. The general kinds of recommendations from an appointed blue-ribbon reform commission are fairly predictable. Economy and efficiency are the major priorities, and recommendations usually follow the tenets espoused in the traditional reform literature.

There are also problems with elected commissions. If the regional reform commission is elected, it is impossible to ensure a representative commission. It is also probable that members of the commission will have particularist and personal agendas that may not be in the best interests of the region.

The commission will be more political by the very nature of the selection process. The same people selected for a blue-ribbon commission would not normally stand for election to an elected commission. An elected commission may not be as connected to the established political leaders because of their inability to firmly control the selection process. In addition, the elected study commission usually suffers from the same continuity problems that blue-ribbon commissions encounter. It, too, generally goes out of existence after it has made its recommendations. Once the study commission makes its proposal, it is usually presented to the voters and must be accepted or rejected *in toto*. It is an inflexible document, not subject to compromise. In the legislative process, the legislative bodies are able to compromise and mold a legislatively enacted proposal until the last minute in order to gain acceptance. In contrast, the referendum process makes no provision for changes from the proposal. Debate continues to the time of vote, but there is no chance to change the proposal in response to the debate.

Media and Business Involvement

Regional reform is often initiated and kept alive by the efforts of the media and the civic and business communities. Metropolitan areas without strong support from these elements of the community tend to show less interest in regional reform. The civic sector and business leadership can influence cautious politicians to initiate the reform process and also provide financial and research support. Pittsburgh and Cleveland are examples of areas with a strong civic and business leadership commitment to regional reform. Unfortunately for the reform effort, the civic sector and business leadership have shown that they are not adept at selling the recommendations to the general public.

Although most attempts at regional reform submitted to voters are defeated, many more are defeated prior to the vote. In many cases, the recommendations of the study commissions are not submitted to the voters. Many metropolitan areas over the years have established a number of metropolitan study commissions. For instance, in the Pittsburgh region at least eight study commissions have made recommendations on regional governance in the last 80 years–only four were submitted to the voters. The first three efforts failed. The last was successful in instituting county home rule for Allegheny County and making changes in the government structure. The metropolitan reform effort often starts out positively, with the participants full of optimism, and it often ends in divisiveness and frustration. The experience in Milwaukee appears to be typical of the general failure of the study commission process as indicated below:

> A committee of leading business figures from the suburbs and the city, the Metropolitan Study Commission, was created by the Republican

governor in 1957. The overall purpose of the commission was to examine ways in which the city and its suburbs could work together to solve their common problems–among them, adequate water supply. The commission reported that officials of various suburban communities saw no particular gain in any kind of metropolitan governance. They supported cooperation but were opposed to the creation of a metropolitan agency, functional or governmental consolidation. On the other hand, Milwaukee officials went on record to urge the development of a metropolitan government and argued that municipalities that could not function effectively on their own should consolidate with the city.

As its work continued, the momentum on behalf of metropolitan government among members of the study commission waned. Conflicts and disagreements broke out among different members, leading to departures and further delays. Even when the leadership of the commission was turned over to the provost of the University of Wisconsin at Milwaukee, a much-admired civic leader, little could be done to restore the original enthusiasm for metropolitan governance. Eventually, the efforts of the commission came to nought. At best, its discussions led to a series of extended reflections on its failure and how such failure might be overcome in the future.[77]

Impact of Traditional Reform

What is the result of successful reform? Have those metropolitan areas that have reformed produced the economies, the efficiencies, and the reduction of inequities that the reformers promised? Are they in a better position to serve the needs of the residents than areas that are more splintered? These questions are not easy to answer since most reforms were not as comprehensive as the reformers envisioned. The urban areas have also grown beyond the boundaries of the original reform, thereby creating, at least to some extent, the same issues that existed before the reform. Studies have been done on the impact of reform in a few areas, so some observations can be made. It must be reiterated that these studies may or may not be generalizable because of the many other variables that might affect the operation of governments. However, the studies are useful in showing differences or similarities which can be further studied and analyzed. In this section research and observations from the literature are given on the three major advantages that are claimed to result from moving to a regional governing system.

1. Improved efficiency and effectiveness in service delivery by eliminating duplication.
2. Greater equity and a more even distribution of resources through a reduction of geographical disparities.
3. Ability to compete more effectively for economic development.

Improved Efficiency

Efficiency is defined as limiting waste and making maximum use of available resources. An effective government is one that reduces the overall costs of government. Intuitively, the consolidation of governments should result in efficiencies and expenditure savings from reduction in duplication of services. At the very least, there should be some savings from reduction in personnel costs. One would suppose this should positively affect the tax rate; however, empirical analysis does not substantiate this supposition. Social scientists J. Edwin Benton and Darwin Gamble did a time series analysis of property tax revenues, public safety expenditures, and total expenditures by comparing two Florida counties with similar socioeconomic characteristics: the Jacksonville-Duval County consolidation and unconsolidated Tampa and Hillsborough County. These researchers found little impact in property tax revenues. After consolidation, between 1969 and 1981 property tax revenue grew by 1.6 percent annually per capita in Jacksonville and 1.8 percent in the control county. Total expenditures in Jacksonville and Tampa had been declining by roughly the same amount prior to the consolidation. The annual per capita growth in expenditures between 1969 and 1981 was actually higher at 0.9 percent in Jacksonville than in Hillsborough County at 0.8 percent.[78]

Public safety expenditures were tracked by Benton and Gamble because public safety is one of the functions suggested by reformers as likely to benefit in overall reduced costs from consolidation. In the Jacksonville case, however, the opposite occurred. Both Jacksonville and Tampa were experiencing 0.1 percent annual per capita decreases in public safety expenditures between 1955 and 1968. After consolidation, the impact between 1969 and 1981 on Jacksonville was a 0.1 percent per capita annual increase while Tampa continued to show decreases of 0.3 percent.[79]

These researchers found that taxes and expenditures were not reduced, nor was the rate of increase. In fact, just the opposite occurred. The average ratio of per capita property taxes to per capita expenditures in Duval County was 0.272 between 1955 and 1968. After consolidation between 1969 and 1981, the average per capita ratio increased to 0.400. In Tampa the average per capita ratio was 0.550 prior to 1969. Between 1969 and 1981 this ratio dropped to 0.500, still higher than Jacksonville's, but then it had been higher before consolidation.[80]

The Benton and Gamble study did not consider quality of service before and after consolidation, nor did it compare quality with the control county. It is clear, however, that the reformers' contention relative to tax and expenditure reduction is not substantiated in the Jacksonville case. It is also not substantiated in the Miami-Dade County reform, which also resulted in increased expenditure levels.[81] This finding should not be surprising given the normal differential in service levels between the central city and its suburbs. A consolidated structure would be under obligation to even out these services, which would tend to increase overall expenditures. Also, there is an increasing body of literature that refutes the notion that highly centralized and bureaucratic administration is more economical than a proliferation of autonomous, smaller administrations.[82]

The impact of the Nashville-Davidson County consolidation on property taxes during the first few years varied depending on the location of the property. Property taxes within the old city boundaries stabilized compared to the other large Tennessee cities, which had property tax increases of 9 percent in Memphis and Knoxville and 37 percent in Chattanooga. Residents in the consolidated area outside the old city boundaries, however, experienced property tax increases of 26 percent, roughly 6 percent above suburbs in other Tennessee counties with large central cities. The differential in the increase can be attributed directly to the consolidation. Davidson County tax revenue started paying for services that had previously been paid only by residents of Nashville, such as the auditorium and the airport.[83] In commenting on whether consolidation saves money, Lex Hester, the former chief administrative officer of the consolidated government of Jacksonville, said:

> [A]s you expand your ability to deliver services, the demand for those services becomes greater, and you are forced to face some problems that you have been sweeping under the rug for years. When you consolidate the services, there is no rug to sweep it under. You have exposed the problem, the demand cries out for solution, much greater than had you just left it alone. So, in effect your budget is going to go up.[84]

Some observers of local government reform suggest that efficiency and effectiveness may, in fact, deteriorate because of consolidation.[85] They contend that bureaucracies may become too large to be effectively managed. They argue that large bureaucracies are not as responsive to citizens or receptive to changes and new innovations in service delivery, as smaller bureaucracies. Furthermore, there is evidence that administrators seek to take advantage of the consolidation to enhance their bureaucratic structures. Another impediment to reducing expenditures in a consolidation of governments is the promises that are often made to obtain voter support. Even though the implication from consolidation is cost savings through a reduction in staff from elimination of duplication, the consolidated government charter often has a provision that no employees will lose their jobs because of the consolidation. Elimination of duplicative personnel would come through attrition and reassignment. Therefore, personnel numbers are fixed in the short term; however, personnel costs are usually not. Charter provisions often stipulate that there will be no reduction in compensation for any employee. In fact, to avoid morale problems in combining previously separate departments, the government with the highest salary and benefits policy usually becomes the model for the employees of the new government. Combining the personnel systems and establishing a new classification plan in the Athens-Clarke County, Georgia, consolidation within the parameters of no job loss and no reduction in any employee compensation, increased payroll costs approximately 6 percent.[86]

In the Athens-Clarke County, consolidation, for example, the county and city parks and recreation departments were kept separate. In what appeared to be bureaucratic turf protection, the landscape maintenance functions of the parks and recreation departments were retained by those departments despite the establishment of a unit in the central services department charged with landscape maintenance. Turf protection also appeared to be the reason for keeping the facilities maintenance crews of the utilities department separate from those in the central services department.[87] Professor Stephen Condrey describes what happened in the Athens-Clarke County consolidation:

> Unification provided a situation whereby the basic common assumption of stability and predictability within the two former governments' organizational units was shattered. An additional consequence was that savvy organizational participants utilized the entropy precipitated by unification as a prime opportunity to add administrative levels ... The result ... was increased hierarchy and bureaucratic structure within the new government. For example, the recreation and parks and arts and environmental education departments both added assistant directors and division managers even though they were only slightly affected by consolidation. Additionally, the finance department added an assistant director position ... and four division heads in a department of 25 people. The most extreme example of bureaucratic empire building was the landscape management division, which proposed an organizational structure with 22 supervisors in an organization with fewer than 30 members.
>
> In sum, unification presented an opportunity for bureaucrats, in some instances, to protect and preserve their territory and to take advantage of the consolidation process to restructure their departments to enhance their personnel, power, and influence ... It appears that dysfunctional aspects of the early restructuring of the organization may last for years to come.[88]

An exhaustive study of nine city–county consolidations, most of which were paired for comparison purposes with a similar sized county in the state, revealed a mixed record of efficiency gains. About half the consolidated counties showed improved efficiency compared to their control county. Conversely, about half showed that expenditures in the comparison counties grew at slower rates than in the consolidated counties. In comparing expenditure growth in different functions that were consolidated, the result was again a mixture of slightly more than half the consolidated counties performing better than the comparison counties. The researchers in this study concluded that consolidation does not necessarily lead to increased gains in efficiency.[89] Likewise, a consolidation study of five Canadian cities found that costs increased or were expected to increase in three and they decreased in two. In one of the two, costs decreased because of an explicit agreement before the consolidation to keep salary increases to 1.5 percent. Researchers found in their analysis of the Clarke County–Athens consolidation that there were cost savings in some departments, but overall, there was an increase in per capita expenditures.[90]

In a study of 62 communities that voted on consolidation between 1970 and 2002, 12 of which consolidated, Faulk and Grassmueck found no significant difference in expenditures between those that consolidated and those that did not. Their research showed that a few of the consolidations actually were able to show cost savings, but they came more from strategic planning and cooperation that was conscious and deliberate. The savings, where they materialized, were not from the economies of scale effect, but from improved local government processes. The researchers stated that even if there are no real cost savings from consolidation, there might be other benefits. They suggested that consolidated governments are better able to institute changes in processes to improve service quality that might not have been possible before consolidation.[91]

Despite the evidence, reformers still lament the waste and duplication from government fragmentation and duplication and tout the savings from consolidation. For example, the most recent regional plan for the New York metropolitan area by the nonprofit, privately funded Regional Plan Association states that the inefficiency of the fragmented governance system of the New York region is "demonstrated by the dramatic rise in government revenues and expenditures . . . These increases, of 21% in revenues and 42% in expenditures over just 16 years, came during a period in which the region's population only grew by about 2%."[92] The authors give no evidence that a more consolidated government structure would have made any difference.

Improved Effectiveness

An effective government is one that achieves its objectives, one that establishes and implements policies desired by the residents and implements them in an efficient manner. There is anecdotal evidence that city–county consolidation has improved effectiveness. In Indianapolis, for example, services have improved under Unigov. Many observers feel that this is a result of the consolidation. In transportation, for example, in the first three years the miles paved or resurfaced increased from 56 miles in 1969 to 265 miles in 1972. While there is disagreement over the impact of Unigov on service levels and quality, a supposedly objective city hall reporter summed up an early assessment:

> Among the other facts that apparently can be documented are those that show the administration is producing record numbers of streets paved, sidewalks built, condemned houses razed, junk cars removed, jobs found for unemployed, low-cost housing units built, and federal grants approved for various programs.[93]

Former mayor Richard Hudnut credits Unigov for "lift[ing] America's twelfth largest city out of a tailspin and [making] it one of the most livable places in America."[94] Indianapolis, which in 1947 was characterized by author John Gunther as "an unkempt city, unswept, raw, a terrific place for basketball and auto racing, a former pivot of the Klu-Kluxers, and in it you may see the second ugliest monument in the world,"[95] has transformed itself and has emerged with a national reputation as a progressive, well-governed city. It is not possible to determine to what extent Unigov is responsible for this transformation. According to James Owen and York Willbern, who have extensively researched it, "Unigov appears to have made substantial contributions to Indianapolis's emergence as a major US city in the 1970s ... Unigov was probably especially effective in transforming the city's internal and external image."[96]

In Nashville, prior to consolidation, the county had no authority to develop and operate public parks. Opportunities to preserve some of the county's natural assets for the public were rapidly being lost as prime land was acquired by developers. One of the first actions of the consolidated government was to begin a program of land acquisition and park development throughout the county. Recreation programs were extended countywide in cooperation with the school system. Additional quality of life improvements included the extension of health services, hospitals, branch libraries, and street lighting on major roads throughout the county.[97] Residents' satisfaction of the consolidation have been positive as indicated by one survey just two years after consolidation, which found a 71 percent level of satisfaction with the new structure.[98] Nashville has realized substantial efficiencies from better use of its physical facilities. The city and county school systems were merged by the consolidation, which allowed better use of school facilities by transferring county students to vacant classrooms in the city. The bond structure of the consolidated government has increased the pool of surplus funds and provided greater investment returns.[99]

Other metropolitan areas experiencing improved services after structural reform include Miami-Dade County and Toronto. In Toronto, suburban water supply, sewage disposal, and school construction crises were resolved, and better services were provided in regional parks development, express highway construction, road improvements, and unified police administration. In Miami services were improved through adoption of a general land use code, uniform traffic laws, and uniform subdivision ordinances. Quality of life was improved through the adoption of countywide air and water pollution regulations.[100]

Equity in the Distribution of Resources

A commonly accepted principle in local government finance is that those who benefit should bear, or at least share in, the costs. Another commonly accepted democratic principle is that those affected by a decision should, either directly or through their elected representatives, have a voice in that decision. In a large, politically fragmented urban area, one jurisdiction often provides a service with residents in another jurisdiction benefitting without sharing equally in the costs of providing the services. Examples include central city parks, zoos, stadiums, and museums enjoyed by suburbanites with the costs of providing the service paid largely by the central city. In addition, spillovers from a decision made by one community often have positive or negative effects on neighboring communities. A shopping mall, garbage dump, or incinerator located in one community has negative impacts on neighboring communities. It seems reasonable that functions that affect the entire region should be funded on a regional basis and that decisions regarding the functions should be made by regional representatives.

Regionalists claim that a government covering the central city and the suburbs would distribute the costs and benefits more evenly. It would reduce the "free rider problem." Suburban residents within the regional government's boundaries would be taxed to support functions in the central city from which they benefit, such as central city museums and zoos. Central city residents would no longer be required to pay county taxes to support services outside their boundaries. All residents would be required to pay their fair share of social welfare costs to the poor, who are predominantly housed in the central city. A regional government would allow for a more equal distribution of facilities such as affordable housing and facilitate more orderly land use planning across the metropolitan area. Public goods and services could be more evenly distributed throughout the region. It would also facilitate integration of races and ethnic groups as there would be no municipal barriers.

As can be observed, regions across the nation vary widely in how equally resources are distributed among municipalities and across racial groups. Intuitively, one would think that fewer municipalities and more centralized government would result in greater equity. However, the findings of research are mixed on the impact of regional government on equal distribution of resources. For example, Jimenez and Hendrick[101] found from their analysis of the literature that the preponderance of the evidence indicates that decentralized government contributes to racial segregation but that the evidence is not quite so clear on income segregation. However, Lewis and Hamilton utilized a regression analysis of 311 primary metropolitan statistical areas from the 2000 census with populations of 100,000 or more to determine the effect of government fragmentation on disparities in metropolitan areas. They concluded from their analysis that while fragmentation of governmental units has some impact on segregation, other factors, such as the region's age, wealth, location, and other elements of the political culture were equally or even more important. They concluded that efforts placed on reducing the number of governments in a metropolitan area as a way to reduce segregation of minorities and promote income and housing equity would not solve the problem alone and would have little impact on segregation.[102]

Nashville is one positive example of the equity benefits from consolidation. Through its consolidated city and county school system, it was able to allocate resources throughout the county, which not only improved racial integration but also the inner-city school system.[103] There are, however, still socioeconomic disparities that regional reform has not overcome. In Indianapolis, for example, there is a perception in the inner-city minority community that they are paying more than their fair share for the level of services they are receiving. They feel that resources have been diverted from neighborhood revitalization to central business district development.[104] In Dade County, the tiered structure has done little to improve disparities between the central city and the suburban municipalities. Indeed, Miami exhibits the same problems that plague other central cities. The suburban affluence is in stark contrast to the poverty in Miami.[105]

In contrast to Nashville, the consolidated city–county of Jacksonville is characterized as one of the most segregated cities in the country. African Americans continue to reside predominantly within the boundaries of the former city. Those who have moved out of the old city moved into what have become predominantly black neighborhoods. Furthermore, the socioeconomic disparities between the old central city and the suburbs remain quite large. Consolidation has done little to alter the high incidence of poverty in the old central city compared to the outlying areas.[106]

Studies related to economic segregation between the city and the suburbs show that more unified areas tend to be less economically segregated. David Rusk, an advocate of regionalism, compared eight fragmented metropolitan areas with eight that were more unified. He found that residents of the central cities in the fragmented areas do much worse in terms of median family income and per capita income than central city residents in more politically united metropolitan areas. Over a 60-year period from 1950 to 2010, the median family and per capita income in the central cities in less fragmented areas as a percentage of the metropolitan area, declined at a slower rate than in the politically fragmented areas. Rusk then categorized 137 metropolitan areas based on the extent of their fragmentation. He found that the percentage of per capita income of central cities to their suburbs in highly fragmented metropolitan areas (his term is zero elasticity) had fallen from 74 percent in 1979 to 65 percent in 2009. During this period, the central cities in more politically united metropolitan areas (his term is hyper elasticity) had maintained rough income parity with their suburbs.[107]

Economic Development

One of the major arguments made for consolidation of governments is the positive effect it would have on development of the region. Proponents of centralization claim that fragmented urban areas cannot effectively compete for economic development. They claim that centralized government reduces harmful inter-municipal competition within metropolitan areas and beggar-thy-neighbor policies designed to attract development from one municipality to another. Larger size expands the taxable resources under the local government's control, allowing it to employ more assets in attracting development. Size does make a difference. The ability to compete with other cities was one of the factors in the consolidation of New York City in 1898. It wanted to keep up with London and remain larger than Chicago, which was growing rapidly. Economic development was also a factor in the consolidation of Toronto. It is now the fifth largest city in North America with increased economic stature and political power within the state, the nation, and internationally.

Some studies conclude that the ability to compete for economic development is enhanced in regions that are more centralized or work together. Orfield found that in the 1990s the Twin Cities produced more jobs per capita than the Chicago region. He claims the reasons were that the Twin Cities was more unified in its approach, able to bring more resources to the process, and had less intra-area dissension than fragmented areas which competed with each other. In the Twin Cities area, the entire region shares in economic development in any part of the region. In the competition to attract Boeing company headquarters to Chicago, many Chicago area governments made proposals. Boeing officials requested that the area governments should pool their resources and work together to produce one united proposal. They did and were successful in attracting Boeing to locate its headquarters in Chicago.[108] A study of metropolitan areas in the United States using shift-share analysis to measure income change from 1972 to 1997 found that those metropolitan areas with more unified local government and less state control were more competitive in economic development than those areas with more fragmented local government and more state control. In other words, the study found that the most successful regions in economic development had local government systems that were more centralized and that had more freedom from state controls. The worst scenario for development was a fragmented local government system in a centralized state system. In fact, the competitiveness score for the more centralized local government structure in a decentralized state system was

6.7 compared to −1.1 in a multiple local government system with little freedom from the state.[109]

All studies, however, do not reach similar conclusions.[110] A review of studies comparing economic development in consolidated counties with non-consolidated counties found no statistical relationship between consolidation and economic development. Generally, the non-consolidated counties in the state fared as well on various aspects of economic development that the studies measured, such as growth in businesses, per capita income, and population growth, as the consolidated counties. They also conducted a statistical analysis of three consolidations that occurred in the 1990s: Augusta-Richmond County, Georgia; Kansas City-Wyandotte County, Kansas; and Lafayette City-Lafayette Parish, Louisiana with similar counties in each state on change in employment levels and growth in business establishments. Their time frame was comparing pre-consolidation levels with two years after consolidation. Their analysis showed no boost to economic development resulting from consolidation. Martin and Schiff[111] analyzed 13 studies and found that most of them reported no advantages for economic development. Likewise, a study of economic development patterns in the Lexington-Fayette County, Kentucky consolidation found no change in economic development as a result of the consolidation. In comparison with development in the unconsolidated Jefferson County (Louisville), the development trends in both counties did not change during the period studied. Jefferson County outpaced Fayette County despite its fragmented government system.[112]

Given the results of the conflicting findings, what can one conclude as to whether economic development of an area is enhanced by a more centralized government system? Thurmaier and Leland, after analyzing economic growth patterns in nine city–county consolidations with paired nonconsolidated counties in which the consolidated counties fared better, concluded:

> The evidence is not overwhelming by any means. Still, difficulties in using exactly the same indicators notwithstanding, the multiple measures used for this analysis compel us to accept the hypothesis that *consolidated governments will have higher economic growth rates than similar nonconsolidated communities due to structural effectiveness gains.* (Italics in the original.)[113]

Notwithstanding Thurmaier and Leyland's conclusion, the jury is still out regarding the effect of consolidated government on economic development. However, one would surmise that with the misalignment between the economic and political boundaries in polycentric metropolitan areas and that economic flows do not stop at political boundaries, regions that work together in economic development activities have an advantage. Businesses look for an area (not city) that has competitive advantages, a skilled workforce, and amenities. They consider the entire area, not just one part. If regions can work together, it might not matter whether the region has a consolidated or a polycentric governing system. It would appear that a more united region can avoid individual local governments competing with each other for economic advantage and that pooling resources for economic development has its advantages over a fragmented approach.

Case Study: Efforts to Obtain Regional Government in the Pittsburgh Area[114]

During the nineteenth century, Pittsburgh expanded its borders by annexing 25 boroughs and townships. In 1907 Allegheny, a city of 130,000, was annexed. Under the provisions of the special legislation setting up the referendum, Pittsburgh's larger number of voters prevailed even though Allegheny bitterly opposed the annexation. As a result of the controversy surrounding the annexation, politicians from the suburban municipalities organized to oppose any further encroachment by the city. This ended further annexation.

An effort was made in 1919 and efforts continued into the 1920s to establish a federated form of metropolitan government, which was successfully defeated by the suburban association. Pressures from the business community and Pittsburgh politicians continued and in 1929 a charter was proposed to the voters that would establish a two-tier government covering the municipalities in Allegheny County. Even though 68 percent of the residents of the county voted in favor of the proposal, the referendum was not successful in meeting the required two-thirds vote in a majority of the municipalities. Because of the overall favorable vote, efforts were made in the 1930s to obtain state approval to authorize another referendum. The growing power and fierce resistance of the suburban politicians doomed these efforts.

Further efforts to obtain metropolitan government ceased. The focus of reform changed to piecemeal transfer of function from the municipality to the county and obtaining county home rule. These efforts commenced in the 1950s. The intent of those supporting home rule was to give the county authority to provide additional services without the necessity of obtaining permission from the state legislature for each service added. Due to opposition from the suburban officials, who saw it as another attempt at metropolitan government, the state legislature would not authorize a referendum although the state did authorize the gradual transfer of functions. There were two votes on county home rule in the 1970s. Both votes were defeated, the second vote more soundly than the first. Finally, in 1998, on the third vote on home rule, the voters approved home rule for the county. (See Chapter 8 for a discussion of the county's effort to obtain home rule.)

Thus ended the almost 100-year effort to obtain regional government reform for the Pittsburgh area after the era of annexation had ceased. Notice that the reform efforts only involved one county, which, at the start of the effort, constituted by far the majority of the population and geography of the metropolitan area. By the end of the effort, the metropolitan area had expanded to a seven-county region with only about half the population within the county. Moreover, the effort at regional reform started as major efforts to change authority relationships between that county and the municipalities and ended up as a simple home rule charter with no additional authority over county municipalities and a scaled-down version of a restructured county government.

Takeaway

Comprehensive government restructuring in urban areas does not have a bright future. Indeed, as noted previously, most of the activity occurred in the 1960s and 1970s. Even during this period, the majority of the proposals on restructuring government were voted down. Those that were successful were not complete consolidations or federations. Most existing governments in each case were left out of the reform. The major exception was Indianapolis, where most of the incorporated municipalities were consolidated into one government. Partial reform does not achieve the objectives of the reformers. Moreover, since most metropolitan areas have grown beyond a single county's boundaries, consolidation of the central county with the central city also does not achieve the reformers' aims of politically unifying the urban area in a multicounty MA. It seems that, for most metropolitan areas, city–county consolidation is a regional reform concept whose time has passed. They will likely continue to occur but not in mature metropolitan areas. The communities that will benefit from city–county consolidation are more rural or developing areas with substantial unincorporated land surrounding the central city. Even in these areas, annexation is more likely to be successful than consolidation.

Tiered government in the metropolitan concept such as existed in Toronto also does not seem to be a viable alternative. It has been disparaged and replaced in major metropolitan areas in Canada and never really was accepted in the United States. It seems that comprehensive restructuring of governments in metropolitan areas is generally a dead issue except possibly in newer-growth areas. If traditional metropolitan reform is dead, what is the future for regionalism in larger metropolitan areas? Future chapters will focus on other means that are used or being explored to achieve regional governance and provide regional services.

There are a number of issues and concerns involving comprehensive structural reform. City–county consolidations appear to be mainly a regional phenomenon, as most have occurred in the South and West. Consolidations have generally only been partial, as most existing incorporated municipalities in the county often remain separate from the consolidated government.

Furthermore, they cover only one county of metropolitan areas that often extend beyond a single county. The major issues with two-tier governments involve the division of responsibilities between the levels and the extension of the upper-tier boundaries to encompass new growth. The Miami-Dade County government has substantial unincorporated territory to which it must provide services. Toronto's metropolitan government has not been able to extend its boundaries to cover additional urban development in the region. Its metropolitan government covers approximately half the population and only a small portion of the developed land area.

Those who oppose or question the viability of traditional reform suggest that urban areas may be better served by a polycentric system of governments. They suggest people may value government that is more accessible, personable, and accountable than one that in the name of efficiency and economy becomes too big, remote, and bureaucratic. Larger governments are also not necessarily more efficient. Furthermore, it is evident from votes on metropolitan reform that the residents prefer the status quo to major reform initiatives. Researchers who have studied reform efforts conclude that there is a general lack of community interest in metropolitan reform. To engender interest and support, reformers must convince voters that there is a crisis in the current system of government. They must also find ways to neutralize or obtain the support of the political leaders, as studies have shown that they are the major variable in the success or failure of a reform initiative. The process of regional reform is also a barrier to achieving regional reform. There is a question whether the referendum is the most democratic way of deciding the merits of reform, since most voters are uninformed and tend to vote for the status quo on complicated issues.

Evaluations of reformed areas show that most of the goals of those advocating change are not met in a consolidation. The claim that more centralized governments are more efficient is not borne out by the evidence. Although services tend to improve when a region moves from a polycentric to a more centralized governing system, the costs of providing services also tend to increase. The record on equality in the distribution of costs and benefits in the reformed governments generally appears to be improved. Integration is improved in a more centralized structure. There is also evidence that a centralized system improves income distribution and growth. There are also mixed results from studies on the effect on economic development from moving to a more consolidated government. However, one could surmise that a more united region could bring more resources to bear and compete more effectively for development than an area that was less united.

Notes

1. John J. Harrigan and Ronald K. Vogel, *Political Change in the Metropolis*, 7th ed. (New York: Longman, 2003), pp. 262–263.

2. Bernard Ross and Myron A. Levine, *Urban Politics: Cities and Suburbs in a Global Age*, 8th ed. (Armonk, NY: M. E. Sharpe, 2012), pp. 245–246.

3. John J. Harrigan, *Political Change in the Metropolis* (Boston: Harper Collins, 1976), pp. 212–217.

4. Kenneth T. Jackson, *Crabgrass Frontier: The Suburbanization of the U.S.* (New York: Oxford University Press, 1985), pp. 142–143.

5. Kenneth T. Jackson and Stanley K. Schultz, (eds.), *Cities in American History* (New York: Alfred A. Knopf, 1972), pp. 367–368.

6. Samuel Hays, "The Politics of Reform in Municipal Government in the Progressive Era," *Pacific Northwest Quarterly*, 55 (October) (1964): 157–165.

7. Chester Maxey, "The Political Integration of Metropolitan Communities," *National Municipal Review* (August 1922), pp. 240–251, quoted in Allan D Wallis, *Inventing Regionalism* (Denver, CO: National Civic League, 1995), p. 10.

8. Jackson, *Crabgrass Frontier*, p. 143.

9. Harrigan and Vogel, *Political Change in the Metropolis,* p. 11.

10. Benjamin Kleinberg, *Urban America in Transformation: Perspectives on Urban Policy and Development* (Thousand Oaks, CA: Sage Publications, 1995), p. 74.

11. Quoted in Harrigan, *Political Change in the Metropolis*, p. 140.

12. Allan D. Wallis, "Governance and the Civic Infrastructure of Metropolitan Regions," *National Civic Review*, 82 (Spring) (1993): 126.

13. William Anderson, *American City Government* (New York: Henry Holt, 1925), pp. 641–642, quoted in Robert L. Bish and Vincent L. Ostrom, *Understanding Urban Government: Metropolitan Reform Reconsidered*, Domestic Affairs Study 20 (Washington, DC: American Enterprise Institute for Public Policy Research, 1973), pp. 7–8.

14. Robert C. Wood, *1400 Governments* (Garden City, NY: Anchor Books, Doubleday, 1961), pp. 51–64.

15. John C. Bollens and Henry J. Schmandt, *The Metropolis: Its People, Politics, and Economic Life* (New York: Harper and Row, 1965), pp. 177–180.

16. Committee for Economic Development, *Modernizing Local Government* (New York, 1966), pp. 11–12.

17. Ibid., p. 10.

18. Advisory Commission on Intergovernmental Relations, *Metropolitan America: Challenge to Federalism* (Washington, DC: U.S. Government Printing Office, 1966). For further reading on the "good" government groups, see Joseph F. Zimmerman, *Government of the Metropolis: Selected Readings* (New York: Holt, Rinehart, and Winston, 1968), pp. 25–48.

19. Bollens and Schmandt, *The Metropolis*, p. 180. See also Advisory Commission on Intergovernmental Relations, *Alternative Approaches to Reorganization in Metropolitan Areas* (Washington, DC: U.S. Government Printing Office, 1962); and Advisory Commission on Intergovernmental Relations, *Improving Urban America: A Challenge to Federalism* (Washington, DC: U.S. Government Printing Office, 1976).

20. Neal Peirce, *Citistates: How Urban America Can Prosper in a Competitive World* (Washington, DC: Seven Locks Press, 1993).

21. David Rusk, *Cities without Suburbs: A Census 2010 Perspective*, 4th ed. (Washington, DC: Woodrow Wilson Center Press, 2013).

22. Brett Hawkins, Keith J. Ward, and Mary P. Becker, "Governmental Consolidation as a Strategy for Metropolitan Development," *Public Administration Quarterly*, 15 (Summer) (1991): 258–259.

23. Allan D. Wallis, "The Third Wave: Current Trends in Regional Governance," *National Civic Review*, 83 (Summer/Fall) (1994): 290.

24. *City-County Consolidation Proposals.* http://www.naco.org. [Accessed July, 15, 2012.]

25. John C. Bollens and Henry J. Schmandt, *The Metropolis: Its People, Politics, and Economic Life*, 3rd ed. (New York: Harper and Row, 1975), pp. 253–254.
26. Ibid.
27. Harrigan, *Political Change in the Metropolis*, p. 246.
28. Bollens and Schmandt, *The Metropolis*, p. 247.
29. Arthur B. Gunlicks, "Problems, Politics, and Prospects of Local Government Reorganization in the United States," in Arthur B. Gunlicks, (ed.), *Local Government Reform and Reorganization: An International Perspective* (Port Washington, NY: Kennikat Press, 1981), p. 14.
30. L. J. Sharpe, "The Future of Metropolitan Government," in L. J. Sharpe, (ed.), *The Government of World Cities: The Future of the Metro Model* (Chichester, England: John Wiley and Sons, 1995), pp. 15–17.
31. Bollens and Schmandt, *The Metropolis*, p. 275.
32. Ibid.
33. Harrigan and Vogel, *Political Change in the Metropolis*, 7th ed., pp. 266–267.
34. Genie Stowers, "Miami: Experiences in Regional Government," in H. V. Savitch and Ronald K. Vogel, (eds.), *Regional Politics: America in a Post-City Age* (Thousand Oaks, CA: Sage Publications, 1996), p. 192.
35. Ibid., p. 194.
36. *Miami-Dade County Government*, http://www.miamidade.gov/info/about_miami-dade_statistics.asp [Accessed November 12, 2012].
37. Nelson Wikstrom, "Central City Policy Issues in Regional Context," in David Hamilton and Patricia S. Atkins, (eds.), *Urban and Regional Policies for Metropolitan Livability* (Armonk, New York: M.E. Sharpe, 2008), p. 39.
38. J. Cohan, "Metrovisions: Toronto Stumbling Six Years after Huge Mergers," *Pittsburgh Post-Gazette*, Sept. 20, 2004.
39. Richard F. Dye and J. Fred Giertz, *The Changing Relationships Among the Levels of Government in the Provision of Services* (Urbana, IL: Institute of Government and Public Affairs, March 1991), p. 3; George A. Boyne, "Local Government Structure and Performance: Lessons from America?" *Public Administration*, 70 (Autumn) (1992): 336.
40. Harrigan and Vogel, *Political Change in the Metropolis*, p. 255; Werner Z. Hirsch, "Local Versus Areawide Urban Government Services," copy of draft paper in possession of author, n.d.
41. Keating, *Comparative Urban Politics,* pp. 103–104.
42. Norton E. Long, "The Local Community as an Ecology of Games," *American Journal of Sociology*, 64 (November) (1958): 251–261.
43. Patricia K. Edwards and James R. Bohland, "Reform and Economic Development: Attitudinal Dimensions of Metropolitan Consolidation," *Journal of Urban Affairs*, 13 (4) (1991): 468.
44. *National Association of Counties*, http://www.naco.org [Accessed July, 15, 2012].
45. Pennsylvania Economy League, Western Division, *City/County Consolidation Background Report* (Pittsburgh PA, Feb. 2007).
46. *Consolidated City-County*, Wikipedia: http://en.wikipedia.org/wiki/Consolidated/city/county [Accessed, June 29, 2012].
47. See, for example, Allen S. Mandel, "Urban Growth and Government Structure: Criteria for Analysis and Redesign," *Public Affairs Comment*, 20 (August) (1974); Roscoe Martin, *Metropolis in Transition: Local Government Adaptation to Changing Needs* (Washington, DC: Housing and Home Finance Agency, 1963), pp. 130–133; Leonard E. Goodall and Donald P. Sprengel, *The American Metropolis* (Columbus, OH: Charles E. Merrill, 1965), pp. 122–161; Melvin B. Mogulof, *Five Metropolitan Governments* (Washington, DC: Urban Institute, 1972), p. 33;

and Vincent Marando, "The Politics of City-County Consolidation," *National Civic Review*, 64 (February) (1975): 76–78.

48. Marando, "The Politics of City-County Consolidation," p. 81; Jay S. Goodman, *The Dynamics of Urban Government and Politics* (New York: MacMillan, 1975), p. 258; Paul Ylvisaker, "Why Mayors Oppose Metropolitan Government," in Michael N. Danielson, (ed.), *Metropolitan Politics: A Reader* (Boston: Little, Brown, 1966), p. 180; David K. Hamilton, "Areawide Government Reform: A Case Study Emphasizing the Charter Writing Process," unpublished Ph.D. dissertation (University of Pittsburgh, 1978), p. 221.

49. Hamilton, "Areawide Government Reform," p. 223.

50. Ibid.

51. Brett Hawkins, "Public Opinion and Metropolitan Reorganization in Nashville," *The Journal of Politics*, 28 (May) (1966): 408.

52. Hamilton, "Areawide Government Reform," p. 224.

53. Walter A. Rosenbaum and Gladys M. Kammerer, *Against Long Odds: The Theory and Practice of Successful Government Consolidation*, Sage Professional Paper 03–022:2 (Beverly Hills, CA: Sage Publications, 1974), p. 30.

54. Hawkins, "Public Opinion and Metropolitan Reorganization in Nashville," p. 410; Henry J. Schmandt, P. G. Steinbicker, G. D. Wendel, "The Campaign for Metropolitan Government," in Michael N. Danielson, (ed.), *Metropolitan Politics: A Reader* (Boston: Little, Brown, 1966), p. 63.

55. Advisory Commission on Intergovernmental Relations, *Factors Affecting Voter Reactions to Government Reorganization in Metropolitan Areas* (Washington, DC: U.S. Government Printing Office, 1962), pp. 15–24.

56. Vincent L. Marando, "The Politics of Metropolitan Reform," *Administration and Society*, 6 (August) (1974): 241.

57. Bruce Shepherd, "Participation in Local Policy-Making: The Case of Referenda," *Social Science Quarterly*, 56 (June) (1975): 55–70. See also Vincent L. Marando and Carl Reggie Whitley, "City-County Consolidation: An Overview of Voter Response," *Urban Affairs Quarterly*, 8 (December) (1972): 187; and Edward McDill and Jeanne Clare Ridley, "Status Anomia, Political Alienation, and Political Participation," *The American Journal of Sociology*, 68 (September) (1962): 205–213.

58. Marion Kelley, "Albuquerque Votes Against Merger," *National Civic Review* 48 (November) (1959): 533–534.

59. See, for example, Robert L. Lineberry and Edmund P. Fowler, "Reformism and Public Policies in American Cities," in Charles M. Bonjea, T. N. Clark, R. L. Lineberry, (eds.), *Community Politics: A Behavioral Approach* (New York: Free Press, 1971), p. 278; James W. Clark, "Environment, Process, and Policy: A Reconsideration," in David R. Morgan and Samuel A. Kirkpatrick, (eds.), *Urban Political Analysis* (New York: Free Press, 1972), pp. 346–356; John M. Kessel, "Government Structure and Political Environment, A Statistical Note about American Cities," in Thomas R. Dye and Brett W. Hawkins, (eds.), *Politics in the Metropolis* (Columbus, OH: Charles E. Merrill, 1967), pp. 289–298.

60. J. D. Williams, *The Defeat of Home Rule in Salt Lake City*, Eagleton Institute, Cases in Practical Politics, Case 2 (New Brunswick, NJ: Rutgers University, 1960), pp. 29–31; Richard M. Bernard and Bradley R. Rice, "Political Environment and the Adoption of Progressive Municipal Reform," *Journal of Urban History*, 1 (February) (1975): 170–171.

61. Edward Sofen, "Reflections on the Creation of Miami's Metro," in Michael N. Danielson, (ed.), *Metropolitan Politics: A Reader* (Boston: Little, Brown, 1966), pp. 205–216.

62. Hamilton, "Areawide Government Reform," p. 22.
63. Larry Gamm, *Community Dynamics of Local Government Change*, Pennsylvania Policy Analysis Services (State College, PA: Pennsylvania State University, 1976), p. 7.
64. James Bowden and Howard D. Hamilton, "Some Notes on Metropolitics in Ohio," in John J. Gargan and James G. Coke, (eds.), *Political Behavior and Public Issues in Ohio* (Kent, OH: Kent State University Press, 1972), pp. 277–278.
65. Joseph F. Zimmerman, "Metropolitan Reform in the U.S.: An Overview," *Public Administration Review*, 30 (September/October) (1970): 537–538.
66. Sharon Perlman Krefetz and Alan B. Sharaf, "City-County Merger Attempts: The Role of Political Factors," *National Civic Review*, 66 (April) (1977): 175–181.
67. Henry J. Schmandt et al., *Metropolitan Reform in St. Louis: A Case Study* (New York: Holt, Rinehart, and Winston, 1961), p. 200.
68. Gamm, *Community Dynamics of Local Government Change,* pp. 28–30.
69. Hamilton, "Areawide Government Reform," pp. 228–230.
70. Bollens and Schmandt, *The Metropolis*, pp. 316–317; David R. Grant, "Nashville Politicians and Metro," in Michael N. Danielson, (ed.), *Metropolitan Politics: A Reader* (Boston: Little, Brown, 1966), pp. 217–229.
71. Hawkins, "Public Opinion and Metropolitan Reorganization in Nashville," p. 410.
72. Stanley Scott and Victor Jones, "Foreword," in C. James Owen and York Willbern, (eds.), *Governing Metropolitan Indianapolis: The Politics of Unigov* (Berkeley and Los Angeles: University of California Press, 1985), p. xxiv.
73. Hawkins, "Public Opinion and Metropolitan Reorganization in Nashville," p. 415.
74. Scott and Jones, "Foreword," p. xxiv.
75. Smallwood's arguments are discussed in Scott and Jones, "Foreword," pp. xxix–xxx.
76. The following is taken from David K. Hamilton, "Lay Local Government Charter Writing Commissions," *State and Local Government Review*, 14 (September) (1982): 124–127; and Hamilton, "Areawide Government Reform," especially Chapter 4.
77. Anthony M. Orum, *City-Building in America* (Boulder, CO: Westview Press, 1995), pp. 138–139. Reprinted by permission of Westview Press.
78. J. Edwin Benton and Darwin Gamble, "City/County Consolidation and Economies of Scale: Evidence from a Time-Series Analysis in Jacksonville, Florida," *Social Science Quarterly*, 65 (March) (1984): 191–198.
79. Ibid.
80. Ibid., p. 196.
81. Ibid.
82. Vincent Ostrom and Elinor Ostrom, "Public Choice: A Different Approach to the Study of Public Administration," *Public Administration Review*, 31 (March) (1971): 203–216; David Osborne and Ted Gaebler, *Reinventing Government* (Reading, MA: Addison-Wesley, 1992), especially chapters 6 and 9.
83. T. Scott Fillebrown, "The Nashville Story," *National Civic Review*, 58 (May) (1969): 199.
84. National Association of Counties, *Consolidation: Partial or Total* (Washington, DC: National Association of Counties, 1973), p. 44.
85. These observers tend to be mainly economists who identify with the so-called public choice school. This is discussed at length in Chapter 6.

86. Stephen E. Condrey, "Organizational and Personnel Impacts on Local Government Consolidation: Athens-Clarke County, Georgia," *Journal of Urban Affairs*, 16 (Winter) (1994): 373–376.
87. Condrey, "Organizational and Personnel Impacts on Local Government Consolidation," p. 380.
88. Ibid., p. 381.
89. Kurt Thurmaier and Suzanne M. Leland, "Promises Made, Promises Kept," in Suzanne M. Leland and Kurt Thurmaier, (eds.), *City-County Consolidation: Promises Made, Promises Kept?* (Washington, DC: Georgetown University Press, 2010), pp. 271–308.
90. Dagney Faulk and Georg Grassmueck, "City-County Consolidation and Local Government Expenditures," *State and Local Government Review*, 44 (3) (2012): 197–198.
91. Ibid, p. 202.
92. Robert D. Yaro and Tony Hiss, *A Region at Risk: The Third Regional Plan for the New York-New Jersey-Connecticut Metropolitan Area* (Washington, DC: Island Press, 1996), p. 204.
93. Ibid., p. 149.
94. William H. Hudnut, III, *The Hudnut Years in Indianapolis 1976–1991* (Indianapolis: Indiana University Press, 1995), p. 64.
95. John Gunther, *Inside USA* (New York: Harper and Brothers, 1947), p. 387, quoted in Owen and Willbern, *Governing Metropolitan Indianapolis,* p. 1.
96. Owen and Willbern, *Governing Metropolitan Indianapolis,* p. 125.
97. Fillebrown, "The Nashville Story," pp. 199–200.
98. Harrigan, *Political Change in the Metropolis*, p. 230.
99. Fillebrown, "The Nashville Story," p. 200.
100. Frank Smallwood, "Metro Toronto: A Decade Later," in H. Wentworth Eldredge, (ed.), *Taming Megalopolis*, vol. 2 (Garden City, NY: Anchor Books, Doubleday, 1967), pp. 669–697; Bollens and Schmandt, *The Metropolis*, p. 279.
101. B. S. Jimenez and R. Hendrick, "Is Government Consolidation the Answer?" *State and Local Government Review*, 42 (3) (2010): 258–270.
102. James H. Lewis and David K. Hamilton, "Race and Regionalism: The Structure of Local Government and Racial Disparity," *Urban Affairs Review*, 47 (3) (2011): 349–384.
103. Fillebrown, "The Nashville Story," p. 200.
104. Owen and Willbern, *Governing Metropolitan Indianapolis*, p. 180.
105. "Miami Voters Just Say No," *U.S. News and World Report*, Sept. 13, 1997, p. 22; Milan J. Dluhy, "Governmental Crisis in Miami Revisited: Public Administrators Lead the Road to Recovery," *PA Times*, 20 (August 1997): 2; Stowers, "Miami: Experiences in Regional Government," p. 189.
106. Bert Swanson, "Jacksonville: Consolidation and Regional Governance," in H. V. Savitch and Ronald K. Vogel, (eds.), *Regional Politics: America in a Post-City Age* (Thousand Oaks, CA: Sage Publications, 1996), pp. 238–240.
107. Rusk, *Cities without Suburbs*, pp. 48, 88.
108. David K. Hamilton, "Developing Regional Regimes: A Comparison of Two Metropolitan Areas," *Journal of Urban Affairs*, 26 (4) (2004): 473.
109. David K. Hamilton, David Miller, and Jerry Paytas, "Exploring the Horizontal and Vertical Dimensions of the Governing of Metropolitan regions," *Urban Affairs Review*, 40 (2) (2004): 147–182.
110. D. Falk and E Schansberg, "An Examination of Selected Economic Development: Outcomes from Consolidation," *State and Local Government Review*, 41 (3) (1999): 193–200.

111. L. L. Martin, and J. H. Schiff, "City-County Consolidations: Promise versus Performance," *State and Local Government Review*, 434 (2) (2011): 167–177.

112. Jered B. Carr, Sang-Seok Bae, and Wenjue Lu, "City-County Government and Promises of Economic Development: A Tale of Two Cities," *State and Local Government Review*, 38 (3) (2006): 140.

113. Thurmaier and Leland, "*Promises Made, Promises Kept,*" p. 293.

114. Much of this section is excerpted from David K. Hamilton, *Areawide Government Reform: A Case Study Emphasizing the Charter Writing Process*. Unpublished Ph.D. Dissertation, University of Pittsburgh, 1978, pp. 50–72.

5 The Impact of Federal and State Government Policies on Regionalism

A decent home and suitable living environment to every American.
—National Housing Act of 1949

The federal government was not involved in domestic affairs in a major way until the Great Depression of the 1930s. Prior to that time, its major domestic role was to promote the general development of the nation through the transportation and communication systems it subsidized or provided. Starting in the 1930s, it became increasingly involved in most aspects of domestic life. It variously supported and helped finance both local government decentralization and functional centralization in urban areas with its policies, starting in the Depression and accelerating in the post-World War II years. The first section of this chapter covers the federal government's actions that aided fragmentation. The second section deals with federal policies that encouraged functional centralization. The final section covers the role of the states. State policies vary from state to state; however, some generalizations can be made. States generally supported centralization through much of the nineteenth century. In the latter part of that century, states started establishing policies that allowed decentralization to take place. From that time until the later part of the twentieth century, state policies generally fostered decentralization. Recently, some states have started to encourage more centralized approaches.

Federal Housing Policies Supporting Fragmentation

The federal government first became involved in housing as a way to stimulate the economy during the Depression and provide housing for the poor. One of the central elements of President Franklin D. Roosevelt's plan to revive the economy in the 1930s was to build directly or provide loans to local authorities for the building of 192,000 public housing units. These were to be built largely in slum areas of the cities. Immediately, forces coalesced to alter these plans. A coalition of labor groups successfully lobbied to include legislation favoring construction on vacant land over slum sites, thereby focusing development in outlying areas. A coalition of building groups including the National Association of Real Estate Boards and the National Retail Lumber Dealers Association successfully pushed for legislation to restrict public housing and to establish the Home Owner's Loan Corporation (HOLC) and the Federal Housing Administration (FHA) to finance and insure the mortgages of homeowners. While the New Deal did not abandon public housing programs, the focus changed to promoting single-family, suburban housing.[1]

These programs fundamentally changed the way housing was built and sold. Previous to the establishment of the FHA, housing construction was quite risky. Most developers were under-capitalized and existed from the sale of one project or house to the next. They borrowed heavily and in an economic downturn often went bankrupt. Before 1932, typical home loans were issued with three-to-five-year maturities requiring 40 to 50 percent down payments. Expensive second and third mortgages were often necessary. With the onset of the Depression, the housing market was in shambles. Many homeowners lost their homes, and banks were left with houses for which there were no buyers. Financing finally became stable with the passage of the National Housing Act of 1934. By insuring lenders against losses in residential investments, the FHA attracted capital into housing. The program extended the term of the loan to 20 and then 30 years and required as little as ten percent down. With insured mortgages, the borrower was also able to receive a more favorable interest rate. The initial interest rate was 5 percent, which was 1 to 2 percent below the interest rate for uninsured mortgages.[2] With insured mortgages and a longer period over which to amortize them, developers were able to make a longer commitment to the development of the area and develop an entire subdivision. By developing an entire subdivision, developers could reduce construction costs through econo-mies of scale and the use of standard designs and precut and prefit pieces. This made the price of homes more affordable. For example, houses sold in the Los Angeles area in the late 1930s for $3,000 to $4,500, which meant a $50 down payment and an FHA-guaranteed mortgage of $30 to $50 per month.[3]

The FHA, by introducing the mutual mortgage insurance system, suc-ceeded in expanding the supply of capital available from lenders for residen-tial development, making mortgage loans more affordable for borrowers. Through the powerful inducement of mortgage insurance, the FHA's Land Planning Division was able to transform residential development practices as well as play a key role in shaping and popularizing local land use regulation. The federal programs also standardized appraisal methods across the country, which provided guidelines for local building codes. The federally developed system of coding neighborhoods into four categories of quality, however, also helped to promote development in the suburbs and devalue the central cities. Its land-planning consultants and manuals served to guide the decision making of private subdivision developers, and its Land Planning Division encouraged state and local governments to establish or restructure planning agencies and zoning and subdivision regulations. This new federal agency, operated to a large extent both by and for bankers, builders, and brokers, exercised great political power in pressuring politicians and public officials to conform to its requirements. By 1940 the FHA had fully established the land-planning and development process and the pattern of the suburbanization movement that followed World War II.[4]

The federal presence in suburban residential growth was specifically geared to accommodate the large builder, whose input was crucial to the formulation of FHA construction standards, the indispensable prerequisite for mortgage insurance programs. As a case in point, Levitt and Sons boasted the largest line of credit ever provided to a private builder and was able to secure FHA production advances and commitments to finance 4,000 homes with monthly payments under $60. By 1949, the larger builders, such as Levitt, accounted for 25 percent of all new single-family housing units and for nearly two-thirds of all such units by 1959.[5]

In a little more than a decade, FHA mortgage insurance was on the way to becoming an institutional key to homeownership, mainly in the suburbs, for millions of American families. In addition, FHA's insurance program served as a model for a similar program to help returning veterans at the end of World War II purchase their own homes. Thus, FHA's mortgage program was joined by a mortgage program of the Veterans Administration (VA), providing easy terms for veterans to buy a home with the government assuming the risk of default. Through these FHA and VA programs, the federal government subsidized a massive wave of homebuilding, most of it outside of central cities. Over time, such government programs profoundly affected the physical development and the social structure of suburbia, as well as the economic and residential condition of central cities.[6]

Having served the initial purpose of stimulating the home construction industry during the 1930s, the long-term function of federal mortgage insurance became primarily that of a program to support the construction of suburban housing. This was partly because both FHA and VA policies made it easier to obtain loans on new housing, as opposed to already existing housing. In addition, the FHA program was particularly oriented toward assisting the purchase of single-family dwellings, which required more land per dwelling unit than multiple-family housing. During the postwar era, large lots were more readily available and lower priced in suburban areas than in central cities. In general, this systematically tended to favor new residential development in the suburbs.[7]

In spite of the agency's declared objective of expanding home ownership for American families, FHA-backed housing built in the suburbs was by no means intended for ownership by all groups. Until 1962, when President John F. Kennedy signed an executive order to ban discrimination in federally aided housing, it was generally FHA policy to restrict loans to white borrowers. The agency went so far as to endorse as a model a racially restrictive housing covenant dating from the 1930s to protect all-white residential areas. For more than a generation of critically important community development, the FHA actively discouraged investment in racially or ethnically mixed central city neighborhoods by advising its appraisers to give low eligibility ratings to properties located in areas that housed minority groups. It was not until the late 1960s that an FHA commissioner clearly declared that such redlining of whole areas was no longer permissible.[8]

The other major discriminatory practice that the FHA maintained from the crucial decades of postwar suburbanization until the early 1970s was income discrimination against lower-income groups. Eligibility requirements tended to exclude not only the unemployed poor but also lower-income working-class families from qualifying for loan guarantees, even though in the aggregate these groups had the most serious housing needs in the nation. A report of the National Commission on Urban Problems indicated that as of the late 1960s only a little more than 10 percent of FHA mortgage funds had gone to groups in the lower 40 percent of the income scale. In fact, "up until the summer of 1967, the FHA almost never insured mortgages on homes in slum districts, and did so very seldom in the gray areas which surrounded them."[9]

The impact of this income bias, which overlapped with, and reinforced the racial bias of, FHA mortgage policy, can be judged by the magnitude of the program. Between the FHA's establishment in the mid-1930s and the emergence of strong criticisms of its policies in the late 1960s, over seven million housing units, or fully 20 percent of all privately financed nonfarm units in the nation, were constructed with FHA-backed mortgages. The VA mortgage guarantee program proved somewhat more accessible to lower-middle-class groups. Almost 30 percent of VA mortgages in 1966 went to families with incomes between $4,800 and $6,000, as against only 10 percent of FHA mortgages that went to such families in the preceding year. Nonetheless, both the FHA and VA mortgage programs tended to exclude the poor and the near poor. For example, by 1966 the programs had provided less than 2 percent of mortgages to families with incomes of $3,600 or less.[10]

The success of the federal housing programs as a stimulus to the housing market and homeownership was nothing short of phenomenal. It significantly increased the volume of mortgage credit, bringing moderate-income families with relatively little savings into the housing market on a large scale. By 1972 the FHA had helped 11 million families buy houses and another 22 million improve their properties. The VA home loan program for veterans had been accessed for almost ten million loans by 1971.[11] The majority of these loans were for homes built in the suburbs.

Overall, it may be said that both programs contributed to a policy of selective suburbanization favoring white middle-class movement to the suburbs. The middle-class demand for low-density living was reinforced by government-sponsored FHA- and VA-insured mortgages and favorable tax policies which reduced the relative price of the single-family, owner-occupied units largely concentrated in the suburbs. By contrast, there was little federal subsidy available for multiple-unit structures typical of apartment dwellings in central cities. The net result was a strong bias in favor of middle-class ownership of new homes in the suburbs. At the same time, within central cities New Deal-initiated public housing projects became an important concentration point for poor and minority populations, adding to the push factors contributing to rapid suburbanization.[12]

The Cleveland region is an example of the impact of the suburban tilt of federal housing policies. Between 1950 and 1990, 373,700 housing units were built in the suburbs while only 43,000 were built in the city. This was at a time when the number of households in the metropolitan area increased by 273,000. The problem of surplus housing first started appearing in the 1960s with housing availability of 1.5 units per household. These surplus units were largely in the city, and many were abandoned. In the 1970s about 40,000 housing units became surplus. The ratio of units per household rose to 2.0; abandonment was rampant. Over the four decades from 1950 to 1990, approximately 100,000 units of housing in the city were made surplus, most of them abandoned. Abandoned buildings significantly add to the blight and deterioration of a neighborhood.[13]

The Housing Act of 1949 was a major component in the federal government's effort to provide for slum clearance and the construction of public housing. This act was the basis for a broad urban redevelopment program aimed at distressed central cities to combat economic and social threats. These threats were the spread of urban slums and commercial blight from decentralization of the central city population and economic resources to the suburbs and other regions of the nation. The main emphasis of the 1949 act was the construction of federally subsidized, low-income housing. However, there was substantial resistance in many cities to public housing. Particularly, many cities in the Southwest and West including Los Angeles and Houston rejected public housing through local referendums. The main beneficiaries of this 1949 housing program were the old industrial cities of the Northeast and Midwest.

A series of amendments starting with the 1954 amendments and a sharp reduction of funding authorization for public housing changed the focus from affordable low-income housing to economic redevelopment. Instead of building low-income housing, the federal grants were used for the commercial revitalization of the central business districts and blighted areas of central cities. To the extent that low-income housing was built in metropolitan areas, it was most often constructed in the central cities, further isolating and segregating the low-income population. The housing that was removed for commercial urban renewal projects was not replaced, further encouraging population deconcentration from the inner city.[14]

In addition to federal housing policies, federal tax policies also encouraged suburbanization through tax deductions for mortgage interest and local property taxes. Indeed, this is the largest federal contribution to home-ownership. The value of these deductions rose from $3.2 billion in 1958 to $62.6 billion in 1986, $27.3 billion of which was for interest expenses. This major incentive for home ownership benefited those with the most expensive homes, as about 60 percent of all homeowners either have no mortgages or take the standard deduction.[15] One researcher concluded from a study that the combined advantage of the federal tax deductions and the federal mortgage programs was a 17 percent increase in the land area of a typical metropolis in the 1950s. This 17 percent increase was in addition to that caused by other measurable factors like population increase, transportation improvements, and local government efforts.[16]

Manufacturing Deconcentration

Federal policies on location of defense industries played a major role in the decentralization of manufacturing from central cities to the suburbs. The rapid increase in American defense expenditures for World War II started in 1940, when President Roosevelt asked Congress for a billion dollars to prepare for expanded military production. Larger requests soon followed. Between 1940 and 1945 the United States created as much industrial capacity as had existed in the country before 1940. According to one researcher, the initial investment in war production facilities was made in the older cities that housed much of the nation's existing industrial capacity. The consequences of this investment were to begin an immense migration to the nation's older industrial cities. Hartford, Bridgeport, Portsmouth, and other industrial cities experienced a rapid in-migration of workers, first from their immediate hinterlands and then from more remote areas. Detroit recruited workers from all over the rural Midwest, and workers left the depressed areas around Scranton and Wilkes-Barre in northeastern Pennsylvania for Connecticut's war industries.[17]

The influx of war workers soon strained the limits of these old centers. Housing, transportation, and even public health facilities were severely burdened. Morale in defense plants declined as workers abandoned defense jobs in the face of poor or nonexistent housing and days that started and ended with hours spent on crowded public transportation. In the face of these difficulties, federal policy makers at the War Production Board, the War Manpower Commission, and other national agencies realized that defense industries would have to be located outside the older central cities where underutilized labor still existed and where the facilities to absorb new migrants were not filled to capacity.[18]

Political considerations may have also played a part in the decision to put war production facilities in the suburbs. Political scientist John Mollenkopf argued that the War Production Board, dominated as it was by representatives of the business community, used this opportunity to weaken the urban political base of the New Deal by investing in the suburbs. Mollenkopf's argument does indeed seem to fit some of the data that emerged from these years. In Detroit, for example, the War Production Board ignored a proposal by union leader Walter Reuther to retool a large number of smaller industrial plants within the central city for defense production. Instead, funds were diverted to adjacent rural and suburban areas. Detroit may be an atypical example because of the bitter period of labor-management confrontation the automobile industry had just experienced. Political tensions between the militant United Automobile Workers and Henry Ford were at their height. The possibility that conflict between the urban New Deal and its conservative opponents in the suburbs may have shaped some of the federal government's wartime investment policies cannot be ignored.[19]

By 1945, it was possible to see the impact of the decision to relocate defense production outside the older central cities. In New York City, $380 million was invested in defense plants between 1940 and 1945, but $492 million was invested in suburban defense plants in the New York metropolitan area. In Detroit the difference was even greater; $326 million went to the central city, while $713 million was invested in the Detroit suburbs. For every dollar invested in urban Detroit, $2 was invested in its suburbs. In Los Angeles, $4 reached the suburbs for every dollar invested in the city. Only in the newly emergent cities of the South and West did the central cities occasionally receive more money than their suburbs.[20]

These patterns of investment brought in their wake a tidal wave of human migration to cities in the Midwest, South, and Pacific Coast, and more especially to their suburbs. Nearly four million American civilians left their homes for new communities between 1940 and the end of 1943. Between 1940 and 1944, the four suburban counties in the Detroit metropolitan area received more than 200,000 migrants. In 1941, Ford completed its Willow Run bomber plant in rural Washtenaw County, 30 miles from Detroit. By 1944, more than 40 percent of the residents of Washtenaw County consisted of war workers and their families who had moved to the area after 1940.[21]

Unlike older industrial factories, most of the new factories producing war materials were low-rise horizontal developments consuming large tracts of land only available outside the built-up areas of central cities. The result of these federal policies was a substantial industrial base of new, highly efficient factories located outside central cities for commercial development following the war. In fact, after 1946, manufacturing employment moved to the suburbs faster than residential population.[22] As war plants were converted to meet the pent-up consumer demand, employment shifted to the suburbs. Population moved to the suburbs to be near jobs and for modern affordable housing through the FHA and VA. Retail and service establishments moved to the suburbs to service the growing industries and population. Suburban shopping malls and office buildings started sprouting in the 1950s and 1960s. The shopping malls and office complexes also became growth nodes attracting employment and population growth.

Federal Transportation Policies

Federal involvement in highway construction started long before the Interstate Highway Act of 1956. By 1940 the federal government had helped the states build 150,000 miles of primary U.S. highways traversing the nation. But the federal government's most ambitious and consuming highway program was started in 1956 with the Interstate Highway Act.[23] This act created a highway trust fund for revenues from the sales tax on gasoline. From this fund the federal government paid for 90 percent of the cost of the construction and maintenance of a comprehensive system of limited-access highways that revolutionized American transportation. This program made land on the periphery accessible to the city and opened up the suburbs to development like no other program had previously. Even though President Dwight D. Eisenhower had advocated the interstate system to connect cities and assist rural areas, he became concerned in 1959 over the impact the program was having on expanding commuting distances to the central city and contributing to sprawl development patterns. However, his executive orders could not reverse the metropolitan development pattern.[24] Interstate Highway Act money was used to build about 5,000 miles of the 42,000-mile system in urban areas to provide belts and spokes that would facilitate commuter travel from the suburbs to central cities.

In addition to the highway trust fund that provides for highway construction and maintenance, road projects are also subsidized by federal general tax revenue, thereby masking the true costs to the user. For example, more than half of the $13 billion awarded by the federal government for highway projects in 1987 came from general revenues, not user fees. Thus, financing the road system that opened up the suburbs and promoted decentralization came not just from the suburban user through gasoline taxes. These highway programs that had serious consequences for the central city were also subsidized through general taxes paid by city residents. Historian Kenneth T. Jackson states: "[T]he outward movement of people and jobs can be seen as a rational response by millions of individuals to the high rate of implicit subsidy awarded to motor car drivers, suburban developers, and private homeowners."[25]

As the federal highway program was contributing to the growth of the U.S. economy, it was helping to decentralize industry and population within metropolitan areas and intensify automobile traffic congestion. As commuters utilized the new interstate highways to get to work, usage of buses, trains, and trolleys declined. In 1990 only 5 percent of all rush hour commuters used public transit, 86 percent used private vehicles, and 73 percent drove to work alone. Although the number of commuters using public transportation increased in 2000 over 1990, due to the increase in the workforce, the percentage of workers commuting via public transit actually declined to 4.7 percent. The heavy reliance on the automobile actually increased in 2000 to 87.9 percent with 75.7 percent driving alone. In 2000, 10.5 percent of all central city workers and only 2.9 percent of all suburban workers commuted by public transit.[26]

In an attempt to reverse the decline in public transit and encourage more concentrated development, the federal government started providing significant funds for mass transit in 1974. However, distribution of federal transportation dollars was and still is biased in favor of road projects over public transportation projects. The bulk of the federal gas tax is used for highways, with only about 6 percent spent on mass transit systems. The federal funds match for public transit New Starts capital projects are capped at 80 percent but depending on congressional appropriations may be only 60 percent. In contrast, highway funding continues to enjoy a federal matching ratio of 90 percent on the interstate highway system and 80 percent for most other projects. In a recent analysis, federal funds provided only 47.2 percent of the capital funds for public transit agencies. There is much more federal red tape involved in public transit projects than for roads. Unlike highway projects, the Federal Transit Administration must approve each public transit project. With the federal match much higher for highways and the bureaucratic approval process much less costly and burdensome, it is much easier to build and maintain roads than it is to build and maintain public transit systems with federal dollars. Moreover, because the amount of transit funding available is so small, there is intense competition for the funds. Consequently, public transit is the orphan of the federal transportation funding system and is heavily dependent on local government for funding and support.[27]

Federal Infrastructure Grants

Federal grants-in-aid to local governments for infrastructure helped foster a culture of independence and autonomy among suburban communities. The large influx of federal grant money started during the Depression years. Water and sewer infrastructure grants are a good example of how the federal government involved itself in supporting suburbanization. Previous to the 1930s, water and sewer systems were largely financed through local resources. During the Depression, the federal government, through the Public Works Administration, paid for 35 to 50 percent of new water and sewer construction. This was discontinued after the war as part of a reaction to New Deal policies. However, it started again with the Water Pollution Control Act of 1948, which provided limited research and planning funds and some low-interest loans for sewer facilities. By 1956, the federal government was back in local infrastructure development in a major way with an amendment to the 1948 Water Pollution Control Act to provide grants for construction of sewer systems.[28]

The federal role in water and sewer expansion was not significant in the early part of the postwar boom. However, as interest rates on bonds started to increase, as construction costs started to inflate, and as many suburban jurisdictions passed the point of depending solely on backyard septic tanks, the role of the federal government grew. By 1966, 47 percent of sewer construction expenses and 22 percent of water construction expenses were paid by the federal government. The federal share of sewer construction costs rose to about 75 percent in 1980, or $30 billion. It is virtually impossible to measure the impact of this spending on decisions to open new suburban developments; however, its impact on land value can be measured. One study found sewered land to be worth two to four times more than unsewered land.[29] Without the federal grants, it is unlikely that suburban development could have proceeded as it did because the costs of developing sewer and water systems in low-density suburban areas are almost three times higher than in high-density areas.[30] Absent the federal grants, it is probable that the high cost and lack of resources for sewer and water construction would have altered the land use by either increasing the density or acting as a brake on development. Not only did federal grants make it possible for suburban communities to provide basic municipal services, but federal financial assistance was provided for other essential civic infrastructure and facilities to enhance the quality of life, such as the building of hospitals and the purchase of land for parks.

The federal government's involvement in urban areas resulted in two developments that encouraged decentralization and independence from the central cities. To the extent that federal programs provided services directly or required the establishment of agencies to provide services that functioned independently of local government, they bypassed the traditional dependent relationship of the residents to their municipality. Suburban governments now had other avenues to meet needs in the region that had often been provided only in the large cities. There were now many foci concerned with planning, programming, and providing what had traditionally been provided by the city.[31] The second development is that the extensive federal subsidies for social support programs in the central cities attracted more low-income people resulting in greater segregation and an increased economic and social gulf between central cities and their suburbs. As central cities struggled to provide for the low-income, largely minority population, the white middle-class flight to the suburbs accelerated, and suburban communities increasingly sought noninvolvement with the city.[32]

During the critical years of the suburban movement, a study of the 37 largest metropolitan areas showed that suburban local governments were receiving a larger share of federal and state grants than central cities. For example, in 1957, 19 percent of central city expenditures in the 37 largest metropolitan areas were contributed by intergovernmental aid compared to 26 percent for their suburban communities. By 1970, these figures had narrowed to 33 percent for suburban communities compared to 31 percent for the central cities. By 1977, central cities were finally receiving a larger portion of their expenditures from intergovernmental aid than the suburbs at 44 percent to 40 percent.[33] However, the character of the intergovernmental aid received by the central cities and the suburbs was vastly different. The central cities received aid largely for social and welfare programs while the suburbs received substantial aid for infrastructure development and provision of basic services, services that central cities had financed largely from their own-source revenue.

Federal Programs Encouraging Regionalism

With the growth in the number of federal grant-in-aid programs to local governments, regional planning and coordination requirements started to be included as requirements in the grants. Section 701 of the Housing Act of 1961, the Federal Highway Act of 1962, the Urban Mass Transit Act of 1964, and Section 702(c) of the Housing and Urban Development Act of 1965 each established requirements for comprehensive planning as a basis for determining the distribution of federal grants and loans for project development. By 1977, 39 federal programs contained specific requirements for regional comprehensive planning.[34]

As the number of federal grant programs supporting state and local planning efforts grew—from 9 in 1964 to 160 in 1977—emphasis on coordination increased as a companion to requirements for comprehensive planning. The objective of coordination was first introduced in 1959 under Section 702 of the Housing Act, amended. It received greater emphasis in Section 204 of the Demonstration Cities and Metropolitan Development Act (Model Cities Act) of 1966, which established a regional review requirement for projects proposed under 30 different federal grant and loan programs.[35] The Model Cities Act required that all applications by local units for federal grants and loans covering a wide range of programs, including airports, highways, hospitals, sewage and water supply facilities, and open space acquisition must be submitted for review to an area-wide "clearinghouse" designated by the Office of Management and Budget (OMB).

Another significant initiative that provided a stimulus for metropolitan planning was the Intergovernmental Cooperation Act of 1968. This act stated: "To the maximum extent possible . . . all federal aid for development purposes shall be consistent with and further the objectives of state, regional and local comprehensive planning."[36] Sections 401 and 402 of the Intergovernmental Cooperation Act required the President to develop rules and regulations that would promote coordination of federal programs at the state and local levels and reduce the current proliferation of federally created single-function special districts at the substate level. This was done in 1969 through OMB Circular A-95 which created a project notification and review system that expanded the review process created by Section 204 of the Model Cities Act. In addition, the A-95 circular established rules and requirements for state- and area-wide agency review of federal grant and aid programs. It also contained provisions for the establishment of state, regional, and metropolitan clearinghouses. As a result of the requirements laid down in the circular, the number of federal programs subject to the review process increased from 30 to 50. A further revision in 1971 expanded the review requirements to cover about 100 federal planning and aid programs.[37] The procedures specified that the comments and recommendations by the clearinghouse were to include information concerning "the extent to which the project is consistent with or contributes to the fulfillment of comprehensive planning."[38]

The intent of the regional planning and coordination requirements was to mandate an area-wide oversight process in the highly fragmented urban area. The theory was that this would force municipalities to combine and co-ordinate their development plans to avoid duplication and overbuilding of expensive facilities, a step down the road to regional governance. The federal grant requirements for regional planning and coordination stimulated the creation and development of regional planning commissions (RPCs) and councils of governments (COGs) for planning and regional coordination among governments. Grants were made available to these organizations for staffing, administration expenses, data collection, and planning studies. By 1973, 53 state clearinghouses, 212 metropolitan clearinghouses, and 238 regional clearinghouses had been designated.[39]

The Impact of Federal Planning and Coordination Mandates

The effectiveness of the planning and coordination requirements varied depending on the region but generally was not as effective as it could have been. There are a number of reasons for this lack of effectiveness. The major reason was that the regional planning agency was advisory only, without any political power to enforce its recommendations. The regional bodies were at least one step removed from the electorate as they were not directly elected.

Without a regional constituency to please, the interests of the political representatives on the agencies tended to be focused on meeting the needs of the community from which they were elected. Moreover, the professional planners working for the regional agencies had little or no support from members of the agency's governing body for area-wide plans and recommendations that were not compatible with the interests of the individual communities. Because of the lack of political power and enforcement authority, the review and comment process on municipalities' federal grant applications was often ignored if the regional agency's recommendations were negative.

Another related problem was the lack of consensus on regional goals. The planning agency operated without any clear direction as to the overall development objectives for the region. Objectives developed by professional planners can only be implemented if they are embraced by the politicians. Without an area-wide constituency, it is improbable that politicians will be able to agree on regional goals, particularly if they circumscribe prerogatives of the individual governments they represent. Moreover, individual communities would not willingly give their authority over land use and development to a regional agency to implement area-wide plans. Thus, regional plans are usually ignored. One study by the Urban Land Institute found that of 102 cities surveyed, only 10 made specific use of plans drawn up by planning agencies.[40]

Another issue involved problems in funding. Federal programs were often underfunded, the funds were too widely dispersed, or the impact of the program was other than expected. An example is the Urban Development Action Grant (UDAG) program. Until the early 1980s, it was the major federal program to stimulate urban economic development in blighted areas. The funds were distributed on a project approval basis; eligible cities made application and federal officials determined which ones to fund. The UDAG grants had to leverage private investment equal to two and a half times the amount of the award. Often this leverage was nothing more than a loan to private developers. Eighty percent of the grants were used in this fashion from 1982 until UDAG's demise from lack of program funds in 1989.[41] The UDAG program for all practical purposes did not stimulate economic development in the region but shifted development from other parts of the urban area to the UDAG development site. In this way the federal government influenced land use and location decisions. The main impact of the grants was to stimulate commercial and retail development in downtown areas of central cities, thereby redirecting development from the suburbs. However, the funds were not sufficient to have a significant impact on growth and development patterns in metropolitan areas.

The sheer number of grants and the variety of grant sources within the federal government made regional coordination problematic. It was estimated that by 1981 the number of separate grant programs was 540, a substantial increase from the 45 that existed in 1961 at the beginning of the Kennedy administration. Not only were the numbers of grant programs extensive; they were often for overlapping purposes. For example, there were 50 different grant programs available for health purposes, 57 for social services, 32 for ground transportation, and 16 for pollution control and abatement. Moreover, some grant programs funded only component parts of a project. This required the grant applicant to make separate applications, possibly to different agencies, for various components of a project. There was a risk of being approved for part of the project and rejected for other parts of the project. The granting agencies did not coordinate their approvals and otherwise had no knowledge of programs being funded by other agencies. Furthermore, the recipient governments knew or cared little about what other local governments were receiving.[42]

The late 1970s represented the zenith of federal grant programs and federal support for regionalism. In addition to the large number of categorical grants, there were 39 federal programs in operation during the late 1970s that supported regional planning. There were 662 COGs and RPCs heavily subsidized by the federal government. Besides these multipurpose regional organizations responsible for planning, comment, and review for a number of federal grant programs, there were over 1,250 special-purpose regional organizations established to serve as the conduit for specific federal grant programs. There were regional housing authorities for Section 8 housing programs, health systems agencies for health-related grants, area agencies on aging for special programs for the aging, consortia for employment and training programs, criminal justice coordinating councils for law enforcement assistance grants, EMS systems agencies for emergency medical service grants, and economic development districts for economic development grants. Each functional agency had its own separate programs and boundaries that did not necessarily coincide with the boundaries of other special- or multipurpose agencies.[43]

The result was a confusing array of federally mandated regional districts, councils, commissions, consortia, planning groups, interstate compacts, regional clearing houses, and a multitude of other regional structures that needed to interact and become involved in the granting process. These regional agencies, each with a separate board and staffed by professionals oriented to the agency's particular function, related with their counterparts at the national level in functionally organized administrative relationships. They did not, however, coordinate well with other programs. Moreover, agencies operating at this substate, regional level tended to be almost invisible to the general public because there was no direct election of board members. Also, their functions tended to be highly specialized, only impacting narrow constituencies, and even these constituencies did not generally experience immediate impacts from their actions.[44]

To improve coordination between federal grant programs, the A-95 review process and Federal Regional Councils were established. As previously stated, the A-95 review process required a review and comment by a regional body on federal grant applications. Federal Regional Councils comprised the regional directors of the major federal agencies in each of the ten regional federal administrative districts. The intent was that these regional directors would meet regularly to coordinate and integrate their programs to ensure maximum effect at the local level. The effectiveness of these coordinating efforts was questionable. However, it became a moot point when the programs were abolished by President Ronald Reagan in 1982 (A-95 review) and in 1983 (Federal Regional Councils) "to decentralize a process that had become too bureaucratic and burdensome, and emphasized procedures over substance."[45] Thereafter, the coordination and integration functions, to the extent they were carried out, became state responsibilities. In addition to reductions in federal grants for substate regional activities, federal administrative structures that supported intergovernmental relationships with regional entities during the early 1980s were eliminated.[46]

Part of the Reagan administration's decentralization agenda was to reduce the dependence of local governments on federal grants. The number of grants was reduced from 540 in 1981 to about 435 by fiscal year 1987.[47] As the Reagan administration reduced federal categorical grant programs and its regional coordination presence, it also reduced funding for regional councils. These councils had been widely viewed by regionalists as the most appropriate agencies to provide a regional focus. Without the federal funding and the major purpose for their existence, the regional council movement, as a major player in regionalism, lost its momentum.[48] Of the 39 federal programs supporting regionalism in 1979, all but one had either been terminated, had experienced significantly reduced funding, or had been redirected from a regional focus by the end of Reagan's first term. However, the shrinking federal grants to subsidize the cost of new development in urban areas along with the states' inability or unwillingness to pick up the slack resulted in greatly reduced grants to support additional fragmentation.[49]

Following the Reagan era, Congress started again in the 1990s to re-emphasize regional planning and coordination in legislation but not on the same scale as previously. There were fewer grant programs and less money to distribute. Fewer regional agencies were required to oversee the distribution of the grants and they were given more discretion in the use of the funds. The major coordination focus of federal grants in metropolitan areas is now transportation and pollution. The federal transportation acts do not provide federal dollars for highway projects that further degrade the air quality in regions failing to meet federal air quality standards. The Clean Air Act requires that metropolitan regions that fail to meet air quality standards take steps to bring the area into compliance or risk losing federal transportation funds.[50]

Federal Transportation Grants Stimulating Regional Cooperation

The Intermodal Transportation Efficiency Act of 1991 (ISTEA) and subsequent federal highway acts are illustrative of federal efforts to promote a regional approach. The differences between the Interstate Highway Act of 1956 and ISTEA are significant. The 1956 act provided funds for roads that fueled suburban development and destroyed many central city neighborhoods. By contrast, highway acts of the 1990s and 2000s moved more into requiring a balanced consideration of everything that goes into modern transportation–highways, transit, bicycles, pedestrians, freight traffic–and required consideration of the impact of transportation projects on land use, pollution and the environment. The role of metropolitan planning organizations (MPOs), which had been a requirement since the early 1970s, was also strengthened. The acts also required more vigorous public participation.[51]

The 1956 highway program and subsequent programs before the passage of ISTEA essentially vested decision making on road projects with the states. A metropolitan planning organization (MPO) composed of local officials was required in each region to oversee and monitor the distribution of federal highway funds. It did not, however, have final say in how the highway funds were to be spent. The state highway department would tell the MPO which highway projects were to be funded.[52] ISTEA and subsequent highway acts strengthened the role of the MPO to provide significantly greater input in regional transportation issues. With the new laws, representatives from metropolitan areas became more important actors in the process. MPOs were given more authority and responsibility in making transportation decisions to meet metropolitan needs. Representation on MPOs was also broadened to make them more representative of the regions they served. Spending shifted from an almost total focus on highway and road building and maintenance to a small portion allocated for mass transit and other forms of transportation. The requirements mandated a more holistic and long-range approach to transportation planning.[53]

Although the authority of MPOs was strengthened, states continue to play the primary role in most transportation decisions in metropolitan areas. There is also great variability among states in the amount of funds MPOs directly control and the structure of the boards. A Government Accountability Office (GAO) study found that state governments resist any effort to reduce their control over transportation funding. Unlike state departments of transportation (DOT), MPOs are not operational organizations. The governor and state DOTs still have veto authority over MPO-selected projects. Although MPOs (in areas with populations over 200,000) also have authority to veto projects, the states control the majority of the funds and have far greater political leverage than the MPOs. Many MPOs are still struggling between parochial local interests and regional interests. Within many regions, local governments continue to compete with one another for their share of the transportation dollars. Finally, MPOs as well as state capacity remains uneven. State transportation planning has largely remained the province of transportation professionals versed in engineering and concrete pouring rather than urban planning, environmental management, or economic development.[54]

There are a number of policies that have been suggested to improve transportation in metropolitan areas. A region–wide focus and approach are essential to solving transportation–induced problems. MPOs should be strengthened and given more decision-making authority over the federal funds allocated for the region. These organizations should also cover the entire commuting area so they can be in a better position to develop plans, set priorities, allocate funds, and coordinate development and implementation of the various transportation systems across the region. In addition, other regional agencies should have more input in transportation planning. All regional agencies that impact or are impacted by transportation policy should coordinate with each other. There should be one overall co-ordinating agency with authority to ensure that transportation decisions are in the best interests of the region. For example, the State of Illinois recently approved the merger of the Northeastern Illinois Planning Commission and the Chicago Area Transportation Study to form The Regional Planning Board (now called the Chicago Metropolitan Agency for Planning) that will make it possible to better coordinate land-use and transportation projects and issues, give the region a stronger voice in competing for federal funds, and better unify the region in order to compete with other regions in the United States.

Voting Rights Act

Another federal initiative that had a minor impact on political fragmentation was the Voting Rights Act of 1965. The act covered 9 states and portions of 13 other states that had used discriminatory practices to restrict blacks from voting. A provision in the act requires prior approval from the federal government before changes can be made in local government boundaries.[55] Any municipal incorporations or annexations in the covered areas have to receive prior clearance. Although it became more difficult to form suburban governments to exclude blacks under this provision of the act, social scientist Nancy Burns studied the impact of the act on local government formation. She found that the Voting Rights Act preclearance provisions did not seem to affect municipal formation significantly one way or another. There was, however, an initial impact on the formation of special district governments. There were fewer special district governments formed in areas covered by the act than in other areas in the 1960s, but this difference became much smaller thereafter.[56]

State Governments and Regionalism

Local governments are created and regulated by the states. All actions of local governments are ultimately subject to the jurisdiction of the state. As discussed in Chapter 3, state policies in the late nineteenth century on annexation and incorporation established the framework that allowed the political fragmentation that now exists in urban areas. Most states established liberal general incorporation laws, which did not require special legislative acts for each incorporation. Under general incorporation laws, if the residents in an area desire to incorporate as a municipality and meet the requirements in the law, they can do so without further involvement by the state. Although the laws vary among the states, the minimum population, land area, and real estate tax base requirements provide for relatively easy incorporation. For example, Alabama requires only a 300-person minimum population, while in Texas only a population of 201 is needed.[57] Depending on the state, communities could incorporate as villages, boroughs, towns, or different classes of cities and provide a more limited range of services than would be required from a large city. This facilitated defensive incorporation to avoid annexation by the city.[58]

The states also supported fragmentation by assisting small local governments to provide basic services and by providing mechanisms to ensure that the fragmented metropolitan area could function. Peter Salins describes the state's role as follows:

> As the federal government was laying the economic foundation for the sprawling, suburbanized metropolitan region, state governments devised the fiscal and jurisdictional arrangements that made sprawling metropolitanization functionally possible. Most states created metropolitan-wide, and in some cases interstate agencies to organize critical regional transportation, infrastructure, and environmental functions. All states developed programs of assistance to local governments, especially for schools, which made it possible for even the smallest jurisdiction with little in the way of taxable commercial property, to offer a full-blown set of municipal services.[59]

State aid programs, in combination with federal aid programs discussed previously, helped to subsidize suburbanization. Just as proportionately more federal aid went to the suburbs than the central cities until after 1970, state aid was also tilted to the suburbs. A study of the 68 largest metropolitan areas showed that the amount of state aid was evenly split on a per capita basis between the central cities and their suburban areas, despite the extensive problems and poverty of the central cities and the relative affluence and prosperity of the suburbs. In fact, some state aid programs provided more money to the suburban communities than to the central cities. Syracuse, New York; Minneapolis, Minnesota; Akron and Toledo, Ohio; Louisville, Kentucky; Oklahoma City and Tulsa, Oklahoma; Dallas, Texas; Phoenix, Arizona; Salt Lake City, Utah; and Seattle, Washington, all received 75 percent or less of the amount of state aid flowing to the suburbs.[60] After 1970, state aid became more oriented to combat the problems of the central cities. By 1977, in the 85 largest metropolitan areas, state per capita aid going to the central cities was 123 percent of the aid going to the suburbs. There were, however, still areas with major disparities. For example, Omaha, Columbus, Louisville, Oklahoma City, Tulsa, Austin, Corpus Christi, Dallas, El Paso, San Francisco, and Salt Lake City were still receiving 80 percent or less than their suburbs.[61] The type of aid was also different. Aid to the suburbs was often for basic services and infrastructure to allow the suburbs to expand and develop, while the aid going to the central cities was often for social welfare services.

State Programs Encouraging Regionalism

Growth Management Laws

A number of states became concerned with sprawl development and the protection of environmentally sensitive areas and started enacting various forms of growth management legislation in the later part of the twentieth century. In 1961, Hawaii became the first state to institute statewide land use controls. Driven by a desire to protect agricultural land, Hawaii established a policy framework for land development and placed major responsibility for implementing policy with a state land development control agency (Land Use Commission).[62] This agency divided the state into four broad categories: urban, rural, agriculture, and conservation. Within each zone, land can only be used for the purposes specified by the law. Thus, for example, extensive urban development is prohibited in the agricultural zone. In the urban areas, local zoning bodies establish more specific types of zones and issue permits for development. However, despite the intent of the law to protect agriculture land from urban encroachment, the director of Hawaii's Office of Planning complained that these state regulatory controls and county zoning maps have had little effect on slowing the conversion of prime agricultural lands into residential subdivisions. The law allows developers with a land use plan that is inconsistent with the stated use for that zone to apply for a special-use permit. He stated that it is business profitability, not land use maps, that sustains the agriculture industry. Land uses that are more profitable will become paramount in land use decisions.[63]

Other states also became concerned with sprawl and adopted various forms of growth management laws. According to an American Planning Association report, a quarter of the states are implementing moderate to substantial smart growth planning reforms. These initiatives generally required statewide, region-wide or countywide plans and development to comport to the plan. They also advocate reinvestment in existing infrastructure rather than building new infrastructure. For example, Maryland designated parts of the urban areas that are already developed and planned for growth as priority funding areas to direct public infrastructure to these areas in an attempt to use state funding to curb sprawl.[64] Maine created the Maine Land Use Regulatory Commission to develop land use controls for unorganized areas. It also passed legislation that a state permit had to be obtained for any development which "may substantially affect the local environment or pose a threat to the public's health, safety, or welfare."[65] The Georgia legislature passed a comprehensive planning law mandating comprehensive and coordinated planning at the state, regional, and local levels. To qualify for many types of state grants, every city and county must develop a comprehensive plan embracing a variety of elements including land use, the environment, economic development, and governmental infrastructure.[66] New Jersey's growth management plan requires counties and municipalities to develop compatible plans for orderly development. Its objectives are to maximize the use of existing infrastructure, preserve open space, and achieve equitable distribution of affordable housing throughout the metropolitan region. In Washington, the intent of state law is to maximize use of existing infrastructure and protect the environment. It also requires the establishment of urban growth boundaries for each metropolitan area, with no urban services to be provided for development outside this boundary.[67]

Tennessee passed a law in 1998 to address growth, annexation, and incorporation in an effort to have all governments in a county cooperate in the development of a growth plan. The requirements are vague as the law does not specify what constitutes a growth plan. The intent, however, is to establish a urban growth boundary that could reasonably be expected to be developed in the next 20 years to which urban services would be provided in order to facilitate orderly expansion and protect agriculture, recreation and wildlife areas. While proponents say that county growth plans are a step in the right direction, they criticize the Tennessee effort as not requiring multi-county growth plans in metropolitan areas containing more than one county. These county growth plans also could be more effective if municipalities within the county had their own comprehensive plans conforming to the countywide growth plan.[68]

Growth management legislation is often enacted in response to public pressures to protect environmentally significant areas such as woodland, coastal areas, and other unique and fragile environments from overdevelopment. The legislation invariably mandates the establishment of a regional comprehensive plan and a regional impact review of major projects in the region. The plans must be developed according to state objectives. The regional reviews of development requests must consider the impacts that spill over the boundaries of the permitting municipality, for example, traffic congestion, need for affordable housing, and so on. Presumably, the development can be denied or altered if it is contrary to the regional comprehensive plan or the regional impact review is negative. Growth management laws often define the growth management boundary as counties, but the boundary may encompass an entire metropolitan area, such as the three-county Portland region. Another boundary definition could encompass a natural resource system such as California's regional water quality control legislation.[69]

California led in growth control legislation protecting environmentally sensitive areas by establishing a coastal zone plan to protect its coast from inappropriate development. This resulted from an initiative by the environmentalists after the state legislature failed to pass a bill protecting the coast following a disastrous oil spill at Santa Barbara in 1969. The initiative passed by a 10 percent margin in 1972, and the California legislature strengthened the effort with subsequent legislation in 1976. As a result of the initiative and the subsequent law, a statewide commission and six regional commissions were established with responsibility for enforcing state guidelines on developments up to three miles in the ocean and up to five miles inland. Under this law, the commissions permit the 127 cities and counties along the coast to approve each development request if they have first submitted and received approval from the commission on their plans in protecting wetlands, endangered species, and public access to the shores. This growth control legislation is extremely controversial. Many of the cities and counties along the coast have not produced acceptable plans and so the commissions have become bogged down in reviewing and individually approving all coastal development proposals ranging from beach kiosks to subdivisions to nuclear power plants. Commission staff has not been able to focus on the broader development issues and long-range plans for protection of the environment. Although there are implementation problems, and even though close to 90 percent of the permits have been approved, the regional commissions have forced changes to make developments more environmentally acceptable.[70]

Smart growth policies have had varying degrees of success. It has generally proven tremendously difficult to prevent continuing fringe development. One could also argue that any redevelopment that has occurred in already built-up areas would have occurred regardless of smart-growth policies. In one study of urban growth in 49 states, it was found that many smart-growth policies did not reduce sprawl. Growth management plans are often voluntary at the local level and very few jurisdictions adopt such plans. According to Bernadette Hanlon, for state planning requirements to be effective at the local level, they either need to be mandatory or incentives are needed to entice local level compliance. Her research indicates that smart growth policies are largely ineffective as long as local governments have exclusive authority over local zoning and land use. It is generally not in any local government's immediate interests to curtail growth or development.[71] An additional problem with area-wide growth management plans is that the top-down regionalism requirements imposed by the states for comprehensive regional plans sometimes ignore the capacity of local governments to develop plans. Although some states provide consultants and technical assistance to develop regional plans, they often do not provide help in resolving differences among groups with divergent interests.[72]

Growth management legislation to protect an environmental system has substantial limitations. For example, in California the regional commission's role is defined around a resource rather than a geographic or economic region, making it impossible to be a vehicle to implement a true regional plan. It was designed with limited objectives focused on resource protection, recreation, and public access to the coast. Regional issues, such as unemployment, social services, economic development, and affordable housing, are not within its jurisdiction. Moreover, the permitting process is still a local government prerogative if there is a commission-approved land use plan in place. The regional commission cannot resolve land use conflicts between adjoining local governments or have input into new city formation or land annexation.[73]

With an increasingly conservative population, there has been substantial push back on any kind of governmental controls over land use. Owners of land outside of growth boundaries complain that the boundaries are depressing the value of their land. Developers claim that housing costs are increased by restricting the amount of land available for development. Based on the claim that its growth control law was restricting development, Florida repealed its 30-year-old growth management law. Some research shows that growth management laws can result in higher housing prices. The National Center for Policy Analysis concluded from its study of the crash of the housing bubble in 2008 that one of the reasons for the rapid increase in housing prices was restrictive land use policies. It compared the loss in house values in metropolitan areas with restrictive land use polices with loss in house values in metropolitan areas without restrictive land use policies. It found that the average loss per house was $67,000 in the more restrictive markets compared to $17,000 in the less restrictive markets. It concluded that the more modest losses might not have set off the financial crisis, or the financial crisis might have been less severe with less restrictive land use policies.[74]

Regional Services and Policy

Increasingly, states are becoming more involved in local and regional affairs. Many states are encouraging and requiring more of a regional approach to services and policy issues. A few states have tackled controversial social issues by enacting laws mandating or incentivizing regional approaches. For example, Massachusetts enacted a law allowing a special state commission to override local zoning ordinances that interfere with the development of affordable housing. The goal of the law is to spread the responsibility for providing affordable housing to all jurisdictions within the state. Illinois passed a law in 2004 requiring all counties and municipalities with insufficient affordable housing to adopt an affordable housing plan. California, New Hampshire and Oregon have programs that require local governments to provide reasonable opportunities for the development of affordable housing.[75] Connecticut encourages the dispersal of affordable housing across urban regions through a fair housing program which requires the establishment of a negotiating committee that must reach consensus on an affordable housing plan for the region. Once the committee reaches consensus, each municipality's governing body in the region must approve it. The state provides financial incentives to regions to facilitate the process and develop acceptable plans. Some states also offer mediation services for disputes arising over zoning and growth management conflicts.[76]

States have become more involved in local government service delivery and administration. There are instances of states taking complete control of school districts and municipalities with financial problems.[77] In addition, many states permit and encourage cooperation among governments. However, voluntary cooperation among independent and competitive local governments is not easy to achieve. One study in four different states found a lack of cooperation between cities and suburbs. The researchers concluded that big city mayors, preoccupied with the pressures of governing their city and its financial problems were unlikely to lead the way and suburban political leaders were often wary of the intentions of big city mayors and feared being dominated by them when they did reach out to the suburbs.[78]

One example of state efforts to encourage coalition building is Michigan, which has authorized local governments to create area-wide public safety authorities to provide police, fire, and emergency medical services with the approval of the voters in the area. Minnesota has also established the Board of Government Innovation and Cooperation, whose function is to increase local government innovation, cooperation, and efficiency by granting temporary exemptions from state rules or regulations to improve the delivery of services. It also makes grants to local governments to encourage and facilitate cooperative efforts.[79]

Changes in Incorporation and Annexation

To reduce local government fragmentation, some states have tightened incorporation procedures in an attempt to encourage annexation rather than incorporation. A few states require new municipalities to be a certain distance from existing government units, or they must receive the approval of the existing municipality in order for the incorporation to take place. Most states require that boundary changes, and in some cases incorporation requests, be approved by a special state-established body or by the judiciary branch. Virginia pioneered this approach in 1904 by requiring judicial determination by a panel of three judges on questions of annexation and merger. The Virginia legislature established general standards for the judges to follow in their decision making. Other states use state-established agencies or boundary review commissions (BRCs) that provide a continuity that is not available in the Virginia process.[80] The organization and powers of BRCs vary from state to state. They may be a state agency, a mixed state-local body, or a strictly local group. They may have power in both annexation and mergers, or just annexation; they may cover the entire state or be restricted to certain areas. They may have power to advise only or may have authority to terminate an action. Most BRCs were established with a set of broad policy goals. Their general purposes are as follows:

- Encourage orderly metropolitan development, discourage sprawl, and promote comprehensive land use planning
- Enhance the quality and quantity of public services
- Limit destructive competition between local governments
- Help ensure the fiscal viability of local governments.[81]

How effective have BRCs been in improving local government structure in metropolitan areas? Since most metropolitan areas are substantially fragmented, some may consider this as closing the barn door after the horse has escaped; however, half of the states with this requirement are in the South, where much of the annexation activity since World War II has occurred. The process is designed to add a rationality to an otherwise politically charged process. One study concluded that BRCs, after 30 years of existence, had not affected annexations and mergers one way or another.[82] It may be that the impact has not been extensive due to its late establishment in the metropolitan age and the severe limitations placed on the powers of the commission.

Although BRCs can provide assistance in dispute resolution, most of them are not empowered to manage growth and boundary changes themselves. Boundary commissions can prevent incorporation but cannot put their affirmative decisions into effect. In general, BRCs respond to individual proposals for boundary changes rather than take a proactive stance in formulating broad strategies for metropolitan boundary adjustments. This situation is a disappointment to those who hope for a "rationalization" of local government patterns, and a comfort to those who believe that an electoral-legal marketplace of boundary decisions is preferable to a centrally planned pattern.

Regulations on Local Government Formation in Selected States

The boundary commission in Alaska is illustrative of the authority and operation of boundary commissions. It is a statewide commission with authority to oversee the establishment and modification of municipal government boundaries. It has authority to act on incorporation proposals, annexation requests, deannexations, mergers and consolidations, municipal reclassification requests and requests to dissolve municipalities.[83] Another example with a slightly different approach is California. Cities can be formed only after approvals have been obtained from a commission composed of representatives from other cities in the region and the county. In addition, the county board of supervisors must approve the incorporation request. One criterion for granting this approval is that the community proposing to incorporate must project a sizable budget surplus during its first few years. Despite these requirements, most incorporation requests are routinely approved.[84]

Under Washington law, an area can incorporate as a city if it has a minimum of 1500 inhabitants. If the area is within five air miles of the boundaries of a city with a population of 15,000 or more, it must have a minimum of 3000 inhabitants. The basic procedure to incorporate includes a petition requirement, review by a boundary review board or the county legislative body in counties without a board, and an affirmative vote of the residents involved.[85] Fifteen cities have incorporated in Washington since 1990. During the two decades prior to 1990, only one city had incorporated in the state. This recent surge in incorporation activity, which also includes a number of failed incorporation attempts, can be attributed, to a great extent, to the rapid population growth in the state over the past decade, particularly in the Puget Sound region where all of the recent incorporations have taken place. The increasing urbanization and sprawl that has resulted has caused many communities to consider incorporation as a means of exercising local control over the community character.[86]

In North Carolina, incorporation is approved only by act of the state legislature. If a community lies within one mile of the limits of an existing city with a population of 5,000 or more, within three miles of a city of 10,000, within four miles of a city of 25,000 or within five miles of a city of 50,000, the incorporation must have the approval of three-fifths of the members of each legislative house. The proposed incorporation must be supported by a petition of 15 percent of the voters of the area to be included in the incorporation. In most instances the legislature seeks the advice of the Joint Legislative Commission on Municipal Incorporations. This commission investigates whether the proposed town is able to provide the services at a reasonable tax rate, its proximity to existing incorporations and other issues.[87]

In South Carolina, from 1895 until 1975, incorporation was by general law under procedures established by the legislature. In 1975 the Local Government Act (or Home Rule Act) modified the process slightly in an effort to discourage the creation of defensive incorporations. An area considering incorporation must have a population density of at least 300 persons per square mile, with some exceptions made for coastal areas. The area should not be within five miles of an existing city, unless the existing city has already refused to annex all or part of the proposed city. A petition must be is filed with the South Carolina Secretary of State. It must include a specific proposal of the geographic limits of the proposed city and show the area's population. The petition must be signed by at least 50 voters and 15 percent of the property owners in the area proposed for incorporation. A referendum is held, and if a majority of the voters approve, an incorporation certificate is issued by the Secretary of State.[88]

Takeaway

Federal government policies have had a profound effect in promoting decentralization in urban areas. Housing policies promoted home ownership and the building of new, single-family, detached houses in the suburbs. The federal government also promoted deconcentration of industry by subsidizing the building of many war production plants in the suburbs during World War II. Federal policies on transportation encouraged and paid for as much as 90 percent of the costs of a limited-access highway system that opened up the suburbs to the central city, providing suburbanites with easy access to central city jobs. Other federal grants helped suburban governments develop infrastructure for the provision of services. This helped to foster a culture of independence and autonomy among suburban municipalities.

Starting with the increases in grant-in-aid programs to cities in the 1960s, the federal government made an effort to induce regionalism by requiring regional planning and coordination for increasing numbers of its grant programs. However, the regional agencies and the coordinating bodies were advisory bodies in most cases and did not have the political power to counter local or state political leaders bent on economic or infrastructure development for their jurisdictions. Moreover, government bureaucracies were more intent on implementing their programs and guarding their turf than they were in coordinating their programs. There were also no political leaders or government bureaucracy to champion a general governance perspective for the region. Therefore, the federal regional planning and coordination requirements were not effective at halting the market forces that the federal government had helped unleash or the determined efforts of local and state political leaders to obtain development for their particular jurisdictions. The regional planning and coordination requirements were dismantled in the 1980s during the Reagan administration. However, with the passage of the federal highway grants legislation starting with the Intermodal Surface Transportation Efficiency Act (ISTEA) of 1991, there has been a return to limited federal government regional planning and coordination requirements.

The states also encouraged decentralization by establishing easy incorporation policies and different forms of local government. In addition, they made annexation more difficult by requiring the approval of residents of the area to be annexed. State grants and policies also helped small suburban communities develop and provide basic essential services, allowing them to remain independent and autonomous. More recently, many states have reversed course by passing legislation requiring statewide land use plans and growth management plans. They have also made it more difficult for new municipalities to incorporate and easier for communities to annex unincorporated territory. In addition, many states have established boundary review commissions to investigate and approve proposed boundary changes in metropolitan areas.

Notes

1. Brian J. O'Connell, "The Federal Role in the Suburban Boom," in Barbara M. Kelly, (ed.), *Suburbia Re-examined* (Westport, CT: Greenwood Press, 1989), p. 184.
2. Ibid., p. 185.
3. Robert Fishman, *Bourgeois Utopias: The Rise and Fall of Suburbia* (New York: Basic Books, 1987), pp. 174–177.
4. Marc A. Weiss, "The Rise of the Community Builders: The American Real Estate Industry and Urban Land Planning," in Barbara M. Kelly, (ed.), *Suburbia Re-examined* (Westport, CT: Greenwood Press, 1989), pp. 150–151.
5. Donald N. Rothblatt and Daniel J. Garr, "Suburbia: An International Perspective," in Barbara M. Kelly, (ed.), *Suburbia Re-examined* (Westport, CT: Greenwood Press, 1989), pp. 23–24.
6. Benjamin Kleinberg, *Urban America in Transformation: Perspectives on Urban Policy and Development* (Thousand Oaks, CA: Sage Publications, 1995), p. 125.
7. Ibid., p. 126.
8. Ibid.
9. Ibid.
10. Ibid., pp. 126–127.
11. O'Connell, "The Federal Role in the Suburban Boom," pp. 185–186.
12. Ibid.
13. Thomas E. Bier, "Housing Dynamics of the Cleveland Area, 1950–1990," in W. Dennis Keating, Norman Krumholz, and David C. Perry, (eds.), *Cleveland: A Metropolitan Reader* (Kent, OH: Kent State University Press, 1995), pp. 248–251.

14. Kleinberg, *Urban America in Transformation*, pp. 134–139.
15. O'Connell, "The Federal Role in the Suburban Boom," p. 187.
16. Ibid.
17. Arnold R. Silverman, "Defense and Deconcentration: Defense Industrialization During World War II and the Development of Contemporary American Suburbs," in Barbara M. Kelly, (ed.), *Suburbia Re-examined* (Westport, CT: Greenwood Press, 1989), pp. 157–158.
18. Ibid.
19. John Mollenkopf, *The Contested City* (Princeton, NJ: Princeton University Press, 1983), pp. 103–109, quoted in Silverman, "Defense and Deconcentration," p. 158.
20. Silverman, "Defense and Deconcentration," pp. 158–159.
21. Ibid., p. 159.
22. Nancy Burns, *The Formation of American Local Governments: Private Values in Public Institutions* (New York: Oxford University Press, 1994), p. 60.
23. David Rapp, "Route 66 Gets a Federal Fix," *Governing*, 7 (March) (1994): 100.
24. O'Connell, "The Federal Role in the Suburban Boom," pp. 187–88.
25. Kenneth T. Jackson, "Forward," in Barbara M. Kelly, (ed.), *Suburbia Re-examined* (Westport, CT: Greenwood Press, 1989), pp. xii-xiii.
26. U. S. Census Bureau 2000. "Journey to Work," Census Summary File 3, Census Table QT-P23. Released October 27, 2006. http://factfinder.census.gov/gttable [Accessed December 7, 2012].
27. David Hamilton, Laurie Hokkanen and Curtis Wood, "Are We still Stuck in Traffic? Transportation in Metropolitan Areas," in David Hamilton and Patricia S. Atkins, (eds.), *Urban and Regional Policies for Metropolitan Livability,* (Armonk, NY: M.E. Sharpe, 2008), pp. 285–286.
28. O'Connell, "The Federal Role in the Suburban Boom," p. 188.
29. Ibid.
30. Real Estate Research Corporation, *The Costs of Sprawl: Detailed Cost Analysis* (Washington, DC: U.S. Government Printing Office, 1974), pp. 90–125, quoted in O'Connell, "The Federal Role in the Suburban Boom," p. 189.
31. Samuel Humes IV, *Local Governance and National Power: A Worldwide Comparison of Tradition and Change in Local Government* (London: Harvester Wheatsheaf, 1991), p. 126.
32. Burns, *The Formation of American Local Governments*, p. 62. Advisory Commission on Intergovernmental Relations, *Central City-Suburban Fiscal Disparity and City Distress 1977* (Washington, DC: U.S. Government Printing Office, 1980), p. 55.
34. Allan D. Wallis, *Inventing Regionalism* (Denver, CO: National Civic League, 1995), p. 17.
35. Ibid., p. 12.
36. Intergovernmental Cooperation Act of 1968, 31 USC, Section 6506, Subsection C.
37. Florida Advisory Council on Intergovernmental Relations, *Substate Regional Governance: Evolution and Manifestations Throughout the United States and Florida* (Tallahassee, FL: Author, November 1991), p. 19.
38. John C. Bollens and Henry J. Schmandt, *The Metropolis: Its People, Politics, and Economic Life,* 3rd ed. (New York: Harper and Row, 1975), p. 209.
39. Florida Advisory Council on Intergovernmental Relations, *Substate Regional Governance*, p. 27.
40. John J. Harrigan and Ronald K. Vogel, *Political Change in the Metropolis*, 7th ed. (New York: Longman, 2003), p. 294.

41. Harold Wolman and Michael Goldsmith, *Urban Politics and Policy: A Comparative Approach* (Cambridge, MA: Blackwell Publishers, 1992), pp. 213–214.
42. George J. Gordon, *Public Administration in America*, 4th ed. (New York: St. Martins Press, 1992), pp. 86–97.
43. Florida Advisory Council on Intergovernmental Relations, *Substate Regional Governance*, pp. 28–36.
44. Gordon, *Public Administration in America*, pp. 92–97.
45. Ibid., p. 98.
46. Florida Advisory Council on Intergovernmental Relations, *Substate Regional Governance*, p. 38.
47. Gordon, *Public Administration in America*, p. 86.
48. Bernard Ross, Myron A. Levine, and Murray S. Stedman, *Urban Politics: Power in Metropolitan America*, 4th ed. (Itasca, IL: F. E. Peacock, 1991), p. 294.
49. Allan D. Wallis, "Governance and the Civic Infrastructure of Metropolitan Regions," *National Civic Review*, 82 (Spring) (1993): 127.
50. Wallis, *Inventing Regionalism*, p. 41.
51. James H. Andrews, "Metro Power," *Planning*, 62 (June) (1996): 8.
52. Ibid., pp. 9–12.
53. Robert Puentes and Linda Bailey. "Improving Metropolitan Decision Making in Transportation: Greater Funding and Devolution for Greater Accountability." Center on Urban and Metropolitan Policy (Washington, DC: The Brookings Institution, October 2003), p. 3.
54. Hamilton, Hokkanen, and Wood, "Are We still Stuck in Traffic? Transportation in Metropolitan Areas," pp. 266–295.
55. Harrigan and Vogel, *Political Change in the Metropolis*, p. 120.
56. Burns, *The Formation of American Local Governments*, pp. 96–97.
57. Advisory Commission on Intergovernmental Relations, *State Laws Governing Local Government Structure and Administration* (Washington, DC: U.S. Government Printing Office, 1993), pp. 2, 22–23; Robert D. Thomas and Suphapong Boonyapratuang, "Local Government Complexity: Consequences for County Property-Tax and Debt Policies," *Publius: The Journal of Federalism*, 23 (Winter) (1993): 3.
58. An example is the resistance by the suburbs to annexation by Milwaukee. In 1955, the Wisconsin state legislature passed the Oak Creek Bill permitting fourth-class townships to incorporate. Thereafter, townships in counties that abutted Milwaukee on its western and northern boundaries incorporated. Through the incorporation of the townships, Milwaukee effectively became landlocked, bordered to its east by Lake Michigan and everywhere else by incorporated neighbors. Anthony M. Orum, *City-Building in America* (Boulder, CO: Westview Press, 1995), p. 121.
59. Peter D. Salins, "Metropolitan Areas: Cities, Suburbs, and the Ties That Bind," in Henry G. Cisneros, (ed.), *Interwoven Destinies: Cities and the Nation* (New York: W. W. Norton, 1993), p. 161.
60. Advisory Commission on Intergovernmental Relations, *Central City-Suburban Fiscal Disparity and City Distress 1977*, pp. 58–59, 78–79.
61. Ibid.
62. Joyce O'Keefe, *Regional Issues in the Chicago Metropolitan Area* (Chicago, IL: Metropolitan Planning Council, Jan. 15, 1991), p. 20.
63. David W. Blane, "Hawaii-The Nation's Smart Growth Laboratory," Presentation to the Western Interstate Region of the National Association of Counties, May 24, 2001. www.naco.dblane-naco.pdf. [Accessed December 12, 2012].

64. Bernadette Hanlon, *Once the American Dream: Inner-Ring Suburbs of the Metropolitan United States* (Philadelphia, PA: Temple University Press, 2010), p. 136.
65. O'Keefe, *Regional Issues in the Chicago Metropolitan Area*, pp. 20–21.
66. David R. Berman, "State Actions Affecting Local Government," *Municipal Year Book 1990* (Washington, DC: International City Management Association, 1990), pp. 59–61.
67. Ibid., pp. 27–29, 41–43.
68. Tennessee Advisory Commission on Intergovernmental Relations. *Land Use and Planning in Tennessee: Part II: Land Use and Transportation Planning* (Nashville, TN: Author, Feb. 2011).
69. Wallis, *Inventing Regionalism*, pp. 17–18.
70. V. Dion Haynes, "California's '72 Coastal Law Comes Under Fire," *Chicago Tribune*, Jan. 24, 1997, sec. 1, p. 6; Harrigan and Vogel, *Political Change in the Metropolis*, p. 238.
71. Hanlon, *Once the American Dream*, pp. 136–137.
72. David R. Berman, "State-Local Relations: Patterns, Problems, and Partnerships," *Municipal Year Book 1995* (Washington, DC: International City Management Association, 1995), p. 62.
73. Madelyn Glickfeld and Ned Levine, *Regional Growth . . . Local Reaction: The Enactment and Effects of Local Growth Control and Management Measures in California* (Cambridge, MA: Lincoln Institute of Land Policy, 1992), p. 85.
74. Wendell Cox, *The Housing Crash and Smart Growth*. Policy Report No. 335. National Center For Policy Analysis June, 2011, www.ncpa.org, [Accessed Sept. 3, 2012].
75. David K. Hamilton, "Affordable Housing Policies in Metropolitan Areas," in David K. Hamilton and Patricia S. Atkins, (eds), *Urban and Regional Policies for Metropolitan Livability* (Armonk, NY: M. E. Sharpe), pp. 185–189.
76. Ibid.
77. James M. Smith, "Re-Stating "Theories of Urban Development: The Politics of Authority Creation and Intergovernmental Triads in Postindustrial Chicago," *Journal of Urban Affairs*, 32 (4) (2010): 427.
78. Hanlon, *Once the American Dream*, pp. 136–141.
79. Berman, "State Actions Affecting Local Government," p. 63; Berman, "State-Local Relations: Patterns, Problems, and Partnerships," p. 63.
80. Bollens and Schmandt, *The Metropolis: Its People, Politics, and Economic Life*, p. 247.
81. Ibid.
82. Ibid., p. 31.
83. State of Alaska, Department of Commerce, Community, and Economic Development, Division of Community and Regional Affairs. Preliminary Report to the Local Boundary Commission, February 2012, Anchorage, Alaska. http://www.comerce.state.ak.us/dca/ic/ibc.htm [Accessed September 3, 2012].
84. Harvey Molotch, "The Political Economy of Growth Machines," *Journal of Urban Affairs*, 15 (1) (1993): 32.
85. Municipal Research and Services Center of Washington. *Municipal Incorporation*, http://www.mrsc.org/index.aspx [Accessed August 30, 2012].
86. Ibid.
87. David M. Lawrence and Kara A. Millonzi, *Incorporation of a North Carolina Town*, 3rd ed. (Chapel Hill, NC: School of Government, The University of North Carolina at Chapel Hill, 2007).
88. Charlie B. Tyer, *Municipal Government in the Palmetto State*, http://www.ipspr.sc.edu/grs/SCCEP/Articles/municipal%20govt.htm [Accessed August 31, 2012].

6 Providing Services in the Decentralized Metropolis

Jurisdictional fragmentation, when combined with overlapping jurisdictions, can provide an institutional framework for a dynamic of metropolitan organization that continually offers new opportunities for coordination and productivity improvement.
— Advisory Commission on Intergovernmental Relations, 1988[1]

As has been shown in previous chapters, governance of urban areas is through a multiplicity of local governments. The major approach to the provision of regional services in metropolitan areas is described and analyzed in this chapter. The special-purpose district approach to regional service delivery became the dominant form in the post-World War II period, particularly after the 1960s. This is a decentralized, functional accommodation to the growing metropolitan area. In addition, the academic justification for a decentralized governing structure is discussed and analyzed. This justification consists of two approaches to understanding and justifying decentralized governance: the public choice approach and the international relations model. Of the two, the public choice model is the most developed. Academics, who support the decentralized approach, argue that it is a more efficient and desirable method for governance in urban areas than a more centralized approach. These approaches are described and analyzed. Finally, the neighborhood government movement, an even more decentralized governance system, is described and analyzed as to its impact on governance in the urban area.

Special Districts

The major method of providing regional services in the fragmented local government structure is through special districts. *Special districts*, a generic term for state or locally created districts, agencies, authorities, and commissions, are classified separately from school districts for census purposes even though school districts are special districts. In order to qualify as a special district, an organization must exist as a publicly organized entity, often as a corporation with the powers to sue, be sued, make contracts, and so on. It must provide a public service and be governed by a board that is popularly elected or appointed by public officials with reporting requirements to the public. Finally, a special district must have substantial fiscal and administrative independence.[2] The powers of special districts are established by state legislation and vary from state to state. They may or may not have the right to levy property taxes. The *district* designation–for example, library or fire protection district–generally infers the right to levy property taxes, while the term *authority*, such as public transit authority or public housing authority, generally infers the power to collect fees, issue bonds, and, in some instances, levy non-property taxes. However, as special districts are either established pursuant to general state-enabling legislation or by special state legislation, the powers and titles of each special district may vary significantly from state to state and even within states.

The vast majority of the special districts, over 90 percent, perform a single function. More than a third provide environmental and conservation services, such as drainage, flood control and soil and water conservation. The next most common special district-provided function is fire districts followed by housing and community development. Most of the units recognized as multiple-function involve some combination of water supply with another service such as sewerage services. Although the vast majority of special districts are contained within one county, about 11 percent extend into two or more counties.[3]

Financing of special districts is through a variety of mechanisms. Only approximately half have property taxing power.[4] The property tax is a minor source of revenue as only 8 percent of total revenue comes from property taxes. This compares to 16 percent for municipalities and 34 percent for school districts. The major source of revenue is from user charges for services such as hospitals, airports, sewerage, water supply, and other utilities. Approximately 53 percent of special district revenue comes from this source. Intergovernmental transfers are the next largest source of revenue at almost 25 percent.[5] Non-taxing districts, funded by user charges and intergovernmental transfers, can be among the most powerful and influential in the urban area in dictating patterns of development or in the delivery of an essential service with political and service impacts throughout the metropolitan area. Two examples are the Chicago Transit Authority and the Port Authority of New York and New Jersey.

Although regional services can be and are provided through different types of local governments, special districts are the most utilized type of local government for regional development. For example, over 51 percent of the expenditures on public transportation, housing and community development, and airports are through special districts. Even though the amount special districts spend on sea and inland port facilities is small compared to other categories of spending, they spend 60 percent of all local government expenditures on this category. Other services often provided by special districts are hospitals at 46 percent of local government spending on this category and utilities (electric, water and gas) at 35.2 percent of all local government spending.[6]

Although special districts have been used to provide services since colonial times, their numbers were few until after World War II. Since that time, special districts have been the fastest-growing type of local government according to the census bureau. However, that growth rate has slowed down since 2002. Between 1982 and 1992 special districts grew by 12 percent and between 1992 and 2002 they grew by 11 percent. However, the growth between 2002 and 2012 has only been 6 percent.[7] Still, there were almost 4.5 times as many special districts in 2012 than there were in 1942 before the start of the suburban movement. There is only a weak relationship between size or population of a state and the number of special districts. Illinois leads the nation, with 3,249 followed by California with 2,765, which actually registered a small decrease from the number it had in 1992. Texas is third with 2,291 and Pennsylvania fourth with 2,243. In contrast, Alaska and Hawaii have 15 each, Maryland only has 76, and Louisiana has 95. Eleven states have over half the special districts.[8]

States authorize the creation of special districts through special act legislation or general enabling legislation. Traditionally, states have been quite liberal in allowing their creation. However, given the proliferation of special districts, the fragmentation of functions from excessive district creation, and the confusion this engenders among the public, some states are making it much more difficult to create special districts. California, Nevada, New Mexico, Oregon, and Washington have established agencies whose function is, in part, to control special district formation. Colorado requires that petitions for a new district demonstrate that there are not already adequate services to the area in question.[9] These efforts to curb the growth of special districts seem to be generally working except in Colorado, where the rate of growth is actually higher since the 1985 requirement was established. Special districts in Colorado grew 52 percent between 1992 and 2007 compared to the national rate of growth of 18.5 percent. In California and New Mexico, however, the rate of increase has been cut substantially below the national growth rate. California cut its growth rate from over 22 percent in the 1982–87 period to just 2.3 percent in the 1987–92 period. Moreover, between 1992 and 2007, California and Nevada actually reduced the number of special districts, Nevada by 10 and California by 32.[10]

Purpose of Special Districts

Although special districts were not a common phenomenon in early American history, there were special districts for road repair, bridge building, tobacco house construction and maintenance, and waterways before the

Revolution. Some of the earliest districts administered relief for the poor and street paving. In 1768, the Maryland Assembly began creating special districts to fund and administer county almshouses. In colonial Philadelphia, residents created special districts to provide poor relief and street paving.[11]

Special districts are created basically for four purposes:

1. To avoid the debt, tax, and other limitations that may be imposed on general purpose governments.
2. To bring a more businesslike, less political atmosphere to the provision of a service.
3. For political reasons, such as to meet federal government grant requirements.
4. To provide a function on a broader territorial scale transcending restrictive local government boundaries for economies of scale purposes (sewerage district), to include the beneficiaries of the function (air pollution district), or to include the natural boundaries of the function (water basin).

Although these purposes are not mutually exclusive, the concern here is with the fourth reason for the formation of special district governments: special districts as a viable alternative for provision of services that cross governmental jurisdictions. An example of the fourth purpose is the development of a long-term water supply from the Colorado River to the Los Angeles area. This could only be accomplished with the participation of a number of communities. Even though Los Angeles had the resources, it wanted to ensure that there were no free riders on the aqueduct that was to be built. The solution was the formation of a water district encompassing the local governments in the four-county area that would benefit. It was not a state issue, and therefore, it was not appropriate for the state to get involved. It was also not feasible to rely on a cooperative agreement since this arrangement would provide no legal organization or binding commitment on the participants, and there was no possibility of issuing bonds to finance the project without the formation of a special district.[12]

Although 87 percent of special districts transcend general-purpose government boundaries, the county is an organizational barrier. Only 20 percent extend beyond the borders of the county, but this is an increase from 13 percent in 1992. Of the multicounty districts, the majority cover only two counties. The Los Angeles water district is one of the few that covers an entire region. Not only are metropolitan-wide districts rare, but districts performing more than one function are also rare. There are only 3,175 or approximately 9 percent that perform two or more functions. Almost half (49 percent) of these multipurpose districts are involved in some combination of water supply and a closely related service such as sewerage.[13] Since multipurpose districts tend to perform closely related functions, they provide only limited governance. Moreover, since few multipurpose districts extend across county lines, this restricts the ability of these districts to provide a regional governance function across the entire metropolitan area. However, those few multipurpose, regional districts can function as a tier of metropolitan government. There are very few of these that qualify for this designation. (This form of government is discussed in Chapter 9.)

Special Districts in Metropolitan Areas

Some writers differentiate between special districts in metropolitan areas that produce services within a single general-purpose government or on a small geographical basis and those that produce services on a countywide or multicounty basis.[14] The term *metropolitan district* is often used to designate districts that cover one or more counties. Even though metropolitan districts may provide only one or two closely related functions, they provide a regional focus for that function. Metropolitan districts can be established to provide a variety of functions such as port facilities, mass transit, airports, sewerage, water supply, parks, public housing, and water pollution control.

The importance of special districts in providing governance functions in metropolitan areas is evident in a perusal of government census data. There are substantially more special districts in metropolitan counties than in nonmetropolitan counties. Table 6.1 provides data on special districts in metropolitan areas. The major growth of special districts, between 1942 and 1972, corresponds with the period of rapid suburbanization. During this period, the number of special districts expanded 634 percent in metropolitan

Table 6.1 Special District Governments in Metropolitan Areas[a]

Year	Total Special Districts	Metro Special Districts	Special Districts % in MA	Average per Metro County	Average per Nonmetro County
1942	8,299	1,097	13.2	4.1	2.6
1952	12,340	2,598	21.2	10.1	3.5
1962	18,323	5,411	29.5	17.5	4.7
1972	23,885	8,054	33.8	18.1	6.1
1982	28,082	11,725	41.0	17.5	7.1
1992	31,555	13,614	43.1	18.4	7.8
2002	35,052	NA			
2012	37,203	NA			

Source: Compiled by the author from U.S. Bureau of the Census, Census of Governments, vol. 1 (Washington, DC: U.S. Government Printing Office, various years).

Notes:
[a] The information on special districts in metropolitan areas is not available after 1992.

counties compared to 119 percent in nonmetropolitan counties. From 1972 until the Census Bureau stopped keeping records of the number of districts inside and outside metropolitan areas after 1992, special purpose district growth in metropolitan areas slowed considerably, growing only 69 percent, about the same percentage as the growth of metropolitan counties. The 1992 census showed that the average metropolitan county has almost two-and-a-half times more special districts than the average nonmetropolitan county.

There is an average of 43 districts per metropolitan area. However, there is a vast variance in the number from metropolitan area to metropolitan area. The median is 23, indicating that a very few metropolitan areas have a substantial number of districts. Led by Houston with 665 special purpose districts, 51 metropolitan areas (18 percent) have over one-half of the districts in metropolitan areas. Nearly 75 percent have fewer than 50 special purpose districts.[15] The number has a greater relationship to state policies than to the number of municipalities in the area. For example, Douglas County, the central county of Omaha, Nebraska MA, has only seven general-purpose governments, but 144 special district governments, the majority of which are involved in sewerage and water supply. Allegheny County, the central county of Pittsburgh, Pennsylvania MA, has 130 municipalities and 149 special district governments. Erie County, the central county of Buffalo, New York, MA, has 18 municipal governments and 33 special district governments, all involved in fire protection.[16]

One of the most famous metropolitan districts is the Port Authority of New York and New Jersey. It provides a good example of how metropolitan districts can impact a metropolitan area. This is a bi-state regional authority governed by a board appointed by the governors of New York and New Jersey. It is involved in a number of transit-related and economic development functions. The Port Authority's income is derived from user charges, as it has no taxing power. It issues revenue bonds for the construction of facilities and retires the bonds through user charges. Although most non-taxing authorities must rely on government grants and loan guarantees because expenditures usually exceed revenues, the Port Authority of New York and New Jersey has consistently had positive fund balances. By 1931, it was operating four toll bridges and the Holland Tunnel, which provided operating surpluses. The next year it opened a freight terminal, and in 1944 it opened a grain terminal. In 1948, it acquired its first airport, and during the 1950s, it took over the remainder of New York's airports. In the 1960s, the Port Authority entered the real estate business and constructed the 110-story World Trade Center. Its transportation-oriented facilities include six interstate bridges and tunnels, two bus terminals, six airports, ten truck terminals, facilities for international shipping, and a railroad system.[17] With the construction of the World Trade Center and other real estate and revitalization activities such as a legal office building in downtown Newark, waterfront redevelopment projects, industrial parks, and a waste-to-energy plant in New Jersey, the Port Authority morphed from a transportation oriented agency to the premier economic development agency for the region.[18]

In its operation and decision making, the Port Authority is not constrained by local government law and regulation. It answers only to the governors of the states in which it operates, with each state having different priorities for the organization. All appointments to the governing board are made by the governors and are divided equally between the two states. (There is no direct accountability to New York City or any other local government officials or any provision for local official input into the board's action.) In addition, with its own revenue base from user charges, the Port Authority is quite independent from government oversight. In one sense, this is positive allowing it to be entrepreneurial and operate like a private, profit making entity. In another sense, it is negative in that it is only loosely subject to the political will of the state with no local or regional political direction. While the Port Authority is one of the few local governments in the New York region to provide a regional governance focus, it has been criticized for its lack of responsiveness to local leaders and for its refusal to integrate development of its transportations systems with mass transit. It resisted pressures to take over the mass transit system (it did not want to get involved in money-losing operations) and focused on building roads thereby increasing pollution and further congesting the highways as well as reducing mass transit ridership. After a number of years, it finally got involved in a limited way in mass transit.[19]

It has had numerous conflicts with local leaders and has played leaders in one state off against leaders in the other state. For example, the Port Authority was able to gain control of the airport facilities of New York by threatening to build the Newark airport into the world-class airport for the region with its large revenue base. Not wanting to be left behind or left out, New York agreed to let the Port Authority have control of its airports. Another criticism is that its involvement in non-transportation has detracted from its core mission. The economic development activities appeared to be politically driven rather than according to some logical, well-thought-out regional development plan. Their motivation seemed to be a balancing of development between New York and New Jersey that focused more on equity than on regional economic efficiency. They have also diminished the resources and management focus needed to fulfill the authority's fundamental transportation responsibilities.[20]

Another example of how special districts can bring a regional focus to a metropolitan area is evident in the Los Angeles region. California followed the federal Clean Air Act of 1970 with its own, more stringent Clean Air Act of 1976 and established air quality management districts (AQMDs) in urban areas that were out of compliance with state and federal air quality standards. Each district was expected to develop a plan to bring its service area into compliance. These districts were given power to issue permits and fine polluting industries. Since about 60 percent of air pollution is from nonindustrial sources such as automobiles, each AQMD is required to establish plans to reduce pollution from this source. This entails establishing policies on land use decisions to reduce sprawl as well as other measures to reduce automobile usage. As AQMDs have no power to regulate land use, they must work through local governments that have strenuously resisted erosion of their freedom over land use decisions.

The South Coast Air Quality Management District (SCAQMD), covering the Los Angeles region, initially pursued its mandate in an aggressive manner. It established a long-range plan that required local governments to enforce regional policies that often conflicted with local self-interests. For example, a requirement that land use decisions be related to reductions in automobile traffic could easily conflict with a municipality's development plans. Not all local governments have complied with the SCAQMD measures. One study in 1992 indicated that only one-third had implemented some of the SCAQMD requirements. In addition, after an aggressive start, the vigor with which the SCAQMD pursued its mandate waned in the past few years as development and job retention became more important to the region. Also, the SCAQMD has turned to market incentives rather than command and control strategies, which reduces the direct pressure on local governments to enforce pollution reduction measures.[21] The effectiveness of market incentives, at this point, is not clear; however, it is suspected that they will have little effect in reducing automobile pollution.[22]

Governance and Accountability of Special Districts

Whether the governing board of a special district is elected or appointed, there is a question of how accountable these boards are to the public. Members of appointed boards are usually appointed by the elected officials of the governments involved in their creation. Appointed board members may regard their first allegiance to the governing body or the elected official that appointed them. In such cases, the public interest is interpreted as what is in the best interest of the elected official of the organization with the appointment power. For districts with a regional focus, the state and municipalities covered by the district often share appointment powers, which further clouds the issue of public accountability. This is particularly so when the governor is involved in choosing board members of a district with a strictly regional function.

An example of an appointed board with a major regional economic impact is the Metropolitan Pier and Exposition Authority of Chicago, which has 13 members, 6 appointed by the governor and 7, including the chairperson, appointed by the mayor. The mayor of the city where the facilities are located, the area that is most affected by the land use decisions of the board, can appoint a bare majority. An even more egregious example is the St. Louis Regional Convention Center and Sports Complex Authority. The mayor of St. Louis and the chief executive of the county can each appoint up to three members to the board, but up to five members are appointed by the governor.[23] In this example, public accountability flows through three political figures representing different constituencies. In particular, the facilities are located in St. Louis, but the mayor of that city does not control a majority of the board appointments. It is questionable whether boards with appointment power divided among governments representing different constituencies and interests adequately represent the interests of the public most affected by board decisions.

When there are political party differences between the central city and the state, the political leaders may become embroiled in an intense political struggle for control of the special district, with its many patronage jobs and contracts. This may further weaken the board's responsibility to the area. This political struggle is occurring in a number of states, with the central city becoming more and more isolated as suburban Republicans gain more power in the state legislatures. Examples are a Republican governor wresting control over the Delaware River Port Authority by ousting the Democratic board members after a lengthy court fight. A powerful Philadelphia Democrat was the major target of this effort. With the removal of the Democratic members, the Republicans gained control of the board, with its jobs and millions of dollars in economic development contracts in the Philadelphia area. In Illinois, in the 1990s the Republicans gained control of the state legislature as well as the governorship. The Republican–dominated state legislature considered a bill to establish a regional airport authority in the Chicago area which would include the jobs and revenue generated by the Chicago-operated O'Hare airport.[24] This effort was thwarted when the mayor of Chicago formed a bi-state airport authority with Indiana and when an election resulted in Democrats gaining control over the Illinois General Assembly.

One way to address the issue of direct public accountability with appointed boards to ensure representation of constituent members is by using constituent unit representation. Through *this* method, those governments the district overlays choose the agency's governing body. This method works best for public accountability purposes when the general-purpose government selects elected members from its own governing body to represent it on the district's board. One problem is the number of governments that might be affected by the function of the special district. There might be too many governments to allow adequate representation on the board. An example of constituent unit representation and its problems is the Regional Transportation Authority, with responsibility for overseeing public transportation and allocating finances between the operating agencies in the Chicago area. There are 15 members appointed from within the 6-county region:

five from the mayor of the City of Chicago; four by the suburban members of the Cook County Board; one director is appointed by the president of the Cook County Board (from suburban Cook County); and one director each is from DuPage, Kane, Lake, McHenry and Will counties appointed by the chairman of their respective county board. The chairman of the board, its 16th member, is elected by at least 11 of the 15 appointed members, with at least 2 affirmative votes from Chicago, 2 from suburban Cook County directors, and 2 from the counties outside Cook.[25] This system almost ensures that the chairman and the board control will be in the hands of the Cook county suburban directors if they can form alliances with the directors appointed from the other counties. The chairman as of this writing is a Republican, which is reflective of the current suburban control. If Chicago were in control, the chairman would likely be a Democrat.

Constituent unit boards may, in fact, further obfuscate, not clarify, accountability. In trying to balance the representation of the constituent governments and ensure that all stakeholders are represented, accountability becomes fragmented among different interests that may be in competition with each other for resources. Constituent unit boards raise questions such as: To whom is the board ultimately accountable? Should one constituency be more represented than another? Will the board become so fragmented between competing interests that it will not be able to function or determine what is in the region's best interest? Is it realistic to expect board members to put parochial agendas aside and work in the overall best interest of the region?

Because special districts generally operate in the shadows, with little public interest or direct public accountability, they are susceptible to political and contract abuse. Executive director and board appointments are often a reward for political support rather than for expertise or a particular desire to serve the public interest. Board members are often less concerned with the operations of the special district and more concerned with individual benefits that might accrue from their appointment. One example of the potential mischief from special districts with little or no accountability was the situation with the Illinois State Toll Highway Authority. Even though this is a state authority, it is similar to a local government special district in that it operates only in one part of the state and, other than the governor's power to appoint the director and the board, it is completely independent. Executive director appointments by the governor are often a reward for political support rather than for expertise in public works or operation of highway systems. During one recent period, four of five executive directors had no expertise or prior experience in the operation of highway systems.

In this toll authority one executive director was convicted for involvement in a scheme to bilk the authority for excessive fees in the sale of its property. This director also, with the board's approval, bought property for more than twice its appraised value. As long as the toll authority satisfactorily provided services, there was little media or public interest in its internal operation. This allowed administrative practices that would not be tolerated by the public in a more visible public organization. Perks that were dropped by the authority because they finally came to light included the following:

- Free toll way passes for board members and others with no pressing public need,
- Special pensions to supplement regular government pensions,
- $30,000 Christmas parties,
- Personal use of the authority's helicopter.[26]

In another example of how abuses can occur when there is lax account-ability and oversight is an investigation of the Delaware River Port Authority, a joint authority of New Jersey and Pennsylvania. This organization is accountable to both states, which gives it substantial independence. Governor Christie of New Jersey, critical of its operation, commissioned an audit of the Authority. The report indicated that The Delaware River Port Authority had wasted millions of dollars in taxpayer money in the past decade, with much of it enriching authority officials as well as friends and political allies. Among the beneficiaries was an insurance executive and Democratic powerbroker, who allegedly orchestrated the payment of $455,000 to his company and an associate in return for recommending a New Jersey insur-ance broker for the authority. In addition, the report concluded that a policy allowing authority commissioners, family members and others free access to its four bridges linking South Jersey with Pennsylvania was rife with abuse, robbing the public of $1.2 million. The report also found the authority donated money to organizations with ties to commissioners, reimbursed its top officials for lavish meals and conferences and put itself deep in debt by undertaking more than $440 million in politically-directed development projects.[27]

Elected boards of special districts often do not fare much better than appointed boards with respect to the issue of citizen accountability or citizen participation in governance matters. If citizens are satisfied with the provision of a service, such as sewer, water, or transportation services, the service provider almost becomes invisible, and citizens have little desire or need to interact with governing bodies of these services. This results in extremely low public interest and low public visibility for board members. The governance issues in most districts tend to be unimportant to the voters. In some municipal utility districts in Texas board elections have not been held for over a decade because the seats are uncontested.[28] Even votes on financial matters in special-purpose districts, other than school districts, generally receive little interest. One writer noted,

> Anecdotally, we also know that only a handful of voters vote in special bond elections ... Developers who plan to issue bonds must first win

voter approval to back the bonds with a pledge of unlimited taxes, even if the voters can be counted on one hand.[29]

In one election in a utility district in Texas to approve a $2.5 million bond and increase taxes to retire the bond, the proposition authorizing the district to issue the bond and levy the taxes to pay the interest and principal was unanimously approved by the four people who voted.[30]

Understanding the lack of citizen involvement and the independence from local general-purpose governments, developers might purposely use special districts as shields from oversight and control. An example of this is the development of Walt Disney World in Florida. One of the Disney Corporation's first actions was to convince the Florida legislature to establish a 40 square mile special district so that the Corporation would not need to obtain local government permits or have any local government oversight for its development. Disney officials dominated the district, which had relatively few residents. They were able to issue public bonds and borrow money at low rates to finance the private theme park. When Disney started to develop its new residential community of Celebration, it de-annexed the land from the district to ensure that the new residents of the municipality would not be able to have a voice in Disney affairs and its development plans for Walt Disney World.[31]

Regionalists argue that an advantage touted for the use of special districts, their technical, businesslike approach and their removal from political pressures, could also contribute to the accountability problem. Most single-purpose districts are based on highly technical, complex functions and require highly technical and skilled employees. Organizations dominated by highly trained people, such as engineers, scientists, and statisticians, exhibit a technical bias and tend to be more remote from public input. The issues are framed in scientific or engineering language, which inhibit public discussion.[32]

Special Districts and Regional Governance

Although individual state policies and procedures are the major determinants of the number and purposes of special district governments, areas that have had regional reform tend to have fewer special district governments than similar counties in the same state. For example, the combined City–County of Philadelphia has just 14 compared with Allegheny County, Pennsylvania, which has 100. The Nashville-Davidson County consolidation only has seven compared to Knox County, the central county of the Knoxville, Tennessee, MA, which has ten. San Francisco City–County has ten compared to San Diego, which has 103. It is also evident that metropolitan areas with few or no special districts can provide services as effectively as those areas with many special districts. Indeed, critics of government fragmentation argue that metropolitan areas function better with fewer special districts.[33]

Special districts add to the complexities of governing metropolitan areas. They constitute another layer of government, each with its own boundaries that do not necessarily conform to other boundaries familiar to residents. This creates confusion and accountability problems for people living within the districts. Low participation and interest levels in special districts are understandable given the crazy-quilt nature of special district boundaries and how they overlap other special districts and municipalities. Voters often do not know what district they are in. For example, two neighbors may be in one special district for one function but different districts for other functions. Moreover, finding the boundaries may be almost impossible. The functions for which special districts are responsible also vary among municipalities. One municipality may be responsible for providing fire services to the residents while the neighboring municipality may receive its fire protection services from a fire protection district. It probably does not matter to the residents who provides their services as long as they receive acceptable service, but it must be frustrating to the elected village officials not to be able to directly influence the level of services provided by special districts in their community.

An example of the crazy-quilt special district pattern is a municipality in a Chicago suburb. It is served by two different park districts whose boundaries do not correspond to any other boundaries. One residential street begins with the residents on both sides belonging to the same park district. However, a few houses farther along the street, the boundary becomes the middle of the street, and then, a few houses farther, the boundary becomes the other side of the street, with the remainder of the residents on the street in the other park district. All the residents are in the same municipality and in the same township. Needless to say, this is a confusing situation for residents and creates special problems for municipal leaders trying to develop and promote a sense of community. This same community of 35,000 is divided into four high-school districts, with students from the community attending two different high schools in two of the districts.

A major criticism of special districts made by regionalists is that their approach to area-wide problems is fragmented and narrowly focused. Rather than promote an overall coordinated approach to regional planning, special districts further splinter regional governance with their focus on the provision of the single functions for which they were created. Regional issues outside the scope of this single purpose are not their concern. Indeed, these districts have no power to address issues outside their scope. For those urban areas with a number of metropolitan districts, the result is either an uncoordinated approach to regional issues or extreme difficulty in coordination when actions of one district have an impact on other functions. Each district's first and most important priority is achieving the purposes for which it was created. Coordination with other governments is a distant second to its first priority. When an agency has been created and charged with a specific task, its success is determined by accomplishing its specific task, not in evaluating whether the objective is appropriate. For example, the San Joaquin Hills Transportation Corridor Agency was created to build a toll road. Its success is in the building of this road. Never mind that 60 percent of the residents surveyed in one poll were opposed to building toll roads. Its institutional independence and single-purpose mandate isolates it from those public forums where wider regional trade-offs can be addressed regarding issues surrounding transportation options, environmental concerns, and land use.[34]

In Texas, municipal utility districts (MUDs), mainly dealing with water issues, constitute a significant percentage of special districts. A developer might create several small MUDs to maintain control by fragmenting potential opposition. In one development alone, 55 MUDs grapple for water and other services. Once a new MUD is formed, it is not required to consider any of the water planning issues that one might argue are critical to its mission, much less land use issues attendant to its development. Neither are MUDs required to form or join metropolitan coordinating bodies addressing such issues. As a result, other local governments that must deal with MUDs' existence often fail to integrate MUDs fully into existing water supply systems. At the same time, by having so many different districts, the economies of scale through building large water systems are lost.[35]

Special-purpose districts compound the problems of regional decision making. They, along with general-purpose governments, pursue policies to maximize internal benefits. In pursuing their individual goals, they may compete or cooperate with other governments. Associate Professor Megan Mullin chronicles boundary disputes among water districts as they compete or their boundaries and find adequate water supplies to serve their customers. She provides the example of a water district near San Antonio that aggressively expanded its service area through annexations, purchases of neighboring water systems and lawsuits. In doing so, it created animosity with neighboring water districts. When it found that it had overextended itself and could not supply the needed water, a neighboring water district grudgingly allowed the district to tap into its water system. The district continued to pursue its aggressive expansion while drawing down increasing amounts of water from the neighboring water district. The result was increased animosity and competition between the two districts to expand their service areas.[36]

Because of the linkages of functions in metropolitan areas, what may benefit an individual municipality or special district's single function may have an adverse impact on other municipalities or functions in the region. For example, a water district might concern itself with assuring water supply without concern for land use decisions affecting water demand. Likewise, a transportation district might concern itself with the functional integration of a single mode of travel but not with the relationship between modes or with the integration of transportation with land use and air quality.[37] Without an overall coordinating body, individual governments are likely to pursue their separate agendas without concern for the impact on other functions or municipalities outside their jurisdiction.

Special-purpose districts also might not be successful in accomplishing their objectives because of the interrelationships between functions. For instance, the Los Angeles County Metropolitan Transportation Authority has been given responsibility to establish an integrated public transit system in the county. It is developing an expensive and extensive rail and bus system. The success of the transit system is dependent upon factors over which the authority has no control, such as compactness and compatibility of land use along the proposed rail corridors. Another issue over which the authority has no control is the location of jobs. The mass transit system is oriented to the downtown area, where only 5 percent of the region's jobs are located. However, the viability of the system will be in its ability to attract ridership. With jobs and population widely dispersed and with no ability to directly influence land use patterns, the success of the authority is problematic. Moreover, transportation corridor agencies in the region charged with building additional highway capacity are independent of the mass transit authority. Actions of the transportation corridor agencies will exacerbate sprawl, further undermining the success of the mass transit project.[38]

The arguments political scientist Roscoe Martin articulated in opposing special districts in cities in the 1960s are, according to regionalists, still applicable today for metropolitan areas. He stated that the special district serves

> to separate the program in question—urban renewal, public housing, and so on—from the mainstream of city affairs. By the same token it divorces the program from city politics, thereby denying it the juices of democracy. If, however, the purpose is to "remove the program from politics," then the special district does not necessarily achieve its end; for it may serve only to substitute for the general politics of the city with the particular politics of a special clientele ... Finally, the promiscuous employment of special districts tends to atomize local government. The resulting fragmentation has serious implications for a concerted attack on local problems, for citizen concern in government, for the visibility of public activities, and for the responsibility of agencies and officials.[39]

Special district governments are thus regarded by regionalists not as a solution but as a contributor to inequity, duplication, confusion, and inefficiency. Local government reformers argue that the extensive creation of special districts is a failure of our local government system. They maintain that these districts add to the complexity of government and cause administrative duplication and functional overlap as well as adding to the tax burden.[40] Professor Joseph Zimmerman, a longtime observer of local government and metropolitan issues, suggests that the trend toward formation of many limited-purpose local governments, as opposed to general-purpose local governments (i.e., full-service municipalities), reflects a widely held bias against government in general. The attitude thus expressed may be: "the government that does the least governs the best!"[41]

A number of studies conclude that special districts spend more per capita for the same function than large general-purpose governments. There are a number of reasons for this. A small part of the increased spending can be attributed to districts' greater orientation toward expensive capital projects. Another reason for the upward spending bias is factors related to service demand as well as the initial decision to utilize special purpose districts instead of relying on general-purpose governments to provide the service. Furthermore, dividing services among special districts or authorities reduces the potential for economies of scope that occur when fixed overhead, such as computing facilities, central administrative staff, and office space, can be shared. Dividing services among general-purpose governments and special districts or authorities reduces the potential for scope economies and creates costs of coordination and duplication. A further factor related to the upward spending bias of special districts is the involvement of special interest groups who seek to maximize the service and encounter little or no competition from other special interest groups seeking alternative spending decisions. The role of a watchful, diverse citizenry is replaced by interest groups with an intense preference in support of the services the particular district provides, such as recreational enthusiasts for park districts, library supporters for library districts and so on.[42]

Support for Special Districts

Defenders of the current system of government contend that special district governments allow highly fragmented areas to be more efficient. Utilizing the special district approach, municipal governments can take advantage of economies of scale to reduce unit costs, reduce duplication, produce regional services in a nonpolitical, businesslike manner, and still maintain the integrity of their individual governments. Such were the findings of studies of the central counties of the St. Louis and Pittsburgh metropolitan areas. These studies found that by overlapping other governments, special districts provided a larger funding or provision base, provided economies of scale and efficiencies, and promoted cooperation among municipalities by bringing them together in joint or group efforts. The studies concluded that rather than duplicate, special districts complemented other units of government. The Special Education District in St. Louis County was given as an example of how a special district can complement other units of government. Because of the higher expenses per pupil in special education and the relatively few students served, the cost per pupil in special education mitigates against a separate program in each district. The special education district provides a needed, non-duplicative service, and it does not require duplicate schools because most special district teachers work alongside regular district personnel.[43]

Those who support special districts over metropolitan government as a way of applying economies of scale to various services, suggest that centralization of regional services in one area-wide government may produce diseconomies of scale. Functions have different cost curves and, therefore, economies of scale will vary for each service. Special districts allow flexibility so that separate districts can be established, with different boundaries to take advantage of the particular economies of scale for each function. Some services may be better and more efficiently provided at a smaller scale, whereas other services may be better provided at a larger scale. General governmental consolidation, therefore, is not necessary and may even be disadvantageous in the search for economies of scale.[44]

Critics of centralized government also counter the economies of scope argument by suggesting that there are organizational economies from focusing on the delivery of one or two related services that offset any loss of scope economies. Organizational economies result from reducing the complexity and bureaucratic barriers that often occur in large, diversified organizations.[45] Proponents also suggest that special districts offer a better method than a general-purpose regional government to capture benefit or cost spillovers that are borne by parties outside the boundaries of the service area. Each special district's boundaries can be established to capture spillovers for that specific function. General-purpose regional government does not have this flexibility. Furthermore, critics contend that a more centralized government might be less responsive and accountable than smaller, decentralized governments because it is more insulated and remote from the true preferences of the voters. Thus, it may engage in what is called *monopoly government*–providing, through waste and empire building, more government services than people really want. One study attempted to measure this Leviathan effect it found that, after controlling for other factors, total spending by all levels of local government combined increased as the share of government functions at the county level increased. Similarly, centralization of functions at the state level appeared to increase combined state and local spending.[46]

The question remains: Is the use of special districts a solution to service delivery in decentralized metropolitan areas? Mullin, from her analysis, claims that it depends on how they are structured and how they address policy issues that cross jurisdictional lines. In some cases they can solve regional policy problems while in other situations they can contribute to making the regional problem worse. They can add to the negative aspects of fragmentation, coordination, and competition, or they can mitigate the problem through functional specialization, a professional, nonpolitical approach to the problem, and by working cooperatively with other jurisdictions. However, interaction among governments and groups in a decentralized governing system might produce consequences unanticipated by those who support special district government as a cure for solving service delivery problems that spill over general-purpose government boundaries.[47]

Explanations and Support for Decentralized Local Government

Public Choice Theory

Public choice theory is an important body of literature that asserts that decentralized government is superior to centralized government at the local level. This theory was developed from economist Charles Tiebout's essay comparing the metropolitan community to a marketplace.[48] Public choice supporters suggest that local governments are analogous to a firm, and they compete with each other in the marketplace for residents and commerce. The more local governments (firms), the better is the competition. Large bureaucratic governments restrain competition and, hence, the allocation of goods and services, restricting choices by consumers. They suggest the marketplace is the most efficient allocation system, supplying only that which is demanded by consumers. Other systems, especially bureaucratic-dominated ones, result in oversupply and the unnecessary production of goods and services.

While traditional theories of local democracy focus on the capacity for collective choice through voting, public choice focuses on individual choice through markets. The individual as citizen is replaced by the individual as consumer. In support of this, public choice theorists claim that individuals see public policy only in terms of individual utility functions, and these functions comprise the only possible conception of the public good and thus of the desirable goal or policy. In public policy the key concept is that of fiscal equivalence; that is, individuals should receive what they pay for in an undistorted market.[49] Public choice supporters believe that politicians and bureaucrats working within government are generally self-serving. The best way to prevent the ill effects of self-serving behavior is to subject governments, as much as possible, to the discipline of the marketplace. One way to do this is to insist that components of government compete with the private sector, thus producing the pressure for privatization and contracting out. Another way—especially relevant at the municipal level–is to have a polycentric system of governments to foster governmental competition.[50]

According to the public choice model, people select the specific tax and service levels they desire by "voting with their feet." The polycentric metropolitan area thus offers a differentiated market through the numerous municipal governments, allowing people to choose the level of services and taxes desired. The politically fragmented metropolitan area is desirable over the one metropolitan government approach, according to advocates of this model, as the diverse needs of citizens are better met. They argue that the one-size-fits-all governmental system is less efficient than a polycentric system because of the benefits of competition. By competing for residents and development, governments keep costs of providing services low while meeting residents' demands for high-quality services.

A substantial body of literature has been developed around the public choice model.[51] Public choice model adherents, while rejecting the unified area-wide government approach, support functional consolidation or co-operation to achieve economies of scale and efficiency in provision of selected services.[52] Therefore, the public choice approach advocates a poly-centric system of government and differentiation in service delivery to meet citizen choices. However, it recognizes that certain services are provided more efficiently and effectively on an area-wide basis through a single-purpose district or authority. Additionally, supporters of this model maintain that regionalists have not recognized the possible benefits of separating provision units from production units. That is, those who make decisions on what services to provide and oversee them (municipalities) are not required to produce (deliver) them. Municipalities can contract with another unit of government or a private or nonprofit producer and thus achieve quality and efficiency without giving up the advantages of a small municipality. In addition, the chaotic and fragmented nature of government that regionalists criticize in urban areas induces competition which pro-motes efficiency. There is thus no advantage in replacing competition of many governments with a monopoly of one government.[53]

A major tenet of the public choice model is that a decentralized polycen-tric system of local governments is more democratic than a centralized system as it is responsive to citizens' needs and gives more opportunity for citizen participation. Supporters of this model claim that a differentiated government system provides a diversity of opportunities for citizens by their location decisions to influence governments to provide a desired bundle of services and policies. By voting with their feet, citizens are participating in governance. As communities compete for citizens and business, they are being responsive. They assert that a centralized governing system destroys the sense of community, reduces opportunities and incentives for public involve-ment in local governance and generally has a negative effect on local level democracy.

Early philosophers claimed that the municipality is the place where communities of like-minded people could come together and make governance decisions. Small populations and compact areas were necessary to enable people to participate in the governing process. Moreover, people in smaller groups shared mutual interests and were better able to arrive at decisions that were mutually agreeable and beneficial to their interests. They felt that the larger the group of people, the more diverse their interests were and the more difficult it would be to arrive at mutually agreeable and beneficial decisions. The New England township form of government was the form that most impressed Thomas Jefferson and Alexis de Tocqueville for its egalitarianism and opportunity for universal participation. They felt that this form of government embodied the ideal of an independent and autonomous system of small governments that maximized citizen participation in the governance process. The township was the perfect manifestation of the sovereignty of the individual. They argued that decisions made at this level were more democratic because more people could become involved.[54]

The public choice approach gained strength in the 1980s as the regional reform movement lost steam. Voters had generally rejected most efforts to introduce centralized regional structures in metropolitan areas, and regionalists were in retreat. During this period, there seemed to be an increase in intellectual support for public choice. Indeed, in 1987, the prestigious Advisory Commission on Intergovernmental Relations (ACIR), previously a strong supporter of consolidation, broke ranks with the regional reform movement and declared for continued fragmentation.[55]

International Relations Approach to Understanding Metropolitan Areas

Political scientists Victor Jones and Matthew Holden were two of the major figures in the application of an international relations analogy to understanding municipal behavior in metropolitan areas. This approach contends that local governments in urban areas behave in many ways like nation-states. They seek first of all to maintain their independence and autonomy. They compete with one another for development. Like nation-states, local governments seek to expand their territory and sphere of control through annexation and consolidation. They form coalitions for defensive purposes, such as suburban leagues of municipalities, and bargain for needed supplies, such as water and sewerage. Local governments develop institutional arrangements, for example, councils of governments to discuss matters of mutual interest. They also develop compacts among themselves, such as interlocal agreements for mutual advantage.[56] Matthew Holden suggested that diplomacy was the key to the functioning of metropolitan areas because independent local governments behave much like nation-states in the international arena, bargaining and jockeying for advantage with other independent local entities.[57] Victor Jones wrote that local governments are

> tough organizations with many political and legal protections against annihilation or absorption by another government … [W]e should not be surprised to recognize among proposals for reorganizing them counterparts of world government, world federation, functional organization, and bilateral and multilateral compacts.[58]

Criticisms of These Approaches

Both the market (public choice) analogy and the international analogy accept and implicitly endorse the fragmented system of government in metropolitan areas, competition among governments, and the unequal distribution of government services and resources. The market analogy embodies laissez-faire capitalism with its competition and winners and losers, while the international analogy posits that decentralized urban areas are in many ways similar to an archaic world where war and power politics govern relations between nations. Like most analogies, these models also have their limits. Local governments are not like nation-states but instead are subject to super ordinate governments, particularly the state, which can create them, abolish them, and establish laws governing their behavior.[59] Local governments also do not behave like firms because they are not as easily created or abolished as private firms. In addition, competing for residents is not the same as shopping for goods and services in the private market. Moreover, local governments may be forced to serve all customers while private markets only serve those who can pay. However, both analogies fairly accurately portray the realities in most metropolitan areas: a multiplicity of fairly autonomous actors operating in a competitive environment which has characteristics of a war of all against all.[60] This, of course, is the extreme opposite of what the regionalists seek. They want to establish a rational system of laws and regional administration to replace the chaos of the marketplace and the irrationality of politics. They also want to ensure that residents of the metropolitan area are treated equally.

Of the two analogies, public choice is more developed.[61] A substantial body of literature has been written to support the advantages of a decentralized system of government over a more centralized approach to regional governance. Obviously, regionalists dispute this in strident tones. They suggest that the market system has inefficiencies in coordination and overproduction and fails to address social issues of inequality.[62] Political scientists John Harrigan and Ronald K. Vogel are quite succinct as they dismiss both the public choice and the international diplomacy models:

> To state that there is a limited analogy between metropolitan governance and either a free market economy or international diplomacy is one

thing; to posit it as a model for the way in which urban services ought to be provided in the metropolis is quite another thing. That transforms an empirical judgment into a normative judgment. Furthermore, it provides a theoretical justification for what is in most metropolises a very inequitable distribution of public services.[63]

Empirical Tests of the Public Choice Model

Most of the empirical research has been to substantiate or refute public choice claims. The research that has been done seems to verify the bias of the researchers, or there is always some doubt as to whether the findings in one area can be generalized to other areas. Some of the public choice assumptions do not translate completely into the real world. For instance, the metropolitan area is not a homogeneous, undifferentiated plane. Certain areas are more attractive than others. In Chicago, for example, housing along the lakefront is more attractive than housing away from the lake. Further, most consumers do not have the ability of unlimited exit. Typically, people move during specific event-related times of their lives, such as a new job or marriage. In addition, voters are limited to living in those communities where they can find affordable housing and be reasonably close to work. This places limits on the number of communities from which people can choose their "desired bundle of services."

In one empirical test conducted in the Detroit region the public choice claims tested were:

1. The extent of homogeneous sorting of individuals into communities based on demand for public service bundles.
2. The extent that residents in each community were satisfied with the level of services.

According to the public choice model, the variance of local spending demands within a community should be lower than statewide spending demands. For example, if income relates positively with demand, the variance of demand for public spending in a high-income community should be lower than the statewide variance because the statewide population will include both high-income and low-income communities. According to the model, people move to areas where they are satisfied with the services. This study showed the *intra-community* variance to be significantly smaller than the overall statewide variance. It found a high degree of grouping by expenditure tastes in the Detroit metropolitan area, tending to substantiate the public choice feature of a homogeneous community.[64] The researchers surveyed the residents in the Detroit region to determine their satisfaction with spending and taxes. They found that two-thirds of the voters wanted no change in the level of public spending. Only 19 percent wanted a large increase or decrease in public spending, which indicated general satisfaction with the level of public services and spending. Satisfaction levels were higher and dissatisfaction levels lower in the Detroit region than in smaller urban areas in the state. This tends to substantiate the public choice hypothesis that in the areas where there are more communities (a greater variety of public expenditure choices) to choose from, there can be a better sorting of residents by communities to produce greater satisfaction with the amount of public spending.[65]

Another test of public choice claims was conducted in the Atlanta metropolitan area. This was a survey of residents' level of satisfaction and their intentions to move. The services that were measured were overall satisfaction with the area where they lived and specifically, the level of satisfaction with the quality of schools and police services. According to the public choice model, residents, who are dissatisfied with their level of services, would have intentions to move. The results of the survey showed that this was not the case. The factors that influence residents' decisions to move were not the dissatisfaction with the quality of police protection or their schools. Instead, the major influence on the intention to move was the level of satisfaction with local employment opportunities.[66]

Another key claim made by public choice advocates, the differentiation of service bundles among municipalities, was researched by Professor Robert Stein. He looked at the variation between communities for the demand of public expenditures. He divided services into common functions such as police, fire, sewerage, sanitation, and so forth, and uncommon functions such as education, welfare, health and hospitals, libraries, parking facilities, airports, and so on. His findings indicate the existence of a highly differentiated set of municipal service bundles. The differentiation occurs for both common and uncommon services, but uncommon services exhibit the greatest variability. Stein's findings indicate that residents have little concern with who provides common services. Common services are generally only a concern when they are not adequately provided. Demand for common services tends to be relatively equal across communities in the same metropolitan area. Because of this similar demand for common services (except in the case of inadequate performance), common services are less likely to be sensitive to the marketplace. The demand for and provision of uncommon services shows the greatest variability, indicating that municipal differentiation of uncommon services is more sensitive to market forces.[67]

Even though conventional wisdom and some research suggest that smaller jurisdictions reduce the barriers to participation with the result that citizens are more involved in local governance, other research indicates that just the opposite occurs. In a comparative study of a centralized and a decentralized metropolitan area, Lowery, Lyons, and DeHoog found that citizens in the centralized area were more involved in governance. They concluded that participation was higher in neighborhoods in the consolidated city because these places have more groups pursuing contradictory goals. They also found that citizen identification to their city was much stronger in the more consolidated metropolitan area than in the decentralized area. Furthermore, they found that citizens living in the area with the more centralized government felt that they had more influence on public policy and that their attitudes on the level of responsiveness of their government were higher than in the decentralized area. They concluded from their research that rather than centralized government reducing involvement and participation, just the opposite occurred.[68]

Another study of voter turnout in central counties of 12 metropolitan areas in the United States used voting in municipal elections as an indicator of participation. The researchers found that while municipal size had little impact on voter turnout, the degree of municipal concentration had a positive impact. They found that while citizens in smaller communities may share common values and may find it easier to vote, they do not vote in greater numbers than citizens in larger communities. Indeed, they found that the counties with less municipal fragmentation and greater centralization had the highest levels of voter turnout. They surmised that "when municipalities encompass a larger part of their urban counties, the county level of policy problems becomes internalized within the politics of the city, thereby stimulating increased political participation." They argued that fragmented governments facilitate demographic sorting and/or segregation, thereby transforming the electorates of each municipality into more homogeneous grouping in which most of the substance of politics is embedded in boundaries between cities. The result is that citizens are left with either orphan issues lacking a forum in which to be discussed or no need to discuss them because their follow citizens are just like them.[69]

Public choice researchers have attempted to rebut and cast doubt upon the generalizability of these studies. Stephen Percy and Brett Hawkins argued that historically stronger counties in the South may tend to confuse citizens as to what level of government provides what service, and that Wisconsin with a county system judged to be neither weak nor strong would be a more appropriate test site. Their findings from studying Milwaukee are that people tend to identify with the most important government whether it is the county or the local community. Surveys of people who moved from Milwaukee indicate a general dissatisfaction with services, taxes, and quality of life. They concluded that services and taxes are a component of decisions to exit. Moreover, those who stay behind may be satisfied simply to voice discontent. The dissatisfaction level may not be high enough to motivate them to exit.[70]

There is no conclusive evidence to validate or discredit the public choice model. No conclusive proof has been generated on either side. This debate, however, is nothing more than an academic exercise, as the majority of urban areas have chosen the more fragmented system championed by the public choice adherents, rendering moot the argument whether the decentralized or centralized system is better. However, the debate continues and supporters of each side still make their claims to superiority. In one example, a study was commissioned by a national organization of the St. Louis and Pittsburgh regions, two of the most fragmented areas in the United States. Interestingly, shortly after the organization issued its report on St. Louis extolling the effectiveness of the fragmented system of government in meeting regional governance needs through a system of overlapping jurisdictions, two regional citizen study groups issued reports completely at odds with these findings. They found confusion, discord, and lack of cooperation as major reasons for recommending a significant reorganization of the fragmented government system in the St. Louis area.[71] As an example of the strictly academic nature of the debate, about the same time that the reports were issued, a committee appointed jointly by the mayor of St. Louis City and the executive of St. Louis County to consider the fragmented nature of the county submitted a plan recommending the consolidation of the 90 municipalities in the county into 37 new cities. This plan was successfully challenged in the courts with the result that there was no vote.[72] it is highly probable, based on previous referendums on regional reorganization in the St. Louis area, that the voters would have also rejected this plan.

Testing the International Relations Model

There has been very little scholarly interest in pursuing this model. Most examples are at the nation-state level and are difficult to translate to the metropolitan area. The European Union (EU) model is the best international example of how this model could work at the metropolitan level. It is an example of independent countries with histories of often warring against each other voluntarily forming a regional body and transferring some of their power to regulate their individual economy to the regional body. The best working example of the EU model is the Greater Vancouver Regional District (GVRD) in British Columbia. It is similar to the EU in that the municipalities voluntarily transfer to the regional body power to provide certain regional services. By so doing, individual municipalities benefit because the service is more economical and efficient to provide on an area-wide basis. Moreover, individual municipalities are unable to provide or regulate certain regional functions, like air pollution control, that impact the quality of life. Therefore it is a win for both the municipality and the region to empower a regional body to perform these functions. Like the economies of individual countries in Europe benefitting from voluntarily transferring authority to the EU to control certain aspects of their economy, the municipalities in the Vancouver area have accrued benefits from voluntarily transferring control over, or sharing aspects of, selected functions to this regional body.

The GVRD can provide whatever functions the members agree on. There are pluses and minuses to a voluntary organization like the GVRD. Building consensus is not easy for 22 municipalities, each with its own parochial agendas and fears of ceding its local prerogatives to an organization over which it has limited control. Controversial issues are either avoided or are discussed for years before any compromise is reached. Probably the major contentious issue with which it has dealt is regional planning. The individual municipalities have yet to approve a development plan for the region which they see as critical for the orderly and sustainable growth of the region. Moreover, the GVRD has not even attempted to develop a regional economic development plan because municipalities would not willingly transfer authority to a regional organization to control and direct economic growth.[73]

Despite that fact that GVRD has minimal power to compel agreement on planning among member municipalities, planning works because the organization works hard to convince the member municipalities of the value of planning. The administrators also try to accommodate members as much as possible. One advantage GVRD has is that there are no counties in British Columbia. Thus, the GVRD can serve as the supplier of area-wide governance without any complaint of duplication or competition from other general purpose, area-wide governments. Indeed, one of the purposes for the establishment of GVRD was to supply services to unincorporated areas that were urbanizing and small municipalities that could not alone provide their own water and sewerage systems.[74]

Artibise et al.[75] note that the GVRD has demonstrated that when municipalities see the advantage of regional action, when they are not forced to join, and when there can be time to refine the proposals and deliberate, consensus can often be achieved. They claim that the GVRD has the most complete knowledge base about the region and is viewed as an objective, non-biased, professional planning agency for the region. They also claim that given time, good ideas will triumph over bad and a deliberative and thorough debate on the issues to reach consensus will result in achieving the regional interest. This might sound a little too rosy to generally apply to regional governance, but at least in the case of the GVRD, it seems to work.

Neighborhood Government Movement

As a corollary to the public choice approach, the late 1960s and early 1970s witnessed the development of a neighborhood approach to governance in many large cities. This movement, the opposite of the traditional reform approach, advocates the decentralization of government in large cities to the neighborhood level. This approach is viewed by public choice advocates as another vindication of the merits of decentralization and the citizen desire for smaller, more intimate government. The neighborhood government approach is driven by citizen frustration and alienation at the lack of responsiveness of large centralized bureaucracies. This movement seeks greater control of government services to the neighborhood, especially control of schools. The intent of the neighborhood government approach is not only to empower residents of the neighborhood in the delivery of government services but to allow the neighborhood to exercise policy-making power in how those services are to be rendered.

As a recent response to decentralization pressures, it is instructive to consider this movement in some detail. Some government functions have been decentralized for years, such as police stations, firehouses, and libraries. However, they have generally acted as extensions of the bureaucracy located downtown. There were usually no mechanisms to obtain systematic community input. Neighborhood participation is also not new to local government. For the most part, however, it has been limited to providing feedback to government initiatives. Thus, most schemes of the past to involve the neighborhood have not opened up two-way neighborhood–city hall communication.

The Advisory Commission on Intergovernmental Relations indicated that decentralization to the neighborhood level can involve any or all of the following elements:

- Territorial decentralization, which geographically brings city hall to the neighborhoods.
- Administrative decentralization, which involves appointment of neighborhood managers and devolution of some administrative autonomy in program responsibility to neighborhoods.
- Political decentralization, which involves devolution of political power and policy-making authority to subunits, that are autonomous. These subunits would have substantial control over fiscal, programmatic, and personnel matters. They would be primarily responsible to the neighborhood constituency and, secondarily, to the central political unit.[76]

Of the three types of decentralization, territorial decentralization is the most common. Territorial decentralization means not just bringing a city hall physically closer but making it more accessible. This could include holding council meetings in neighborhoods, establishing a special telephone number for complaints, or using an ombudsman to receive and follow through on complaints within the administration. Another type of territorial decentralization is to select representatives from the neighborhoods to form a community-wide advisory committee to elected officials. Dayton, Ohio, is an example of territorial decentralization. It has established a system of neighborhood boards elected by the community, which serves as a conduit for communication between the city and the neighborhoods.[77]

Political decentralization is the devolution of substantial amounts of political power, policy-making, and authority over personnel to the neighborhoods. An excellent example of political decentralization is St. Paul,

Minnesota, which has devolved substantial political authority to 17 district councils, with representatives elected by the residents in each district. Each council has a city-paid administrator and a neighborhood office. The councils have substantial powers, including planning and advising on the physical, economic, and social development of their areas, jurisdiction over zoning, authority over the distribution of various governmental services, and substantial influence over capital expenditures. Neighborhood representatives comprise a citywide committee to give priority ranking to capital development projects in the city. Besides representing the service needs of the area to the major city agencies, the councils are involved in such activities as the operation of community centers, crime prevention efforts, and the production of a district newsletter. Although it has not decentralized on the scale of St. Paul, Birmingham, Alabama, has also experimented with political decentralization. Neighborhood residents elect representatives to neighborhood associations which control use of federal funds provided to their areas through the Community Development Block Grant (CDBG) program and work with community resource staff on finding solutions to neighborhood problems.[78]

Administrative decentralization is the establishment of neighborhood service centers to work with (and for) neighborhood groups to provide community services. A recent movement in this direction is the increasing popularity of community policing. Under this concept, two-way communication occurs between the police and residents. Police are considered extensions of the community, not the central office. They work closely with community groups and tailor programs and activities to fit the needs of the neighborhood. There is a substantial amount of autonomy from the central office. Decentralization of a number of government services involves the establishment of a neighborhood service center from which services are coordinated. A neighborhood manager monitors and coordinates services. The manager works with neighborhood groups and the central bureaucracy in the provision of services.

Administrative decentralization has been operating in a few cities for some time. In the 1970s, New York established "little city halls" to provide complaint centers in neighborhoods and facilitate community participation and oversight of city services. In one instance, the neighborhood organizations successfully mobilized opposition to a major development initiative pushed by the city. The central administration backed down in the face of opposition from the neighborhood groups. This experiment has evolved into substantial decentralization with the establishment of 59 community boards to coordinate services, comment on land use decisions, and propose capital budget expenditures.[79]

An area that has sparked decentralization pressures and controversy is education. Efforts at decentralizing public education were attempted in New York and Detroit in the 1960s, and Chicago decentralized its school system in 1988. In New York the decentralization plan called for 32 nine-member school boards elected every three years to oversee the system's 750,000 elementary- and middle-school pupils. High schools and special programs remained under the control of the central bureaucracy. Local boards were to hold educators accountable by controlling district jobs, budgets, programs, and policy. Boards could hire almost all staff from principals to non-pedagogical employees such as paraprofessionals and school aides. Although teachers remained outside board appointment power, boards controlled their promotions. Controversy followed the decentralization. One result has been an escalation of patronage and corruption. With the vast reservoirs of jobs and money at their disposal, the local school councils became patronage centers of unprecedented proportions. One observer likened them to the heyday of Tammany Hall. A majority of the local school boards ran their districts like fiefdoms where jobs were doled out to campaign workers, lovers, and family, or sold for cash.[80]

Controversy also resulted from Detroit's efforts to decentralize its school system. Decentralization occurred when the central school board tried to impose a desegregation plan that involved the busing of 9,000 children. The state legislature outlawed busing and gave more power to the neighborhood school boards.[81] The Chicago system decentralized through locally elected school councils with substantial autonomy from the central bureaucracy. This experiment produced successes and failures. The failures tend to be more publicized than the successes. Problems have been reported such as how some schools cannot find enough people to stand for election to fill the seats, and how school councils mismanage funds, change test scores for council members' children, intimidate teachers and principals, and fire school principals for no apparent reason. An assessment of the Chicago school system indicated that decentralization did not achieve the local control that the reformers envisaged. The system is also more complex and probably less governable now than before decentralization. The report concludes that "the job of the principal is probably harder, rather than easier, to perform in a focused, goal-oriented way; the leverage of local communities over school operations has not obviously been enhanced in any predictable sense."[82]

However, some changes were made that hold promise to make the Chicago school decentralization system work better. Probably the major change was the state legislature making the mayor of Chicago directly responsible for the success of the school system. The mayor immediately placed trusted city administrators, not educators, in charge of the school district. With the mayor's political backing, the new chief administrative officer installed systems to monitor operations of the school councils. If a council is not following guidelines and there are problems in the school, the central administration can put the school on probation. If the school council does not resolve the problem, the central administration can relieve the school council, the principal, and the teachers of their positions. Following the takeover, the central administration can hire a new teaching staff, a new principal, and call for new school council elections. A number of schools have been reconstituted in this manner. Given this potential threat to their authority, school councils are becoming more responsible in the operation of their schools.

Ultimately, the successful implementation of neighborhood government requires strong support from political leaders. However, politicians often resist neighborhood governance out of fear that the neighborhood groups will become too independent and ungovernable, and that their role will be marginalized by the neighborhood centers. Neighborhood service centers, with direct ties to central administration, are not dependent on the political leaders for their services. This changes the dynamic between the elected official and the neighborhoods. This tension and potential loss of political power would be mitigated only if the neighborhood service center was under the direct control of the politician representing the neighborhood.

This devolution of power to neighborhoods is also generally resisted by the bureaucracy. Reasons for bureaucratic resistance involve the disruption of established routines and opposition to relinquishing their exclusive control of service delivery. Bureaucratic resistance also originates in a normative system that values fairness, impartiality, and efficiency. Agencies that must husband scarce resources are reluctant to distribute benefits just because communities want them. Professional administrators, concerned with citywide issues, question the legitimacy of parochial demands. Administrators complain that with decentralization of services they lose all economies of scale, and neighborhood service centers can lead to favoritism among residential groups in the delivery of services. Moreover, they contend that the concept of trying to do things uniquely for all the neighborhoods is impossible, and the expectations of the neighborhoods can never be satisfied given the resource limits. The end result may be increased citizen frustration and alienation over their inability to obtain the desired services, which will reduce, rather than increase, the amount of participation.[83]

Assessment of Neighborhood Government

A problem with neighborhood government involves the very purpose for neighborhood governments: to give residents more control over services provided in the neighborhoods. The potential for patronage and corruption is compounded with decentralization. The rampant patronage and corruption in the decentralized New York City school system is evidence of the dangers of political devolution of power. New York's experience is contrary to the public choice assumption that local, fragmented government is more responsive because local voters are more involved and can more easily remove elected lower-level officials if things go wrong. The New York City findings suggest that devolution to local levels may neither increase voter participation nor result in greater responsiveness to citizens. Devolution may indeed simply replace one unresponsive elite—bureaucrats–with another unresponsive elite–political hacks.[84]

The problems associated with neighborhood government seem to outweigh any advantages gained from improved citizen participation. Neighborhood control can be divisive to the overall best interests of the neighborhood, city, or region. By providing a forum for the articulation of localized grievances, neighborhood government can undermine efforts to benefit the city as a whole. In some instances, enhancing neighborhood power has led to racial and income exclusion, and not-in-my-backyard (NIMBY) conflicts that have often blocked the development of socially necessary facilities. Moreover, neighborhood control does not appear to empower the poor. Many efforts have resulted in disappointing levels of involvement by low-income residents, renters, and minorities. Neighborhood government's potential to promote social equity is further undermined when such efforts pit one neighborhood against another in competition for public resources.[85]

Neighborhood institutions do not reliably produce effective representation. Some neighborhoods simply lack the leadership cadre and institutions necessary to articulate the interests of residents. To the vexation of many participants, a few individuals with irritating personalities may dominate a neighborhood organization, eventually driving out other potential contributors. Additionally, the small size of the neighborhood presents planners and community groups with economic, political, and logistical difficulties. First, neighborhoods are not economic units in their own right. The creation of many small programs tailored to individual neighborhood needs necessarily sacrifices the economies of scale characteristic of centrally administered programs.[86]

Although people still advocate neighborhood government and experiments continue, the vigor of the drive for neighborhood government of the 1960s and 1970s has subsided. The generally poor results from the 1960s and 1970s decentralization experiments, along with continuing resistance by political leaders and the bureaucracy, have changed the focus of community governance. There is still interest in neighborhood participation and involvement but not in establishing strong neighborhood sub-city governments. Neighborhood advisory councils are becoming a more accepted and promoted form of community participation. For example, local school boards in New York City in 1997 were stripped of much of their hiring and budgetary powers.[87] Efforts at neighborhood power and involvement are not dead, but the focus has shifted from obtaining power over government institutions to working with government institutions to promote neighborhood revitalization.

Special Districts in One California County

Although the number and use of special districts vary by state and county, this section is illustrative of the use of special districts in one county to give some indication of how special districts affect governance and services. Sacramento County, California has seven cities, no townships and over 100 special districts providing a wide arrange of services throughout the county. The population of the county is 1,374,724. Sacramento with a population of 453,781 is the largest city in a metropolitan area that includes eight counties and has a metropolitan area population of 2,149,127. Special districts in the county provide the following services:

- The Sacramento Metropolitan Air Quality Management District (SMAQMD) created by state legislation. It has no direct authority over vehicle emissions. It develops plans and regulations, monitors air quality, reviews land use and transportation-related projects to minimize air quality impact, and it educates the public. Sources of funding include state and federal grants and permit fees.
- Cemetery districts: Sacramento County is served by four independent cemetery districts governed by boards of trustees that are appointed by the Board of Supervisors to govern operations of the district.
- Drainage and water district to manage storm drainage, flood control, and provide potable water.
- Eleven fire districts provide protection outside the cities of Sacramento and Folsom.
- The Sacramento Regional Solid Waste Authority regulates waste collections and recycling services for businesses and apartments.
- Flood control districts for the purpose of providing maintenance on flood control levees on the rivers.
- The Sacramento-Yolo Mosquito and Vector Control District provides mosquito and vector control services to both Sacramento and Yolo counties.
- Districts providing a variety of functions such as a countywide district that provides street and highway safety lighting services within Sacramento County and the City of Rancho Cordova, two districts that provide park and recreation services, and a district that provides multiple functions including street and highway sweeping, road maintenance, soil conservation and drainage control in a specific development.
- Municipal utility district providing electric service and street lighting.
- Parks and recreation districts to provide park and recreation facilities and programs.
- Reclamation districts are authorized to reclaim land by the construction of levees, provide irrigation water, provide proper drainage facilities, and provide for the operation and maintenance of facilities and levees.

- Resource conservation districts have the authority to conduct activities that include: control of runoff water, prevention or control of soil erosion, development and distribution of water, improvement of land capabilities, dissemination of information and the conducting of demonstration projects in soil conservation.
- Sanitation districts provide wastewater collection, treatment and disposal services.
- Sacramento Regional Transit District Authority and the Sacramento Transportation Authority to provide public transportation services.
- A variety of water districts to provide potable water and irrigation functions.[88]

After reading the array of services that the special districts provide to the citizens of the county, one can see the fragmented nature of the service delivery and can imagine the difficulty of coordinating the various services and governments providing the services. Citizens in the county are not able to just go to one government for their services, which is confusing to citizens. There are also accountability issues because many, if not all, of the districts have appointed board members and provide services that do not receive much citizen or media interest. One would also think that the multiplicity of governmental entities would create additional costs in facilities, equipment, and personnel.

Takeaway

In the politically fragmented urban areas in which most Americans live, the provision of regional services is complex and complicated. The methods of providing regional services vary from one metro area to another. However, standard vehicles for provision of these services in this decentralized government system are similar throughout the country. A major method for provision of regional services is the special-purpose district. These districts proliferated in metropolitan areas with the suburbanization movement following World War II. Recently, some states have started to restrict the formation of special districts to reduce fragmentation in service delivery. Problems in governance of special districts include lack of accountability to the public whether the board members are elected or appointed. Appointed members are accountable to their political mentors who appointed them. Because of the lack of citizen interest in the operation of special districts, the public accountability of elected boards is also problematic. The result of lack of accountability may be board actions that are often not in the public interest.

Critics contend that special districts add to the complexities of governing metropolitan areas. They create confusion among residents and frustration in community political leaders, who are unable to directly influence the level of services special districts provide to their constituents. Special districts approach their assigned function with a single-minded focus and do not coordinate well with other governments or regional agencies. Fragmentation of services through special districts reduces the potential for economies of scope. Defenders of special districts argue that they are an effective way to provide services in a decentralized local government system. They suggest that special districts provide flexibility in obtaining economies of scale for each function, encourage cooperation among governments, and reduce tendencies of large multifunction agencies to become bureaucratized.

The public choice model, developed by economists not only as an explanation for the decentralized political system but as an advocate of it, has been hotly debated in the academic community by proponents and opponents of decentralization. Whether the public choice approach is, in fact, superior to the approach advocated by reformers is largely an academic question. The citizens have already cast their ballots for decentralized government. In fact, a manifestation of the public choice approach is the neighborhood government movement. This movement, as opposed to the centralization movement, is an attempt to decentralize government in large cities and empower the neighborhoods relative to local government services. The results of this movement, with some exceptions, have not been positive.

Notes

1. Appraisal by the Advisory Commission on Intergovernmental Relations of governance in the St. Louis area summarized by Donald Elliott, "Reconciling Perspectives on the St. Louis Metropolitan Area," *Intergovernmental Perspective*, 15 (Winter) (1989): 18.
2. U.S. Bureau of the Census, *1992 Census of Governments*, vol. 1 (Washington, DC: U.S. Government Printing Office, 1994), pp. ix-x.
3. U.S. Census Bureau, *2007 Census of Governments: Local Governments and Public School Systems by Type and State*, www.census.gov/govs/cog/govOrg Tab03ss. html [Accessed Sept. 20, 2012].
4. U.S. Bureau of the Census, *1992 Census of Governments*, vol. 1, p. xii.
5. U.S. Census Bureau, *2007 Census of Governments: Local Government Finances by Type of Government and State*, Table 2, www.census.gov/govs/cog/govOrg Tab03ss.html [Accessed Sept. 20, 2012].
6. U.S. Census Bureau, 2007 Census of Governments: *Local Government Finances by Type of Government and State*, Table 2, www.census.gov/govs/cog/govOrg Tab03ss.html [Accessed Sept. 20, 2012].
7. The figures for 2012 are preliminary and are subject to change.
8. U.S. Census Bureau, *2007 Census of Governments: Local Government Finances by Type of Government and State*, Table 2, www.census.gov/govs/cog/govOrg Tab03ss.html [Accessed Sept. 20, 2012].
9. Ibid.
10. Census Bureau. Census of Governments 2007. Local Governments and Public School Systems by type and State and Census of Governments 2002. Special purpose local governments by State: 1952–2002 vol. 1 Table 5 p. 5. http://www. census.gov/govs/cog/GovOrgTab03ss.html [Accessed Sept. 23, 2012].

11. Nancy Burns, *The Formation of American Local Governments: Private Values in Public Institutions* (New York: Oxford University Press, 1994), p. 46.

12. Ibid., p. 29.

13. U.S. Census Bureau, *2002 Census of Governments: Government Organization* Vol. 1:1 table 9. Special District Governments by Function and State (Washington, DC: 2002: U.S. Government Printing Office), p. 14.

14. John C. Bollens and Henry J. Schmandt, *The Metropolis: Its People, Politics, and Economic Life*, 3rd ed. (New York: Harper and Row, 1975), p. 264.

15. Kathryn A. Foster, "Specialization in Government: The Uneven Use of Special Districts in Metropolitan Areas," *Urban Affairs Review*, 31 (January) (1996): 289–290.

16. U.S. Bureau of the Census, *1982 Census of Governments*, vol. 5 (Washington, DC: U.S. Government Printing Office, 1994), pp. 19–109.

17. Gerald Benjamin and Richard P. Nathan, *Regionalism and Realism: A Study of Governments in the New York Metropolitan Area* (Washington, DC: Brookings Institution Press, 2001).

18. Robert D. Yaro and Tony Hiss, *A Region at Risk: The Third Regional Plan for the New York-New Jersey-Connecticut Metropolitan Area* (Washington, DC: Island Press, 1996), p. 207.

19. Benjamin and Nathan, *Regionalism and Realism: A Study of Governments in the New York Metropolitan Area*.

20. Ibid.

21. Alan L. Saltzstein, "Los Angeles: Politics without Governance," in H. V. Savitch and Ronald K. Vogel, (eds.), *Regional Politics: America in a Post-City Age* (Thousand Oaks, CA: Sage Publications, 1996), pp. 63–65.

22. Scott A. Bollens, "Fragments of Regionalism: The Limits of Southern California Governance," *Journal of Urban Affairs*, 19 (1) (1997): 112–115.

23. Ibid., app. A.

24. Charles Mahtesian, "Semi-Vendetta Cities and the New Republican Order," *Governing: The Magazine of States and Localities*, (June) (1996): 31–32. Also see Chapter 2 for a more detailed discussion of the increasing political isolation of the central city in state politics.

25. *Regional Transportation Authority*, http://www.rtachicago.com/about-the-rta/board-of-directors.html [Accessed Oct. 10, 2012].

26. Rogers Worthington, "Tollway Chief Targets Image Problem," *Chicago Tribune*, June 3, 1997, sec .2 p. 1.

27. New Jersey Comptroller: *Delaware River Port Authority Wasted Millions, to Benefit of Leadership by Christopher Baxter*, March 29, 2012, http://www.nj.com/news/index.ssf/2012/03/nj_comptroller_deleware_river.html [Accessed Oct. 10, 2012].

28. Sara C. Galvan, "Wrestling with MUDs to Pin Down the Truth About Special Districts," *Fordham Law Review*, 75 (6) (2007): 3054.

29. Ibid, p. 3055.

30. Burns, *The Formation of American Local Governments*, p. 12.

31. Bernard Ross and Myron A. Levine, *Urban Politics: Cities and Suburbs in a Global Age*, 8th ed. (Armonk, NY: M. E. Sharpe, 2012), p. 236.

32. Bollens, "Fragments of Regionalism," p. 117.

33. U. S. Census Bureau, *2002 Census of Governments: Government Organization*, Table 161:1. www.census.gov [Accessed October 12, 2012].

34. Bollens, "Fragments of Regionalism," p. 113.

35. Galvan, "Wrestling with MUDs To Pin Down the Truth About Special Districts," p. 3070.

36. Megan Mullin, *Governing the Tap: Special District Governance and the New Local Politics of Water* (Cambridge, MA: The MIT Press, 2009), pp. 107–112.
37. Allan D. Wallis, "Governance and the Civic Infrastructure of Metropolitan Regions," *National Civic Review*, 82 (Spring) (1993): 130.
38. Bollens, "Fragments of Regionalism," pp. 111–113.
39. Quoted in Arthur B. Gunlicks, "Problems, Politics, and Prospects of Local Government Reorganization in the United States," in Arthur B. Gunlicks, (ed.), *Local Government Reform and Reorganization: An International Perspective* (Port Washington, NY: Kennikat Press, 1981), pp. 18–19.
40. Ross and Levine, *Urban Politics: Cities and Suburbs in a Global Age*, pp. 255–256; Wallis, "Governance and the Civic Infrastructure of Metropolitan Regions," p. 130.
41. Zimmerman, "Special District Growth Reflects Anti-Government Bias," p. 407.
42. Galvan, "Wrestling with MUDs to Pin Down the Truth about Special Districts," p. 3068; George A. Boyne, "Local Government Structure and Performance: Lessons from America?" *Public Administration*, 70 (Autumn) (1992): 336; Kathryn Ann Foster, *The Political Economy of Special-Purpose Government* (Washington, DC: Georgetown University Press, 1997), pp. 183–191.
43. Advisory Commission on Intergovernmental Relations, *Metropolitan Organization: Comparison of the Allegheny and St. Louis Case Studies* (Washington, DC: U.S. Government Printing Office, 1993), pp. 14–15.
44. Richard F. Dye and J. Fred Giertz, *The Changing Relationships Among the Levels of Government in the Provision of Services* (Urbana, IL: Institute of Government and Public Affairs, March 1991), p. 3; Boyne, "Local Government Structure and Performance," p. 336.
45. Jonas Prager, "Contracting Out Government Services: Lessons from the Private Sector," *Public Administration Review*, 54 (March/April) (1994): 181.
46. Dye and Giertz, *The Changing Relationships Among the Levels of Government in the Provision of Services*, pp. 4–5.
47. Mullin, *Governing the Tap: Special District Governance and the New Local Politics of Water*, pp. 121, 179.
48. Charles M. Tiebout, "A Pure Theory of Local Government Expenditures," *Journal of Political Economy*, 44 (October) (1956): 416–424.
49. Michael Keating, *Comparative Urban Politics: Power and the City in the United States, Canada, Britain, and France* (Aldershot, England: Edward Elgar Publishing, 1991), pp. 108–109.
50. Andrew Sancton, *Governing Canada's City-Regions: Adapting Form to Function* (Montreal: Institute for Research on Public Policy, 1994), p. 42.
51. See, for example, Vincent Ostrom, Charles Tiebout, and Robert Warren, "The Organization of Government in Metropolitan Areas: A Theoretical Inquiry," *American Political Science Review*, 55 (December) (1961): 831–42; J. M. Buchanan, "Principles of Urban Fiscal Strategy," *Public Choice*, (Fall) (1971): 1–16; J. Zax, "The Effects of Jurisdiction Types and Numbers on Local Public Finance," in H. Rosen, (ed.), *Fiscal Federalism: Quantitative Studies* (Chicago, IL: University of Chicago Press, 1988), pp. 79–106; D. Kenyon and J. Kincaid, (eds.), *Competition Among State and Local Governments: Efficiency and Equity in American Federalism* (Washington, DC: Urban Institute Press, 1991).
52. R. Parks and R. Oakerson, "Comparative Metropolitan Organization: Service Production and Governance Structures in St. Louis, MO, and Allegheny County, PA," *Publius*, 23 (Winter) (1993): 19–30.
53. David Miller, R. Miranda, R. Roque, C. Wilf, "The Fiscal Organization of Metropolitan Areas: The Allegheny County Case Reconsidered," paper presented

at the North American Institute for Comparative Urban Research Conference, June 16–18, 1994, pp. 3–4.

54. R. T. Gannett, Jr., "Bowling Ninepins in Tocqueville's Township," *American Political Science Review*, 97 (1) (2003): 1–16; G. Weiher, *The Fractured Metropolis: Political Fragmentation and Metropolitan Segregation* (Albany, NY: State University of New York Press, 1991); Harold Wolman, "Local Government Institutions and Democratic Governance," in D. Judge, G. Stoker, and H. Wolman, (eds.), *Theories of Urban Politics* (Thousand Oaks, CA: Sage Publications, 1995), pp. 135–139.

55. Keating, *Comparative Urban Politics*, p. 111.

56. Bollens and Schmandt, *The Metropolis*, p. 35.

57. Matthew Holden, "The Governance of the Metropolis as a Problem in Diplomacy," *Journal of Politics*, 26 (August) (1964): 627–647.

58. Victor Jones, "The Organization of a Metropolitan Region," *University of Pennsylvania Law Review*, 105 (February) (1957): 539, quoted in John Kincaid, "Metropolitan Governance: Reviving International and Market Analogies," *Intergovernmental Perspective*, 15 (Spring) (1989): 23.

59. Abolishing local governments once they are created is highly unusual, although establishing laws affecting their behavior is common.

60. Kincaid, "Metropolitan Governance," p. 23.

61. The international relations model has not had much attention since it was proposed in the 1950s, and has only recently been revived by John Kincaid. See Kincaid, "Metropolitan Governance," pp. 23–27.

62. Harold Wolman and Michael Goldsmith, *Urban Politics and Policy: A Comparative Approach* (Cambridge, MA: Blackwell Publishers, 1992), pp. 17–18.

63. John J. Harrigan and Ronald K. Vogel, *Political Change in the Metropolis*, 8th ed. (New York: Longman, 2006), p. 257.

64. Edward M. Gramlich and Daniel L. Rubinfeld, "Micro Estimates of Public Spending Demand and Test of the Tiebout and Median-Voter Hypotheses," *Journal of Political Economy*, 90 (31) (1982): 536–39. The study included virtually all the area within 40 miles of downtown Detroit. Within this area it was presumed possible for all voters/consumers to find a community with individuals of like tastes in public expenditures.

65. Ibid.

66. Richard N. Engstrom and Nathan Dunkel, "Satisfaction with Local Conditions and the Intention to Move," *Cityscape: A Journal of Policy Development and Research*, 11 (1) (2011): 143–146.

67. Robert M. Stein, "Tiebout's Sorting Hypothesis," *Urban Affairs Quarterly*, 23 (September) (1987): 140–60.

68. David Lowery, W. E. Lyons, and R. H. DeHoog, "Institutionally Induced Attribution Errors: Their Composition and Impact on Citizen Satisfaction with Local Government Services," *American Politics Quarterly*, 18 (1992): 169–196; W. E. Lyons and David Lowery, "Government Fragmentation Versus Consolidation: Five Public-Choice Myths about How to Create Informed, Involved, and Happy Citizens," *Public Administration Review*, 49 (November/December) (1989): 535–542.

69. K. Kelleher and David Lowery, "Political Participation and Metropolitan Institutional Context," *Urban Affairs Review*, 39 (6) (2004): 720–757.

70. Stephen L. Percy and Brett W. Hawkins, "Further Tests of Individual-Level Propositions from the Tiebout Model," *The Journal of Politics*, 54 (November) (1992): 1149–57.

71. Elliott, "Reconciling Perspectives on the St. Louis Metropolitan Area," pp. 17–18.

72. Donald Phares, "Bigger Is Better, or Is It Smaller? Restructuring Local Government in the St. Louis Area," *Urban Affairs Quarterly*, 25 (September) (1989): 5–17.
73. David Hamilton, *Measuring the Effectiveness of Regional Governing Systems* (New York: Springer, 2013).
74. Ibid.
75. A. Artibise, K. Cameron, and J.H. Seelig, "Metropolitan Organization in Greater Vancouver: 'Do it yourself' Regional Government," in D. Phares, (ed.), *Metropolitan Governance without Metropolitan Government?* (Burlington, VT: Ashgate Publishing, 2004), p. 210.
76. Advisory Commission on Intergovernmental Relations, *The New Grassroots Government? Decentralization and Citizen Participation in Urban Areas* (Washington, DC: U.S. Government Printing Office, 1972).
77. Jeffery M. Berry, Kent E. Portney, and Ken Thomson, *The Rebirth of Urban Democracy* (Washington, DC: Brookings Institution, 1993), p. 13.
78. Ibid.
79. H.V. Savitch, "Postindustrialism with a Difference: Global Capitalism in World-Class Cities," in John R. Logan and Todd Swanstrom, (eds.), *Beyond the City Limits: Urban Policy and Economic Restructuring in Comparative Perspective* (Philadelphia, PA: Temple University Press, 1990), pp. 153–156.
80. Lydia Segal, "The Pitfalls of Political Decentralization and Proposals for Reform: The Case of New York City Public Schools," *Public Administration Review*, 57 (March/April) (1997): 142–43.
81. Harrigan and Vogel, *Political Change in the Metropolis*, pp. 206–207.
82. Laurence E. Lynn Jr. and Teresa R. Kowalczyk, *Governing Public Schools: The Role of Formal Authority in School Improvement*, working paper, Series 95–3 (Chicago, IL: Irving B. Harris Graduate School of Public Policy Studies, University of Chicago, June 30, 1995), p. 23.
83. Susan S. Fainstein and Clifford Hirst, "Neighborhood Organizations and Community Planning: The Minneapolis Neighborhood Revitalization Program," in W. Dennis Keating, Norman Krumholz, and Philip Star, (eds.), *Revitalizing Urban Neighborhoods* (Lawrence, KS: University Press of Kansas, 1996), pp. 106–107.
84. Segal, "The Pitfalls of Political Decentralization and Proposals for Reform," p. 147.
85. Fainstein and Hirst, "Neighborhood Organizations and Community Planning," pp. 109–110.
86. Ibid.
87. Segal, "The Pitfalls of Political Decentralization and Proposals for Reform," p. 149.
88. *Directory of Sacramento County Service Providers*, http://www.saclafco.org/Service Providers/SpecialDistricts/ListingbyCategory/default.htm [Accessed Oct. 12, 2012].

7 Providing Services in Decentralized Metropolitan Areas Through Intergovernmental Cooperation and Contracting

We must move from our devotion to independence, through an understanding of interdependence, to a commitment to human solidarity.
—U.S. Catholic Conference[1]

With the increasing political fragmentation of local governments in urban areas following World War II, it was impossible for many local governments to adequately deliver services due to an inadequate tax base. As discussed in Chapter 1, the two major purposes for development of local governments are to provide services and to more precisely regulate economic and social activity. The power to regulate is also the power to exclude. These purposes could be contradictory, as governments with small territory tend to be more homogeneous and are better able than larger governments to regulate economic and social activity to reflect the desires of the community. But communities also need to be large enough to encompass a tax base sufficient to finance services without prohibitive taxes. During the nineteenth century, becoming part of a larger municipality solved the service delivery problems often at the expense of being able to effectively regulate and exclude. During this time, the service purpose generally was paramount as many communities sought to become part of the larger central city to obtain its superior services. (See the discussion in Chapter 3 on annexation.) The exclusiveness purpose has been dominant since then, particularly since World War II. Communities explore all possible service delivery options before exclusiveness is forfeited.

The cooperation movement was a phenomenon of the rapid increase of municipalities in metropolitan areas after World War II and the increasing realization that many local government problems and issues needed to be addressed on a broader basis. Cooperation during the 1960s and 1970s came about for the following reasons:

- The establishment of forums for discussion of regional issues without any compulsion on the part of member governments to take action,

- The increasing costs of services and the public pressure not to increase taxes,
- Involvement in regional bodies to meet federal requirements to be eligible for grants.

Cooperative action was an acceptable alternative to consolidation because it did not threaten the political independence of the individual municipalities. Moreover, regional bodies were useful forums through which politically independent municipalities could discuss regional issues and take collective action as necessary to accommodate regional service needs. The use of special districts to provide services, as discussed in Chapter 6, is one method of accommodating the service delivery needs of the myriad local governments in metropolitan areas. This chapter looks at cooperation among governments and contracting as a means of providing services and addressing regional issues. I analyze the structures and mechanisms of cooperation emanating from the rapid suburbanization movement of the post–World War II period and expand on the federal government's involvement in this movement. (Chapter 10 looks at the new regionalism movement that has gained momentum since the 1990s.)

Theoretical Basis for Cooperation

The concept of cooperation is based on the collective action theory that was explicated by Olson in 1965.[2] Collective action refers to the cooperation or agreements between individuals or entities to achieve common goals or acquire benefits and avoid costs they would not acquire or avoid if they acted alone. It is assumed that local governments engage in collective action with other governments or contract services to nongovernmental entities when it is in their best interests to do so. Obviously, economic incentives are a major reason for entering into collective action agreements. There are, however, noneconomic reasons for governments to engage in collective action. There can be sanctions for not engaging in collective action, such as being excluded from the benefit of the agreement that other local governments enjoy. There can be pressures to become involved to maintain friendly relations with other local governments, to be viewed as a leader or to gain prestige and to be seen as a player and not isolated from other local governments in the metropolitan area. There will, of course, be an incentive to not incur the cost of the collective action if the local government can obtain the benefit as a "free rider," that is, enjoy the benefit without joining. The general conditions for local governments to become involved in a cooperative action are:

- They must have a common goal,
- The transaction costs and other costs of the collective action must be less than the benefit received from the agreement,

- The benefit is excludable—only members of the collective action benefit,
- The benefit must be non-rivalrous—the consumption of the goods by one government does not diminish the consumption by another member government.

By definition, cooperation is voluntary, and participating governments enter into cooperation willingly. There is no coercion; however, there may be major disincentives for not cooperating. For example, the federal government has induced cooperative efforts through its grant programs. The governments entering into the cooperative arrangements maintain their independence, but lose individual control over the production of the service. They generally have varying amounts of oversight of the function and theoretically can withdraw from the cooperative arrangements with sufficient notice if they are not pleased with the service. Withdrawal from a cooperative service agreement, however, may not be easy because of pressure from other members to the agreement and the difficulty of re-establishing an in-house means of service provision or finding another outside provider.

Municipalities seem to be more willing to cooperate in some areas than in others. For example, local governments are generally willing to cooperate in the provision of systems maintenance functions, such as the development and maintenance of physical infrastructure. Suburbs are less willing to cooperate in the provision of lifestyle services, including planning, zoning, education, and police protection. Indeed, communities incorporate to gain control over these lifestyle functions to protect their neighborhood, social standing, and property values from outside threats. They are more willing to cooperate in providing equal access to sewerage and water supply because these functions do not impede upon lifestyle choices, are noncontroversial, and are essential for maintenance of public health throughout the region.[3]

There are two levels of cooperation: the policy or governance level and the service delivery or functional level. The policy level deals with broad issues involving regional governance, such as regional political issues and issues regarding broad policy. Also addressed at this level are service delivery issues such as what services to deliver on a regional basis and broad policy on how those services are to be delivered. The functional level is where administrative decisions are made on the details of regional service delivery. The separation of provision (responsibility for the service) and production (delivery of the service) allows substantial flexibility in service delivery. Individual local governments that are responsible for the services do not necessarily have to produce (deliver) the service. This separation of provision from production is embodied in the concept of alternative service delivery. Cooperation in service delivery can be for all or part of a function.

Early Developments in Interlocal Cooperation

Cooperation among governments became extremely important in addressing regional governance issues when it became evident that most metropolitan areas would not accept a federated or a consolidated governmental system. Cooperation, as a solution to regional issues, was advocated as early as the late 1950s and early 1960s. It was also apparent to students of local government that cooperation was an essential element in the popular home rule movement which advocated more independence for local governments. Regionalists were concerned that home rule would induce more parochial thinking and actions at the expense of a regional approach to addressing area-wide problems. They maintained that governments could not use home rule to isolate themselves from the rest of the metropolitan area; they still needed to be involved in regional issues. One of the early writers, political scientist Luther Gulick, in writing about the effects of home rule, makes a case for cooperation:

> We now recognize that every major local governmental responsibility has broader regional connections . . . What becomes of home rule under these circumstances? The answer is clear . . . It is time to rise above local politics on regional matters and to work together . . . The price of home rule in the metropolitan areas is cooperation, institutional and political.[4]

Other early writers Arthur Bromage,[5] Edward Banfield, and Morton Grodzins also advocated cooperation as a solution to problems of coordination. Banfield and Grodzins developed a model of voluntary cooperation as the best approach for addressing metropolitan problems. Collective actions by governments, according to Banfield and Grodzins, are the best way to handle such services as public transportation, air pollution control, water and sewer systems, and solid waste management. Their model is interesting because it calls for the central city mayor to be the leader in the cooperation movement. The mayor in their model would "transcend the interests of the central city and think in terms of the entire metropolitan area."[6] The model crashed around this assumption. Most central city mayors were too busy worrying about central city problems to reach out to the suburbs and try to unite them in common initiatives. Those that did were usually rebuffed as they had no power to compel the suburbs to submit to their leadership. Moreover, in most metropolitan areas, any efforts by central city mayors in this direction were usually resisted by the suburbs as a grab for power and the precursor to metropolitan government.

The cooperation movement of the 1960s and 1970s focused mainly on pragmatic service delivery issues, ignoring broader governance issues. By addressing specific service delivery issues, various aspects of policy were decided, but the discussion on regional issues did not usually go beyond the specific function. In this sense municipalities sought to maintain as much separation and autonomy as possible. Individual governments seemed to be suspicious of each other's motives, creating cooperation barriers, particularly between central cities and suburbs. In fact, much of the cooperation in this period was not between the central city and the suburbs but between suburban governments. Cooperation was often forced by federal programs that required regional entities to review and comment on local government proposals for federal government grants.

Informal and Formal Cooperation

As opposed to formal cooperation with its written understandings and contracts, informal cooperation is unwritten, informal understandings between politicians or administrators from different jurisdictions. There is no binding legal agreement between governments, but it is generally the kind of day-to-day cooperation not readily visible or recognized. It may be an understanding between administrators or between political leaders that information, equipment, services, and the like will be shared when possible. It is often a "handshake" agreement in the sharing of crime laboratories or police records by police departments, park districts' use of school swimming pools for summer recreation programs, the sharing of jails, and fire departments aiding neighboring communities to fight fires. Informal cooperation is widely practiced but rarely documented, so there is no way of determining how widespread it is.

An example of informal cooperation between local governments is that between San Diego and Tijuana. Local law-enforcement agencies work, often informally, with their counterparts across the border. Officials from both communities often meet to coordinate disaster response plans, to share intelligence on crime and gangs, and to promote economic development. This international cooperation is based on handshakes between locals. These cooperative efforts are informal because formal agreements would require international treaties that would need to be developed and approved by both national governments.[7]

The three major kinds of voluntary formal cooperation in service delivery are interlocal service agreements, joint-powers agreements, and contracting with the private or nonprofit sectors. Joint-powers agreements involve two or more units of local government agreeing to work together in the financing and delivery of a service to their citizens, such as sharing of facilities. A variation of the joint-powers agreement is parallel action whereby two or more governments pursue mutually agreed-upon commitments separately even though the results are designed to benefit both parties. Interlocal service agreements are legally binding agreements entered into by two or more governments under which one government agrees to provide a service to the other(s) at an agreed-upon cost. The quantity and quality of the service are stipulated in the agreement.[8] Privatization is a form of an interlocal service agreement except that the contract is with a private or nonprofit organization. The local government maintains responsibility for the provision but contracts for the production of the service.

Privatization of Services

Municipalities have contracted services such as garbage and solid waste collection for a number of years. Contracting with private or nonprofit organizations has become quite popular as an alternative form of service delivery. Not only are more governments involved, but no local government function is immune from being privatized. A National League of Cities random sample survey with 332 responding administrators from cities 25,000 or more in population representing all sections of the country revealed strong support for government contracting at 93 percent. However, 69 percent of the respondents would prefer to provide the services in-house if given the option. They felt the greatest benefits to government outsourcing of services were cost savings (35 percent), greater flexibility in service delivery (32 percent), staffing (14 percent) and higher quality services (13 percent). They felt that the greatest problem in outsourcing was holding contractors accountable at 47 percent. Other problems were the loss of in-house expertise at 24 percent while 13 percent indicated that they did not experience the expected cost savings. One problem expressed by one-quarter of the respondents was the small number of vendors from which to choose. While 69 percent expressed satisfaction in their performance, the major areas of dissatisfaction were in responsiveness, quality, timeliness of delivery of the service, and service continuity. Actual cost compared to projected cost and compliance with terms of the agreement and law were less of a performance issue.[9]

The International City/County Management Association (ICMA) conducted a randomized, stratified survey of chief administrative officers of local governments with 1600 respondents. The survey found that municipal officials generally favor contracting and about 50 percent have studied the feasibility of privatizing services. The major reasons given for considering contracting were external fiscal pressures and the desire to decrease costs of service delivery. The major obstacles to privatization were reported as opposition from elected officials, local government employees, and labor contract restrictions.[10] Table 7.1 shows the ten services reported in the ICMA survey most commonly provided in-house, through interlocal cooperative agreements or by a separate authority, and through contracting out the service. It also shows the overall percentage of the delivery of that service by that mode of delivery.

It is clear from Table 7.1 that the major mode of delivery is still by government employees. Administrative services are overwhelmingly delivered by government employees. As to the other alternative delivery

Table 7.1 Ten Services Most Frequently Provided Through each Mode of Service Delivery

In–house	% of Total Service Delivery	Partially In–house	% of Total Service Delivery	Interlocal Service Agreement / Authority	% of Total Service Delivery	Privatized	% of Total Service Delivery
Clerical Services	92	Street Repair	52	Welfare Intake	59	Vehicle Towing	65
Payroll Services	89	Tree Trimming	47	Job Training	59	Solid Waste Collection Commercial	56
Personnel Services	89	Elderly Services	42	Mental Health Services	58	Daycare Facilities Operation	54
Police Patrol	88	Vehicle Maintenance	38	Child Welfare	53	Legal Services	52
Traffic Control	84	Building and Grounds	34	Public Health	52	Electric Utility	48
Public Information/ Relations	83	Cultural/ Arts Programs	34	Drug/Alcohol Programs	49	Solid Waste Collection Residential	47
Code Enforcement	82	Traffic Signals	33	Prison Operation	44	Solid Waste Disposal	43
Data Processing	75	Parks Maintenance	25	Tax Assessing	40	Hospital Operation	40
Snow Plowing	74	Legal Services	24	Public Transit	40	Tree Trimming	33
Parks and Recreation Operation	73	Parks and Recreation Operation	22	Hazardous Materials Disposal	38	Hazardous Materials Disposal	32

Source: ICMA, Profile of Local Government Service Delivery Choices, 2007, http://bookstore.icma.org/data_sets_c42.cfm [Accessed Nov. 24, 2012].

methods, only a handful is over 50 percent delivered by that mode. Even many of those services that are often provided through alternative forms of service delivery are also provided at least partially by government employees. For example, even though tree trimming is often privatized, it is more often partially provided by government employees. The types of services that are most often provided by interlocal service agreements or authorities are social welfare services. Although aspects of solid waste collection and disposal are often privatized, the major service that is most often privatized is vehicle towing. It is also interesting that day care operation is also generally privatized. Surveys to determine the incidence of contracting have different results depending on the date of the survey, who is surveyed and the questions asked. Most surveys are convenience surveys conducted by associations of their members and thus might not reveal the true nature of contracting services or interlocal cooperation.

Cooperation among Local Governments

Cooperation often starts with sharing of information. It may progress to sharing of resources and to a formal joint-powers agreement, with each government continuing to provide the service but specializing in a certain area and providing this unique service to the other government. For example, one government could provide ambulance services and fire protection while another government provides fire investigators; one government could share its crime laboratory with another government that shares its police academy. Another form of cooperation is shared purchasing of supplies and services. This could range from joint-purchasing contracts for supplies to pooled risk management and joint purchasing of health insurance plans. Sharing of resources could extend to many different functions and parts of functions. The possibilities of cooperation and sharing in the provision of services are endless. Examples of sharing just from the New York region include:

- One community in New York dissolved its 23-member police force and contracted the services with a nearby community.
- In Long Island two communities are pooling garbage to make more efficient use of recycling plants.
- In New Jersey two school boards have agreed to jointly hire a private food service company, resulting in reduced food service costs to the school districts.[11]

Bulk purchasing is an area where cities cooperate to reduce costs. A city in the Boston region purchased new LED streetlights on a purchasing contract with Boston that is projected to save the city $250,000 for the purchase and $80,000 a year in electricity costs. The city manager claims that 30 years ago cooperation with other cities would not have been the mode of operation, but cities are now under extreme pressure to find ways to be more efficient.[12] Some municipalities seeking to cooperate through contracting out services to other governments are not always welcomed by the government providing the contract. One city in Michigan, seeking to contract police services with the county, is receiving resistance from the sheriff even though his department and authority would be substantially strengthened through the contract with the city. For the city in question, it sees the contract with the county as a means to close a budget gap and still provide a satisfactory level of service. City officials indicate that without the contract with the county, the city would be forced to lay off 15 firefighters and 25 police officers.[13] In one survey by the National League of Cities, it was found that over half the responding cities with populations over 100,000 and three-fourths of the cities with populations over 300,000 were involved in interlocal agreements. What is encouraging about this survey is that larger cities were actively involved contrary to earlier times when larger cities exhibited neither the need nor the desire to cooperate with other local governments.[14]

Cooperation seems to be quite common in limited-service municipalities. *Limited-service municipalities* are those that do not have jurisdiction over the full range of services delivered to residents of the municipality. For example, limited-service municipalities may have separate park districts, library districts, township governments, fire protection districts, and so on. In these instances, the cooperation is often between the municipality and the separate special districts providing services within the municipality. Cooperation is also more common between municipalities in close proximity to each other, municipalities with small- to medium-sized populations, and municipalities sharing parts of a function, not the total function. An example is a Chicago suburban municipality where the park district, the high-school district, and the village have cooperated in various activities and projects. The park district and the high-school district jointly constructed and use a swimming pool and a gymnasium. The village and the park district work together on the development of parks with multiple uses, such as storm-water retention and recreation activities. The village joined with a number of other nearby municipalities to develop a shared data-processing center.[15]

There are numerous examples of communities joining in cooperative endeavors. A unique cooperative agreement in the Des Moines, Iowa metropolitan area involves 15 cities and 3 counties including Des Moines. Two communities share the same fire chief. All the communities share training programs and emergency dispatch technology. Administrators from each government involved in the cooperative agreement have been directed by a resolution passed by the political leaders to aggressively look for opportunities for cooperation and seriously evaluate cooperative proposals from other governments. The intent is to institutionalize a culture of intergovernmental cooperation within the governments.[16]

A further example is Fulton County, Georgia, where neighboring jurisdictions' different ordinances regarding animal control created conflict and confusion among residents. To solve this problem, the incorporated jurisdictions contracted with the county and adopted the county laws on animal control. To reduce political conflict in service delivery, the county then subcontracted with the Humane Society, a politically neutral organization, for the delivery of the service. An example of the cost savings from sharing under-utilized equipment and personnel is the joint-powers agreement between Los Angeles County and 12 cities in the county. Many of the cities involved in the joint-powers agreement have occasional need for certain equipment and manpower but not enough to justify purchasing their own. The county provides the equipment and the personnel for use by the 12 cities on an exchange-rental basis.[17] Cooperative endeavors might also extend to sharing buildings. In Salinas, California, for example, the city and the county have entered into an agreement to develop a joint government center. The officials feel that it is not only a symbolic message to the county that the two governments are working together but that it will be easier to jointly cooperate in providing and coordinating services.[18]

As discussed in Chapter 2, communities often vigorously compete with each other for economic development. Examples were provided in the chapter of how competition for development creates winners and losers and animosities among municipalities. Some areas are starting to accept the idea that the economy of the municipality does not stop at the municipality's border and that working together to promote the region for economic development provides benefits to all municipalities. In one example, the communities along Lake Minnetonka in the Minneapolis metropolitan area are banding together to promote development along the lake to make it more attractive for tourists. Working together, they are able to pool marketing dollars for better results and also attract major developers. Plans include connected bike trails, a coordinated schedule of festivals, and a scenic road around the lake. These are all projects that require the cooperation of the 14 communities located on the lake.[19]

What facilitates successful cooperation? A number of factors are important including managerial, geographical, economic, and political. Prior successful experience in cooperative endeavors often leads to additional cooperative initiatives and not only in the same function. New technology requirements or opportunities that require substantial investments may result in the formation of partnerships to share the costs or benefits from economies of scale of the new technology. Geographical proximity facilitates successful cooperation. Homogeneity of communities, not only in demographic characteristics but in socioeconomic characteristics, will be an advantage in developing partnerships. Obviously, positive encouragement and leadership from political officials are important to develop lasting cooperative ventures. If the perception is that the function needs to be individually controlled, it will not be a viable candidate for sharing. Involving stakeholders in the community in the planning and implementing of the cooperative venture is important to its success. Economically, the cooperative venture should show that it will be cost effective and the result will be beneficial to the partners.[20]

Interlocal Agreements and Service Consolidations

Interlocal agreements (ILAs) are a longstanding form of cooperative service delivery. However, there has recently been greater emphasis on ILAs as a way to provide services in decentralized metropolitan areas. It is a mechanism for local governments to voluntarily enter into agreements to take advantage of economies of scale to provide services more effectively and efficiently and continue to maintain their independent status. In other words, the community continues to have responsibility for the provision of the service but has combined with one or more other governments for the production of that service. ILAs might be formed with any other government, but the county is often a major partner in these services. (See the discussion on the Lakewood Plan in this chapter and county contracting in Chapter 8.) An ICMA survey of local government managers in North Carolina found that 94 percent had established ILAs for one or more services. The most identified services included tax collection, building inspection, dispatching, water and wastewater, recreation and planning. The reasons given for the ILAs included potential efficiencies, improved service delivery, better coordination of resources and enhanced public accountability.[21]

One study of ILAs in the Kansas City Metropolitan area by political scientists Kurt Thurmaier and Curtis Wood found that there was no central repository of ILAs and, even within communities, officials did not have complete knowledge of the number of formal and informal ILAs in which they were involved. The researchers found that engagement in ILAs tended to be more a social phenomenon than an overt means of attempting to save money. Administrators form social networks with each other through local meetings of professional associations, involvement in councils of governments or even through attendance at the same graduate school programs. These networks are often the means to start conversations that lead to exchange of ideas and the formation of cooperative working agreements between their departments and government functions.[22]

More formal long-term agreements must, of course, be sanctioned by the governing bodies of the involved governments. These interpersonal networks, often referred to as conjunctions, thus facilitate the development of ILAs. According to research by Leroux and Carr on the effect of administrative and electoral conjunctions in Wayne County, Michigan (Detroit), there was a positive relationship between the existence of these relationships and the likelihood of their jurisdictions entering into ILAs for maintenance-type services of roads, solid waste, watershed management, and wastewater treatment. For lifestyle services, administrative conjunctions were less likely to lead to ILAs in economic development and public housing but were likely to be found in public safety and parks and recreation services. Networks among elected officials were shown to have a positive effect on development of ILAs for all of the lifestyle functions studied with the exception of public housing.[23]

Cooperation and consolidation proposals are more frequent because of the existence of organizations such as the Intergovernmental Cooperation Council consisting of all municipal governments in Milwaukee County and civic organizations concerned with government efficiency. A study of potential efficiency and cost savings of the potential merger of fire services in five municipalities in the Milwaukee area by this organization was stimulated by a proposal from a civic organization. This study projected a one million dollar saving in annual operating costs and four million dollars over the next five years in vehicle replacement costs. The savings would be in the reduction of administrative personnel—for example, one fire chief instead of five and a reduction of rolling stock from 40 to 25.[24]

Fire services are a prime candidate for consolidation. Fire departments lend themselves to a regional model because firefighters from different agencies generally have agreements to assist each other in major fires and industrial accidents. Public safety consumes the largest chunk of a municipality's budget with fire services representing a significant part of the public safety budget. With budget shortfalls, particularly in recessionary periods, fire services are one of the first services to merge. A number of cities of all sizes in California, grappling with the budget shortfalls of the 2008 recession and the slow recovery, have consolidated or are seriously considering consolidation of fire departments. They are contracting with the county, with an area-wide authority or merging their services with other cities. For example, Santa Ana, the second largest city in Orange County has contracted with the Orange County Fire Authority to handle fires and medical calls in the city. The city faces a $30 million budget gap, and the elimination of its fire department is projected to save $10 million a year.[25] The merger of fire departments and fire protection districts in DuPage County in the Chicago metropolitan area is also being recommended as a way to save taxpayer money. A member of the county board complained that there "is just too much government. We simply cannot continue to afford the services we have at the same taxes and if we don't find better ways to deliver local, county and state services, taxes are going to go up." He indicated that fire districts are one of the best opportunities to achieve consolidation at the local level.[26]

Another area that the business community is pushing to consolidate or coordinate services is in code enforcement. Cities and counties usually have two sets of codes and separate departments established to enforce the codes.

Since most developers work across boundaries in many different jurisdictions, it creates delays and confusion in being forced to comply with numerous building codes. The city of Wichita and Sedgwick County have agreed to consolidate code enforcement into one department and have one building code to make it more efficient and cost effective.[27]

Some municipalities are going beyond consolidation of services because of the fiscal pressures from the slow recovery from the Great Recession. Bedford City, Virginia, which has been an independent city since 1968, has reached an agreement with the county to revert back to town status so that it can again be part of the county. In essence, the city of 6,000 would disincorporate and its services would be provided by the county. City officials, who initiated the process, claim that the change would save taxpayers' money and result in more efficient services.[28]

Advantages and Disadvantages of Cooperation and Contracting

Cooperation through interlocal agreements and by contracting out service delivery with the private or nonprofit sectors introduces many of the concepts sought by regionalists. These concepts include reducing the number of service producers, eliminating administrative duplication, obtaining economies of scale in the production of the service, and encouraging local government officials to think regionally, not parochially. Cooperation can serve as a model for the improvement of organizational or institutional arrangements to enhance the efficiency and quality of service delivery. It can also be a model for the development of other cooperative strategies within the region. In addition, cooperation has symbolic advantages. Cooperation between governments indicates to the community at large that government is changing and becoming more innovative to better meet the needs of the residents. It is an indication of a new political and administrative culture responding to the economic challenges and service needs of the community. Moreover, cooperation removes the production of the service from the political arena, theoretically making it more professional and businesslike, while the political leaders still retain decisions on policy.

Obvious reasons for cooperation are to obtain cost savings or to improve the quality and effectiveness of services. Agreements that bring local governments into a single unit for service delivery purposes also provide more uniformity in the delivery of the service as well as a larger funding base. The larger funding base allows the acquisition of more technologically sophisticated equipment than might otherwise be possible. Through cooperative agreements, a local government can obtain a service or a product that it cannot produce itself or can produce only at a prohibitively high cost. For example, eight small municipalities in St. Louis County, Missouri, contracted with the county police department for comprehensive police services. The eight municipalities avoided the substantial capital expenditures necessary for the establishment of individual municipal police departments including station construction, physical facilities, automobiles, and equipment. Thus, cooperative agreements can solve a problem affecting several local governments without changing the basic structure of the local government system, and without significantly restricting the freedom of action or autonomy of the recipient governments. Contracting with another organization does not require voter approval in most cases, and they can usually be terminated on relatively short notice.[29] Finally, the municipality may also benefit from competition in the marketplace. If there are a number of organizations bidding to provide the service, the resulting cost savings could be substantial. Some of the advantages of competition in both cost savings and improved services are:

- Competition induces greater efficiency. Although savings from contracting vary, private firms generally deliver services more economically than public organizations. However, this is not necessarily the case if public sector organizations have to compete with private sector organizations. In these instances, the costs for public sector organizations are roughly the same.
- Competition forces public monopolies to respond to the needs of their customers. In a competitive environment, an organization must be responsive to its customers or it will lose them.
- Competition rewards innovation. The old standard ways of providing services may not be the best. Through competition, new ideas and better ways of providing services are continually sought.
- Competition boosts the pride and morale of public employees. In competitive situations, people seem to work harder and feel more satisfaction when they know they have done a good job.[30]

A government may obtain benefits from organizational economies by having the service produced by an outside organization. Organizational economies result when a function simply becomes too large and complex for the municipality to effectively and efficiently manage. "Contracting out permits the government authorities to side step some of these bureaucratic barriers, focus on their most critical operations, and relegate the remainder to contractors."[31] Osborne and Gaebler refer to this as steering rather than rowing; it is referred to as focusing on the core business in the private sector.[32] The intent of organizational economies is to reduce the potential for inertia and make organizations more responsive to the needs of consumers.

Despite the general advantages described above, cooperative agreements may not be the panacea for the delivery of every function. Local governments should not automatically opt for cooperation but should carefully consider the advantages and disadvantages of cooperative action for each situation.

Professor Jonas Prager argues that public organizations should only consider an interlocal agreement or contracting out when they cannot take advantage of scale economies or scope economies by producing the service in-house. An organization would realize scale economies when it is either too small or too large to take advantage of the optimal scale. "Thus, a central crime laboratory, with experienced technicians and specialized knowledge, is not likely to be efficiently utilized by a small, low-crime community."[33] Prager cautions, however, that scope economies must be carefully considered before a government chooses to enter into a contract on the production of a service. Scope economies result when employees can be cross-trained to perform a number of functions. He writes:

> Sometimes an operation may be too small to achieve high levels of efficiency, yet can be combined with a second activity that uses similar resources. Municipal street maintenance crews can be trained to drive snow plows and even to handle infrequent calls for rescue and first aid services. In a small community, hospital-based social workers need not be limited to their hospital patients. They can handle the social predicaments of dysfunctional families, home-bound senior citizens, drug-addicted teenagers, alcoholics, and so on. Perhaps the jack of all trades is the master of none, but when masters of all trades are financially unsupportable, the jack-of-all-trades is surely more cost-effective.[34]

A recent survey by the ICMA found that although 45 percent of the respondent local governments had considered intergovernmental agreements for service delivery, only half of those had actually established an agreement to share or coordinate service delivery. There are barriers that make the development of interlocal agreements problematic. Communities have divergent interests, which create difficulties in developing a collective action framework. There are also transaction costs involved in developing interlocal agreements that might outweigh the presumed benefits of the intergovernmental arrangement. Transaction costs include any relationship barrier between possible partners or within organizations. One barrier is the impact on politicians and administrators and the extent to which the co-operative efforts are in their self interests. Another transaction cost is involved in obtaining usable information in finding acceptable partners, determining costs and benefits, establishing protocols to police and enforce the agreements and protecting the independence of the individual partners.

On the other hand, a successful partnership can build a level of trust among partners that reduces the transaction costs for additional partnerships to near zero and readily facilitate additional partnerships. Over time, embedded relationships with other governments can result in an extensive regional governance network.[35] Another major concern is the potential loss of local control. Contracts are a step removed from local political control and, therefore, less accountable to the citizens or to their elected officials. In addition, cooperative arrangements are normally developed for a single, limited-purpose function. A municipality may be involved with a number of cooperative arrangements with different municipalities, making it hard to coordinate all of the services to the municipality. Multifunction cooperation agreements would avoid scattering functions among various boards and reduce the need for coordination.

A further disadvantage is that the cooperation may be terminated at the whim of an individual party to the agreement, particularly those agreements that are informal. This forces the recipient municipality to make alternative arrangements on short notice. Besides the threat of untimely termination, cooperative agreements, especially informal agreements, are particularly susceptible to high-level personnel changes and personality conflicts that may make it difficult to maintain or even develop agreements in the first place. One example of the inability to come to an agreement was a municipality in the Calgary, Canada region. The municipality needed an increased water supply for a development and wanted to buy water from the neighboring city of Calgary, which controlled the water rights to the nearby river. Calgary refused to cooperate. The municipality was forced to look elsewhere. Instead of a three-kilometer water line to Calgary, the municipality was faced with a 62-kilometer line at a cost of more than $40 million.[36] Occasionally, the contracting municipality becomes prisoner to the entity producing the service if there is little competition or interest from other service providers. In such cases, the government receiving the service may face the option of substantial cost increases or poor service, or the prospect of resuming the service in-house at considerable expense if the municipality previously eliminated its in-house capability.

The limited jurisdictional authority of the agency providing the co-operative service is a potential disadvantage. For example, if cooperating governments establish an organization to produce a service with only advisory powers, the organization must build consensus to effectively produce that service. Obtaining consensus from each municipality to the agreement on the various aspects of the service delivery might be impossible because of the parochial concerns of individual municipalities. Thus, actions of one municipality may reduce the benefits to the other municipalities. In addition, since most cooperative agreements cannot compel participation, the nonparticipation of one or two of the larger municipalities can impede and hinder the effectiveness of a regional approach. Although most would agree that the will or interests of the majority should not be frustrated by resistance from a small minority, local governments consider their autonomy a higher value. Therefore, governments resist the establishment of cooperative bodies that have decision-making power over participant communities.[37]

The paucity of competition from organizations available and willing to bid on contracts is a common problem. The advantages of outsourcing are potentially lost when there are too few companies competing for the contract. One ICMA survey found that the percentage of municipalities experiencing inadequate vendor supply grew from 25 percent in 1992 to 31 percent in 2007. Even when competitive public service markets exist, they may erode over time. It requires substantial transaction costs to create public service markets and the effort may not be successful. A set of three or more bidders is the minimal number to meet competitive thresholds. Obviously, the more bidders, the better the concept of the market works. There are also geographical differences in competitive location. Studies have found that suburban municipalities are generally in a more competitive environment than rural municipalities or central cities.[38]

Measuring performance and monitoring the contract or the interlocal agreement is often not done well. One study found that over half of the municipalities surveyed did not evaluate contract service delivery. Some suggest that the hollowing out of the workforce due to contracting has led to a reduced capacity to monitor and evaluate contracts. Studies have also shown the pervasive influence of politics in the awarding and managing of contracts. One study of information technology found that higher levels of contracting correlated with reduced local government internal management capacity.[39]

The Lakewood Plan

One form of interlocal agreement that involves contracting an array of services from one government is called the Lakewood Plan. The Lakewood Plan takes its name from a community in the Los Angeles metropolitan area that incorporated in 1954. The incorporation was a defensive mechanism to resist the imminent annexation by the city of Long Beach. Prior to incorporation, services were provided by Los Angeles County. As with other municipalities upon incorporation, Lakewood was expected to provide municipal services to its residents. The municipality faced substantial start-up costs. To avoid the capital investment necessary to commence the services, the community leaders sought to have Los Angeles County continue to provide services to the city. The county received approval and was given the power to contract with newly incorporated municipalities to provide services. Lakewood purchased an array of services from the county, including police and fire protection as well as some 39 other services. Although the city had sufficient population to provide its own services (it had over 50,000 inhabitants upon incorporation), the community leaders determined that it was to the community's tax advantage to contract with the county. The county bureaucrats, concerned with the diminishing size of their departments due to the large number of incorporations, were also willing to provide services to the municipality.[40]

The Lakewood Plan led to the creation of a number of incorporations of small cities that obtained most of their services from the county. The arrangement offered communities, especially smaller communities, the ability to secure high-quality, professional services at costs below what they could provide individually. Many unincorporated areas took advantage of this plan to incorporate to protect their area from being annexed by larger municipalities. These "contract" cities were thus able to provide needed services and maintain their independence and autonomy. The result was a large increase in the municipal fragmentation of incorporated cities that used their municipal powers to keep out unwanted residents or development. For example, Rancho Palos Verdes enacted land-use regulations that blocked new development to preserve the community's exclusive, estate-like character.

Other areas incorporated to avoid the higher taxes that would come from being annexed. The City of Industry incorporated as a "tax island" to shelter the railroad yards, factories, and warehouses within its borders from the higher taxes that would have resulted from annexation to another community. In order to meet the minimum population of 500 required for incorporation, the city had to count the patients and employees of a local psychiatric sanitarium. The City of Industry levies no taxes on industrial or residential property.[41] One example of the problems and issues that can result from incorporations that either start out or end up as "tax islands" is the city of Vernon, California. Currently, fewer than 100 residents live in this city. It has 1,800 businesses and a tax base of $334 million. It has no parks, one school and only one residential street. The city manager received an annual salary of $785,000 in 2009, and the person he replaced earned $1.65 million. All but a handful of the residents work for the city. Its officials are all related to the employees. Most live in city-owned houses or apartments. There are currently efforts in the state legislature to disincorporate the city and have city services provided by the county. The city would not be able to incorporate under current law requiring 500 residents. At one time it had 500 or more residents but the expanding industries bought up most of the homes and demolished them.[42]

An obvious disadvantage of the Lakewood Plan is that the community sacrifices some control over the quantity and quality of services and, therefore, must be satisfied with more standardized services rather than services tailored to their specific needs. Although Lakewood Plan municipalities have substantial bargaining power to influence the delivery of services by threatening to withdraw if their needs are not met, the county makes the final decisions on the quantity, quality, price, and style of the services delivered. This severely restricts Lakewood Plan communities from the independence enjoyed by other communities producing their own services. A common practice is for newly incorporated municipalities to initially contract with the county for virtually all their municipal services. Over time, however, they often withdraw from some of the services. The municipality withdraws because it either determines that it can perform certain services more efficiently than the county government, or the municipality's leaders decide to undertake a function on their own for such nonfinancial reasons as the desire for greater community control over the service. Communities that have terminated contracts with the County of Los Angeles have cited the desire for more specifically tailored services as a major reason for terminating their contracts.[43]

A major disadvantage of the Lakewood Plan concept for regionalists is that it fosters political fragmentation. By enabling municipalities to contract all of their services from the county, it encourages local government fragmentation by providing an easy way to receive services upon incorporation. There is little incentive to seek annexation to improve services. Even areas with small populations can incorporate and receive services at a reasonable cost. After the Lakewood Plan was enacted, the number of incorporations increased from only two between 1930 and 1940 to 32 in the next 20 years.[44] There was no incentive to seek other forms of regional government, as the county was, in effect, serving regional needs.

The number of services purchased varies by each municipality. The Lakewood Plan is attractive to municipalities because of its flexibility in choice, addition, or elimination of services. In 2010, the city of Maywood, a poor Latino community, in the face of mounting budget shortfalls, dismissed its entire municipal workforce. It contracted with the county for police services and with a neighboring municipality and private firms for its other services.[45] The Lakewood Plan concept has been extended to not just contracting a large array of services with the county. The concept is to outsource a number of major functions to other public, private or nonprofit organizations as exemplified by the city of Maywood.

A few cities across the country have taken outsourcing to extremes where most of their services are not provided by their own employees. Examples include Crestwood, Illinois, a community of close to 12,000 population with 21 employees, Weston, Florida, a city of 66,000 population with 9 employees, Centennial, Colorado, a city of over 100,000 with little more than 50 fulltime equivalent employees, and Sandy Springs, Georgia a city of 93,000 with 7 public employees, which boasts the largest public–private partnership in providing municipal services in the nation. These cities are poster cities for providing services at low costs to the taxpayers. For example, Crestwood for years rebated a large portion of property taxes back to the residents in the form of a check each year. The rebate included portions of the taxes the residents paid for school and county taxes. Citizen satisfaction surveys give the cities high marks for services. Weston was ranked as the 63rd best place in America to live by *Money Magazine* in 2012. Services are seamlessly provided by these communities and residents might not even know that the employees they are dealing with are not city employees.[46]

Regional Councils

Regional councils are cooperative, regional organizations composed of counties, towns, and often special districts. The purpose of regional councils is to increase communication, cooperation, and coordination among local governments in planning and implementing programs that address regional issues. The basic characteristics of regional councils are:

- They are multijurisdictional because they encompass more than one local government. They may be within one county or they may be composed of a number of counties in a metropolitan area.
- Their prime purpose is to achieve local government cooperation across legal boundaries.
- They can be multifunctional. Rather than just focus on a single function (like a single-purpose special district), regional councils may deal with a variety of broad public issues, such as transportation, health, public safety, and environmental quality.
- Regional councils are advisory in nature and, with few exceptions, lack the normal governmental powers of taxation, regulation, and direct operation of public facilities.
- Membership is voluntary and members can withdraw at any time.[47]

The traditional role of regional councils was to bring an area-wide focus to physical planning in such areas as land use, economic development, the environment, and housing. Regional councils, however, also provide non-planning assistance by serving as a vehicle for the resolution of multi-jurisdictional issues and by providing some direct services to member governments. A survey of regional councils found that over three-fourths of the councils were involved in information services, economic development activities, housing and community development, and environmental planning. Councils serving populations over one million were more extensively involved in regional activities than those serving smaller populations. For example, over 70 percent of the councils serving large populations were involved in six of nine possible regional program areas, compared to only four of nine program areas for councils serving medium populations and five of nine program areas for councils serving small populations. However, in some of the more controversial areas, such as housing and community development and health and human resources, the smaller councils were more involved than the larger councils. Table 7.2 shows the breakdown of the percentage of councils involved in each program area.

Regional Planning Commissions

Two major variations of regional councils are councils of governments (COGs) and regional planning commissions (RPCs). RPCs were the earliest

Table 7.2 Regional Council Program Participation, by Size of Council[a]

Program Area	Small[b]	Medium[c]	Large[d]	All
Transportation Planning	55%	36%	39%	51%
Land Use Planning	72	67	87	70
Health and Human Resources	60	51	43	50
Public Safety	36	60	43	37
Economic Development	84	80	83	80
Environmental Planning	73	87	96	80
Management/Technical Services	61	60	74	65
Information Services	84	89	100	85
Housing, Community Development	78	76	74	78

Source: Adapted from National Association of Regional Councils, "1993–94 Regional Council Survey: Program, Activity Characteristics," *Regional Council Data Series*, Report no. 5 (Washington, DC: August 1995), pp. 2–7. Reprinted with permission of the National Association of Regional Councils, 1998.

Notes:
[a] A survey of 357 regional councils conducted in 1993–94.
[b] Serves a population of less than 300,000.
[c] Serves a population between 300,000 and one million.
[d] Serves a population of more than one million.

type of regional councils to be developed. These area-wide agencies were established primarily for comprehensive planning purposes. The emphasis was on land use or development and use of facilities by more than one governmental jurisdiction. The first regional planning commission was set up by Los Angeles County in 1922. That same year New York organized a committee to carry out an extensive survey of the New York metropolitan region and to prepare a general plan for its development. This survey and the planning reports of this pioneering group inspired similar work in Philadelphia; Chicago; St. Louis; Washington, DC; Boston; and other metropolitan areas. Despite its success, growth of RPCs was slow, as only 18 metropolitan planning agencies were created between 1922 and 1945. The pace of creation increased somewhat when another 22 were created between 1945 and 1955. In the five years after Congress passed the Housing Act of 1954, which under Section 701 provided urban planning assistance to metropolitan areas, more than 100 metropolitan planning agencies were created. By late 1967 there were 216 RPCs, but this figure had only increased to 253 by 1970 due to the rapid growth of other types of regional councils.[48]

Most regional planning commissions are officially created under a specific state act or general enabling legislation. Representatives on the governing body are predominantly citizens appointed by the local governments or by the governor. The basic regional council program involves developing plans and recommendations in specific functional areas, such as air pollution control, solid waste disposal, transportation, law enforcement, water quality, land use, manpower, and economic development. RPCs are useful in providing a forum for communication among local governments and for the establishment of goals and priorities for the region.

The basic weakness of a regional planning commission is that it is only advisory and lacks a parallel regional government with the powers to implement its decisions. This is in contrast to a municipal planning commission which is also advisory but is part of an implementing government. The RPC must rely on the enforcement powers of local governments to implement its decisions. Because local government political officials often are not on the boards, RPCs have difficulty implementing their plans. Moreover, because RPCs are not political bodies, the emphasis has been on less controversial areas. Even in these areas, RPC recommendations are often not implemented.[49]

Councils of Governments

COGs are voluntary associations composed of local governments. Their major purposes are the following:

- To provide a forum for discussion of issues and challenges of general concern to member governments,
- To determine policy and priorities on these issues,
- To implement decisions through the member governments,
- To coordinate federal, state, and local programs with a regional impact.[50]

Member governments designate an elected official to represent them on the COG. They consider policy and programs of a regional nature. Their emphasis is on short-term policy relative to pragmatic programs such as technical assistance, joint purchasing, mutual police aid agreements, training programs, solid waste disposal, and the like. The decisions by the COG are not binding on member governments. It is, therefore, the individual member's decision whether to join a COG initiative. To ensure that the COG remains mainly a deliberative body, and because all members generally do not join COG initiatives, any decision to establish a regional program is usually implemented by forming an independent organization for those municipalities that wish to participate.[51]

The COG movement began in the Detroit area in 1954 when Edward Connor, a Detroit city councilman and president of the Wayne County Board of Supervisors, and his counterparts from neighboring counties formed the Supervisors Intercounty Committee. The number of COGs grew slowly until the 1965 amendments to the Housing Act of 1954, which made Section 701 planning assistance funds available to councils of governments and other regional organizations for professional staffing, administrative expenses, data collection, and regional planning studies for land use, transportation, housing, economic development, resource development, community facilities, and environmental improvement. Almost overnight, COGs became important metropolitan organizations. In the space of two years the number of COGs grew from 35 in 1965 to 103 in 1967.[52]

Prior to the passage of the 1965 amendments to the 1954 Housing Act, COGs were chiefly funded by membership dues. RPC funding, on the other hand, came from a variety of revenue sources including local taxes, membership dues, interlocal service agreements, user fees, state and federal grants, and contracts.[53] With the change allowing access to federal funding, COGs became the dominant form of regional organization. The reason for their dominance was that they had political representation on their governing bodies, whereas the regional planning commissions were governed by boards composed of appointed citizens. To be more politically acceptable, regional planning commissions started transforming themselves by appointing local government political leaders to their boards. By the late 1960s and early 1970s, there was generally little distinction between most regional planning commissions and councils of government. Although many metropolitan areas still have distinct COGs and RPCs, many of their functions overlap. For the remainder of this discussion, COGs and RPCs, unless otherwise indicated, are referred to as regional councils.

Decline of Regional Councils

The federal–regional council partnership peaked in 1977 when regional councils were involved in up to 40 federal grant programs. Eight key federal program areas included housing planning assistance, highway and mass transit planning and programming, area-wide planning for services to the aging, economic development planning, air and water pollution control planning, manpower development planning, criminal justice planning, and the A-95 program review and comment process for local government grant proposal (see Chapter 5). By 1977, federal funding assistance to councils was approximately $800 million, which represented 75 percent of the nation's total council funding.[54]

Commencing with the Reagan Administration, there were significant changes in the extent of federal involvement in metropolitan areas. The federal government terminated programs that promoted cooperation and regionalism. Many regional grant programs were phased out. By the early 1990s, only 13 programs still existed. The A-95 review process was rescinded, eliminating regional review for many continuing federal grant programs. Several regionally oriented grant programs were turned over to state administration with no requirement for continuing a regional review. With the withdrawal of the federal government from promoting regionalism, the federal share of regional councils' budgets declined from 75 percent in 1977 to 45 percent in 1988.[55]

With the reduction in federal funding for regional activities during the Reagan Administration, 126 councils, almost 20 percent, closed their doors by 1988.[56] In order to survive, the remaining councils had to significantly alter their operations. As the traditional planning programs promoted and funded by the federal government plummeted, regional councils developed other sources of funding and purposes to justify their existence. They became much more responsive to the needs of their dues-paying membership and more involved in brokering or entrepreneurial activities. States started using regional councils to generate regional infrastructure or growth plans and as a conduit in some states for programs for the region, such as economic development assistance.[57]

One federally-funded RPC that has survived and, in fact, has prospered is the metropolitan planning organization (MPO). The MPO is the designated council to oversee the planning and distribution of federal highway funds in metropolitan areas. With the passage of the 1991 Intermodal Surface Transportation Efficiency Act (ISTEA) and subsequent highway legislation distributing highway funds to states and metropolitan areas, MPOs became the vehicles for the distribution of federal highway funds in metropolitan areas. MPOs are required to, among other things, develop and maintain a long-range transportation plan and a transportation improvement program for the region. They are also required to consider the environment, particularly the impact on air quality. Although most MPO funds distributed through MPOs are used for highways, they are required to do multimodal planning and a certain portion of the funds must be used for mass transit and other types of transportation.

The planning function is still the major activity of most councils. A survey of regional councils reported that among councils serving populations one million or over, 94 percent were involved in planning; councils serving populations between 500,000 and one million reported 88 percent involvement. However, councils serving less than 500,000 reported more focus on membership services and less involvement in the planning function. The survey further found that council directors were optimistic about the future of regional councils, especially for those councils serving large populations. They felt that councils can play an important role in various activities involving the regional economy, transportation, environmental, and infrastructure issues, but a lesser role in regional issues involving housing, education, substance abuse, and health.[58]

Federal funds remain the largest single source of revenues for councils. The second highest source of operating revenue is a combination of contractual services, charges for informational services, membership fees, support from the private sector, and miscellaneous sources. State sources constitute the third largest source of funds with the remainder coming from other local sources. State funds to regional councils are allocated for such purposes as education, parks and recreation, housing, and the environment. Significant regional activities include distributing and monitoring the use of pass-through funds. Pass-through funds are funds that are not expended by regional councils but rather distributed to other regional organizations or local governments for specific programs. This would include such federal programs as the Job Training Partnership Act to fund private industry councils, Environmental Protection Agency funds, and federal highway funds. The largest share of pass-through funds comes from the federal government at almost three-quarters of the total.[59]

Councils and Regional Governance

Proponents of regional councils claim that they are an alternative to consolidated or metropolitan government. They claim that councils are an incremental reform that provide a form of metropolitan governance and have been useful without being painful. Cynics argue that their purpose is defensive and psychological. They claim that COGs were created to give the illusion that something is being done in order to address regional problems to prevent any more powerful or drastic regional governmental reorganization. Regional council supporters had high expectations. The Advisory Commission on Intergovernmental Relations (ACIR), an early advocate of councils, described them as "being a useful means of stimulating a greater cooperation among governmental officials, creating public awareness of metropolitan problems, and developing an areawide consensus on more effective use of handling these problems." The National Association of Regional Councils touted regional councils as organizations where "local officials are able to define and direct the proper course for the solution of area-wide problems that cannot be solved within a single jurisdiction."[60]

The reformers' high expectations for councils have, with few exceptions, not been met. They have failed to develop strong political support from the state or among local governments in the region. They remain as advisory and planning bodies without the means to implement their plans. COGs' continued dependence on federal government funding and lack of support among local governments is evident by the large numbers that folded with the cutback in federal financial and programmatic support. One study of COGs in Allegheny County, Pennsylvania, concluded that councils have been effective only with external inducements or when financial problems forced independent governments into cooperation in order to provide a needed service.[61]

The major function of regional councils, to promote regionwide coordination through planning, has been largely ineffective mainly because they had no authority to implement their plans. The review and comment process was often ignored by federal agencies and was treated simply as a bureaucratic hurdle by the applicant governments. Councils also avoided controversial planning problems to avoid confrontations with member governments. A further problem was the source of the councils' authority. They derived their authority from federal agencies. This created problems when councils sought to develop working relationships and legitimacy with local governments. As federal authority and resources have been withdrawn, councils' ability to establish local legitimacy has been essential to their survival. Acceptance and financial support at the local level are critical, as state governments have generally provided little financial or programmatic support. Finally, councils have been able to create only a weak sense of the region for planning purposes and almost no political or administrative regional identity.[62] Charles Shannon, a former COG employee, writes on councils' failure at regional governance as follows:

> COGs have tended to "intergovernmentalize" everything and, in the process, cloud our vision of the metropolitan forest by dealing with too many small trees ... The failure of COGs is only in part of their own making. Local governments have expected COGs to serve as a collective voice for them, which is often not the same as a regional voice. State governments have assiduously avoided the fundamental issues of structural reform in metropolitan areas, and the federal government, through its various programs, has often subverted local agendas by promoting federal ones.[63]

The difficulty of attempting to bring a regional perspective to a decentralized system of governance is evidenced from a survey of executive directors of regional councils in Florida. In order to carry out their activities, they must work and interact with municipalities, counties, other regional agencies, state agencies, and federal government agencies. In the survey, the directors indicated that major difficulties arose because local governments did not understand the regional councils' roles, lacked an intergovernmental perspective, and underutilized the regional councils. Regional governance through the councils could be more effective, according to the council executive directors, with more adequate, stable funding, more authority, less parochialism of council members, and more willingness of local government to cooperate.[64]

One assessment of regional councils indicates they have been valuable in formulating plans for land use, transportation, sewer and water facilities, and the conservation of natural resources. But serious questions can be raised about whether these plans are sensitive to the need for social change and whether they give equal weight to the interests of all parts of the region. There is a major question about representation. In 60 percent of the councils, each member government has an equal vote regardless of the size of its population.[65] This gives disproportionate power to smaller jurisdictions at the expense of the larger jurisdictions resulting in the favoring of suburban issues. In fact, one study of 98 COGs found a general rejection of the idea that central city problems should be one of their focal points.[66] Because of their general suburban orientation, critics complain that most regional councils consider physical development primarily in the suburbs and ignore issues of interest to the central city, such as affordable housing and public transportation.[67] There was an especially sharp conflict between Cleveland and the Northeast Ohio Areawide Coordinating Agency (NOACA). This agency was formed to meet federal A-95 review demands and to obtain federal grants. Cleveland was given only one vote on the COG so NOACA was heavily dominated by suburban governments. Because Cleveland's interests were being ignored by the COG, the city withdrew from the COG. The Department of Housing and Urban Development threatened to strip NOACA of its A-95 review power, which would have been a major financial blow, if it did not adopt the one person, one vote principle. NOACA relented, but even with the proportional representation on the council, Cleveland is still a minority member of the council. The longstanding suspicions of the central city by the suburbs will likely mean that the 75 percent suburban-dominated board will continue to be wary of Cleveland's proposals.[68]

An assessment of the Metropolitan Washington Council of Governments (MWCOG), the premier council in the Washington, DC, area, concludes that it has only been as effective in regional governance as its member governments have allowed. With no formal government authority and dependent upon federal and state grants, contracts, and member contributions, MWCOG is effectively precluded from addressing the most serious problems facing the region. It is a voluntary organization, and members have left or threatened to leave over various issues. Montgomery County, Maryland, for example, withdrew in 1963 and returned only after it won concessions on representation. Because of the diversity of the governments it represents, stands on controversial issues are impossible for MWCOG. A proposed strict model gun control law advocated by the District of Columbia caused considerable opposition in suburban Maryland. Likewise, because of suburban opposition, MWCOG has been unable to support a commuter tax for the District of Columbia or take action that appears to favor one area of the region over another. For this reason it has not been able to involve itself in economic development activities.[69]

Another problem with the effectiveness of regional councils is they have no regional constituency and no regional political leadership. Political officials appointed to the council represent their own organizations' interests over those of the regional body. Their primary allegiance is to the voters who elected them. Because of the makeup of the council's governing body and the lack of an area wide constituency, it does not seem likely that regional leadership will develop through these organizations. Further, councils cannot be seen as a step toward structural change and possible metropolitan government because they are criticized as spending most of their time on survival or organizational maintenance rather than the augmentation of power—and this goal has tended to supersede others of a programmatic nature. They try, on the one hand, to demonstrate to federal authorities that they are worthwhile investments and, on the other hand, to reassure local units that they constitute no threat to them. They have generally shied away from any effort to enhance their authority vis-à-vis other local governments. They have been severely criticized as being overly timid in attempting to define their role and stake out their jurisdictional field.[70]

Councils are invariably underfunded and understaffed which severely circumscribes their ability to play a major role in regional issues. The constant potential for membership withdrawal with the loss of financial contributions and programmatic support hangs over each regional council as it attempts to deal with metropolitan issues. As per the example of MWCOG above, councils avoid particularly controversial issues and often disregard the regional perspective in their review of members' federal grant applications. In these reviews COGs are generally supportive, as critical comments and opposition would risk alienating their members.

Critics feel that councils will not be able to provide an effective regional governance role without giving them more authority and making them more independent. They argue that councils should be empowered to veto local projects, if they are not in accordance with area-wide plans, and should be authorized to directly provide functions to residents. Professor Donald Norris contends that councils will not survive local or state politics or provide effective regional governance without substantial changes. He argues that they must have status and authority within the intergovernmental system. He recommends the following changes for councils to be effective in regional governance:

- They must be permitted and required to provide specified services directly to citizens within the region in order to establish an identity with citizens and officials from local governments.
- They should have their own tax base or independent source of revenue and not be dependent upon other governments for their financial viability.
- They should have exclusive domain for delivery of specified services that are not duplicative of, or competitive with, services provided by other local governments.[71]

Besides the opposition from governments to enhancing the role of regional councils, they also face increased competition from other regional organizations. These include a variety of private sector associations, non-profit organizations, foundations, environmental organizations, economic development agencies, and chambers of commerce that have recently established or discovered a regional mission. With all the other organizations becoming involved, the potential for regional councils to be dominant organizations in regional governance will be seriously eroded without some restructuring and aggressive leadership.[72]

On the positive side, regional councils have furthered regionalism if just by providing a focus and a forum for discussion and debate on selected regional issues. Some councils have been instrumental in fostering regional action on selected issues. The Northwest Municipal Conference, discussed below, is an example of a COG that has been successful in engendering action on a number of regional issues. On balance, regional councils can be judged as neither disasters in regional governance nor as wildly successful. One observer writes positively about regional councils' contributions to regional governance as follows:

> [T]here are grounds for viewing COGs and other regional authorities with favor, for they are learning devices, which serve to acquaint public officials and the community in general with the nature of areawide problems and the necessity of approaching them on a coordinated basis. They have helped to create a sense of regional community and provided a number of services that may have been lacking before. Finally, given previous failures in the establishment of regional governing structures, the COG has been a major achievement—worth all of the effort and resources that the federal and local governments have put into it, provided the COG is seen developmentally, and not as a final form.[73]

Supporters of regional councils suggest that they can remain important players in regional governance as long as they continue to be used by state and federal governments for planning activities and grant distribution. With federal and state programs to administer, councils can provide a regional influence. The Southern California Association of Governments (SCAG), covering the Los Angeles region, has become a strong regional force in multiple functions because of powers granted it through state and federal agencies. It is the designated metropolitan planning organization (MPO) for distribution of federal transportation funds. It is also the regional agency with planning and review powers in pollution control under the federal Water Pollution Control Act of 1972 and the amendments to the Clean Air Act of 1990. In addition, the state has designated SCAG to implement state policy in housing, hazardous-waste management, air quality, and environmental review.[74]

Professional associations also recognize the need for regional cooperation and advocate an expanded role for regional councils. The International City Management Association's Futures/Vision Consortium indicated in its 1991 report that local governments face problems that cannot be addressed by single jurisdictions and recommended regional approaches to address common issues. A report on the future of regionalism, issued by the National Association of Regional Councils, says recognition of the region as the

> playing field for public and private activity is increasing: not because of federal requirements but because of the practicalities of business activity, the larger geographical realm in which people live and work, and the need for more realistic public decision making.[75]

Even though regional councils are controversial, social scientists Patricia Florestano and Laura Wilson-Gentry found strong support for them in a survey of Maryland, a state with a legal and political tradition of strong, independent local governments. Survey respondents were state and local appointed and elected officials. They were almost unanimous in their support for councils' traditional roles. Over 90 percent thought councils should remain a regional forum and continue reviewing regional projects, and over 80 percent wanted councils to continue their roles of seeking federal funds and helping to set regional goals. They were less willing to support more activist roles in implementing state programs (63 percent opposed), delivering services (56 percent opposed), or documenting compliance of constituent governments (48 percent opposed). While realizing the value of regional councils in assisting in regional solutions, state and local officials are divided on the issue of expansion of councils' roles. The survey, however, documented strong support (73 percent) for councils serving as umbrella agencies for regional planning efforts.[76] The researchers were cautious in their conclusions from the survey on the future roles of regional councils in Maryland:

> Overall, little support is shown for activist roles, but there is support for improving current functions. Second, there is little major difference between elected and appointed officials on most of these issues, although the elected officials generally tended to be slightly more positive about all aspects of regional activity. On the whole, we are less positive than when we started that regionalism and regional agencies will play a major role in solving state and local problems in the future. While we do not believe such agencies will go out of business, our data does not indicate that they will greatly expand their roles in years to come.[77]

Regional Councils in Two Metropolitan Areas

Northwest Municipal Conference

To further understand how regional councils operate, following are descriptions of the operation of two regional councils. The Northwest Municipal Conference (NWMC), a COG in the Chicago area, began in

1958 with eight northwest suburbs as members. The conference met monthly to discuss mutual problems (water supply, flood control, refuse disposal, police and fire coordination, and zoning in unincorporated land), exchange viewpoints, develop common solutions, and speak as a body for achieving common goals. Over the years, the NWMC expanded to some 42 local governments in the north and northwest Chicago suburbs. Each municipality has a representative on the conference's board of directors. All municipalities have an equal vote regardless of their population size. NWMC is not a planning or research organization but an organization whose major purpose is to provide member services. Regional issues of interest to member governments are discussed and, occasionally, decisions are reached and action taken.

The conference is only as effective as the active participation of its members. Members are involved through a committee structure, where the real work of the conference takes place. These committees oversee a substantial conference program. The largest single expenditure, approximately 25 percent of the budget, goes for legislative activity. The conference serves as the voice for its members promoting municipal interests and concerns at the county, state, and national levels. Its legislative role has evolved and expanded over the years. It maintains a fully staffed office in the state capitol during each legislative session and schedules and co-ordinates testimony from member municipalities on municipal issues. The lobby activity of the conference is chiefly directed at the state, where it seeks to have an annual legislative agenda accepted by the state legislature. Efforts are made, however, to influence public opinion on key state legislative issues as well as Cook County ordinances of interest to conference members. The conference also is involved with the congressional delegation from the area on actions in Washington, DC, of concern to member municipalities.

In addition to lobby activities, member services include promoting regional cooperation and serving as a vehicle for regional activities that benefit member governments. Among its intergovernmental cooperative accomplishments are the following:

- Entry-level screening for firefighters and police officers. It coordinates physical agility testing and administers written exams. Test results from the physical and written tests are provided to the member municipalities for their hiring processes.
- Training and education programs for local government officials and employees. It conducts surveys, maintains an information clearing-house, and provides staff assistance to many cooperative ventures not requiring separate staff or organizations.
- Intergovernmental Personnel Benefit Cooperative, a pooled health insurance cooperative for members.

- A joint-purchasing cooperative for consumable supplies and an auction for the disposal of members' surplus property, such as cars, trucks, heavy equipment, and some small public works-related equipment.
- The conference was instrumental in organizing the Solid Waste Agency of Northern Cook County (SWANCC) charged with implementing recycling and solid waste disposal plans for members.
- NWMC served as the forum for discussions that resulted in the forming of organizations to bring water from Lake Michigan to supplement members' well water.
- Through the conference, a model cable television ordinance and an organization were established to be a consumer advocate for residents concerning local cable franchises, operations, programming, and rate regulations.
- NWMC led a coalition that brought additional commuter rail service to the northwest suburbs.[78]

As an organization existing to serve its members, there is little involvement with federal initiatives. The two exceptions are in manpower and transportation. The conference is involved in the Private Industry Council of Northern Cook County as the public sector partner. It provides oversight duties and prepares quarterly reports of the activities of the council. Although it is not the federally designated metropolitan planning organization for the region, NWMC receives some federal funds for transportation planning. It performs technical studies and data collection and serves as a liaison between member municipalities and various regional and state transportation agencies.

The Intergovernmental Cooperation Council in Milwaukee[79]

The council consists of Milwaukee and the other 18 municipal governments in Milwaukee County. Council activities often go beyond the borders in reaching out to other entities on intergovernmental cooperation projects. The intergovernmental cooperation commitment is to engage in regional planning, engage in ongoing, open and meaningful discussions to ensure a cohesive approach to decision making and problem solving for the region, and to share the benefits and costs of regional initiatives. Milwaukee is the major staff support to the council. Some recent intergovernmental cooperative projects and concerns are:

- Recently, Milwaukee and the city of Wauwatosa worked together to transform a former landfill into a park with residential opportunities. This joint effort resulted in environmental, recreational and tax revenue benefits.

- Milwaukee and neighboring municipalities have agreements with a variety of utilities to provide services and infrastructure. These agreements include public works services, such as recycling.
- Milwaukee has Mutual Aid Agreements with neighboring communities regarding fire services. The City provides hazardous material (HAZMAT) and biological threat abatement services for the region.
- Milwaukee and Waukesha Counties have a fuel purchase agreement that substantially reduces cost of fuel.

The Milwaukee County Intergovernmental Cooperation Council provides a means for all 19 cities and villages in the county to discuss and resolve contentious issues. As technology continues to advance, the process of sharing information, maps, vital statistics, and more becomes even easier, which enhances decision-making. Milwaukee is aggressive in wanting to develop cooperative agreements. It has developed a cooperation plan and has listed a number of goals that it wants to accomplish through intergovernmental cooperation. Goals in its cooperation plan include improving communication and working relationships between the city and its government partners, promoting a more comprehensive and coordinated metropolitan approach to planning, development and service delivery, and cooperating with other governments on revenue streams and efficiencies.

Takeaway

In decentralized metropolitan areas, cooperation and contracting services are an alternative means of service delivery. It is claimed that through these mechanisms more efficient and effective service delivery can be achieved. Cooperation, interlocal service agreements, and contracting with the private sector also introduce more of a regional perspective. A unique form of interlocal agreement is called the Lakewood Plan. This plan involves contracting for the provision of a number of services by one government from the county. Under this concept one government could contract for most, if not all, of its services from another government, from the private sector, or from a combination of the public, nonprofit and private sectors. Various forms of contracting have become increasingly popular across the country as a significant alternative source of service delivery.

Cooperation in service delivery is becoming more popular in this environment of fiscal austerity and budget constraints. However, the problems associated with cooperation and contracting should be carefully assessed before local governments embrace the concept. The problems involving accountability, transaction costs, reduction of local control and other issues should be carefully considered before entering into any cooperative agreement.

Other cooperative mechanisms to promote regionalism are regional councils known as councils of governments (COGs) and regional planning commissions (RPCs). The effectiveness of regional councils is dependent upon funding, membership, and commitment. Generally COGs are effective on issues only when their members reach consensus. Many COGs do not cover the entire metropolitan area or do not cover the major governments within their geographical area. It appears that smaller and poorer municipalities are more prone to join and participate in COG programs because of the financial benefits. Wealthy communities often remain outside of COGs and do not participate as much in regional activities. All communities involved in COGs tend to be involved only to the extent of their self-interest, not to further regional governance. Federal subsidies were an important funding stream for the development of regional councils and remain an important funding stream for their functioning. The future of the regional council movement is heavily dependent on external funding sources and on outside incentives for local governments to come together in cooperative endeavors.

Notes

1. National Conference of Catholic Bishops, "Economic Justice for All: Pastoral Letter on Catholic Social Teaching and the U.S. Economy," 1986, p. 448. http://www.usccb.org/upload/economic_justice_for_all.pdf [Accessed Jan. 14, 2014].
2. Mancur Olson, Jr., *The Logic of Collective Action: Public Goods and the Theory of Groups* (New York: Schocken Books, 1965).
3. Donald F. Norris, "Killing a COG: The Death and Reincarnation of the Baltimore Regional Council of Governments," *Journal of Urban Affairs*, 16 (2) (1994): 157.
4. Quoted in Frank Smallwood, "A New Approach: Three Alternatives Outlined to Make Our Traditional Home Rule Doctrines Compatible with Modern Needs," *National Civic Review*, 56 (May) (1967): 251.
5. Ibid.
6. Quoted in Lawrence S. Leiken, "Governmental Schemes for the Metropolis and the Implementation of Metropolitan Change," *Journal of Urban Law*, 49 (1972): 673.
7. Bernard H. Ross and Myron A. Levine, *Urban Politics: Cities and Suburbs in a Global Age*, 8th ed. (Armonk, NY: M. E. Sharpe, 2012), p. 252.
8. Ibid., p. 251.
9. Amanda M. Girth and Jocelyn M. Johnston, *Local government Contracting*, National League of Cities Research Brief on America's Cities, February 2011, http://www.nlc.org/build-skills-and-networks/resources/research-reports [Accessed Nov. 24, 2012].
10. International City Management Association, *Profile of Local Government Service Delivery Choices, 2007*, http://bookstore.icma.org/data_sets_c42.cfm [Accessed Nov. 24; 2012].
11. Lasa W. Forderaro, "Towns Sharing Services to Cut Costs," *New York Times*, July 15, 1991, sec. A, p. 16.

12. Chuck Rasch, "Recession-Battered Cities Combine Services," *USA Today*, October 18, 2012, wwwlusatoday.com/story/news/nation/212/10/18/recession [Accessed October 24, 2012].
13. Mark Tower, "Saginaw City Official to Return to County Committee Wednesday with Policing Counter-Proposal," December 4, 2012, http://blog.mlive.com/saginawnews_impact/print.html [Accessed Dec. 5, 2012].
14. "City Fiscal Outlook Better, Infrastructure Top Concern," *PA Times*, Aug. 1, 1995, p. 1.
15. Melissa Reiser, "Governments Learn to Work Together," *Arlington Heights (Ill.) Daily Herald*, Mar. 1, 1990, sec. 5, p. 1.
16. Josh Hafner, "Cities and Towns are Collaborating More Often to Provide More and Better Services to Residents," Nov. 12, 2012, www.desmoinesregister.com/article 20121113/news [Accessed Nov. 13, 2012].
17. National Association of Counties Research Foundation, *Interlocal Service Delivery* (Washington, DC: National Association of Counties, 1982), pp. 10–11.
18. "Joint City, County Government Center Planning ok'd," *The Californian*, May 1, 2012, www.thecalifonian.com/fdcp/?unique+1336664968078 [Accessed May 5, 2012].
19. Kelly Smith, "To Boost Tourism, Cities turn to Lake Minnetonka's Liquid Assets," July 15, 2012, www.startribune.com [Accessed July 16, 2012].
20. Raymond Cox, Service *Sharing: The Akron Experience*, Presentation at the Annual Urban Affairs Association Conference, Pittsburgh, April 19–21, 2012.
21. Chuck Abernathy, "Practical Strategies for Consolidation," *Public Management*, (October) (2012): 20–22.
22. Kurt Thurmaier and Curtis Wood, "Interlocal Agreements as Overlapping Social Networks: Picket-Fence Regionalism in Metropolitan Kansas City," *Public Administration Review*, 62 (5) (2002): 585–596.
23. Kelly Leroux and Jered B. Carr, "Prospects for Centralizing Services in an Urban County: Evidence From Eight Self-Organized Networks of Local Public Services," *Journal of Urban Affairs*, 32 (4) (2010): 461–465.
24. Mike Johnson, "Report: Fire Department Consolidation would Save 5 Communities Millions," *Journal Sentinel*, May 30, 2012, www.jsonline.com/news/milwaukee/report [Accessed Jan. 9, 2013].
25. Abby Sewell, "Santa Ana Disbands Fire Department in Bid to Rescue Budget," *La Times*, March 6, 2012, www.latimes.com/news/local/la-me-fire-dept-cuts-20120306,0,518723 [Accessed March 7, 2012].
26. Bob Goldsborough, "Consultant: DuPage County Fire Departments should Merge to Save Taxpayer Money," *Chicago Tribune*, May 10, 2012, www.chicagotribune.com/news/local/ct-met-dupage-comm [Accessed May 10, 2012].
27. Deb Gruver, "City, County to Consolidate Code Enforcement Departments," *The Wichita Eagle*. August 30, 2012, www.kansas.com/2012/08/29/ [Accessed Aug. 31, 2012].
28. Justin Faulconer, "Bedford City unveils potential last city budget," *News Advance*, May 1, 2012, www2.newsadvance.com/news/2012/may/01/Bedford-city-unveils-potential-last-city-budget-ar-1883911 [Accessed May 2, 2012].
29. National Association of Counties Research Foundation, *Interlocal Service Delivery* (Washington, DC: National Association of Counties, 1982), pp. 11–12.
30. David Osborne and Ted Gaebler, *Reinventing Government: How the Entrepreneurial Spirit Is Transforming the Public Sector* (Reading, MA: Addison-Wesley, 1992), pp. 80–84.
31. Ibid., p. 181.

32. Ibid., pp. 25–48.
33. Jonas Prager, "Contracting Out Government Services: Lessons from the Private Sector," *Public Administration Review*, 54 (March/April) (1994): 180.
34. Ibid.
35. Sung-Wook Kwon and Richard C. Feiock, "Overcoming the Barriers to Cooperation: Intergovernmental Service Agreements," *Public Administration Review*, 70 (6) (2010): 876–884.
36. Matthew J. McKinney and Shawn Johnson, *Working Across Boundaries: People, Nature and Regions* (Cambridge, MA: Lincoln Institute of Land Policy, 2009), p. 5.
37. National Association of Counties Research Foundation, *Interlocal Service Delivery*, p. 12.
38. Amanda M. Girth, Amir Hefetz, Jocelyn M. Johnston, and Mildred E. Warner, "Outsourcing Public Service Delivery: Management Responses in Noncompetitive Markets," *2012 Public Administration Review*, 72 (6) (2012): 888–889.
39. M. Ernita Joaquin and Thomas J. Greitens, "Contract Management Capacity Breakdown? An Analysis of U.S. Local Governments," *Public Administration Review*, 72 (6) (2012): 808.
40. John C. Bollens and Henry J. Schmandt, *The Metropolis: Its People, Politics, and Economic Life*, 3rd ed. (New York: Harper and Row, 1975), p. 303.
41. Ross and Levine, *Urban Politics: Cities and Suburbs in a Global Age*, pp. 252–253.
42. John Rogers, "California Officials Could Put End to High-Paid Los Angeles Suburb," *Lubbock Avalanche-Journal*, December 26, 2010, p. A4.
43. Bollens and Schmandt, *The Metropolis: Its People, Politics, and Economic Life*, p. 303.
44. John J. Harrigan, *Political Change in the Metropolis*, 5th ed. (New York: HarperCollins College Publishers, 1993), p. 292.
45. Ross and Levine, *Urban Politics: Cities and Suburbs in a Global Age*.
46. http://www.westonfl.org; http://centennialcolorado.com/index.aspx?NID=460 [Accessed Jan 21, 2013].
47. National Service to Regional Councils, *Regionalism: A New Dimension in Local Government and Intergovernmental Relations* (Washington, DC: 1971), p. 4.
48. Ibid., pp. 4–5.
49. Ibid.
50. Ibid., p. 6.
51. Ibid.
52. Ibid.
53. Florida Advisory Council on Intergovernmental Relations, *Substate Regional Governance: Evolution and Manifestations Throughout the United States and Florida* (Tallahassee, FL: November 1991), p. 53.
54. Charles P. Shannon, "The Rise and Emerging Fall of Metropolitan Area Regional Associations," in J. Edwin Benton and David R. Morgan, (eds.), *Intergovernmental Relations and Public Policy* (Westport, CT: Greenwood Press, 1986), p. 65.
55. Norris, "Killing a COG," p. 156.
56. Florida Advisory Council on Intergovernmental Relations, *Substate Regional Governance*, p. 38.
57. Patricia Atkins, "From the Mauling to the Malling of Regionalism," *Public Administration Review*, 53 (November/December) (1993): 583–584.
58. Sherman M. Wyman, "Profiles and Prospects: Regional Councils and Their Executive Directors," *1994 Municipal Year Book* (Washington, DC: International City/County Management Association, 1994), pp. 43–56.

59. Florida Advisory Council on Intergovernmental Relations, *Substate Regional Governance*, pp. 68–71.
60. Shannon, "The Rise and Emerging Fall of Metropolitan Area Regional Associations," pp. 64–71.
61. Joseph A. James and David Young Miller, *An Assessment of the Eight Councils of Governments in Allegheny County* (Pittsburgh, PA: Pennsylvania Economy League, 1994), pp. 1–3.
62. Shannon, "The Rise and Emerging Fall of Metropolitan Area Regional Associations," pp. 66–68.
63. Ibid., p. 71.
64. Florida Advisory Council on Intergovernmental Relations, *Substate Regional Governance*, pp. 173–230.
65. Wyman, "Profiles and Prospects," p. 50.
66. John J. Harrigan and Ronald K. Vogel, *Political Change in the Metropolis*, 7th ed. (New York: Longman, 2003), p. 298.
67. Arthur B. Gunlicks, "Problems, Politics, and Prospects of Local Government Reorganization in the United States," in Arthur B. Gunlicks (ed.), *Local Government Reform and Reorganization: An International Perspective* (Port Washington, NY: Kennikat Press, 1981), p. 20.
68. Harrigan and Vogel, *Political Change in the Metropolis*, p. 298.
69. Jeffrey Henig, David Brunori, and Mark Ebert, "Washington, D.C.: Cautious and Constrained Cooperation," in H.V. Savitch and Ronald K. Vogel (eds.), *Regional Politics: America in a Post-City Age* (Thousand Oaks, CA: Sage Publications, 1996), pp. 107–109.
70. Gunlicks, "Problems, Politics, and Prospects of Local Government Reorganization in the United States," p. 21.
71. Norris, "Killing a COG," pp. 165–166.
72. Wyman, "Profiles and Prospects," pp. 43–56.
73. Gunlicks, "Problems, Politics, and Prospects of Local Government Reorganization in the United States," p. 21.
74. Scott A. Bollens, "Fragments of Regionalism: The Limits of Southern California Governance," *Journal of Urban Affairs*, 19 (1) (1997): 115–116.
75. Quoted in Patricia S. Florestano and Laura Wilson-Gentry, "The Acceptability of Regionalism in Solving State and Local Problems," *Spectrum: The Journal of State Government*, 67 (Summer) (1994): 27.
76. Ibid., p. 30.
77. Ibid., p. 32.
78. Northwest Municipal Conference, nwmc-cog.org [Accessed Oct. 15, 2011].
79. The majority of the information for this section is taken from City of Milwaukee, *Intergovernmental Cooperation*, www.cityofmilwaukee/intergov(1)pdf [Accessed Jan. 9, 2013].

8 The County and Regional Governance

Increasing metropolitan scale and development of megalopolises will generate additional pressures for transfer of functional responsibilities.
—Advisory Commission on Intergovernmental Relations, 1976[1]

In this chapter the county's evolution (or potential) as a major provider of regional services is considered. The county's evolution from an administrative arm of the state to a major role in regional services may occur through a comprehensive restructuring or on an ad hoc basis, one service at a time. The best example of comprehensive county restructuring was that of Miami-Dade County, which was discussed in Chapter 4. Most of the increase in the number of county functions occurs through the piecemeal transfer of functions. Regional reformers accept the county as a reasonable alternative to traditional metropolitan government or city–county consolidation because it covers a larger geographical area than the city and is an already established and accepted government. The major problems with this solution to regional governance are the traditional limited role of the county and the multi-county metropolitan area. It is possible that county political leaders would reach out to neighboring counties and community leaders to form partnerships and coalitions on regional governance issues. However, regionalists argue that the county government structure must be reformed to make it a more representative government including a separation of the legislative and executive functions. In addition, the county must have greater independence from the state.

Consideration of the county as a major provider of regional services started in the 1930s as part of the county home rule movement, but it received serious consideration as a viable alternative to traditional reform in the late 1960s and 1970s. This chapter begins with a discussion of the traditional role of the county in the local government system, followed by an analysis of the home rule movement including the various proposals to restructure the county. The county's increasing role in the provision of regional services is discussed and a comparative analysis of two counties and their regional roles is provided. Finally, the prognosis for the county as a regional government is analyzed.

The Role of Counties in the Local Government System

The traditional role of the county is to serve as an administrative arm of the state in providing certain state-mandated services and limited local government functions in unincorporated areas. The county has no choice or option in the provision of state-mandated functions. Many services, including indigent services and recordkeeping, are even beyond the policy or fiscal control of the county and are client- or formula-driven. Other mandated services allow the county some discretion in the level of services provided, for example, the extent of road construction and maintenance. The county's responsibility in unincorporated areas is to provide limited municipal services including police protection, roads, parks, and recreation. In addition, in many states the county may provide services jointly with municipalities (or for them) through interlocal agreements.[2]

When an area incorporates, the municipality takes over the county's limited municipal functions, but the county continues providing state-mandated administrative functions, such as legal recordkeeping, the judicial function, welfare, and health services. For instance, keeping the peace becomes a municipal function after the incorporation. The county's police responsibilities in incorporated areas are to provide specialized assistance, as requested, and to serve the needs of the judicial system. Upon incorporation, the municipality also assumes the major development function for the area, such as building and maintaining local streets. The county continues to be responsible for maintaining its road system but its road-building function within the incorporated municipality generally ends.

Although county services vary by state and region of the country, counties are the largest providers of human and social services (welfare, hospitals, public health, and corrections). The county has only a minor role in physical development and maintenance (highways and streets, sewerage, water supply, parks, recreation, libraries). Public safety, sanitation functions, physical development and maintenance activities have traditionally been considered as municipal-type functions. The county's role in local government may be limited or extensive depending on the policies of the state, the existence and responsibilities of townships, and the size and age of the municipality. One study of 162 counties in 50 of the largest metropolitan areas found that counties in the West, in aggregate, provide the most services, with an average of 16.2 services per county, followed closely by counties in New York, New Jersey, and Pennsylvania with an average of 16.0. Counties in the South were third with an average of 14.5 services. The weakest counties in providing services are in the Midwest and New England. Midwest counties provide an average of 12.6 services, and New England counties provide 10.3 services. Counties in the South and West are the most involved in the nation in infrastructure and physical development functions. Involvement in these functions (streets and highways, sanitation, sewerage, public transportation, and utilities) indicates the importance of counties in these parts of the country relative to the other regions. However, Pennsylvania, New Jersey, and New York, as opposed to the remainder of the Northeast region, also exhibit strong county roles which are almost equal to southern and western counties in providing developmental functions.[3]

Early Development of County Government

Modern county government reflects the heritage of the many nationalities of people who originally settled in America. These colonists brought government traditions with them but the unique needs in different areas in the colonies required adaptation. Counties in New England were limited mainly to judicial functions while towns were vested with significant governing authority. These governing structures met the economic and security demands of concentrated communities. In New York and Pennsylvania, both counties and cities developed substantial political authority. Further south, counties in Virginia emerged as the dominant local governmental power.[4]

Sociology professor Roland Liebert contends that the need for a uniform system of justice was a major impetus for the development of the county system in America. During most of the colonial period, commerce and industry were primarily matters of individual enterprise by isolated townsmen or were organized into small shops with strictly local employment. A neutrally acceptable judicial system for protection and enforcement of civil agreements or commercial contracts was developed and applied by each municipality. However, as trade increased among the colonies and companies grew, locally interpreted law was not acceptable. Contracts made in one place were sometimes not honored in another, as each locality sought to protect its own economy. As commerce grew and interdependence between colonial cities developed, it became clear that a uniform system of justice to resolve contract disputes was needed.[5]

After independence, the new nation established a uniform system of justice covering contracts and agreements. Cities no longer had power to develop and administer law in this area. To administer the judicial system, keep legal records, and perform other minor administrative functions, counties, as geographically defined administrative districts, were established in most states. Significantly, those cities that had a colonial tradition of judicial autonomy often retained administrative responsibility for these state-supervised functions. That is, although counties were established in these areas, colonial cities maintained a large degree of autonomy, and the county's role was less significant. Municipalities in the entire region of New England maintained a significant degree of autonomy from the county. Philadelphia, New Orleans, and San Francisco consolidated with their counties. City–county separation was another method to maintain city autonomy. This was done in St. Louis and Baltimore, and is mandated for cities in Virginia when they reach a certain size. In the more rural areas of the former colonies and in western territories, there were no local government traditions. As new cities were established and grew, they typically remained subject to the administrative functions assigned to counties by the state.[6]

The county's role in the local government system thus evolved differently depending on the area of the country. That heritage continues to affect the county as it continues to change in the twenty-first century. The variation in county service delivery is one indicator of the differences in the importance of counties in the various regions of the country. In New England, as discussed above, counties provide fewer services than in other areas. Two New England states (Connecticut and Rhode Island) have no counties. Starting with the Depression and accelerating with the suburban movement after World War II, the county, in most parts of the country, assumed new services or significantly expanded services and has become a much more important actor in local governance.

Reforming County Government Structure

The county was generally not considered a target in the progressive reform era. In the early era of regional government reform, most of the attention was placed on extending city boundaries, first through annexation and then by extending city boundaries to include the entire county and eliminating the county as an entity. The county did not initially receive attention as a viable alternative in the regional reform movement because it provided limited services. It was viewed as an administrative arm of the state—an arbitrary geographical division of the state for convenience in implementing state laws. Because of the lack of interest in county government reform, one of the early reformers, Henry S. Gilbertson, characterized the county as the "dark continent of American politics."[7]

Belatedly, attention was focused on the county as a potential regional government. The reformers sought to reorganize county governments and authorize them to provide more extensive municipal and regional functions. In 1929 the National Municipal League prepared a model county manager charter recommending the same appointed manager system as that advocated for municipal government.[8] In order to achieve the reformers' goals, the county had to have more freedom from state constraints. Home rule would provide this freedom. Without home rule powers, the county could only provide those services authorized by the state. With home rule powers, the county would be able to provide all local government services except those specifically prohibited by the state. One other caveat in county home rule was the relationship between the powers of the county and municipalities within the county. County home rule would not supersede or replace authority of municipalities to provide a service.

Reformers argued that with home rule powers, the county could be reorganized and authorized to provide municipal and regional services.[9] According to reformers, county government, as it existed, was structurally and functionally not capable of being an effective provider of municipal services. The major criticisms were:

1. The structure of county government requiring numerous elected administrative officials diffuses the political leadership thereby rendering the county incapable of effective government.
2. Problem solving in a non-centralized administrative system with no chief executive is problematic.
3. The county lacks the legal authority to provide the broad range of services which people expect.
4. Additional dysfunctional features are lack of a civil service system; lack of trained, capable personnel; and restricted taxing powers.[10]

The Advisory Commission on Intergovernmental Relations (ACIR) recommended the following regarding restructuring of counties in 1962:

• States should enact legislation authorizing governmental units wholly within a county to transfer responsibility for specific governmental services to the county by coordinating mutual action of the governing bodies concerned.
• States should enact enabling legislation to permit county governments, individually or jointly, to establish machinery for the performance of service functions desired and required by their residents.
• Counties should be permitted to adopt, pursuant to simple petition or referendum administrative procedures, and optional forms of county government.
• Municipalities and counties should be given all residual powers of government not denied by the state constitution or by general law.[11]

Most proposals for modernizing county government center on creating an elected executive similar to a strong mayor system or an appointed manager similar to the city manager system and centralizing administrative authority over most county services. Although 37 of the 47 states with viable county governments have adopted some form of county home rule power, 13 restrict home rule to certain counties or limit the grant of home rule powers. Only 24 states provide broad grants of home rule powers to all their counties including extensive taxing and service provision authority and the power to frame and adopt their own county charters. According to research by the National Association of Counties, of the 3,068 counties, approximately 800 have an appointed or elected county manager/administrator form of government. Only 153 have adopted a charter form of government giving them broad powers.[12]

What are the results of reformers' efforts to restructure and enhance the municipal powers of county government? The success of adoption has been disappointing to those regional reformers who had hoped for home rule counties to assume strong regional governance roles. Some states are more active in adoption of home rule than other states. New York with 21 and Louisiana with 23 lead in home rule charter adoption. Florida is next with 19 followed by California with 13. These four states have 50 percent of the home rule counties. A number of states that allow home rule or charter adoption have, so far, had no adoptions.[13]

Home rule referendums have been held in numerous counties, but most have not been approved by the voters. Since the 1970s, interest has waned in county home rule, and efforts to adopt charters have declined. Interest has been mainly confined to a few states. For example, in the 1990s the majority of the home rule activity took place in Colorado, Florida, Louisiana, Maryland, and Montana. The efforts in most of these states were not successful. Voters in Colorado defeated all six proposed charters; Maryland rejected all eight proposed charters, and Montana soundly rejected 11 of the 12 charters presented to the voters. Florida and Louisiana had the most success with six of seven charters passed in Louisiana and five of nine approved in Florida. Overall, 71 charters were presented to the voters between 1990 and 1998 with 23 accepted for a 32 percent acceptance rate.[14]

Many county home rule proposals have been submitted to the voters more than once. In Oregon, for example, four counties have failed on three attempts. In other counties, successful home rule votes have often required numerous efforts. Four of the eight successful charters in Oregon were approved on the second or third vote. Montana requires its county governments to review their structure every ten years and submit an alternate form to the voters. Out of 56 counties, voters have approved only three changes: two city–county consolidations and one county manager form. Voters in Illinois have rejected all 11 efforts (two counties tried twice) to obtain an elected executive system of government.[15] In Pennsylvania only about a third of the home rule charters or optional plans (7 of 21 attempts) have been accepted by the voters. The major activity and success in Pennsylvania was during the 1970s. Pennsylvania voters in the 1980s, with only one exception, voted against even the formation of government study commissions, rejecting five of six efforts. The one exception was in Schuylkill County in 1982, where the voters approved a county government study commission but rejected the home rule charter developed by the commission. Of the seven home rule counties in Pennsylvania, five were approved in the 1970s, Allegheny County home rule was approved in the 1990s and Luzerne County voters approved home rule in 2010 on the third try. The voters had previously rejected proposals in 1974 and 2003.[16]

Politics of County Reform

County home rule is controversial because it invariably involves restructuring and additional grants of authority. Those opposed readily assert that a restructured county, freed from state constraints, is the first step to usurping local community control. Opponents often make the connection between county home rule and metropolitan government. Since the voters defeat most metropolitan government or city–county consolidation proposals, successful county home rule efforts are also problematic. Studies of unsuccessful efforts to obtain county home rule suggest most of the same factors that are evident in voter rejection of more comprehensive regional reform efforts. Voters tend to equate the two as an attempt to subvert municipal government. For example, a study of an unsuccessful effort to gain home rule for Summit County, Ohio found that residents generally remain apathetic to county home rule. The apathetic voter either stays home or tends to vote the status quo. Educating voters and drawing supportive voters to the polls are important in obtaining voter approval.[17] The perception of a crisis in county government service delivery is important in mobilizing supportive voters. A home rule charter was ultimately approved for Summit County in 1979. It remains one of only two counties in Ohio that have home rule charters. The other county is Cuyahoga County.

Most county restructuring efforts do not make it to a vote. In one Ohio county a self-appointed citizens' committee composed of a small group of business leaders spent eight months developing a home rule charter for the county, which proposed the establishment of a county executive form of government and the elimination of elected county row offices. There was immediate opposition from a number of elected county and local government officials when the charter was unveiled. Concerns were voiced over the "extreme" centralization of power within a single executive. There was also concern over whether the county's home rule authority would allow it to dictate to other local governments and would usher in metropolitan government. Finally, those skeptical of the proposal questioned the need to change a government that was working well. The future of this initiative is in doubt because there has not been enough support to obtain the requisite number of signatures to even put it on the ballot.[18]

One researcher identified three variables that primarily account for adoption or rejection of charter change attempts by the voters. The most important variable is the number and types of groups traditionally involved in local government decision making. The more groups involved and the more educated on local government issues they are and the greater the chances of their active support for a home rule charter. Group involvement leads to greater newspaper coverage of study commission proceedings and relatively smaller changes in the structure recommended which improves the chances for success. Also, the more groups involved in campaigning for acceptance of the recommendations, the greater the chances for a successful conclusion.[19]

The other two variables identified by this researcher are (1) the amount of conflict generated with respect to the study process, and (2) the campaign and the stand taken by local politicians on the study commission's recommendations. Recommendations are more likely to succeed where almost no conflict is generated and where local political leaders are supportive. It was found that party affiliation and socioeconomic status are factors in the presence or absence of conflict. Conflict is more prevalent in communities with more Democratic Party voters and residents who have relatively lower income and are less educated, working-class people. Community conflict is also likely where local political officials oppose the recommendations. Elected officials will generally be more supportive of incremental changes than major changes.[20] Without the active support of political leaders, county home rule is extremely difficult to obtain. Political officials, unless they have been discredited, generally have a broad base of support and can exercise an extensive amount of influence with voters. Therefore, an additional element affecting political support is the number of elected officials in the proposed county home rule charter. The more elected officials retained, the greater the chances of gaining voter approval.[21]

Although opposition to county government reform remains strong and the rate of success is miniscule, there is continuing interest in reform in some areas. Two large counties ushered in new charters in 2011. Voters in Cuyahoga County in Ohio and Macomb County in Michigan approved new county charters.[22] Frederick County, Maryland in November 2012 joined the ranks of home rule counties by voting overwhelmingly to change their county charter with 62.6 percent in favor.[23]

Efforts of One County in the Quest for Home Rule[24]

The Pennsylvania General Assembly passed Act 62, the Home Rule Charter and Optional Plans Law (53 PS 1–201–211, 2–203), in 1972 establishing the process for municipal and county governments to obtain home rule. The process established by Act 62 provided for a nonpartisan election for the establishment of a study commission. The commission could then propose a home rule charter, an optional form of government, or decide that no change is needed. Immediately after the act was passed, there was a flurry of home rule activity across the state. However, the pent-up desires to explore home rule faded quickly.

Allegheny County made two attempts to obtain home rule in the 1970s. Both the 1972 and the 1977 attempts were soundly defeated. Because of the crushing defeat of the 1977 effort, the issue of county home rule was not further addressed for 16 years. In 1993 the release of a report by the county controller calling for home rule placed it back on the public agenda. Because of the failure to obtain home rule in the 1970s under the provisions of Act 62, those supporting home rule in the 1990s sought other ways to proceed. The state legislature passed a new law applicable only to Allegheny County that stipulated an appointed, rather than an elected, government study commission. The stipulated process for appointing a charter writing commission also would ensure that the commission would be fairly representative of the political parties. Following passage of the act, a commission was established. This commission operated like a typical blue ribbon commission with little controversy. Indeed, the basic structure of government had been stipulated by the enabling legislation, so the potential for controversy on basic structure and other issues that had embroiled the other commissions was mitigated.

In contrast to the 1970s home rule vote campaigns, there was substantial and active leadership support for the 1998 charter. All three serving county commissioners, all but one of the former county commissioners, the former mayor of Pittsburgh, half of the row officers, and a number of state legislators and municipal officials actively campaigned for the charter. Unanimous support of the county commissioners for home rule was unprecedented in Allegheny County reform efforts. An additional contrast to the 1970s was the full and active support of each of the government study commission (GSC) members. All eight members played active roles in the campaign leading up to the vote. The business community had invested considerable effort in lobbying the legislature for passage of the enabling act for the process and the business-funded and led Pennsylvania Economy League had provided staff support to the 1998 GSC. It also invested considerable resources in the vote campaign. Business-led civic associations, particularly the influential Allegheny Conference, and the Pennsylvania Economy League largely directed the Allegheny 2000 Citizens Committee, the home rule advocacy group. Those supporting the home rule charter spent over one million dollars on the vote "yes" campaign, while the organized opposition reported less than $100,000 on the vote "no" campaign.

Despite the huge disparity in the amount of resources expended by the supporters and the opponents, and the non-controversial nature of the charter, the success of the change effort was in doubt. An effort to increase the sales tax for building new sports stadiums and for general development actively supported by the business and political leadership had been handily defeated just six months earlier. The voters were wary of any changes, particularly changes pushed so strongly by the business and political leadership. Many voters chose not to vote on May 19, 1998, the day of the election. Less than 29 percent of the registered voters voted and over

13 percent of those casting ballots did not vote on the home rule question. Voters from the heavily Democratic city and older, depressed suburbs voted against the charter, but the charter lost in the city by only 5,000 votes. The vote from the growing, higher-income suburbs made up the deficit in the city. Still, the charter was only narrowly approved by a razor-thin margin of just 564 votes out of 210,882 votes cast, with 105,723 voting for home rule and 105,159 voting against it.

Allegheny County voters had three opportunities to vote on home rule charters. The charter proposed by the first GSC had many reform elements, but also some controversial populist elements designed to improve participation and access for women and minorities. Politics played a much stronger role in the election of the GSC in 1977. The political leaders were active in pushing their candidates and their particular agendas. The GSC became embroiled in partisan politics. The final commission, an appointed commission, behaved like a typical blue ribbon commission by striking a balance between reform and moderation to make the charter more acceptable to politicians and voters. The business community was the architect of the enabling legislation establishing the appointment process and the parameters of the commission. Moreover, the business-supported civic community provided staff support in the charter writing process and was heavily involved in the campaign for voter approval.

It is evident that the method of selection of the GSC and the writing process were important factors in the success of home rule in Allegheny County. The elected GSCs became too controversial and lost the support of the political leaders and the business community. Indeed, the political leaders not only did not support the elected GSCs' recommended charters, many of them fought actively against them. In contrast, the political leaders and the business community supported the charter submitted by the appointed commission. It is highly likely that Allegheny County would not have achieved home rule status in 1998 if the study commission had been elected rather than appointed.

The Urban County

County services can be divided into traditional, municipal and regional. Traditional county services are such functions as recordkeeping, including land records and vital statistics; property tax assessment and collection; public safety, including police protection in unincorporated areas, courts, prosecution, and jails; public health and welfare services; elections; and maintenance and construction of roads in unincorporated areas. Municipal services are generally provided in unincorporated areas where the county acts as the local government to the residents. Depending on the county's involvement beyond the traditional mandated services to unincorporated areas, services may include fire protection, libraries, neighborhood parks and recreation, refuse and garbage collection, and more extensive local police protection. In many instances, these services are provided by a local special district, or each resident arranges his or her own provision. In some instances county municipal services may be provided in incorporated areas but this requires an interlocal agreement. Regional services are provided countywide in both incorporated and unincorporated areas and include mass transit, airports, junior colleges, solid waste disposal, regional parks, comprehensive land use plans, community development and housing, culture and recreation services, and environmental control. Municipal services would be classified as regional if they are provided countywide.[25]

One type of county government reform championed by reformers as an alternative to comprehensive regional reform has become known as the *urban county*. A county is, or is developing into, an urban county if one or more of the following is evident:

- An increase in the number and complexity of municipal-type functions provided by a county in unincorporated areas,
- Transfer of a function, usually mandated by the state, from incorporated municipalities to the county for provision on a countywide scale,
- Intensification of a long-established function or the assumption of a new one by the county government for provision throughout the county,
- Expansion of cooperative agreements under which a county provides services to municipalities;
- A comprehensive reorganization that simultaneously reallocates municipal functions between municipalities and the county. This has only been accomplished in Miami-Dade County, as was discussed in Chapter 4.[26]

Despite county government structural deficiencies and the limits and controls imposed by the states, services provided by counties are increasing. Traditional services have expanded to meet the needs of the residents and to take advantage of programs as they have become available. As population expands into unincorporated areas, the county's role in providing municipal services increases. One observer has identified the county's provision of regional services as its fastest-growing role, with such functions as transportation, air quality, conservation, landfill and toxic sites, growth management, and economic development increasingly provided by the county. These functions are typically environmental or quality of life issues that address long-range problems. As counties increase and expand their services, they gain political power and increased autonomy from the state and increased stature and visibility as a major local government in the community. In some areas of the country, their service expansion, especially in the provision of regional services, make them the dominant government in the region.[27]

Urban counties are a post-World War II phenomenon. As urban areas rapidly grew, counties were required to provide more extensive services to the growing populations in unincorporated areas. Regional services were provided either through a state-created special district or by the county through a department or an authority. Milwaukee County, the central county of the Milwaukee MA, is an example of how the county's role in service provision expanded in the twentieth century. Until the Depression, both the city of Milwaukee and Milwaukee County provided health and welfare functions. The city's services were much more extensive than those provided by the county and served a much larger population. During the Depression, the city was unable to provide for the health and welfare needs of its population. The federal government provided an array of programs directly to cities to put people back to work and thus became an increasing presence in what had previously been a fairly closed resident–local government relationship. In addition, the county stepped in and provided welfare and health services in Milwaukee when the city was not able to meet these needs.[28]

The federal and county involvement in providing for the residents of Milwaukee affected the traditional city resident–intergovernmental relationship, not just during the Depression but afterward. The city became more dependent on other governments and the county started evolving into a major service provider, not just in unincorporated areas but in incorporated areas as well. The change in the city–county relationship during this period and its lasting effect is evident by tax changes. In 1930, 72 percent of the total taxes levied on Milwaukee's citizens went for city expenditures and only 16 percent went to the county. By 1940, the county's share of tax revenue had climbed to 33 percent. The county's percentage has remained relatively stable at roughly 30 percent. Besides assuming a greater role in health and welfare, the county also assumed responsibility for the city's parks. Thus, the county became and has remained an active provider of services previously delivered only by the city.[29]

Not only are counties becoming more involved in regional service delivery, but the transfer of functions from municipal to county governments is also evident. Particularly, financially distressed central cities are seeking to shed functions to cut expenses. Counties can justifiably provide financial support or assume administration of functions previously provided by the central city that benefit the entire county, such as sports stadiums, zoos, parks, art museums, and other cultural facilities. For example, Pittsburgh in the early 1990s announced that it would no longer continue funding cultural facilities, museums, and recreational facilities that were enjoyed as much or more by suburbanites as by city residents. The city's decision not to continue its financial support resulted in the establishment of a regional asset district to fund these facilities on a countywide basis.

The growing interest in transfer of functions from municipalities to the county level has been reported in a number of surveys. One survey of 33 municipalities in a metro area in Florida found 30 percent of responding municipalities were interested in transferring one or more functions to the county. Table 8.1 reports the results of another survey of municipalities interested in transferring functions to the county. The majority in the survey gave reasons associated with the municipality's inability to adequately provide the service. Almost as many indicated their desire for saving money by achieving economies of scale and eliminating duplication. The major functions transferred to the county are specialized public safety functions, such as police and fire training and crime labs. The next most transferred functions are selected public works functions.

Counties in Florida and Los Angeles County, California, provide extensive municipal services. More than 50 percent of the population in Florida lives in unincorporated areas, and this population depends on counties for the majority of their services. The municipal services provided by Florida counties in these unincorporated areas include residential street construction and maintenance, waste collection and disposal, water and sewer services, and fire and police protection.[30] Los Angeles County not only provides for the municipal needs of the unincorporated population in the county, but also provides services to incorporated municipalities through contractual agreements. These arrangements are known as the Lakewood Plan (see the discussion of the plan in Chapter 7). The county is authorized to provide 58 different services to municipalities ranging from animal control, building

Table 8.1 Reasons Given by Municipalities for Wanting to Transfer Functions to the County

Reason Given[a]	%
Achieve economies of scale	58
Eliminate duplication	44
Lack of facilities and equipment to adequately provide the function	41
Fiscal restraints	29
Lack of personnel	26
Inability to provide adequate services	22
Jurisdiction or geographic limitations	21
Federal aid requirements/incentives	20

Source: Susan MacManus, "Decentralization Expenditures and Responsibilities," in Robert J. Bennett, (ed.), *Decentralization, Local Governments, and Markets: Towards a Post-Welfare Agenda* (New York: Oxford University Press, 1990), p. 160. Reprinted by permission of Oxford University Press.

Note:
[a] Municipalities gave more than one response. Therefore, the percentages do not total 100.

inspection, law enforcement, fire protection, and engineering to traffic signal maintenance, lane striping, industrial waste regulation, and subdivision final map check. Many cities have availed themselves of these contractual opportunities. The county has approximately 1,600 agreements, ranging from as few as 7 services in one city to as many as 45 in another city. As a consequence of its services to unincorporated areas and its contractual agreements, the Los Angeles County Sheriff's Department has one of the largest police forces in the nation. In addition to municipal services, the county is also involved in provision of selected regional services including an extensive parks system and a large, diversified recreation program.[31]

Transfer of functions from one level of government to another is widely supported by reformers as a way to bring about regional reform as an alternative to the elusive voter-approved government restructuring. The ACIR, in advocating the transfer of functions, found the benefits to be similar to the advantages of government consolidation or metropolitan government.[32] The county's role as a provider of municipal services has grown, but many counties in metropolitan areas still are not involved in municipal service provision. Moreover, county governments are not always receptive to becoming involved in additional functions because of the financial constraints on their own-source revenue and the decreasing amounts of intergovernmental aid to fund services. In addition, there are often state-imposed obstacles. Some states do not allow voluntary transfer of functions between levels of government, and others impose conditions such as voter approval.[33]

As discussed in Chapter 7 California counties pioneered the use of counties to provide an array of services to municipalities through the Lakewood Plan. Recent research on interlocal agreements (ILAs) between counties and municipalities in California found that existing interlocal agreements between municipalities and counties tended to lead to additional contracts. In other words, municipalities and counties, after realizing the advantages that accrued from one interlocal agreement, tend to be more open to exploring additional cooperation.[34] According to research conducted by Leroux and Carr in an urban county in Michigan, maintenance-type services are the types of services that are most often contracted at the county level while ILAs for lifestyle services tend to be less centralized. They studied four maintenance functions (roads and bridges, solid waste disposal, watershed management, and wastewater treatment) and four lifestyle functions (economic development, public safety, parks, and public housing). They found that almost 100 percent of the ILAs for roads and bridges construction and maintenance and solid waste disposal were with the county. While the other two maintenance services were also highly centralized, they were less so as there were other providers resulting in municipalities establishing ILAs with other governments. When municipalities contracted lifestyle services, it was usually with other municipalities.[35]

Counties are often major players in ILAs and service sharing agreements. The county has a larger population and tax base than the city and therefore can offer economies of scale and a greater sharing of the tax burden than the more geographically constrained municipal governments. The county usually is also required to provide most, if not all, of the same services in unincorporated areas that municipal governments provide within their boundaries. With two departments providing similar services, it seems to make sense that the two departments could consolidate or work out agreements to share resources and equipment to benefit both the county and the cities within the county. With the budget pressures, more and more cities and counties are starting to consolidate functions or share services. A few examples of the many initiatives follow:

- Chippewa Falls, Wisconsin and Chippewa County are working out arrangements to merge the city's and the county's dispatch center.[36]
- Anderson City and Anderson County, South Carolina will vote on whether to consider sharing services with the county. The county and the city currently work together on the collection of property taxes and wastewater treatment. The county collects property taxes for the city and the county purchases wastewater treatment services from the city.[37]
- Camden, New Jersey is merging its police force with a county-run force.[38]

The County as a Re-distributor of Resources

The increased responsibilities of the county providing services in the city have substantial impact on the county's distribution of resources. County services are not uniformly distributed throughout the county. As indicated previously, the county's responsibilities in unincorporated areas are greater than in incorporated areas. However, unless there are specific contractual agreements, the county tax rate is usually uniformly applied across the county so that all residents pay the same rate regardless of where they live.[39] Therefore, there appears to be a redistribution of resources from the incorporated areas to the unincorporated areas. Moreover, large central cities have traditionally augmented the county's health and welfare functions, whereas smaller incorporated municipalities do not. Additionally, county expenditures in terms of road building in less developed areas, development and maintenance of county parks, and so on tend to be more concentrated outside the central city. Thus, conventional wisdom views the county as a redistributor of resources from the central city to outlying areas.[40] The redistribution of resources is a major issue in the reformers' contention that fragmented government in urban areas exacerbates and perpetuates inequality. They maintain that the high-cost poor are concentrated in the central city, isolated from the affluence of the suburbs, while the county's tax receipts are being redistributed to the suburbs to support the county's more extensive services in unincorporated areas.[41] The question of the county's role in resource distribution is dependent on at least the following variables:

- Whether the major source of locally raised revenue for the county is the central city or the suburbs,
- The numbers and types of functions provided by the county in incorporated and unincorporated areas,
- The location of the recipients of those functions.

Because the county's role varies in each urban area, even within states, it is impossible to give a definitive answer to the redistribution question. However, in urban counties where the county has assumed more functional responsibilities, particularly for welfare-related services, there may be a tendency for redistribution from the affluent suburbs to the central city. Social scientists Brett Hawkins and Rebecca Hendrick studied the distribution of benefits in Milwaukee County between the suburbs and the central city. They studied the distribution of eight county services funded heavily from the property tax: capital indebtedness, correctional institutions, mental health, the museum, parks, social services, transportation for the handicapped, and the zoo. They found that for every function studied, the benefits to the central city exceeded its tax contribution. In other words, the county is redistributing property tax revenue from the suburbs to the city.[42]

The Hawkins and Hendrick study of Milwaukee County, therefore, found just the opposite of the conventional thinking regarding county tax redistribution. However, as was discussed earlier in the chapter, Milwaukee County has assumed a number of municipal functions and expanded its services over the years. It is thus more heavily involved in service provision than many other counties. Therefore, this research cannot be interpreted as representative of counties generally. Research on more counties and grouping by types of services would need to be done before this finding could be generalized. However, it seems probable that those metropolitan counties providing extensive services are redistributing resources from the affluent suburbs to the less affluent central city. The Milwaukee study supports the reformers' contention that the urban county could be a solution to the problems of inequality and maldistribution of resources in politically fragmented areas.

Restraints on the County Assuming a Larger Regional Role

Counties in most states are still severely restricted by the state in the types of functions they can provide. As stated earlier, there are very few home rule counties. Counties, therefore, are still basically considered administrative arms of the state with the majority of their services mandated by the state. Most counties cannot assume a function without express permission from the state legislature. Because there is less flexibility in what the county can and cannot do that directly affects the quality of life for residents, county political leaders are generally less visible and not as engaged with the public as municipal political leaders are. Thus, they have less local political influence with the public than municipal political leaders. Their political influence in the state legislature is generally not as great as that of the larger cities. These are undoubtedly reasons why county political leaders have not assumed greater roles in regional governance.

Another reason the county is not involved in more services is that there are restrictions on county taxes. Counties have a larger property tax base than cities because they cover more territory. However, they are restricted in most states to the property tax as their sole own-source tax revenue. Given the public's opposition to property tax increases (other than for restricted school-funding proposals in some areas), a large property tax increase to raise the amount of revenue needed to fund additional services is not politically feasible. The county may, therefore, choose not to provide additional services or accept transfer of functions even when authorized or requested to do so.

Home rule for counties is also not the panacea for greater county involvement in local and regional governance for many of the reasons discussed above. They generally lack political influence, they are still regarded as administrative arms of the state, and even county political leaders often do not take advantage of their home rule powers. Moreover, home rule counties generally do not have the authority to supersede local government ordinances. This limitation makes it extremely difficult for the county to become a major player in regional and local governance issues. Home rule counties may also not be able to eliminate elected row offices without a referendum, which makes an improved administrative structure problematic. An advantage to home rule counties that should not be an impediment is the tax restriction. Home rule counties usually can levy taxes on other objects, which is one of the possible reasons for the frequent rejections by voters of home rule.

Another impediment for the county in regional governance is the multi-county metropolitan area. To effectively provide political leadership in regional governance in multi-county metropolitan areas, counties must form coalitions with other counties. This may not be possible without home rule powers or state approval. It is also highly unlikely that county political leaders will be willing to develop coalitions and collaborative relationships to address regional governance issues with counties they are competing with for economic growth. There may be differences in the problems confronting counties. The central county has more welfare-related and redevelopment concerns, whereas suburban counties have fewer welfare-related issues and are concerned with initial development issues. With divergent interests and growing political and economic power, the suburbs have little incentive to become involved with the central county in what could be perceived as the central county's effort to use suburban resources to solve its problems.

Given these constraints, it requires aggressive and farsighted county political leaders to rise above the historical traditional, legal, and political barriers and become involved in municipal and regional governance issues. It is much easier to focus on the traditional county functions rather than to become involved in nontraditional county functions despite state authorization. County political leaders often are forced into assuming additional functions only if compelled by state mandate or if subjected to substantial pressure by outside groups.

Prognosis for the County Assuming a Larger Governance Role

Despite the limits and controls imposed by the states, many counties are gaining political power and increased autonomy. Regardless of the lack of success in home rule charter adoption, counties have assumed a growing list of services. Particularly, counties in urban areas are becoming more involved in providing or brokering municipal and area-wide services. Many are playing a significant and expanding role in service delivery. Most county governments are under pressure to assume responsibility for a growing number of services, especially as mature cities face increased costs of providing services at a time of stringent fiscal limitations. For some time, county expenditures have increased at a greater rate than those of municipalities. For instance, one study showed that as early as the decade of the 1970s, county per capita expenditures in 50 of the largest metropolitan areas increased 143 percent, compared to 118 percent for the municipalities in these counties. The study also showed that in all regions of the country, except New England, metropolitan counties provide, on average, more services than their suburban municipalities. Furthermore, the number of services these counties provide has increased. For example, in developmental services, traditionally reserved for incorporated municipalities, the study found that metropolitan counties increased the number of services from an average of 1.7 to 2.0 while suburban municipalities decreased services from 3.3 to 3.1. In redistributive services (health and welfare, etc.), the counties increased services from an average of 2.5 to 2.7 per metropolitan county while the municipalities remained static at 0.8 services.[43]

Counties are developing more political independence from the state, particularly the suburban counties in states where the locus of legislative control has shifted to the suburbs. This evolution to more political autonomy was confirmed by a survey of county officials by the National Association of

Counties (NACO). The survey revealed that 49 percent of responding officials from counties in metropolitan areas felt that they had substantial independence from the state.[44] Furthermore, when compared with other local units, counties are increasingly performing an important intergovernmental role in the federal system. Being inextricably linked to the state, counties have become an extension of the state for administering federal programs, especially social welfare programs, for which states have key administrative responsibilities. There is no question that counties are becoming more important to local governance.[45]

Despite the problems and concerns, reformers are still hopeful that the county can assume a stronger role in regional governance. They are hopeful the county can become a focal point for regional policy-making and program implementation. The county is receiving increasing attention as the logical vehicle for the delivery of selected services in metropolitan areas. One of the latest services that has been recommended to be transferred to the county level is emergency management.[46] However, considering the problems and issues of the county assuming a greater regional role, the evidence does not presently support political scientist Scott Fosler's statement that counties will have "leadership responsibility for determining how America's urban regions will be governed [as] the front line agents of governance in the new urban regions."[47] Although some counties have made progress in increasing the number and types of services and have obtained some political independence from the state, much more progress needs to be made before most metropolitan counties can claim a leadership role in regional governance. Moreover, the legal and political environment within which a county operates varies widely from state to state and from urban area to urban area. Leadership roles in regional governance will be determined by the environmental conditions and institutional arrangements in each urban area.[48]

Comparative Study of Two Counties and Their Involvement in Regional Governance

Whether counties can play a leadership role in regional reform will be determined by their progress in achieving urban county status and developing multicounty coalitions to address regional problems. Some counties are much further along this trail than others. For example, on a continuum from non-involvement to heavy involvement, Cook County, the central county of the Chicago metropolitan area, would be close to the non-involvement end, while Allegheny County, the central county of the Pittsburgh metropolitan area, would be close to the opposite end. This section is an in-depth comparative analysis of Cook County and Allegheny County. The rational for the comparison is that Allegheny County, as a non-home rule county (it only gained home rule status in 1998) has been involved in regional governance activities for many years while Cook County has been a home rule county since 1970 and has been minimally involved in regional activities.

Illinois granted counties home rule in the 1970 state constitution for those counties willing to reorganize their form of government from the traditional commission form to an elected chief executive form. Cook County, the only Illinois county with an elected chief executive officer, became a home rule county when the constitution took effect. The intent behind the county home rule provision was the desire for counties to become major actors in regional service delivery. The constitution provided for broad home rule powers and stated that the "Powers and functions of home rule units shall be construed liberally."[49] The constitution also provided for broad powers of intergovernmental cooperation for local governments. With authority to provide a broader array of services in unincorporated areas, it was hoped that counties would reduce the proliferation of municipalities and special districts.[50]

Despite the broad grant of power, there were limitations. The legislature had the authority to limit or exclude functions by a three-fifths vote or by state preemption. The court could also render a decision that the function in question does not pertain to the government and affairs of the home rule county. A major constraint to the home rule county's authority was a provision stipulating that a county home rule ordinance could not supersede a municipal ordinance. In the event that an ordinance enacted by a home rule county conflicted with a municipal ordinance, the municipal ordinance would prevail within its jurisdiction regardless of whether the municipality was a home rule unit.

Soon after obtaining home rule authority, Cook County political leaders commenced exercising this new freedom from state constraints. The initial use was in the area of taxation and finance. It established a tax on the sale of automobiles, alcoholic beverages, and gasoline. It also issued bonds without a referendum and instituted a vehicle fee (wheel tax) on vehicles in unincorporated areas to help pay for police protection in these areas as well as a tax on motor homes. Some observers feel that this early and extensive use of home rule power to institute new taxes was a major factor in the defeat of home rule efforts in other counties as no other county in the state has obtained home rule status.[51]

The county also used home rule power to make a few changes in its government structure. It abolished the office of the elected coroner and established a medical examiner's office staffed by professionally trained personnel. It empowered the county auditor to audit the accounts of all special districts under the county board's direction. It abolished the elected comptroller and established an appointed one. It also established a commission to consider additional uses of its home rule powers. This commission made a number of controversial recommendations including the consolidation of duplicate functions provided by both the county and municipalities, such as environmental protection and public health. In addition, the commission proposed a major role for the county in policy issues of a regional nature and the gradual assumption of special district functions.[52] After the initial flurry of home rule action on financial matters, a few changes in structure, and consideration of what to do with their newly acquired powers, relatively little more was done to streamline the county structure, consolidate services, or become more involved in regional governance. Cooperative endeavors between the county and municipalities have not been pursued.

Why has the county not used its home rule powers to streamline its government and become more involved in regional governance? Court decisions have not been supportive of an expanded county role. The court's interpretation of the municipality's authority to supersede county ordinances went so far in one example to grant a municipality extraterritorial power to negate a portion of a Cook County zoning ordinance applicable only in unincorporated areas.[53] Another reason is the political divide between Chicago and the suburbs, and the historical dominance of the county by Chicago. There was no political support from either party for using the county's home rule powers to streamline county government or to involve the county in service delivery and governance issues beyond that which it was already doing. County government is dominated by the Democratic Party with Chicago as the chief orientation of the party. The president of the board, except for one brief four-year period, has been a Chicago Democrat since Cook County gained home rule status. There was little interest by Chicago Democrats for the county to assume a stronger role in governance that might detract from Chicago's dominant political position in the county and with the state legislature. Moreover, the board members outside the city tended to be Republican and were not excited about the prospect of having a county government dominated by the Democrats and Chicago becoming any more involved in suburban governance.

Because of the political divide between the city and the suburbs, regional services were usually provided by establishing more neutral, less political special districts through the state. An example is the establishment of the Regional Transportation Authority in 1974 to oversee funding of the public transit system in the region. Even though it covered more than one county and was opposed by suburban counties and some Cook County suburban county commissioners, it was established by the state with Chicago's active involvement. Chicago needed a larger geographical area to fund the Chicago Transit Authority (CTA).[54] There is no indication that the county was involved in a positive way in its establishment.

The county's tax structure has mitigated against the county's involvement in providing additional services. Its heavy dependence on the property tax for revenue, the public perception that the county is inefficient and wasteful of the tax revenue, and the fear of taxpayer backlash from tax increases has kept the county from becoming involved in additional services. Building and operating the new Cook County hospital has created a financial burden on the county.

There is also little engagement from the private sector with the county. The orientation of the private sector is with Chicago. The county is not involved in the economic and community development issues that are of interest to the private sector except in the few unincorporated areas. Moreover, the majority of the residents do not consider the county as part of the local service continuum. It is often viewed as simply a recordkeeper and tax collector. Residents look first to their municipality for local services and then to the state or a special district for services that the municipality does not provide.

Contrast the experience of Cook County with that of Allegheny County, the central county of the Pittsburgh metropolitan area. This county did not achieve home rule status until 1998. Prior to home rule, it had the traditional three-member commission and extensive elected row officer system. Since the entire county is incorporated, it does not have the traditional role of providing limited municipal functions in unincorporated areas. Its only traditional role is serving as the administrative arm of the state in the mandated functions of assisting the poor, maintaining county roads, administering the criminal justice system, administering the property assessment and collection system, and recordkeeping.

As early as 1951, a study commission recommended that the county become more involved in provision of local government services through the transfer of a number of functions from municipalities (mainly Pittsburgh) to the county. In addition, the commission recommended that the county change its structure from the commission system and establish a home rule county. This report was criticized by municipal political leaders as an attempt by the county to grab power and was rejected. Yet, over the years with the state's blessing, a number of municipal functions were transferred to the county on a piecemeal basis, and the county became substantially involved in municipal and regional functions. This was accomplished largely because of financial constraints on municipalities, and because county leaders were willing to assume the services.

Thus, the county evolved from providing a limited array of functions in the early 1950s to become a major provider of regional and municipal services. The list of municipal and regional functions in which Allegheny County is involved is substantial. These include a county-established mass transit authority, economic development planning, a community college system, environmental programs, financial support for libraries and cultural activities, pollution control programs, solid waste disposal, a regional parks system and recreation programs, an international airport, and public housing programs. A 1992 study by the Advisory Commission on Intergovernmental Relations found that Allegheny County's regional role was particularly important in enabling the region's highly decentralized local government system to effectively provide services. The county's regional roles were described as follows in the study:

- Provision of certain countywide services such as an arterial highway network and a county parks system.
- Provision and production of selected components of functions that benefit from economies of scale or broad-based coordination such as police and fire training, the investigation of serious crimes, and police forensic analyses.
- Planning, information gathering, and facilitating coordination and problem solving for issues that transcend municipal boundaries.
- Funding for innovative municipal initiatives and ventures that have an interlocal character.[55]

In Allegheny County, aggressive leadership and a willingness to enlarge the county's role were essential for the county to become more involved in nontraditional county functions. In addition to taking over functions, the county has become involved in policy issues. County and city political leaders worked with private sector leaders to obtain funding from the state and other sources to renovate the convention center, build new stadiums for the professional sports teams and refurbish the cultural district in Pittsburgh.[56] Another example of the county's regional activities is the establishment of a regional public–private development partnership involving all the counties in the Pittsburgh MSA. Allegheny County political leaders worked with the private sector to develop this partnership. This multi-county partnership has been successful in lobbying for favorable state legislation and funding for projects and favorable interpretation of federal environmental regulations.[57]

Table 8.2 is an indication of the regional services provided by, heavily subsidized by or controlled by, the county or a county-controlled authority comparing Cook and Allegheny counties. Allegheny County is much more involved and in control of regional functions than Cook County government. Authorities in both counties provide a large portion of the regional services. The difference is that in Allegheny County, the authorities are county-established and controlled authorities while the authorities in Cook County are state-established. The authorities in Cook County have boards that are either elected or the appointment power is shared with the state or Chicago exercising major control.

The comparative study of Cook County and Allegheny County suggests that state constraints are less a barrier to the county assuming a larger regional role than local political traditions and the aggressiveness of county political leaders. Even though Allegheny County was a non-home rule county with greater state constraints than Cook County, its political leaders have been much more involved in regional governance activities. Cook County, even

Table 8.2 Comparison of Selected Regional Services Provided Directly by the County, Subsidized by, or Provided by a County-Controlled Authority

Regional Function	Provided by or under the Control of Allegheny County	Provided by or under the Control of Cook County
Public Transportation	Yes	No
Parks and Recreation	Yes	Yes
Community College System	Yes	No
Airport	Yes	No
Public and Subsidized Housing	Yes	Yes
Cultural and Sports Facilities	Yes	No
Economic Development	Yes	Yes
Sanitation (Wastewater Treatment)	Yes	No
Environmental Protection	Yes	Yes
Emergency Management and Security	Yes	Yes

Source: Calculated by the Author

though it is a home rule county, continues to provide mainly traditional county services. It has made little effort to provide regional leadership or become involved in the provision of regional services.

Takeaway

The county's role in local governance has changed considerably over the years. Its role is dependent on a number of factors including the authority granted to counties by the state and the aggressiveness with which that authority is pursued by the county. The efforts to change the traditional commission form of government to a strong executive and obtain county home rule have had minimal success. However, the county's local governance role has become more significant in urban areas through interlocal agreements, transfer of functions from municipalities to the county and the increased need for, and complexity of, traditional county functions. The political calculus is an important factor in how involved the county is in provision of regional services regardless of the authority granted by the state.

The county is receiving increasing attention as the logical vehicle for the delivery of selected services in metropolitan areas. Considering the problems and issues of the county assuming a greater regional role and the increasing areal growth of metropolitan areas into multi-county units, the evidence does not presently support political scientist Scott Fosler's statement that counties will have "leadership responsibility for determining how America's urban regions will be governed [as] the front line agents of governance in the new urban regions."[58] Although some counties have made progress in increasing the number and types of services and have obtained some political independence from the state, much more progress needs to be made before most metropolitan counties can claim a leadership role in regional governance.

Notes

1. Quoted in Susan MacManus, "Decentralizing Expenditures and Responsibilities," in Robert J. Bennett, (ed.), *Decentralization, Local Governments, and Markets: Towards a Post-Welfare Agenda* (New York: Oxford University Press, 1990), p. 158.
2. Tanis J. Salant, "County Governments: An Overview," *Intergovernmental Perspective*, 17 (Winter) (1991): 7.
3. Mark Schneider and Kee Ok Park, "Metropolitan Counties as Service Delivery Agents: The Still Forgotten Governments," *Public Administration Review*, 49 (July/August) (1989): 345–52.
4. Blake R. Jeffery, Tanis J. Salant, and Alan L. Boroshok, *County Government Structure: A State by State Report* (Washington, DC: National Association of Counties, July 1989), pp. 3–4.
5. Roland J. Liebert, *Disintegration and Political Action: The Changing Functions of City Governments in America* (New York: Academic Press, 1976), p. 43.
6. Ibid., pp. 43–44.
7. Henry S. Gilbertson, *The County, the Dark Continent of American Politics* (New York: National Short Ballot Association, 1917), quoted in Herbert Sydney Duncombe, *County Government in America* (Washington, DC: National Association of Counties Research Foundation, 1966), p. 27.
8. Roger H. Wells, *American Local Government* (New York: McGraw-Hill, 1939), p. 81.
9. Ibid., pp. 120–121.
10. Ibid.
11. Advisory Commission on Intergovernmental Relations, *State Constitutional and Statutory Restrictions Upon the Structural, Functional, and Personal Powers of Local Government* (Washington, DC: U.S. Government Printing Office, 1962), pp. 63–78.
12. Kathryn Murphy, *County Government Structure: A State by State Report* (Washington, DC: National Association of Counties, March 2009).
13. Ibid.
14. Ibid.
15. Salant, *County Home Rule: Perspectives for Decision-Making in Arizona*, (Tucson AZ: Office of Community and Public Service, University of Arizona, 1988) pp. 23, 63, 76.
16. Pennsylvania Economy League, *Background Materials for the Ad Hoc Working Group Studying Home Rule Options for Allegheny County* (Pittsburgh, PA: Pennsylvania Economy League, April 1994), sec. 4, p. 3. and Michael P. Buffer, "Voters say 'yes' to home rule," Standardspeaker.com, November 3, 2010, http://standardspeaker.com/news/voters-say-yes-to-home-rule-1.1058604 [Accessed Feb. 1, 2013].
17. John H. Bowden and Howard D. Hamilton, "Some Notes on Metropolitics in Ohio," in John J. Gargan and James G. Coke, (eds.), *Political Behavior and Public Issues in Ohio* (Kent, OH: Kent State University Press, 1972), pp. 285–292.
18. Morgan Delp, "Group Works to Change County's Government Structure," *Toledo Free Press*, June 22, 2012, www.toledofreepress.com 2012/06/22/ [Accessed June 25, 2012].

19. Larry Gamm, *Community Dynamics of Local Government Change,* Pennsylvania Policy Analysis Service (State College: Pennsylvania State University, 1976), pp. 30–31.
20. Ibid., pp. 30–33.
21. Thomas P. Murphy, *Metropolitics and the Urban County* (Washington, DC: Washington National Press, 1970), pp. 239–246; Vincent L. Marando and Carl Reggie Whitley, "City-County Consolidation: An Overview of Voter Response," *Urban Affairs Quarterly,* 8 (December) (1972): 191.
22. Charles Taylor, "New Year Brings New Governance to Two Counties," *County News,* 43 (2) Jan 31, 2011.
23. Ryan Marshall, "Frederick County Could Abandon Commissioner-based Government," July 11, 2012, www.Gazette.net /apps/pbcs.dll/article?AID= 20100711/NE [Accessed July 12, 2012]; Frederick County, Maryland website. http://msa.maryland. gov/msa/mdmanual/36loc/fr/html/fr.html [Accessed Jan. 17, 2012].
24. The following is taken from David Hamilton, "Government Study Commissions and County Home Rule," *International Journal of Public Administration,* 27 (10) (2004): 737–765.
25. Advisory Commission on Intergovernmental Relations, *The Challenge of Local Government Organization* (Washington, DC: U.S. Government Printing Office, 1974), p. 61.
26. John C. Bollens and Henry J. Schmandt, *The Metropolis: Its People, Politics, and Economic Life,* 3rd ed. (New York: Harper and Row, 1975), p. 299.
27. Salant, "County Governments," p. 7.
28. Anthony M. Orum, *City-Building in America* (Boulder, CO: Westview Press, 1995), pp. 107–109.
29. Ibid.
30. Robert D. Thomas, "Counties in Transition: Issues and Challenges," *Intergovernmental Perspective,* 17 (Winter) (1991): 12.
31. Bollens and Schmandt, *The Metropolis,* pp. 299–301.
32. MacManus, "Decentralizing Expenditures and Responsibilities," p. 159.
33. Ibid, pp. 158–164.
34. Eric S. Zeemering, "California County Administrators as Sellers and Brokers of Interlocal Cooperation," *State and Local Government Review,* 41 (3) (2009): 174–177.
35. Kelly Leroux and Jered B. Carr, "Prospects for Centralizing Services in an Urban County: Evidence From Eight Self-Organized Networks of Local Public Services," *Journal of Urban Affairs,* 32 (4) (2010): 455–459.
36. "City, County to talk about Merging Dispatch Centers," *The Chippewa Herald,* September, 4, 2012, http://chippewa.com/news/local [Accessed Sept. 9, 2012].
37. Charmaine Smith-Miles, "Anderson City Council to Vote on Whether to Study Sharing Services with County," May 8, 20112, http://independentmail.com/news/2012/may/08/ [Accessed May 9, 2012].
38. James Osborne and Darran Simon, "With New County-run Force Camden Police Layoffs Loom," August 8, 2012, http://articles.philly.com/2012/08/08/news/33101357 [Accessed Aug. 9, 2012].
39. In many unincorporated areas of counties, residents often request a higher level of county service, for example, additional police patrols for which they pay an additional amount.
40. Some counties, particularly some involved in consolidations, have instituted a differential tax system for different levels of service. This is mainly to ensure that the more rural areas receiving fewer services in a consolidated city–county

government do not subsidize those residents receiving higher-level urban services.

41. This image is not completely accurate as the federal government and some state governments redistribute tax revenue from taxpayers in the affluent suburbs to support central city welfare recipients and to meet other central city expenditures.

42. Brett W. Hawkins and Rebecca M. Hendrick, "Do County Governments Reinforce City-Suburban Inequalities? A Study of City and Suburban Service Allocations," *Social Science Quarterly*, 75 (December) (1994): 755–71.

43. Schneider and Park, "Metropolitan Counties as Service Delivery Agents," pp. 347–350.

44. R. Scott Fosler, "The Suburban County: Governing Mainstream Diversity," *Intergovernmental Perspective*, 17 (Winter) (1991): 36–37.

45. Robert D. Thomas and Suphapong Boonyapratuang, "Local Government Complexity: Consequences for County Property-Tax and Debt Policies," *Publius: The Journal of Federalism*, 23 (Winter) (1993): 17.

46. See William L. Waugh Jr., "Regionalizing Emergency Management: Counties as State and Local Government," *Public Administration Review*, 54 (May/June) (1994): 255.

47. Fosler, "The Suburban County," p. 37.

48. Thomas and Boonyapratuang, "Local Government Complexity," pp. 17–18.

49. Illinois Constitution. Article VII Section 6 Subsection (a and m).

50. Diana Smith Canfield, *Illinois Home Rule and American Democracy: A Study of Anticipations, Consequences, and Prospects for the Future*, PhD dissertation, 1979, Northern Illinois University, pp. 143–146.

51. James Banovetz and Thomas W. Kelty, "Home Rule in Illinois: Image and Reality," *Illinois Issues*, 1989, p. 9.

52. Cook County Home Rule Study Commission, Report: *Summary of Recommendations*, July 19, 1976 (Chicago, IL: Cook County Board of Commissioners).

53. Canfield, *Illinois Home Rule and American Democracy*, p. 198.

54. R. Pearson, "Chicago Now 2nd City to its Suburbs," in "Chicago: A work in progress," *Chicago Tribune Special Reprint,* published originally February 7–14, 1999.

55. Advisory Commission on Intergovernmental Relations, *Metropolitan Organization: The Allegheny County Case* (Washington, DC: U.S. Government Printing Office, 1992), p. 83.

56. Pennsylvania Economy League, *1999 Annual Report* (Pittsburgh).

57. R. Stafford, Executive Director of the Allegheny Conference on Community Development, personal interview, March, 2001, Pittsburgh; Allegheny Conference on Community Development, *Remaking our Region: Building New Partnerships for Change Creating a New Vision for Growth* (Pittsburgh: 1993).

58. Fosler, "The Suburban County, pp. 36–37.

9 Unique Approaches to Regional Governance and Fiscal Regionalism

Governance is critical to providing equity for the region's society, particularly public education, And governance is crucial to protecting our environment as we reform land use regulations that currently encourage sprawl and work to integrate environmental and economic accounts.

—Regional Plan Association[1]

Special districts and cooperation among governments in providing services were topics of previous chapters. The use of special districts to provide regional services in decentralized areas was discussed in Chapter 6. In Chapter 7 councils of governments and regional planning commissions as ways governments cooperate in addressing regional policy and service issues were discussed. Major criticisms of these approaches were the increased government fragmentation from the use of special districts and the lack of authority of voluntary organizations to implement their decisions. This chapter covers regional entities that provide a stronger regional governance impact. This is a hybrid approach to governance of metropolitan areas that attempts to address these two issues. It uses a special district or a council of governments approach to provide regional governance. The major difference from the approach discussed in the previous chapters is that the organizations have authority to provide more than one service, have authority to coordinate other special districts providing regional services, or have authority over other governments to implement their plans and policies.

It is appropriate to differentiate between this approach and other regional limited-purpose districts that may have more than one function, such as port authorities and development authorities. In fact, port authorities and development authorities are sometimes combined into one district. The Port Authority of New York and New Jersey, discussed in Chapter 6, is one such district. It operates not only public transit and highway transportation systems but harbor and airport facilities as well and is also heavily involved in economic development activities. Another example is the Bi-State Development Authority in the St. Louis region. This authority has responsibility for the mass transit system as well as for economic development activities in the vicinity of the mass transit stations and other facilities it operates. These districts, however powerful their regional influence may be, still have limited ability to influence and coordinate the majority of regional activities. They cannot be considered as providing an overall regional governance function that is similar to the approach discussed in this chapter.

Another form of regional governance discussed in this chapter is fiscal regionalism. Although highly controversial, tax revenue sharing for specific purposes is receiving increased attention. The first local tax-sharing plan that is still in operation was instituted in the Minneapolis-St. Paul region to reduce region-wide disparities. Tax-sharing plans have been established in other places for such purposes as economic development and to more equitably fund specific regional facilities that are located in one jurisdiction but are utilized by residents throughout the region.

Although these approaches to regional governance are relatively new, they are engendering increasing interest among observers and practitioners. The concepts and an analysis of these approaches through case studies of metropolitan areas where they have been implemented are presented in this chapter. Case studies of governance by regional special district covered in this chapter are Portland, Oregon; Minneapolis, St. Paul, and Vancouver, British Columbia. Regional tax-sharing programs in Montgomery County, Ohio, New Jersey Meadowlands, Denver, Pittsburgh, and the Twin Cities areas are analyzed. Finally, the future viability of these forms of regional governance is assessed.

Strengths and Weaknesses of Governance by Regional Districts

General strengths of these approaches are that they provide a regional co-ordination and integration function over multiple regional services. They provide a general regional focus to the metropolitan area. They also possess the legal authority to make and implement regional plans. There is a certain amount of flexibility in this metropolitan arrangement that more structured solutions to the problems of regional governance do not offer. These types of governments usually start with limited powers and, if they are successful, evolve to meet additional needs of the region. It is difficult, however, to create and develop them. Building a strong political base for these regional agencies is problematic, particularly if board members are not directly elected and their functions are not the types that capture the general interest of the public. Moreover, even though these regional districts provide or coordinate a number of functions, they do not provide all the regional functions and are restricted in their coordination authority. Their impact and potential are limited by the number of functions, their authority over these functions, and their ability to attract political support.

Regionalists still view this form of metropolitan government as a highly desirable solution to problems of regional governance. Richard Babcock, a specialist in land use law, suggests that regional control of basic infrastructure functions such as sewerage, water, transportation, and solid waste disposal for the total metropolitan area is the best method of regulating land use, reducing sprawl, and channeling development because "growth follows the availability of infrastructure."[2] He suggests this is a more desirable form of regional governance than the traditional city–county form of con-solidation because most metropolitan areas encompass more than one county. Babcock cites the example of the Nashville metropolitan area that grew beyond its city–county consolidation and is suffering from lack of a region-wide tier of government to coordinate and direct infrastructure development. Babcock writes:

> There are seven collar counties around metropolitan Nashville, and they are all suffering the consequences of uncontrolled and unplanned growth. Between 1970 and 1980 the Nashville-Davidson County population grew only 6.7 percent. By contrast the population growth rates in surrounding counties ranged from 27.2 percent to 68.8 percent. The work force growth in the central county was just the opposite of the population growth. In 1970, 24 percent of the work force in the surrounding counties worked in Davidson County. In 1980, the figure was 46 percent. In 1970, tax rates in the surrounding counties were 25 percent lower than Nashville; in 1980, they were slightly above Nashville . . . Water is a serious problem in a number of collar counties . . . Similar problems exist for sewer, solid-waste disposal, and public transportation.[3]

Regional Governance in Portland

In response to the growing public concerns about the high costs and poor services from the large number of small, single-purpose districts in the Portland area, the state legislature authorized the creation of the Metropolitan Services District (MSD). This was a metropolitan, multipurpose district established by vote of the residents which could be given a tax base and assigned as many functions as the voters chose. The voters approved the MSD in 1970 but did not give it independent taxing powers. The MSD covered the entire three-county metropolitan area and had extensive authority to provide regional services. Its board of directors consisted of seven members appointed from local government elected officials: one from each county commission, one from Portland, and a municipal official from each county representing the municipal governments in that county.[4]

Despite its extensive powers, the MSD was cautious in exercising this authority, perhaps because of its lack of independent taxing powers. For the first few years its only function was planning a regional solid-waste disposal system financed by a small regional tax on the disposal of used automobile tires. In 1976, the MSD assumed the operation of the Portland Zoo, a facility with a larger attendance from the metropolitan area than from Portland. The agreement was contingent upon voter approval of a regional property tax to fund the zoo's operation.[5]

Other issues and concerns were surfacing in the early 1970s that were fostering a regional focus. One major issue was the negative effects of sprawl. Three groups coalesced as ardent supporters of regional growth management measures: agricultural interests, environmentalists, and business groups. The agricultural interests were concerned about the loss of prime farmland in the Willamette Valley. The environmentalists (including the governor) were concerned with pollution and protection of the environment. Businesses, dependent on the agricultural economy, supported growth management.[6]

The result of this movement was the passage in 1973 of Oregon Senate Bill 100, requiring cities and counties to prepare comprehensive plans that conformed to goals set by a state commission. One of the goals required all incorporated cities to draw urban growth boundaries large enough to accommodate growth projections for 20 years. The law required the boundaries to be reviewed and adjusted if necessary every five years. The state commission was authorized by the legislation to preempt local land use authority and withhold state grants if local plans did not meet state goals. The drawing of the urban growth boundaries in the Portland area was initially assigned to the Columbia Regional Association of Governments (CRAG).[7] This council was the designated regional planning agency for the area. CRAG suffered from the same problems that other councils of governments (COGs) exhibited. Its dependence on members for financial and political support hampered its ability to gain approval of urban growth boundaries. In 1978, voters approved the merger of CRAG into a reconstituted Metropolitan Services District. The governing board of the district was changed from 7 appointed members to 12 elected members plus an elected executive officer. Metro, as the reconstituted organization was named, had the combined authority of the two predecessor agencies. In 1979, during its first year, the state approved an urban growth boundary for the region. This was a major accomplishment that CRAG had been unable to achieve.

Metro covers the three-county Oregon portion of Portland metropolitan area, which includes 25 cities and 1.5 million people. (The Washington portion of the Portland region adds another 600,000 people.) Metro's responsibilities have increased over the years. In 1980 it assumed responsibility for regional solid-waste disposal when it took over operation of the one existing, publicly owned regional landfill. In 1986, voters gave Metro approval to issue general obligation bonds to build and operate the Oregon Convention Center. In 1995 and again in 2006, voters approved bonds to develop a system of regional parks. In 1990, Metro assumed management responsibility for the Portland Center for the Performing Arts, Portland Civic Stadium, and Portland Memorial Coliseum. Subsequently, the operation of the coliseum was later given to the Oregon Arena Corporation. Although Metro does not control the transit system, it is the designated MPO for the region and is thus heavily involved in transportation planning. Other regional services that are not within its purview include sewage and water services, and airports.[8]

A major change occurred in 1992 when voters approved a home rule charter for Metro, freeing it from the necessity of obtaining approval from the state legislature for any additions in services. The charter also reduced the size of the governing board from 12 to 7 members elected by district and continued the elected executive officer. Metro's primary responsibility under the charter is stated in its preamble: "planning and policy making to preserve and enhance the quality of life and the environment for ourselves and future generations; and [provision of] regional services needed and desired by citizens in an efficient and effective manner." To this end, Metro was charged with adopting a "future vision" for the region and a framework plan to guide growth. It also has been given the authority to require the region's cities and counties to change their policies to ensure the compatibility of local government plans with the regional framework plan. Metro has made substantial progress in achieving its planning responsibilities. In 1995, the Region 2040 Growth Concept was adopted which does the following:

- Encourages compact growth development near transit lines to reduce land consumption,
- Preserves existing neighborhoods,
- Identifies rural reserve areas that will not be included within the urban growth boundary,
- Sets goals for permanent open space with the urban growth boundary,
- Recognizes that cooperation with neighboring cities outside the urban growth boundary is necessary to address common issues.

The 2040 Regional Framework Plan, based on the above concepts, integrates land use, transportation, green space, and other issues of metropolitan significance to bring about a coordinated, consistent approach to development. Although the home rule charter makes regional land use planning Metro's primary responsibility, it also gives it a continuing significant role in the delivery of regional services. Metro continues to provide the regional services for which it had responsibility prior to the adoption of the charter. The home rule charter grants Metro authority to provide additional regional services and work with local governments on solving issues of a regional nature. The majority of Metro's budget comes from user fees at 46 percent. Property tax revenue is a significant source of income at 19 percent and sales taxes bring in 7 percent. Grants at 9 percent and intergovernmental revenues at 5 percent are other revenue sources.[9]

Assessment of Portland's Metro

Observers generally give the Portland region high marks in containing sprawl, reducing environmental problems, and maintaining a viable central city. The urban growth boundary has succeeded in its goal to reduce sprawl and promote infill development that has strengthened Portland's neighborhood and the region's older suburbs. The urban growth boundary is a 28,000 acre tract surrounding the metropolitan area. Residents of the Portland MSA drive less and enjoy cleaner air than do residents of other similar sized areas. While other areas experienced significant sprawl development, the Portland area has expanded slowly and in a planned fashion. It added little more than four square miles to its urban area between 1979 and 1997. In 1997, an additional seven square miles were added. In 2010 an additional 1,985 acres were added to the urban area with the expectation that it would accommodate growth over the next 20 years.[10]

A powerful tool for Metro is the state-mandated urban growth boundary. Infrastructure expansion is confined within the growth boundary. This is a powerful weapon for Metro's efforts to contain growth and provide for orderly infrastructure development. Developers, who were initially suspicious of the program, became supporters when more land was zoned for multifamily residential use, and the average single-family residential lot was reduced allowing for more intensive use of the land. The zoning requirements also allow for more efficient use of public infrastructure.[11]

Regional growth management controls have been effective in keeping the central city viable. Shopping and activity in the downtown after business offices close are encouraged by building and zoning regulations which mandate that downtown buildings must devote at least 50 percent of their frontage to retail space. Regional planning channels retail and commercial development along public transit lines. Mixed-use zoning encourages the building of projects that mix single- and multifamily housing in the same development, all within walking distance of shopping, work, and public conveniences. Public transportation has been enhanced through the diversion of money earmarked for a new freeway into a light rail system and improved bus service. Traffic during rush hour is still congested, but 40 percent of downtown workers use public transit.

Growth management has had a positive effect on the environment. Portland has had no violation of federal air quality standards since 1991, compared to an average of 100 days a year before the establishment of the growth boundary.[12] The growth management boundary has also had a positive effect on containing sprawl. Between 1970 and 2000, the growth in urban land was actually slower than the growth in population. Between 1979 and 2007, the urban area within the boundary increased less that 20 percent while the population increased more than 46 percent. This is roughly 30 percent lower than would be expected given the area's degree of political fragmentation. Compared to other large metropolitan areas, Portland has done remarkably well in containing sprawl.[13]

Portland still has strip development, blight, and housing prices that have mirrored the changes in the economy. This is not dissimilar from other western cities. The projection that the urban growth boundary would have a negative effect on housing prices is difficult to determine. When housing prices rose in the Portland area, they soared all over the West. Denver and Salt Lake City, two cities without growth boundaries, also experienced a similar rise in housing prices. In Denver, for example, they increased 44 percent during a similar period of a 26 percent increase in Portland. However, due to the constraints placed on builders because of the urban growth boundary, housing is probably less expansive in Portland. Builders construct town houses and relatively small homes that are squeezed onto small plots of land. The homes often have relatively tiny backyards and no side yards.[14]

The Portland region is not too dissimilar to other metropolitan areas in the provision of regional services. Most regional services are provided by single-purpose districts. Metro does not provide water, sewer, police, transportation, public housing, economic development, and most other regional services. It is, therefore, not a comprehensive two-tier government. Metro's success lies in its authority to coordinate functions and address regional planning issues. As an elected regional coordinating organization, it brings together local and regional interests to deal with issues of a regional nature. The powers and resources of other established governments in the area have not been diminished. By serving as a forum for discussion and action on regional policies, it has provided an effective regional governance structure and process for a decentralized system of government.[15]

Vancouver Regional Governance[16]

Municipalities in the greater Vancouver region, realizing the benefits of regional provision of certain services, supported the creation of regional districts that benefitted from economies of scale or from joint production. The provincial government also supported regional governance but wanted a more unified approach. After some effort the municipalities agreed to the establishment of the Greater Vancouver Regional District (GVRD). One stipulation in the municipalities' support was the opt-out clause. According to the opt-out provision, municipalities were required to be part of the district, but they had the option of choosing the functions in which to participate. If a municipality opted out of a particular function, it would be required to provide the function on its own. In 1970 after the concept of a regional multipurpose authority was well established, this opt-out provision was abolished by the province upon recommendation of the regional district board itself.[17]

When the GVRD was established in 1967, the provision of public hospitals was the only statutory function granted directly by legislation. However, the legislation establishing regional districts empowered the province to establish a district, set its boundaries, assign its functions, and name it without requiring further legislative action. This provided the flexibility for the provincial leaders to establish districts to meet the needs of the different areas of the province without further legislative approval for the inevitable changes in functions that would occur over the course of time. It also allowed the executive arm of the provincial government to oversee and maintain control by requiring provincial approval for any changes sought by the district. It was not given direct taxing authority so its main source of revenue is from utility user charges and other charges to municipalities for its services. Although it cannot directly tax, it can levy taxes to municipalities, which they collect for the district. However, less than 10 percent of its revenue is derived from property taxes.

The GVRD encompasses a substantial portion of the Vancouver metropolitan area including 22 municipalities, 1 First Nations community and 1 unincorporated area. The board of directors is composed of elected mayors and council members appointed from each municipality. There are currently 37 members of the board. Each municipality receives one vote for every 20,000 residents and no member may hold more than five votes. As a result, a small municipality has one director and one vote while Vancouver, the largest municipality, has 6 directors and 27 votes. A very persuasive person with one vote might be able to sway the entire board. For example, a person from a small community, who was well known in the art world, was able to convince the board to adopt a cultural plan although it had previously been rejected by the board before this individual became a member. The board has evolved from appointed to elected and is now back to appointed. Direct election only lasted for four years from 1974 to 1978 after which it reverted to appointment by member municipalities from among their elected officials. Election of the board was fiercely resisted by the municipalities as a step to metropolitan government.[18]

The first function the board assumed in 1968 was debt financing of municipal projects. There was general support for this function because financing projects using the combined assessed valuation of the entire region reduced overall borrowing costs to the municipalities. Building on the success of this function, the board started acquiring other regional functions and evolved to a multi-function district.[19] The GVRD provides services directly, oversees services other districts provide, and is a regional planning agency. It currently provides or oversees the following functions:

- Water, sewer, and solid-waste disposal and recycling. These functions are delivered through the municipalities, so that the GVRD does not have a direct interface with the residents of the municipalities.
- Twenty-two regional parks.
- Low income housing for 10,000 people.
- Air quality management.
- Regional growth management planning.
- Selective services to member municipalities including labor relations, emergency communications and planning.

Regional Planning in Vancouver

Finding the balance between local control and regional priorities and issues is extremely contentious. Shortly after the GVRD was formed, it attempted to develop a regional growth management plan. For the regional plan to be effective, the local plans had to conform to the regional guidelines. Many suburbs resisted this intrusion on local prerogatives, and it became so contentious that the province removed the GVRD's regional planning power in 1983. With the explosive growth and development in British Columbia in the early 1990s, there was an evident need for a plan to channel the development. The mayor of Vancouver, who was also the chair of the GVRD board at the time, persuaded the board to make a serious planning effort. The result was a cooperative effort and a product that was accepted by the municipalities. This plan was approved in 1996 by the GVRD and recognized as the official growth and development plan by the provincial legislature. This regional plan did not require the municipalities to cede any authority to the regional body. The GVRD thus did not have any powers to implement the plan. The implementation of the plan was to be through a consensus-based strategic planning process. That this consensus process was not effective is evident by the continued helter-skelter development of the region. The reason that the region did not decentralize and spread out more is due to a provincial act that generally protected agricultural lands from development.

In the face of the continued unplanned development that was transforming the metropolitan area, the province was persuaded to restore planning powers to the board with the stipulation that any regional plan have the acceptance of all municipalities. If a municipality objected to the plan agreeable to the majority, it would go through an involved dispute resolution process in an effort to bring it into agreement. Once the plan is accepted, each municipality is obligated to prepare a regional context statement showing how its plan is consistent with the regional plan or how it will be brought into conformance with the regional plan. These statements must be approved by the GVRD board.

The attempt to develop a regional plan to replace the first plan started in 2001. The intent was to develop a green, sustainable development plan. There was also substantial public support for a sustainable development plan to protect regional environmental assets. Although provincial officials review and approve other GVRD plans, such as water and waste management plans, it has taken a hands-off approach to the growth planning and has not applied any pressure or provided planning guidelines. The requirement that all municipalities must approve any regional growth plan means that the planning process is long and drawn out. The GVRD has no means to make individual municipalities conform or agree to regional goals or guidelines. All planning is based on consensus—each municipality determines whether it is in its individual best interest to agree to a regional plan. Although the provincial government has taken a permissive approach to this development plan, it has effectively established an urban containment boundary in that it has protected agriculture land from urban development. Municipalities must obtain approval to be able to develop on provincially designated agricultural land. The GVRD is the approval agency for development on agricultural lands within the greater Vancouver area.

Providing Regional Services in Vancouver

An example of the problems of regional coordination and fragmentation in the Vancouver metropolitan area is public transit. In 1998, the province created the Greater Vancouver Transportation Authority with members of the board appointed by, and subject to, the policies of the GVRD. The authority had power to control all transit, roads, and regional transportation functions in the region. Previously, the transit system had been controlled by a provincial agency although it had been funded by local taxes and fees.[20] Board members were chosen from among GVRD board members. Thus, the GVRD was able to coordinate the public transit system in carrying out its growth management and air quality responsibilities. Due to friction between the GVRD and the province over rail transit development priorities and major highway construction, the province changed the transportation board makeup to eliminate control by the GVRD. The province now appoints the board, which consists primarily of business representatives. A mayors' council, composed primarily of GVRD board members, is an advisory body to the transportation board, but this council has little power beyond its ability to veto property tax increases.

Another contentious issue is public housing. The GVRD has been involved in providing housing since the 1970s. It became involved because the national government was providing money to build low-income housing and the GVRD recognized it as an unmet need in the region. Most of the housing was built during this time period and scattered throughout the metropolitan area with no housing complex larger than 100 units: 70 percent of the GVRD housing units are market rate with 80 percent of housing revenue received from rents. Although it has housing units in Vancouver, most of the units are in the suburbs. The major demand is for affordable housing in the city. The GVRD has long waiting lists for its Vancouver housing but has difficulty finding tenants for its housing in the suburbs. The GVRD is not the only provider of subsidized housing as Vancouver also has public housing units. It is, however, the only provider in the suburbs. Below market-rate housing does not carry the stigma that it does in the United States. Indeed, mayors in some suburbs complain that they do not have any GVRD housing units in their municipalities.

Assessment of Greater Vancouver Regional Planning District

There are pluses and minuses to a voluntary organization like the GVRD. Building consensus is not easy for 22 municipalities, each with its own parochial agendas and fears of ceding its local prerogatives to an organization over which it has limited control. Controversial issues are either avoided or are discussed for years before any compromise is reached. Probably the major contentious issue with which it has dealt is regional development planning.

There are advantages and disadvantages to the consensual, local prerogative regional governing system model. One disadvantage is the local choice. There are some functions in which municipalities have no choice if the regional function is to be effectively provided. For example, municipalities cannot choose whether to become involved in the regional planning process. Regional planning is extremely difficult if the regional planning body has no power to force the individual municipalities to agree on the regional plan. Moreover, transportation planning, a critical component of any regional plan, is not under the GVRD's jurisdiction, which makes the planning process that much more difficult. In addition, once the regional body assumes a function and a municipality agrees to be in the function, it is extremely disadvantageous to the delivery of the service for a member to opt out.

Artibise, Cameron, and Seelig[21] note that the GVRD has demonstrated that when municipalities see the advantage of regional action, when they are not forced to join, and when there can be sufficient time to deliberate and refine the proposals, consensus can often be achieved. They claim that the GVRD has the most complete knowledge base about the region and is viewed as an objective, non-biased, professional planning agency for the region. They also claim that given time and sufficient deliberation, good ideas will triumph over bad. A deliberative and thorough debate on the issues to reach consensus generally will result in achieving what is in the best regional interest. Although the process might be slow and uneven, and controversial issues may be kept off the table, the GVRD does have success in many areas and is viewed as a strong regional governing presence in the Vancouver region.

The Twin Cities Metropolitan Council

The Twin Cities Metropolitan Council grew out of an effort in the 1960s by the Citizens League, a group of business- and civic-minded citizens. The Citizens League organized study groups, breakfast meetings, and seminars that focused on regional problems and possible regional governance structure. By 1967, a consensus developed for the establishment of an elected metropolitan council with operating control over regional services. What emerged from the state legislature was a "weaker" metropolitan council with some coordinating powers over regional services. The council consisted of a 14-member council and a chair appointed by the governor from state senate districts subject to senate approval. The number of council members was subsequently increased to 16 due to senate redistricting. Although not as strong as the council recommended by the Citizens League, there was a difference between the powers of the Metropolitan Council and other state-created regional councils. Unlike many other state-created councils, its jurisdiction extended over the entire seven-county metropolitan area. It was given the charge to prepare reports and make recommendations to the legislature on air and water pollution, parks and open space, sewage disposal, taxation, assessment practices, storm drainage, and consolidation of local services. The council's authority over public transit was restricted as the legislature established a separate agency to plan, construct, and operate new transit systems in the metropolitan area.[22] Whereas many metropolitan regional councils were advisory in nature and could only review and comment on local governments' federal grant proposals (the A-95 review process), the Metropolitan Council was given the power to review and reject plans of metropolitan districts if they were inconsistent with the council's regional development policies.

Although the council is appointed, the senate district method of representation means that neither the city nor the suburbs are over-represented. Moreover, gubernatorial appointment subject to senate approval gives the council a political base in the state legislature that is lacking in most other regional councils. The aggressiveness with which the council exercises its powers is also dependent on the orientation of the members appointed to the council. Initial appointees to the council were advocates of strong regional governance. As a result, the council moved quickly to solidify its position and establish itself as a regional governing presence. It adopted a regional development guide and began turning down development projects that conflicted with the guide, even when local governments supported them.[23]

The council tackled inadequate sewage disposal that was contaminating the water supply, the region's most urgent problem. It developed a plan to establish a number of semi-autonomous sewer districts administered by a metropolitan-wide board. The legislature approved the plan in 1969.

Implementation of the sewer plan succeeded, but not without some controversy. The council moved into social planning becoming the regional planning agency for criminal justice and for health. In 1971, the council was given authority over a new regional board responsible for parks and open spaces, but many of its other proposals were not accepted by the state legislature. In fact, as the council sought increased control over regional bodies, such as the Metropolitan Airport Commission, it became embroiled in controversy. In addition, as it sought to expand its leadership into other regional issues, there was increasing opposition. For instance, the council's efforts to establish a regional housing authority met with fierce opposition from municipal officials.[24]

Despite the opposition and legislative defeats, council persistence led to a number of major regional innovations. A major accomplishment was a fiscal disparities plan to equalize tax revenue in the region. This council-supported initiative was approved by the state legislature in 1971. (The fiscal disparities plan is discussed later in this chapter.) Another major triumph was the approval of a plan requiring each local unit of government to prepare comprehensive plans in conformance with the Metropolitan Council's regional plans and policies. Other significant accomplishments in the first decade of its existence included the development of a regional approach for solid-waste disposal. It also forced the affluent suburbs of Golden Valley to develop a plan for low- and moderate-income housing. The council exercised its veto authority over capital projects to stop plans for a second airport and a rapid rail transit system. In addition, it created a regional parks system by issuing bonds and giving the money to the counties to purchase land and develop parks.[25]

During the 1980s, the council seemed to lose its influence over regional policy and evolved into a bureaucratic agency. This was probably because its success in the 1970s added a proliferation of programs it was required to oversee and also because of controversial council appointments. A *Minneapolis Star Tribune* editorial on June 15, 1984, summarized the council's situation:

> With metropolitan services and urban-growth controls largely in place, the council's mission is no longer clear. Its committees are bogged down in detail. It has just gone through a year and a half of turmoil under a controversial chairman. And it seems increasingly vulnerable to attempts by a forgetful Legislature and jealous local governments to erode its authority and effectiveness.[26]

Although the council had been at the center of regional activities in the 1970s, this was no longer so in the 1980s. It was bypassed on decisions regarding the siting of major regional facilities, including the World Trade Center, the racetrack, a new professional sports stadium, and the Mall of America shopping center. In addition to being bypassed on significant land use decisions, there were other signs that the council was losing its dynamism. The council found itself in a decade-long controversy with the transit commission over the management of the bus system, planning for transit policy, and the development of light rail transit. It also was criticized for permitting expansion of the metropolitan service area. The *Minneapolis Star Tribune* accused the council of becoming an "easy mark for leapfrog developers and tax-base hungry fringe suburbs."[27]

In the 1990s, the council regained some of its lost stature. It was reinvigorated with council appointments more supportive of regionalism. It re-emphasized regional planning, a focus that it lost in bureaucratic monitoring of day-to-day operations during much of the 1980s. In addition, the council was given direct operating authority over mass transit with the abolition of the Metropolitan Transit Commission in 1994. Likewise, the legislature abolished the Metropolitan Waste Control Commission and gave its operations to the council. Having direct operational authority was a major change from the council's previous role of serving strictly as a planning and coordinating agency.

The council is now the major regional governing entity in the area. It oversees the Metropolitan Urban Service Area, which provides regional services and facilities. It is the designated MPO for the Twin Cities region. It serves as the region's public housing authority. Its planning functions include water supply, regional parks, and all forms of transportation. The council's primary source of revenue is user charges at 39 percent. Its second source is property taxes and a share of the motor vehicle excise tax at 28 percent. It also receives 24 percent of its revenue from the state and federal governments.[28]

As the council took on more activities and acquired more regional authority, its efforts to rein in sprawl diminished. During the first years of its existence, it tried to direct growth to existing infrastructure rather than build new developments. Since the mid-1990s, it has been more reluctant to curb urban growth. Although its future plan, Blueprint 2030, contains smart growth recommendations and advocates strengthening the area's land use controls, increased density and infill development is not a high priority. Its rural zoning regulations have become also less restrictive and more tolerant of large-lot exurban development.[29]

Assessment of the Twin Cities Metropolitan Council

The Metropolitan Council was conceptualized as a planning, policy-making, and coordinating body. The implementation was left to other organizations. Within the first decade of its existence, the council evolved into an organization with extensive regional authority. It appointed the members of most metropolitan commissions, had approval over their capital budgets, and established the developmental policies for the districts. After it lost its regional policy focus and became bogged down in bureaucratic minutia in the 1980s, it lost its credibility with the state legislature. With only specific powers granted by the state, it had to obtain the legislature's approval for any changes or additions to its grant of authority. With the council's political base dependent upon the support of state government, to the extent the legislature and governor were supportive, the council got much of its agenda approved. In most instances, however, the council's proposals were controversial to the point that few initiatives were ever approved as proposed. The council has been more effective in addressing the pressing physical issues in the 1960s and 1970s than the pressing social issues since then. Its base of political support proved insufficient to be effective in the controversial social issues. In fact, as an appointed rather than an elected body, it has not been able to develop an independent political base, provide regional political leadership, or withstand the parochial interests of state and local politicians.[30]

Since the establishment and early successes of the Metropolitan Council, the support for regionalism has eroded in the region. The business leaders who were a major source of support for the establishment of the council have retired. The large corporations that were locally owned and controlled in the 1960s, such as Pillsbury and Dayton–Hudson, provided financial and leadership support for regionalism. These corporations are no longer locally controlled and their top officials are less involved and less committed to local issues. It is highly unlikely that the Metropolitan Council, if it did not already exist, could be created in the current environment.[31]

Although the area faces substantial problems, it is making progress. While sprawl continues to be a problem, the area experienced 15 percent less sprawl between 1970 and 2000 than would be expected given the number of local governments. (There is a relationship between government fragmentation and sprawl.) The location of jobs continues to decentralize. Comparing the Twin Cities to Portland with its urban growth boundary, the Portland area experienced a greater percentage of job growth in cluster development between 1990 and 2006. The difference was 31 percent of 14 percent. Congestion is a problem and has been increasing more rapidly than in Portland with its cluster development and greater use of its public transportation system. Hours of delay per traveler in the Twin Cities increased 43 percent between 1993 and 2003 compared to only 12 percent in Portland.[32]

One problem that the Met Council has is that the urban area has grown beyond its boundaries. It has no jurisdiction over two urbanized counties in Minnesota and two in Wisconsin that are now part of the Twin Cities metropolitan area. This means that developers, residents and businesses have options that limit the council's ability to pursue aggressive growth management activities. In addition, with a board appointed by the governor, the entire board can go from 100 percent Democrat to Republican after an election. This impacts the stability of the board and the consistency of its policy direction.

On balance, the council must still be considered a success in addressing regional issues in comparison to the regional councils of other metropolitan areas. Why was the Twin Cities successful in developing a regional governance structure while other metropolitan areas are not? There are a few factors that seem to make a difference in the progressive regionalism that made it possible to establish the Metropolitan Council:

- *The absence of racial and ethnic diversity and the general homogeneity of the population.* In 1970, blacks composed only 4 percent of the Twin Cities' population. Even in 2011 blacks and Hispanics comprised only 7.5 percent of the metropolitan population, much less than in other major metropolitan areas. Even though the region lacks some of the richness of ethnically diverse metropolitan areas, homogeneity has probably made the development of a cohesive community easier.[33]
- *The type of economy in the Twin Cities region.* The region never experienced the industrialization that occurred in other, older metropolitan areas. Furthermore, the type of businesses that developed in the region was locally owned. There were more corporate headquarters in the Twin Cities per capita than in any other metropolis except Boston. Roughly half the people in manufacturing worked for locally based firms, the highest proportion in the country. Ninety percent of those employed by firms with headquarters in other areas are in firms that were originally created by local entrepreneurs and subsequently sold to outside firms. The labor force was also more highly educated than in other areas. One study ranked the Twin Cities highest among the top 25 metropolitan areas in the proportion of high-school graduates. An educated workforce and independence from outside control fostered a commitment to place, self-reliance, and involvement in community issues outside of the workplace.
- *The involvement of the business and civic sectors in public affairs.* The Citizens League was a catalyst in the establishment of the Metropolitan Council. The long time commitment of wealthy families and leaders from the business community have been key to developing and maintaining a strong regional governance presence. They not only help to fund regionalism but are actively involved in the Citizens League and other forums promoting regionalism.[34]

Efforts to strengthen the role of the council have met with only limited success. For example, fair-share affordable-housing bills that would strengthen the role of the council in the distribution of affordable housing throughout the region were vetoed by the governor in 1993 and 1994. In the early 1990s, the council came close to being abolished by the state legislature. Annual amendments to appropriation bills to eliminate the council have gained support. The governor publicly chided the council in 1991 to improve or it would be abolished. A 1994 bill to make the council an elective instead of an appointive body was narrowly defeated. However, a major reorganization of the council was approved in the session to give it operating authority over regional sewer and transit systems. The reorganization moved the council from a $40 million-a-year regional planning agency with loose supervisory control over regional agencies to a $600 million-a-year agency with operational authority. Although failure to become an elective body to establish an independent base of support was a setback, the reorganization was viewed as a significant step in reinvigorating the council.[35]

As the council took on more activities and acquired more regional authority, its efforts to rein in sprawl diminished. During the first years of its existence, it tried to direct growth to existing infrastructure rather than build new developments. Since the mid-1990s, it has been more reluctant to curb urban growth. Although its future plan, Blueprint 2030, contains smart growth recommendations and advocates strengthening the area's land use controls, increased density and infill development is not a high priority. Its rural zoning regulations have become also less restrictive and more tolerant of large-lot exurban development.[36]

Fiscal Regionalism

Tax revenue sharing is the distribution to municipalities of the proceeds of a pool of locally raised revenue contributed by participating governments. Tax revenue sharing can be contributions from a portion of the property tax base, a dedicated portion of the sales tax, or simply an assessment to each municipality determined by the tax base of the community. Contributions to, and distributions from, the pool are usually based upon some predetermined formula that takes into account the affluence and relative needs of each municipality. In this scenario, municipalities with a lower tax capacity contribute less and receive more from the pool than communities with a higher tax capacity. Tax revenue sharing is intended to:

- Reduce competition among communities for commercial and industrial properties to add to their tax bases.
- Create a fairer distribution of tax benefits from properties that impact on and are supported by surrounding communities.
- Reduce disparities in tax bases.
- Promote orderly urban development, regional planning, and smart growth by reducing the impact of fiscal considerations on the location of business and residential growth of highways, transit facilities, and airports.[37]

In metropolitan areas without tax revenue sharing, communities retain all the tax revenue from development within their borders. With communities in the region competing with each other for development to improve their tax base, this competition can reduce the economic base of neighboring jurisdictions if businesses are enticed to relocate. The region as a whole may be worse off because a business relocating may cause blight and higher taxes in the community losing the business, and the winner municipality may not realize any additional tax revenue for years because of the tax incentives and other inducements it offered to the business to attract it. There are also the added expenses for the winner municipality in providing municipal services to the new business.[38] With a tax revenue sharing plan, the incentive for municipalities to compete with other municipalities in the region for economic development is lessened because a portion of the increase in tax revenue is contributed to the pool to be shared with other municipalities. With a tax revenue sharing system, development is still extremely important, and the municipality, where development occurs, still retains much of the increased tax revenue. However, the entire region benefits from the development. Therefore, development becomes more of a regional effort instead of an intra-area competition. Rather than try to entice firms to move from one municipality to another in the region with tax rebate packages, the region's communities work together to attract development from outside the region and retain and help existing businesses grow.

Development in one municipality has ripple effects on other municipalities in the area. Neighboring governments incur costs, such as increased police and road maintenance costs, but do not share in the benefits. Tax revenue sharing is a way to compensate municipalities for the spillover costs from development outside their borders. In addition, studies show that the ability of a community to attract development is linked to the fiscal health and attractiveness of its neighbors.[39] Development that is not coordinated with other municipalities promotes sprawl and increased congestion and pollution. Economic development without some coordination with land use planning in the region ultimately has a negative impact on the area's quality of life.[40] Tax revenue sharing, to the extent that it can reduce intra-area competition for economic development, promotes a more orderly use of land.

Another issue is the equitable funding of the costs associated with facilities that are housed in one municipality but are used by residents throughout the region. These regional assets include parks, libraries, and cultural and sports facilities. Most of these entities, like many public services that enhance the quality of life, are not able to charge entrance fees that cover the cost of developing and maintaining the asset. While some of the costs can be covered through fund-raising, governments generally provide a substantial subsidy to keep these entities viable. Much of the government cost has traditionally been absorbed by the municipality where the facility is located, usually the central city. A fair and equitable system would spread these costs over the municipalities in the region whose residents benefit from being within easy commuting distance of these regional assets.

Tax Base Sharing in the Twin Cities

Only a few metropolitan areas have established programs to address the fiscal issues involved in the unequal distribution of the tax base and regional resources. The first tax-sharing plan in the nation, and still the most extensive, is the Fiscal Disparities Act of 1971 passed by the Minnesota legislature for the Twin Cities metropolitan area. This controversial legislation passed by just one vote in the Minnesota Senate on its second try. Although 75 percent of the suburban senators voted against the bill, it passed because of the combined support of the rural senators and those from Minneapolis and St. Paul. The legislation passed easily in the House because of a coalition of representatives from the central city and poor suburbs as well as substantial rural support. While central city and suburban support was for the benefits these areas would gain, much of the rural support was due to personal relationships and appeals to a sense of fairness. The bill's chief sponsor was a Republican representing a poor suburb. This helped to garner support from other suburban and rural Republicans. Democratic legislators from Minneapolis, St. Paul, and the low-tax suburbs also supported the legislation. The legislation became law in 1975 after it was upheld by the Minnesota Supreme Court.[41]

The act established a tax base sharing program among municipalities in the Twin Cities metropolitan area. Each municipality contributes 40 percent of the growth in assessed valuation of its commercial and industrial property from the base year of 1971 to a pool. Residential property and the remaining 60 percent of the increase in assessed valuation of the commercial and industrial property are taxed according to determinations made by the local taxing bodies. The distribution of the pool is based on fiscal capacity, defined as equalized market value per capita. This means that:

* If the municipality's fiscal capacity is the same as the metropolitan average, its percentage share of the pool will be the same as its share of the area's population;
* If its fiscal capacity is above the metro average, its share will be smaller;
* If its fiscal capacity is below the metro average, its share will be larger.

By 1991, the fund had grown to 31 percent of the region's total commercial and industrial assessed valuation; 157 communities were net recipients, and 31 were net contributors. The largest net recipient in 1980 was Minneapolis, which became a contributor[42] and has recently slipped back into recipient status. It switched to being a net loser in 2011 after being a net gainer from 2002 through 2010. The city of St. Paul historically has been the largest single beneficiary. Currently, the regional tax base pool of about $500 million represents about 39 percent of the region's total commercial/industrial tax base and 12 percent of its entire tax base (residential included).

The tax revenue sharing scheme has had a substantial impact on equalizing disparities among municipalities. Within the region, tax base disparity (as measured by per capita commercial/industrial value per capita) among communities with population over 10,000 is now 3 to 1. In the absence of the law, the disparities would be 10 to 1.[43] The disparity continues to decrease as in 2000 it was approximately 12 to 1, but for cities with populations over 9,000, the ratio of tax base disparity was 5 to 1. Before the law went into effect for municipalities over 9,000 the disparity was 12 to 1.[44] When compared with other metropolitan areas, the system has worked quite well. With the fifth-highest level of government fragmentation out of the fifty largest metropolitan areas, it is 35 percent below the level of fiscal inequality predicted by the level of fragmentation.[45] A study of school districts in the Chicago region found that the ratio of richest to poorest school districts was 28 to 1, a ratio 7 times greater than in the Twin Cities region.[46]

However, disparities remain, and fiscal zoning and competition for tax base is intense. Critics say it artificially props up tiny towns and pulls large sums out of increasingly distressed suburbs, while lavishing millions upon affluent communities at the urban fringe. The winners in this competition are usually the high-tax-capacity, developing areas with few social problems and comparatively low taxes. The losers are the low-tax capacity, fully developed areas with many social problems and high taxes. In addition, the tax revenue sharing system has distributional inequities. Cities with a higher than average commercial base but with low-valued homes and increasing social needs, such as Minneapolis, have until recently contributed tax base to the pool. At the same time, municipalities with fast-growing residential areas, usually in upper-income communities that have eschewed commercial development, receive money from the system because their overall property market values are lower than many lower-income communities with commercial and industrial development.[47]

Examples of the problems attendant with the revenue sharing law are Bloomington, Burnsville and Prior Lake. In the decades since the law was written, once-comfortable donor suburbs such as Bloomington and Burnsville have grown stressed by aging housing, roads and sewers and new populations of struggling immigrants, while former cornfields in exurban townships and remote suburbs have grown wealthy, at least in terms of their residents' incomes. Prior Lake, a recipient suburb with its fancy lakeside homes, has been able to keep its tax rates lowest in Scott County while adding major amenities: a splendid city hall, an architecturally upscale fire station, a water treatment plant, lots of new parkland. Prior Lake has very little industrial or commercial property and has made no effort to attract commercial/industrial development.[48]

New Jersey Meadowlands Tax Sharing Program

The New Jersey Meadowlands Commission (NJMC) was established for the purposes of protecting a fragile environmental area. NJMC is the zoning and planning agency for the 30.4 square mile Meadowlands District created in 1969. The district consists of 45,000 acres, including 19,500 land acres, in portions of 14 municipalities and 2 counties. Its mission is protecting and promoting the environment, ensuring orderly economic development and growth, and providing and facilitating shared regional services such as solid waste management. To implement this mission it established zoning and land use controls that allowed some communities to have economic development while others growth was restricted. To compensate communities that were not allowed to grow, a tax-sharing plan was established.[49]

Tax-sharing in New Jersey is not an attempt to minimize fiscal disparities, but to reduce the fiscal impacts of land use regulation. The Hackensack Meadowlands Master Plan for the area, adopted in 1972, formed a regional approach to zoning. As it was being developed, legislators saw a need to create a tax revenue sharing plan to share the benefits of development as they zoned certain areas for industrial, commercial and residential use and others for parks, highways, open space and other nontaxable uses. Towns that were designated for development share a portion of the revenue they collect from new ratables with neighboring towns that were zoned for nontaxable uses, such as landfills and protected marshlands. The tax-sharing plan was designed to balance inequities whereby each community would get a proportionate share of the property taxes from "new" (post 1970) development, regardless of where it occurs.[50]

Each community contributes 40 percent of the taxes on properties developed after 1970 to a pool, or "Inter-municipal Account." From that pool, each community receives a payment for school pupils living in the area equal to the cost of educating these children, as well as a payment reflecting the percentage of property the community has in the Meadowlands District. Some communities receive more than they contribute, others less. A tax-sharing stabilization fund was created by the state to stabilize the adjustment payments of both the paying and receiving municipalities. It accomplishes this objective by capping the amount paid by a paying municipality to no more than 5 percent above the previous year's obligation. In the case of receiving municipalities, the amount is capped so that it receives at least 95 percent of the previous year's receipt.[51]

The impact of the zoning and the tax-sharing on communities in the Meadowlands District is substantial. For example, Kearny has 36 percent of its land area in the district. The land in the district is only 6.9 percent of the total assessed value of the town. If the land in the district were to perform at the same level as the non-district properties, an additional $45.9 million a year in tax revenue would be generated. Thus the $3,863,134 that Kearny received in 2012 in tax-sharing payments is very low when compared to potential tax revenue it could have received had the land been allowed to be developed. Over the 40 year period the land in the district was restricted in its development, the remainder of the town land was developed. This restricted development has placed a disproportionate financial burden on non-district properties to fund the cost of providing municipal services and capital improvements in the district. For example, the Kearny fire department has responded to numerous calls, the water department has made numerous repairs on the water transmission system in the district and has also maintained, replaced, and repaired numerous hydrants. The utilities department has invested in improving the sewer system in the district.[52]

Kearny received only $92 million in tax revenues from district lands in its boundaries between 1973 and 2005 and received $60 million from the tax-sharing pool. The town that paid the most into the revenue sharing fund, Secaucus, paid $55.6 million into the tax-sharing fund from the $655.5 million in district tax revenue it collected during this same period. Using the 2010 populations for each municipality and their most recent equalized property valuations, the stark variation in economic development between Secaucus and Kearny becomes even more evident: there is $143,540 in assessed property valuation for each Secaucus resident and just $59,155 for each Kearny resident. For 2011, that translated into an average property tax bill of $6,338 in Secaucus and $8,960 in Kearny.[53]

It is an understatement to say that not all communities are pleased with the concept. Those communities contributing to the pool are not happy with the plan, while the recipients are supportive. The paying communities are seeking to reduce the percentage that goes into the pool or to end the system altogether. They complain that the tax-sharing plan in its current form is outdated and financially harmful to their communities The recipient communities resist indicating that the payments are critical to their budgets because of the zoning that has not allowed them to pursue economic development.[54]

Tax-Sharing in Montgomery County, Ohio

As opposed to the state-mandated tax-sharing scheme in the Twin Cities and New Jersey, the tax-sharing plan in Montgomery County is voluntary. It addresses both interlocal fiscal disparity and counterproductive competitive behavior. This program was established by the Montgomery County Commissioners in 1992 to attract jobs and retain the county's tax base, reduce interlocal competition for development, enable the county to successfully compete as a region in national and international markets, and to share the benefits of countywide economic prosperity among all jurisdictions in the county. This program started with an initial ten-year life.

The county contributes $5 million a year or $50 million over the ten years, to a pool to be distributed to participating municipalities and townships for economic development purposes. Municipalities must also contribute to the pool according to a formula based on the growth of their property and income tax collections. No more than 13 percent of the jurisdiction's growth in property and local income tax revenue is subject to contribution. Twenty-nine of the thirty-two local governments, including Dayton, the area's largest city, agreed to participate in the program.[55] Municipalities cannot join or opt-out during the ten-year period. Money is disbursed from the fund by a selection committee composed of officials from the participating jurisdictions and business leaders. The projects are selected that have the greatest area-wide economic impact. Cooperative inter-jurisdictional projects are favored. Proposals that would induce inter-jurisdictional competition for economic development are not funded.[56]

The results of the pool sharing formula have been positive in fostering greater interlocal cooperation and providing benefits for the region as a whole. The fund has also had a modest impact on reducing the fiscal disparities between the rich and poor jurisdictions.[57] Smaller jurisdictions particularly have benefitted from collaborative economic development strategies and industrial park development. Dayton has also benefitted from the program by using the fund to attract new businesses to the distressed western side of the city. Cooperative endeavors supported by the program include combining most of the participating municipalities to create the Regional Fire Alliance to foster cooperative fire services. The program is a modest step in the direction of regional governance and the reduction in intra-area competition for economic development. After 19 successful years, ED/GE was renewed for another 9 years in 2011.

Regional Asset Districts

Another innovative approach to revenue sharing is the sharing of local tax revenue to support regional assets. The Denver region pioneered this concept. It has also been adopted in Allegheny County, Pennsylvania. *Regional asset districts* are funding, not operating, districts. The intent of the districts is to broaden the tax base to provide financial support for facilities enjoyed by residents throughout the region, which have traditionally been financially supported largely by the municipality where they are located. Regional assets, most of which are located in the center city, include museums, sports facilities, cultural facilities, and recreation facilities. Obtaining the approval of suburban residents to raise their taxes to support regional assets regardless of where the facilities are located, is a major step forward in regionalism.

The City and County of Denver operates many of the major cultural and scientific facilities of the region, including the Denver Zoo, the Museum of

Natural History, the Denver Botanic Garden, and the Denver Art Museum. For many years, these facilities received state operating subsidies in recognition of the fact that they had statewide significance. In fact, a survey of patrons found that most were residents of the suburbs and other areas of the state. In 1982, the legislature ended its $2 million annual subsidy; city support for these institutions also was drastically reduced. Faced with the possibility of losing these regional assets, voters of the six-county metropolitan area were asked in a 1988 referendum to support creation of a Scientific and Cultural Facilities District (SCFD). The district would levy a 0.1 percent sales tax to support these and some 200 other arts and cultural organizations located throughout the six-county area. The referendum passed by a 3 to 1 margin. This method of regional funding was replicated by the Denver region through the establishment of another district to finance the construction and operation of a baseball stadium for the Colorado Rockies baseball team. Again, suburban voters perceived that a Denver-based facility was of regional significance, and they agreed to support it with a special levy.[58]

Adapting the Denver model, a regional asset district was established in Allegheny County, Pennsylvania. This district was not approved by the voters. Enabling legislation was approved by the Pennsylvania legislature in December of 1993 and was subsequently activated by vote of the Allegheny County Commissioners. The regional asset district covers only the county, not the entire Pittsburgh region. It can extend support to a broader range of facilities than the Denver district. However, most of the supported facilities are located in Pittsburgh. The district receives half of the revenue from a 1 percent, countywide sales tax. The other half is divided among county and municipal governments, a major portion of which must be used to reduce the property tax.[59]

The district is administered by a seven-member citizen board. The board members cannot be elected officials, public employees, or even relatives of elected officials. Four members of the board are appointed by the Allegheny County Commission, two are appointed by the mayor of Pittsburgh, and the seventh is chosen by the other six members from a list of nominees provided by regional agencies in the area. The governor is also allowed to appoint an eighth nonvoting member. The board members decide which regional assets are eligible for funding. Although a few assets are specifically excluded, such as schools, health care facilities, and parks with less than 200 acres, virtually everything else can qualify. Six of the seven board members must approve before funding can be provided to any agency. The tax generates approximately $85 million for the district which can be distributed each year. Libraries at 31 percent and parks at 29 percent are the two principal beneficiaries of the program. Among the other special facilities that receive funding from the district's sales tax are the Pittsburgh Zoo, Three Rivers Stadium, the Aviary, Phipps Conservatory (a botanical garden), and the museums and science center of the Carnegie Institute. In addition, numerous smaller annual grants are made to a variety of cultural organizations. The district has awarded over $1.4 billion in operating grants including $54 million in capital grants for projects like accessibility, critical infrastructure and equipment since 1995.[60]

The Pittsburgh region's move toward regionalism is in sharp contrast to its historical resistance to any initiative that had the appearance of metropolitanism. In this instance, Pittsburgh was no longer able or willing to continue operating and subsidizing major cultural and recreational facilities from local tax revenue. The civic, political, and business leaders realized that the region must cooperate in a countywide funding scheme or these facilities that enhance the quality of life for the entire region might be lost. This was accomplished through a legislative initiative rather than a vote. A referendum would have taken much longer with only a slight probability of success.

Future Viability of These Forms of Governance

Regional districts and tax revenue sharing schemes like the ones discussed above are relatively rare in the United States. However, there is increasing interest in them among those concerned with regional governance as a way to provide structure in addressing regional issues. A few metropolitan areas are considering combining single-purpose districts into multipurpose authorities. Political and business leaders in these areas are starting to realize that combining single-purpose districts into multipurpose districts or establishing an agency with strong coordinating and planning authority over regional districts is necessary to achieve effective regional governance. In the Richmond, Virginia, region, for instance, a multipurpose district has been proposed to combine water, sewer, solid-waste, and transportation services into one agency. An umbrella regional planning and service agency also has been recommended for the Denver region. The Denver proposal would combine planning functions with coordinating responsibilities for regional services as well as actual service delivery responsibilities for selected single-purpose districts. This agency would have the power to generate financial resources and ensure that regional policies and plans are implemented. Functions that it would coordinate or provide include all water supply, transportation, health care, pollution control, solid-waste disposal, and open space management.[61]

Regional tax revenue sharing is a concept that is gaining in popularity. This form of regional governance is more acceptable than the multipurpose special districts such as the Portland, Vancouver or Twin Cities model. This is probably because tax revenue sharing agreements deal with a small portion of a municipality's tax revenue and usually are focused on a portion of additional revenue from new taxes or new development. More municipalities also seem to be net recipients rather than net contributors. Despite the potential benefits for the region, any changes in the regional governance system from the status quo are vigorously resisted as an encroachment on the autonomy and independence of governments. Therefore, chances of approval of these types of regional governing systems are more likely to be implemented if they are approved by state legislative action than by voter approval. Regionalists are avid supporters of these approaches because they provide structures through which regional delivery of services can be coordinated. Moreover, disparities among municipalities can be reduced and there can be a structure to aid in developing a culture of regional governance.

Many observers claim that the Portland, Vancouver, and Twin Cities areas are unique and their regional governance structure could not be adopted elsewhere. Every metropolitan area is unique, and the conditions existing in one do not easily translate to another. To date, no other metropolitan area in North America has adopted a form of regional governance that is like those described above. The conditions that will influence the type of regional governance system vary from area to area. No two systems described in the case studies in this chapter are completely similar. They are variations of a basic model that could be adopted in other metropolitan areas to provide a regional governance function within a decentralized government system.

Takeaway

Given that government restructuring is not likely to happen in most metropolitan areas, there are still many regional issues that must be addressed. A few metropolitan areas have made efforts to address these issues by establishing unique regional bodies with some authority to provide or oversee regional services. Regional planning in a few metropolitan areas has also been strengthened by giving the regional planning body some authority over the local governments to ensure that regional plans are followed. While all metropolitan areas have some kind of regional planning commission or agency, most of these only have authority to plan and make recommendations. Only a few metropolitan areas have dabbled in fiscal regionalism. Sharing locally raised taxes or giving a part of their tax base to equalize fiscal disparities throughout the region is generally a nonstarter in communities required to give of their resources. If shared taxes are used for specific services or facilities that bring a general benefit to the entire region, they are more likely to be accepted by the public.

The type of regionalism described in this chapter provides the permanence of a legal structure and a force of law, which in many respects is superior to voluntary cooperation and collaboration. The viability and duration of voluntary cooperation and collaboration depend on the willingness of the participants to become involved and continue in the arrangement. Although few regions currently have multipurpose regional districts or tax-sharing programs like the ones discussed above, there is increasing interest in these concepts in some metropolitan areas. It seems reasonable that these approaches could be used as models to address regional governance issues plaguing metropolitan areas without major disruption of the current decentralized system of government.

Notes

1. Robert D. Yaro and Tony Hiss, A *Region at Risk: The Third Regional Plan for the New York-New Jersey-Connecticut Metropolitan Area* (Washington, DC: Island Press, 1996), p. 81.
2. Richard F. Babcock, "Organizational Approaches I: Implementing Metropolitan Regional Planning," in Joseph F DiMento and LeRoy Graymer, (eds.), *Confronting Regional Challenges: Approaches to LULUs, Growth, and Other Vexing Governance Problems* (Cambridge, MA: Lincoln Institute of Land Policy, 1991), p. 82.
3. Ibid., pp. 84–85.
4. Arthur C. Nelson, "Portland: The Metropolitan Umbrella," in H. V. Savitch and Ronald K. Vogel, (eds.), *Regional Politics: America in a Post-City Age* (Thousand Oaks, CA: Sage Publications, 1996), p. 259.
5. Henry G. Cisneros, *Regionalism: The New Geography of Opportunity* (Washington, DC: U.S. Department of Housing and Urban Development, March 1995), pp. 21–22.
6. Christopher Leo, "Is Urban Sprawl Back on the Political Agenda? Local Growth Control, Regional Growth Management, and Politics," paper presented at the annual meeting of the Urban Affairs Association, Toronto, April 18, 1997.
7. Christopher Leo, "Regional Growth Management Regime: The Case of Portland, Oregon," paper in possession of the author, n. d.
8. Myron Orfield and Thomas F. Luce, Jr., "Governing American Metropolitan Areas: Spatial Policy and Regional Governance," in Catherine L. Ross, (ed.), *Mega Regions: Planning for Global Competitiveness* (Washington, D.C.: Island Press, 2009), p. 257.
9. Ibid.
10. Bernard Ross and Myron A. Levine, *Urban Politics: Cities and Suburbs in a Global Age*, 8th ed. (Armonk, NY: M. E. Sharpe, 2012), p. 260; Nick Christensen, "State Commission Unanimously approves UGB Expansion," *Metro News*, June 14, 2012, http://news.oregonmetro.gov/1/post.cfm/state-commission-unanimously-approves-ugb-expansion [Accessed Feb. 19, 2013].
11. Lincoln Institute of Land Policy, *Alternatives to Sprawl* (Cambridge, MA: 1995), p. 20.
12. Bob Ortega, "Growth Controls Haven't Curbed All Ills in Portland Area," *Chicago Tribune*, Jan. 28, 1996, sec. 16, pp. 1, 6.
13. Orfield and Luce, Jr., "*Governing American Metropolitan Areas*," pp. 255–257.
14. Ross and Levine, *Urban Politics*, p. 225.
15. Nelson, "Portland: The Metropolitan Umbrella," pp. 268–269.
16. Substantial portions of this section are taken from David K. Hamilton, *Measuring the Effectiveness of Regional Governing Systems: A Comparative Study of City Regions in North America* (New York: Springer, 2013), pp. 98–106.

17. P. Tennant and D. Zirnhelt, "Metropolitan Government in Vancouver: The Strategy of Gentle Imposition," *Canadian Public Administration*, 16 (1973): 124–138.
18. A. Artibise, K. Cameron, and J. H. Seelig, "Metropolitan Organization in Greater Vancouver: 'Do it Yourself' Regional Government," in D. Phares, (ed.), *Metropolitan Governance without Metropolitan Government?* (Burlington, VT: Ashgate Publishing, 2004), p. 206.
19. Tennant and Zirnhelt, "Metropolitan Government in Vancouver," pp. 124–128.
20. P. H. Wichern, "Metropolitan Government in Canada: The 1990s," in D. Phares, (ed.), *Metropolitan Governance without Metropolitan Government?*, p. 49.
21. Artibise, Cameron, and Seelig, "Metropolitan Organization in Greater Vancouver: 'Do it Yourself' Regional Government," p. 210.
22. Barbara C. Crosby and John M. Bryson, "The Twin Cities Metropolitan Council," in L. J. Sharpe, (ed.), *The Government of World Cities: The Future of the Metro Model* (Chichester, England: John Wiley and Sons, 1995), pp. 91–94.
23. Ibid., pp. 94–95.
24. Ibid., pp. 96–97.
25. John J. Harrigan, "Minneapolis-St. Paul: Structuring Metropolitan Government," in H. V. Savitch and Ronald K. Vogel, (eds.), *Regional Politics: America in a Post-City Age* (Thousand Oaks, CA: Sage Publications, 1996), p. 219.
26. Quoted in Crosby and Bryson, "The Twin Cities Metropolitan Council," p. 99.
27. Quoted in Harrigan, "Minneapolis-St. Paul: Structuring Metropolitan Government," p. 219.
28. Orfield and Luce, Jr., "*Governing American Metropolitan Areas*," pp. 252–256.
29. Ibid.
30. Harrigan, "Minneapolis-St. Paul: Structuring Metropolitan Government," pp. 214–223.
31. Ibid., pp. 220–223.
32. Orfield and. Luce, Jr., "*Governing American Metropolitan Areas*," pp. 259–270.
33. U. S. Census Bureau, "Selected Population Profile in the United States 2011," *American Community Survey 1-year Estimates*. http://factfinder2.census.gov/faces/tableservices/jsf/pages/productview.xhtml?pid=ACS_11_1YR_S0201&prodType=table [Accessed March 23, 2011].
34. John Brand and Ronnie Brooks, "Public-Private Cooperation for Urban Revitalization: The Minneapolis and Saint Paul Experience," in R. Scott Fosler and Renee A. Berger, (eds.), *Public-Private Partnership in American Cities: Seven Case Studies* (Lexington, MA: D. C. Heath, 1982), pp. 164–165; C. James Owen and York Willbern, *Governing Metropolitan Indianapolis: The Politics of Unigov* (Berkeley, CA: University of California Press, 1985), pp. 188–191.
35. Myron Orfield, *Metro Politics: A Regional Agenda for Community and Stability* (Washington, DC and Cambridge, MA: Brookings Institution and Lincoln Institute of Land Policy, 1997), pp. 114–131.
36. Orfield and. Luce, Jr., "*Governing American Metropolitan Areas*," pp. 252–256.
37. Tax Base Sharing, www.nyslocalgov.org/pdf/Tax_Base_Sharing.pdf [Accessed March 14, 2013].
38. William J. Pammer Jr. and Jack L. Dustin, "Fostering Economic Development Through County Tax Sharing," *State and Local Government*, 25 (Winter) (1993): 58.
39. See the studies by Larry C. Ledebur and William R. Barnes, *City Distress, Metropolitan Disparities, and Economic Growth* (Washington, DC: National League of Cities, 1992); and H. V. Savitch, D. Collins, D. Sanders, J. P. Markham,

"Ties That Bind: Central Cities, Suburbs, and the New Metropolitan Region," *Economic Development Quarterly*, 7 (November) (1993): 341–57.
40. Pammer Jr.and Dustin, "Fostering Economic Development Through County Tax Sharing," p. 59.
41. Orfield, *Metro Politics*, pp. 143–144.
42. Worcester Municipal Research Bureau, *Considering Regional Government for Worcester–Part II: Proposals for Comprehensive Regional Governance*, Report No. 95–2 (Worcester, MA: Apr. 3, 1995), p. 12.
43. Steven Dornfeld, "Tax-base sharing law gets a closer look in Twin Cities," *MinnPost*, Feb. 9, 2012, http://www.minnpost.com/cityscape/2012/02/tax-base-sharing-law-gets-closer-look-twin-cities [Accessed March 13, 2013].
44. Tax Base Sharing, www.nyslocalgov.org/pdf/Tax_Base_Sharing.pdf [Accessed March 14, 2013].
45. Orfield and Luce, Jr., "*Governing American Metropolitan Areas*," pp. 273–275.
46. Orfield, *Metro Politics*, p. 163.
47. Ibid., p. 87.
48. David Peterson, Katie Humphrey and Laurie Blake, "Twin Cities Tax-share Program Receives Scrutiny," *Star Tribune,* January 31, 2012, http://www.startribune.com/local/138366989.html?refer=y [Accessed March 14, 2013].
49. "Mayor Santos Defends Tax Sharing in the Meadowlands District," News Release, April 16, 2012. http://www.kearnynj.org/node/1112 [Accessed March 13, 2013].
50. Tax Base Sharing, www.nyslocalgov.org/pdf/Tax_Base_Sharing.pdf [Accessed March 14, 2013].
51. Ibid.
52. "Mayor Santos Defends Tax Sharing in the Meadowlands District".
53. Ibid.
54. Michael Copley, "Outside Study Proposed in Meadowlands Tax-sharing Dispute," NorthJersey.com January 13, 2013, http://www.northjersey.com/news/186658851_outside_study_proposed_in_meadowlands_tax-sharing_dispute_dispute_may_get_legal_aid.html?c=y&page=3 [Accessed March 13, 2013].
55. Eileen Shanahan, "Going It Jointly: Regional Solutions for Local Problems," *Governing: The Magazine of States and Localities,* (August) (1991): 72–73.
56. William R. Dodge, *Regional Excellence: Governing Together to Compete Globally and Flourish Locally* (Washington, DC: National League of Cities, 1996), p. 164.
57. Pammer and Dustin, "Fostering Economic Development Through County Tax Sharing," pp. 67–68.
58. Allan D. Wallis, "The Third Wave: Current Trends in Regional Governance," *National Civic Review*, 83 (Summer/Fall) (1994): 290, 305–306.
59. Cisneros, *Regionalism: The New Geography of Opportunity*, p. 24.
60. "RAD Works Here," http://www.radworkshere.org/interior.php?pageID=16 [Accessed March 20, 2013].
61. Dodge, *Regional Excellence*, pp. 303, 331–332.

10 Collaborative Regional Governance

The city and its suburbs are interdependent parts of a single community bound together by a web of transportation and other public facilities and by common economic interests. Increasingly, community development must be a cooperative venture toward the common good of the metropolitan region as a whole.
—John F. Kennedy, State of the Union Address, 1961

Collaborative regional governance goes beyond cooperative governance described in Chapter 7 to include and embrace the involvement of nongovernmental entities. It recognizes that in decentralized metropolitan areas, effective governance requires the involvement of the private and nonprofit sectors. Starting approximately in the 1990s, a new approach to regionalism took shape. Many advocates for regional reform of local governments shifted away from the traditional government structure approach. Rather than advocating a regional government structure, they started focusing on ways to govern decentralized regions. Instead of the normative approach of a restructuring of local governments to reduce their number, the focus became how regional governance happens or can happen. With the previous focus on local government structure, the thinking was that if the structure can be rationalized, regional governance problems will be solved.

The new approach to regionalism rested on the assumption that governance did not take place in a vacuum. There were major forces other than political leaders and public administrators that had a major influence on local government public policy and implementation. This approach took its theoretical underpinnings from community power studies. The seminal study that started this movement was Floyd Hunter's 1953 study of who controls public policy in Atlanta. He claimed a small group of business elites had the major influence in determining policy.[1] Robert Dahl followed with a study of New Haven in which he claimed that business elites were not the major influence on governance. He argued from his findings that decision making in cities was more pluralistic with different actors and groups involved depending on the policy issue.[2] These theories have been debated and argued, and additional theories have been developed to further refine the initial theories or contribute new ones. The point here is that the studies showed that nongovernmental actors had a major influence in governance of cities.

Other studies focused on the impact of the urban economy and how economic decisions affect urban policy. Urbanists for some time have explored the relationships between the governmental and nongovernmental sectors in the governance of cities. The political economy approach postulates that there is a dependent relationship between politics and economics and that local governance results from interaction between economic and government actors.[3] A major focus for political economy theorists is the nature of the relationship between politics and economics in urban decision making. Urban regime theory is one theory that attempts to explain this relationship. Urban regime theory rejects the claim made by some political economists of economic determinism and embraces the concept that urban policy-making results from a complex relationship between economic and political actors. Urbanist Clarence Stone, a major force behind the development of urban regime theory, asserted that the underlying concept of urban regime theory is the centrality of the relationship between the forces that control the political process and those that control the economy. Stone wrote:

> Urban regime theory assumes that the effectiveness of local government depends greatly on the cooperation of nongovernmental actors and on the combination of state capacity with nongovernmental resources ... The reality is that government and business activities are heavily intertwined, as are government and nonprofit activities.[4]

According to the urban regime theory supporters, an urban regime is an informal coalition of public and private interests working together to make and carry out governing decisions. Governance of the urban area is, therefore, a collaborative process of informal partnerships between public and private actors. Although there are a number of other political economy theories purporting to explain the relationship between politics and economics in urban decision making, urban regime theory is one of the most developed and accepted theories by urban researchers.[5]

Urban Regime Theory and Regional Governance

Urban regime theory concepts are being recognized and advocated as an alternative to regional government in fragmented metropolitan areas. Regional collaboration is an extension of regime theory concepts to regional governance. The major concepts underlying regional collaboration are similar to urban regime theory. The term given to this form of regional governance is *New Regionalism*. (I use the terms new regionalism and regional collaboration interchangeably in the remainder of this book.) The two major concepts involved in new regionalism are cooperation between governments and collaboration with the private sector in making and implementing public policy. Basic regional governance does not require private involvement. Regional services can be delivered and governments can cooperate among themselves without the involvement of the nongovernmental community. However, new regionalism is more than just interlocal government cooperation. It involves nongovernment actors working with government to address public policy issues.

There are some differences between city and regional governance that create problems in transferring the regime theory concepts to regional collaboration. Indeed, the major drawback in the application of regime theory at the regional level is the lack of traditional political institutions with regional authority with which the nongovernmental community can form coalitions. Moreover, the private sector still tends to have a central city focus on governance.[6] However, there is evidence that this focus on the central city is changing with the continuing decentralization of corporations to suburban locations. Business Professor Rosabeth Moss Kanter's research has noted a marked increase of business groups involved in regional issues in the last 20 years. In addition, while collaboration between the private and political sectors in city governance has been the modus operandi for decades, it is a new concept in most regions. Even in those regions with a history of public–private partnerships, the evidence suggests that the collaboration has not been consistent.[7]

Indeed, the traditional big business orientation to the central city has largely been displaced by a number of factors in addition to the dispersion of corporate headquarters and manufacturing facilities to the suburbs. Although there is still a focus on the downtown of the central city, the ties are not as strong as they once were. Hanson and his colleagues, after studying corporate civic engagement in 19 metropolitan areas with headquarters of Fortune 500 companies, found that the commitment of CEOs of major companies to the central city has eroded. Likewise the civic associations through which these corporate executives work or become involved in city governance issues have also experienced lowered capacity to make an impact. Among their conclusions are the following:

- There are less home-grown CEOs of major corporations with the result that they do not identify with the city. Corporation executives have less autonomy and time to unilaterally engage in civic activities. CEOs are subject to increasing pressure to produce for their board and the shareholders.

- The focus is more on resolving regional issues because of the dispersion of headquarters and facilities across the region. Transient executives often do not live in the center city and are more familiar and interested in regional issues of concern with their corporation than particular central city problems. Their orientation might be more on state and federal issues than local issues.
- Increased reliance on civic associations to initiate agendas, mobilize corporate resources, and staff projects reinforces the tendency toward cautious action. Association executives are employees and cannot command the economic power that CEOs of hometown businesses could in earlier years. Civic association executives must rely on their skill to mobilize support for their plans, and are dependent upon the agreement and action of their board and funders to achieve results.
- The mergers of CEO-led civic associations with regional organizations have increased interest in regionalism. Regional associations are often larger than the former small group of corporate titans of yesteryear. These groups are less cohesive and more formal in their decision making and therefore more cautious in what they undertake. Because of the difficulty of obtaining action, many CEOs withdraw and assign second-tier executives to represent their corporation on the boards and committees of the association. This reduces the power and authority of the civic associations.[8]

There are many community leaders from the private and nonprofit sectors seeking regional solutions for economic and social issues. The pressure for regional solutions, therefore, is more likely to come from the nongovernmental leadership. Because of the resources that the business community contributes to collaborative governance, new regionalism usually has an economic focus: a comprehensive functional approach to enhance the orderly economic development of the region. This development focus is not on how to deliver one service requiring a regional approach but on how numerous functions and services can be provided for the economic benefit of the entire region. This economic focus encourages the addressing of infrastructure issues, such as transportation, and social issues, like affordable housing and education. In some instances, collaborative alliances may form to address only one issue, but the same core people may be involved in a number of single-purpose alliances. The result is an interlocking web of people involved over time in a number of regional issues so that even single-purpose issues receive a broad focus.

Characteristics of New Regionalism

As indicated above, new regionalism involves both cooperation and collaboration. Cooperation was discussed in Chapter 7 and entails governments working together to provide a service or to solve some regional problem. Cooperation, as indicated in Chapter 7, has been an alternative service delivery method for many years in many states; however, its incidence has substantially increased in the last few years as local governments have become more financially strapped and the public has resisted tax increases.

New regionalism is more than cooperation. Public–private collaboration, then, is an essential component of new regionalism. Collaboration connotes multi-sector involvement among independent actors. Collaboration is a concept where both public and private actors work together for mutual benefit and where it is generally not possible for any one actor to effectively achieve the goal alone. Entering into the collaboration is a voluntary action, and no one actor is totally in charge of the collaborative effort and receives all the benefit. One definition of collaborative governance is a governing arrangement involving one or more public agencies working with one or more nongovernment entities in a collective, deliberative, consensus-oriented decision-making process to make or implement public policy or manage public programs or assets.[9]

Professor John Donahue characterizes collaboration as "joint efforts by public and private actors, each wielding a degree of discretion, to advance a goal that is conventionally considered governmental." According to Donahue, collaboration is a public–private partnership but is more precise in its meaning because the latter term has been associated with everything from a "contract for hauling urban garbage to a compact for ending global poverty."[10] Professor David Warm contends that while cooperation involves two or more parties working together in a mutually beneficial way, collaboration necessitates actually combining resources into a mutual endeavor involving joint responsibility and rewards to achieve a goal that cannot be achieved independently.[11]

In the context of local government, collaboration is often confused or used interchangeably with concepts like networking, coordination and cooperation. Collaboration implies something more. It involves working across institutional boundaries to engage outside individuals and entities in a highly connected way that essentially reshapes the processes of decision making or service delivery. While cooperation involves two or more parties working together in a mutually beneficial way, collaboration necessitates actually combining creativity, expertise, knowledge, and other resources in a mutual endeavor. Collaboration itself is not the goal but a means to achieve the goal that cannot be arrived at without the collaborative effort.[12] Cooperation and collaboration in new regionalism reinforce each other. Collaboration leads to cooperation which leads to further cooperation and collaboration. Thus, both the broader regional policy issues are addressed as well as the administrative means to jointly implement the policies. While each addresses different processes, both cooperation and collaboration should be present in new regionalism. Allan Wallis identifies major characteristics of collaborative governance or new regionalism as follows:

- *Governance versus government.* Advocates of regionalism today tend to speak in terms of governance rather than government. The change in terminology reflects a shift in focus from formal structural arrangements to informal structures and processes for setting policy and mobilizing action. In part, de-emphasizing government recognizes that the public opposes reforms that would effectively create a new layer of government.
- *Cross-sectoral versus uni-sectoral involvement.* Responsibility for achieving effective regionalism is no longer viewed as primarily falling to the public sector. As the change in terminology from government to governance implies, it is an effort requiring the active involvement of the for-profit and nonprofit sectors, frequently working together with the public sector. Each sector has unique capacities and specific areas of legitimacy. Cross-sectoral arrangements make it possible to combine these in ways that allow for a far more effective mobilization of effort.
- *Collaboration versus coordination.* A major objective of regionalism in the past was improved coordination of public sector planning and action. Today, the cross-sectoral character of regional governance stresses collaboration over coordination. The objective is not simply to know what others are doing, but to develop arrangements that mobilize the unique capacities and legitimacy of each sector working together to accomplish specific tasks of regional scope.
- *Process versus structure.* The importance of collaboration places new emphasis on process over formal structural arrangements. While process in the past has served the objectives of data analysis and planning, the processes employed today focus on developing a regional vision and goals, formation of consensus among critical stakeholders, and, ultimately, mobilization of resources to meet objectives.
- *Networks versus formal structures.* The increased emphasis placed on collaboration and process is also indicative of the fact that regionalism today operates through network-like organizations as opposed to formal structures. Organizations in a network at any one time reflect the specific task or project being undertaken. Nevertheless, such networks tend to have a stable core of stakeholders who share significant interest in specific strategic arenas.[13]

Those advocating a new regionalism approach to the problems of governing decentralized metropolitan areas focus on process instead of structure. They seek regional governance solutions through a process that is all-inclusive, involving both the private and nonprofit sectors working with governments in a collaborative effort to address regional issues. Through an issue-oriented process involving a broad cross-section of leaders in the region, they hope to achieve consensus and action on regional issues. New regionalists recognize that the traditional reform recommendations of local government consolidation or the formation of a new, extensive metropolitan government are no longer appropriate for two reasons: (1) increased understanding of the weaknesses of large-scale governments, and (2) local resistance to the creation of new governmental institutions.

The agenda for the new regionalism movement is not necessarily to establish a permanent structure or to centralize power in one structure. Instead, the purpose is to institute a process to make decisions on regional issues, broker cooperative arrangements among governments in the region, and induce state legislation when necessary to implement regional solutions. The process is not a one-time effort but a continuing effort to focus attention on regional governance issues. Those advocating this type of reform hope that, over time, a culture of regionalism and cooperation will be instilled in the area and that government leaders and residents will see the wisdom of establishing a regional structure to institutionalize the process.

A major difference from past regional governance efforts is the involvement of the private sector in working directly with government to foster regional governance. The private sector through a variety of organizations, such as the Committee for Economic Development and better government associations, has long advocated regional government reforms. These organizations, however, usually maintained an arm's-length relationship with governments on reform issues. This was due to their advocacy of abolition of most local governments, a position that was obviously unpopular with most local government politicians. In the new regionalism movement, business leaders are making efforts to work closely with governments on regional governance issues. This approach is usually based on an economic development imperative to enhance the economy of the region. The focus is not on efficiency, effectiveness, and equity in service delivery but on addressing regional issues that plague and hinder the economic viability of the region, such as environment, transportation, job creation, and housing concerns. These issues, as discussed in Chapter 2, are increasingly perceived as pressing problems that must be addressed on a regional basis. Economic development issues are also increasingly perceived as pressing issues that must be addressed on a regional basis. Likewise, nonprofit organizations are interested in regional governance issues from a social service perspective. They are interested in promoting social equity and equal access throughout the metropolitan area.[14]

Basic regional governance does not require private involvement. Regional services can be delivered and governments can cooperate among themselves without the involvement of the nongovernmental community. However, new regionalism is more than just delivery of services. Collaborative regionalism involves addressing regional policy issues in addition to delivery of services. Governance issues that involve solving problems and implementing policies that affect regional development cannot be adequately addressed without the involvement of the nongovernmental sector. Public–private coalitions, then, are an essential component of new regionalism. It is a collaborative, nonhierarchical process that involves participants from both the public and private sectors. There is a commitment among participants to consensus building and shared leadership in resolving issues. The participants invariably have their own self-interests but usually develop a group synergy that extends their scope of influence, range of expertise, and legitimacy that they lack on their own. Consequently, the collaborative effort is held together by the advantages each participant perceives through mutual involvement.[15]

Government leaders' interests run the gamut, from bringing economic development to their community, to providing adequate services, to protecting or improving the quality of life for their residents. There is an increasing awareness among government leaders of the need to work with each other and with leaders from the private and nonprofit sectors to effectively achieve their goals. Therefore, each sector has particular self-interests in collaborating in regional governance. To achieve their self-interests, they must be willing to share power and resources.

Collaboration and Regional Governance

As previously stated, regional collaborative governance is based on the realization that no single government in a decentralized, polycentric system can effectively meet regional challenges. Participation of all interested parties is important if there is to be successful resolution of regional problems, and positive cooperative action is likely to be more effective and lasting than negative, top-down mandates. Moreover, this regionalism movement recognizes that creativity and experimentation are better than a heavy-handed bureaucratic approach. Regional problems are more likely to be solved by focusing on substantive problems than on the structure or the process.[16]

The regional governance that is emerging is different from the regional council movement of the 1960s and 1970s. Instead of organizations to help resolve regional problems, councils in the 1960s and 1970s were often seen as extensions of the federal government, as paper shufflers and gatekeepers of federal grant programs, and as somewhat adversarial by the local governments in the region. While these notions still exist, they are less pervasive, regional entities today are seen more and more as vehicles to resolve regional governance issues. A major focus in the 1960s and 1970s was to obtain federal grants through regional councils, not to resolve regional governance issues. Councils, composed mainly of local government representatives, encountered turf problems, and member governments were often concerned that cooperation would lead to loss of power and authority. The current collaboration and cooperation is much more involved in problem solving with participants actively trying to find ways to cooperate and work together. With the pressures on governments to provide acceptable services and with the expectation to do so without increasing resources, there is more of an urgency and less turf-guarding in the new regionalism movement.[17]

Collaboration with the private and nonprofit sectors and the spirit of cooperation between local governments is also fueled by the increasing awareness of the interdependence of metropolitan areas and the need to cooperate and work together. This is particularly evident in economic development. The once-dominant heavy industry with its extensive investment in facilities is being replaced by service and high-tech businesses that are mobile and easily relocated. In the industrial era, the commitment to an area by a business was often solidified by access to capital, the location of the headquarters in the area, and the heavy investment in immobile facilities and equipment. Now, it is likely that plant facilities, financial capital, and the headquarters for a firm are located in different metropolitan areas and possibly in different nations. Plant and equipment investments are also not as extensive and immobile as they once were. For firms to be competitive in an increasingly mobile and globalized economic environment, the adequacy and quality of public services throughout the region are important considerations for attracting and retaining growth. Providing services and the siting of regional facilities that support growth require collaboration and cooperative efforts.[18]

Relationships are critical to collaboration. In a collaborative environment where negotiations, give and take, and compromise are essential, building trust is required to achieve success. If the parties trust each other, there is far less likelihood for the parties involved to be apprehensive as to what the other organizations' real motives are. Trust between stakeholders also increases the ease of reaching agreement and deciding a course of action. Because collaboration is never neat and tidy, the group members need a strong sense of mutual trust to make things work. Moreover, in a crisis there might not be time to come to an agreement as to who is to take the lead. With relationships already established, it is much easier to work through sticky issues in a timelier manner.[19]

Collaboration is a nonhierarchical process where all parties come to the table as relatively equal participants in decision making. Because all participants are peers, a commitment to consensus building is a prerequisite to the success of the endeavor. There is no set formula for success other than the desire to cooperatively work together and set aside parochial interests for the good of the whole. Under new regionalism with no hierarchical structure and overall authority, a new form of leadership and a different way of making policy are required. These are not leaders in the traditional sense of having positional authority over others, and they should not be in a position to directly benefit from a specific solution. Decisions need to be made in a cooperative and collaborative environment. Facilitators cannot be connected with any specific government involved or any private or nonprofit enterprise that stands to gain from a proposed solution. In other words, their agenda should be simply to facilitate the collaborative process to reach mutually acceptable solutions. Developing consensus and overcoming independent member opposition are essential to obtain action that is in the overall best interest of the whole. Entrepreneurial leadership is required to provide governance in a setting where no one is in charge. David Chrislip and Carl Larson, in their research on collaborative leadership, identified the environment needed for successful regional collaboration:

> Participants come from the public and private sectors and from the broader community. They are not members of a single organization but rather come from many different organizations and institutions. Their training, experiences, and values differ markedly. There are many different values—religious, educational, political, industrial, and so on—represented ... [S]trategies for getting results in situations demanding collaboration are unclear ... There is no agreement on the problems themselves, on possible solutions, or even on how to move ahead ... [Leaders] rely on the group to work with the content and substance of the issues. Their task is to see to it that the process is constructive and leads to results, not to impose their own answers to collective issues. The questions they face have only the answers the group can agree upon ... The answers must emerge from the interaction of the stakeholders.[20]

What is required to be a successful collaborative leader? One study asked people, who were identified as successful collaborators, what they considered necessary to be a successful collaborative leader. They indicated first and foremost, the collaborative leader must have requisite personal attributes with the main attribute being open-mindedness, followed by patience. Other attributes that were important but mentioned less were having self-confidence, being willing to take risks, and being flexible, unselfish and persistent. After personal attributes, interpersonal skills were important including being a good communicator, an excellent listener and adept at working with people. Group process skills were third on the list, which included being an effective negotiator, facilitator, and collaborative group problem solver. Strategic leadership was also important including ability to articulate a vision and think strategically in developing goals, structures, inputs and actions to achieve the objectives of the collaboration.[21]

An excellent example of a collaborative leader compared to a non-collaborative leader occurred in the Katrina hurricane disaster. The director of the Federal Emergency Management Agency (FEMA) when Katrina devastated New Orleans was Michael Brown. FEMA performed poorly under his direction and he was replaced with Thad Allen, who was brought in to manage the cleanup. Brown argued that he was not able to control other agencies that were not under his formal control. There were no clear lines of authority and the levels of government were not coordinating their activities. No one provided the leadership and the coordination that was required for a smooth response. Instead the response was sporadic and tied up in bureaucratic red tape, finger pointing and fights over who had authority. Plans had not been worked out in advance and so no one was responsible for coordinating the overall response.

Brown, in control of the lead agency with the most resources but without authority over the other relief agencies, neglected the key requirement for a successful resolution with many stakeholders involved. He needed to take the lead in forming partnerships and collaborations with the myriad other agencies to address the disaster. He did not lead in a collaborative way and instead responded with a hierarchal, silo mindset. In contrast, Thad Allen took a collaborative, nonpolitical approach to the Katrina aftermath. He did not engage in finger pointing or recriminations with the governor or the mayor of New Orleans. Instead, he quietly forged a working relationship with them and involved them in his cleanup plans. He had planning meetings with stakeholders and coordinated the efforts of organizations that brought in resources to assist in the cleanup. Working collaboratively and open communication were key to his success in the Katrina cleanup. The contrast between Brown's and Allen's leadership styles reflects key differences between the bureaucratic hierarchical approach and the collaborative approach.[22]

Besides skilled facilitation for successful regional collaboration, there must be results from the process. Groups that do not see some results from their efforts will soon lose interest and commitment. Action-oriented groups will engender increased participation from those who want to have a voice in the process. To be successful, collaboration should include all relevant stakeholders. Involvement in the process must be broad-based and inclusive rather than exclusive. Although there is a danger that inclusiveness may bring in those whose agenda is to derail the process, there is a greater danger of failure by excluding some groups whose support is necessary for the collaboration to succeed.[23]

Collaboration should be strategic in nature to have the greatest chance of success. All too often, a group of well-intentioned participants come together but with limited forethought about the purpose, structure, processes, or outcomes of the collaboration. This mirrors the notion of "muddling through" and hoping that something good will result. Occasionally something good does result but often inertia, fatigue and frustration are the outcomes. It should be intentional, goal-directed, with agreed upon rules and procedures. There should be basic agreement on the problem and participants should be carefully chosen and should be invested in the process and committed to seeking a solution. Participants should be willing to work across boundaries and leaders should be consensus builders.[24]

Problems with Collaboration

A major criticism of public–private collaboration is that the public sector is an unequal partner in the collaboration. Teisman and Klijn claim that while there is an intensified interaction between public and private partners, there is little joint decision making and continuity in cooperation. In effect, there is much talk, but the partnership is not truly equal. It is not the same as joint ventures in the private sector with shared decision making. This blending of public and private only goes so far as the participants come from two different orientations. The public sector is political, hierarchical, and a command system while the private system is market driven. Although there may be some shared decision making, the final decision and method of implementation of the policy is determined by the public sector, making any partnership an uneven partnership. An additional concern is the free rider problem. In some instances, governments may be able to stay out of the cooperative and collaborative arrangements and still receive benefits.[25]

Another issue with new regionalism is that its main focus is economic development and other issues might not receive adequate attention. Although activities that promote economic development will impact social issues to some extent, such as affordable housing, new employment centers, or adequate transportation for commuter access or movement of goods, the emphasis is not on social problems. The social issues might not receive the holistic attention that is required to effectively address them. In addition, community groups often have goals that are not consistent with business-led economic development initiatives such as growth management and protection of the environment. The question remains as to how new regionalism initiatives with heavy business influence can effectively extend to social issues beyond economic development. According to Ross and Levine, outside the economic development arena, the achievements of new regionalism have been relatively minimal.[26]

The most important public benefit from collaborative initiatives is jobs, which are generally either temporary, low-paying, or do not go to the people in the region who most need them.[27] The goal of the private sector in a collaborative effort is for the public sector to facilitate private development. This may be a worthwhile goal, critics contend, if the residents benefit with increased employment opportunities, lower taxes, or better services. Yet, the evidence suggests that benefits are not enjoyed equally throughout the region. The majority of jobs created by downtown development usually require considerable education or technical training. These jobs are filled predominately by suburban or city residents who are already employed or employable without the government subsidies. The trickle-down effect on general prosperity is minimal because the development creates an island of prosperity in a sea of poverty.[28]

Redevelopment disproportionately favors downtowns over neighborhoods and the well-educated over the unskilled.[29] A criticism of the downtown redevelopment focus is that the area's other needs tend to be inadequately addressed, if at all. For example, researchers of Cleveland's touted renaissance charge that the public–private partnership has not adequately addressed the decline of manufacturing or the increase in poverty and racism that cloud the prospects for future development.[30] Furthermore, critics charge that public involvement may distort the private market to the advantage of some private firms and the disadvantage of others. There is also concern that the government may assume questionable risks for which the taxpayers may be ultimately responsible. Finally, in the rush to assist private development in order to achieve a public goal, public health, safety, and welfare objectives may be sacrificed. In any cooperative venture with the private sector, the government's obligation to protect the public's welfare should not be compromised. The government should not improperly expropriate private resources or unnecessarily provide a benefit to particular private organizations at the expense of other private organizations.[31]

The involvement of the private sector and its prominent role in public–private ventures raises important questions of democracy and accountability. Just who is, and is not, represented in these decision-making bodies? (These same issues can also be raised, more or less, relative to metropolitan-wide special districts.) Private developers, business leaders, and business-led civic organizations often dominate special districts and new regionalism initiatives. Neighborhood groups are less organized, less connected to the political establishment, and command fewer resources. They are at a distinct disadvantage in influencing public policy compared to the business community. Latino and African American activists have been hesitant to support new regionalism because of their fear that it might be insensitive to many of the concerns of minority communities.[32]

To summarize, there are many institutional and political obstacles to collaboration including conflicting goals and missions of the collaborators, inflexible administrative and legal procedures, and constrained financial resources. The incomplete legal foundation for collaboration raises questions about authority, transparency and accountability. The context of collaborative governance may not fairly balance private interests and public authority. Critical interests may not be represented and collaborative processes may bias decisions toward the participants with the greatest resources. Collaboration can be a way of advancing self-interested goals.[33] In responding to the critics, law professor Judith Wegner contends that there is a legal framework of state laws and case law that provides protections against government overreaching in facilitating private development. A clear public purpose must be demonstrated for government involvement in the private sector. In addition, government power to provide tax incentives or expenditures of resources in public–private ventures is strictly regulated by requirements regarding due process. Often, voter referendums provide opportunity for citizen approval of the potential impact on the public welfare from public–private ventures.[34]

Despite these statutory and legal assurances that the public interest is protected in public–private partnerships, there remains a concern of a fundamental conflict of interest. Government interests are different from private interests, and its role as regulator conflicts with its role in assisting in development.[35] It is clear that business is needed to provide investment, employment, and taxes, and business needs government to provide public services and establish the parameters for development. However, goals and needs diverge. The community experiences an imbalance of information because it knows less of the business corporation's goals and needs than the business corporation knows of the community's affairs. Thus, there is an information advantage favoring the private sector in cooperative ventures. Also, large corporations may gain or maintain an advantage over smaller businesses by extending their influence through public–private partnerships.[36] In any event, benefits bestowed on the partnering corporations by public sector incentives shift public service costs to consumers and corporations not involved in the cooperative efforts.

There are, however, examples of citizen groups that have been effective in developing partnerships and regional alliances to achieve goals that were not economic-development based. For instance, in Ohio a regional alliance calling itself the First Suburbs Consortium joined with farmers to support an Agricultural Preservation Act to preserve farmland by limiting sprawl development that saps the vitality of older communities. Church groups and nonprofit associations came together in an alliance to pressure Minnesota to pass regional fair-share housing and social justice legislation. In Oregon a coalition of environmentalists, farmers, downtown business interests and neighborhood activists came together to support growth management measures that preserved green space and agricultural land in the Portland metropolitan area.[37]

Elements That Foster Successful Collaborations

The initiation of collaboration can come from either the public or private sector. The key to successful collaboration is a willingness to work together by both public and nongovernmental leaders, a viable civic infrastructure to organize and facilitate the process, and a leader from either side to initiate the process. The civic infrastructure is the necessary support system that nurtures and sustains the regional cooperation effort. Even with a strong civic infrastructure, there must be leaders on both sides to promote public–private regional collaboration. A willingness by the civic community to engage in collaboration will come to naught if the public sector leaders are not prepared to cooperate.[38]

Even business enterprises seem to do better in networked environments. A study of similar businesses in closed environments versus networked environments appears to give credence to the value of regional collaboration and networks in promoting growth and development. The areas studied were the Route 128 Beltway around Boston and California's Silicon Valley. Both areas enjoyed roughly the same employment levels in 1975, had common origins in postwar military spending and university-based research, and were heavily engaged in computer-related businesses. Although both regions faced downturns in the 1980s, Silicon Valley quickly recovered while Route 128 continued to struggle to reverse its decline. Professor AnnaLee Saxenian argues that the different experiences of these two regions are due to the environment in which its companies operate. She states:

> Silicon Valley has a regional, network-based industrial system that promotes learning and mutual adjustment among specialist producers of a complex of related technologies. The region's dense social networks and open labor markets encourage entrepreneurship and experimentation. Companies compete intensely while at the same time learning from one another about changing markets and technologies through informal communication and collaborative practices. Loosely linked team structures encourage horizontal communication among firm's divisions and with outside suppliers and customers. The functional boundaries within firms are porous in the network-based system, as are the boundaries among firms and between firms and local institutions, such as trade associations and universities.
>
> In contrast, the Route 128 region is dominated by autarkic corporations that internalize a wide range of productive activities. Practices of secrecy and corporate loyalty govern relations between these firms and their customers, suppliers, and competitors, reinforcing a regional culture that encourages stability and self-reliance. Corporate hierarchies ensure that authority remains centralized, and information tends to flow vertically. Social and technical networks are largely internal to the firm, and the boundaries among firms and between firms and local institutions remain far more distinct in this independent, firm-based system.[39]

Vibrant Civic Sector

For successful collaboration between the business and political communities to take place, the business sector has to be organized. In regime theory a thriving civic sector is an important vehicle through which nongovernmental actors influence public policy.[40] It is also an essential element in new regionalism. Political scientist Robert Putnam found in his research of regional government in Italy that civic networks are important for regional governance because they foster communication and interaction among diverse groups. Civic engagement overcomes barriers of suspicion and mistrust and promotes community-regarding behavior and cooperation in resolving community issues. Civic involvement on the basis of shared interests transcends narrow self-interests and promotes cooperative behavior for the good of the whole.[41]

That is why, for example, conservation groups, while providing for the particular needs of their members, also serve the broader community in promoting wetland protection. However, a web of competing interests balances the interests of the conservation group with the interests of groups pushing economic development. Thus, the civic infrastructure moves the discussion to a higher level that transcends individual government boundaries and balances narrow interests of individual associations with the interests of other associations.

Additional research[42] shows the importance of the civic sector as a neutral zone between government and business where issues can be discussed and relationships can be developed without political boundaries and immediate business agendas interfering. Civic agency leaders often are former successful politicians or high-level business executives who have credibility with both business and political leaders. These leaders are able to bring the various stakeholders together and facilitate discussion and action on decisions. Civic agencies can also function as neutral third parties in providing staff support and conducting research to keep issues on the public agenda. There are a number of examples in the literature of successful resolution of difficult regional public policy issues that were brokered by a neutral civic agency.[43]

A Committee for Economic Development study of public–private cooperation also concluded that "civic leaders—people who care about their cities and are willing and able to take action—are the impetus for public–private cooperation that can be the vehicle for overcoming otherwise compelling forces of deterioration." This study identified the following as essential for a vibrant civic infrastructure:

- A positive civic culture rooted in a practical concern for the community as a whole that encourages citizen participation;
- A realistic and commonly accepted vision of the community that takes into account strengths and weaknesses in identifying what the community can and should become;
- Effective building-block civic organizations that blend the self-interest of their members with the broader interest of the community and translate that dual interest into effective action;

- A network among the key groups that encourages communication among leaders of every important segment and facilitates the mediation of differences among competing interests,
- The inclination to nurture civic entrepreneurs–leaders whose knowledge, imagination, and energy are directed toward enterprises that will benefit the community, whether in the public sector, the private sector, or both;
- Continuity in policy, including the ability to adapt to changing circumstances, which minimizes uncertainty and fosters confidence in individual and group enterprises.[44]

Private Sector Leadership

Even as the business sector has an important, if not the dominant, private sector role in urban regime studies, business leadership is necessary to build an effective regional regime. Successful business-initiated and supported collaborative regionalism is dependent on the continuing and personal involvement of the top leadership from the private sector in a civic agency dedicated to fostering partnerships on public policy issues. Business leaders generally exercise their influence through civic agencies in providing financial support and actively serving on agency boards and committees. Civic agencies must be perceived to be neutral and non-biased toward any individual interest involved in the process. They cannot be perceived as connected with any specific government involved or any private or nonprofit enterprise that stands to directly gain from a proposed solution. Their agenda should be simply to facilitate a collaborative process to reach mutually acceptable solutions on public policy issues.

Kathryn Foster and David Henton and his co-authors maintain that the interests of private sector leaders are often the impetus for regional governance collaboration. Since they establish the agenda, their issues reflect the interests of the private and nonprofit sectors, including economic growth, service cost and quality, and intraregional disparities. According to Foster, the public sector leadership has a weak regional focus, whereas corporate, civic, and academic leaders are more regionally focused. They generally see their interests as regional rather than restricted by political boundaries.[45] Harvard University Professor Rosabeth Moss Kanter claims that business groups are increasingly recognized as a major force in advocating regional approaches to economic development issues. She calls these business groups *shadow governments* and writes,

> It is taken for granted in many places that the problems of metropolitan regions will not be solved without business involvement, and many informal or unofficial public leadership roles have been handed to the private sector, reflecting an assumed primacy of the economy over the polity.[46]

Crisis or Opportunity

Empirical regime studies show that a crisis or opportunity is often required to energize the private sector to become involved in public policy. An identifiable crisis can mobilize not only the business community but the political leaders and residents of the area to jointly work towards acceptable solutions. Without a crisis or an appealing opportunity, the possibility of achieving success in new regionalism initiatives is considerably less. Indeed, the crisis or opportunity needs to capture the attention of the leaders of the community in order for the leaders to put in the time and effort to work towards a solution. Examples in the literature are usually of the community leaders responding to an economic development crisis.[47] Occasionally, however, the business community responds to an opportunity as was the case in Atlanta and Salt Lake City where city and suburban business and government leaders collaborated on the Olympics. Through the necessity of collaboration to bring to fruition the Olympics, networks and relationships were formed that continue as the leaders address regional problems confronting their region.

Broad Community Involvement

Regional public–private collaborations are more successful if they are broad-based coalitions. There are numerous examples in empirical studies of the importance of broad community support for successful regional governance initiatives. In Pittsburgh the business organization, Allegheny Conference on Community Development, convenes broad-based task forces of community leaders from all sectors to study public issues, make recommendations, and advocate for their acceptance. In the structural reform effort in Indianapolis, the role of the League of Women Voters and the Chamber of Commerce was important in keeping the reform issue on the public agenda. The Greater Indianapolis Progress Committee, a bipartisan citizens group representing a wide spectrum of the community, was probably the most successful of numerous government-sponsored study groups. This group has been institutionalized as a valuable component of the civic community.[48]

Another area with a strong civic infrastructure that has had substantial success in instituting mechanisms for regional governance is the Twin Cities. The Twin Cities has the familiar civic organizations such as the Urban League, the American Association of University Women, the Urban Coalition, the United Fund, and the League of Women Voters. But they also have several organizations that are unique. These organizations are characterized by their ability to involve business leaders in public affairs in intimate and sustained ways. The Citizens League is one of the country's most successful private, business-oriented, civic research organizations.

The League was created in 1952 as an outgrowth of years of informal discussions on public issues among civic-minded Twin Cities businessmen. Since the early 1960s, the League's main task has been to identify important issues before they become critical, study them, assess possible responses, and recommend a preferred approach. Membership is open to anyone who is willing to pay the minimal annual dues–there are about 3,000 individual members and 600 supporting firms and foundations.[49]

Public Sector Involvement and Support for Regional Collaboration

Absent political involvement and support, the business community would not be able to achieve success with its regional agenda. However, without business support and pressure, there would be little interest in the political community for a regional orientation. Obviously, for business to maximize its influence in regional governance issues, there must be public sector leaders who are receptive to partnering with the private sector, and they must be in a position to affect public policies. The major problem is that there is generally no government structure at the regional level with authority over the geographical area similar to a municipal government. Without this structure and the need to build a regional constituency, political leaders are less invested in regional issues. This makes coalition building more difficult. Because there is no regional political constituency, it also makes the business sector that much more critical in initiating new regionalism.

Political leaders increasingly realize that development and governance issues are moving to a regional level, and their authority is limited beyond their boundaries unless they unite in joint efforts. Moreover, business leaders are anxious to engage political leaders in partnerships, because they realize that their businesses can better compete in a global economy from a well-governed region that is focused on quality-of-life and development issues. Examples of public and NGO collaboration are numerous. One such example is in the Peoria, Illinois area, which is not known as a vibrant, forward-looking, well-governed area. A public–private partnership has been established to plan for the future development of the area. A vice-president from the major employer, Caterpillar, is co-chair along with the mayor of Peoria and the superintendent of the public school district. Representatives from the Peoria Civic Federation, composed major employers in the area, and the Greater Peoria Council of Governments are included on the steering committee. The partnership is broad based with task forces to study and make recommendations on delivery of local government services, public education, culture and tourism, economic development, and transportation.[50]

Government leaders generally are interested in regional issues only to the extent that these issues affect their individual municipalities. Regional issues that might engender regional involvement range from bringing economic development to their community, to providing adequate services, to protecting or improving the quality of life for their residents. Although some federal and state policies may promote regional planning and cooperation among local governments, politicians from all levels generally avoid regional governance issues unless there is public support for a particular issue.[51] There is little or no incentive for federal, state, or local political leaders to involve themselves in regional governance issues because there is no regional voting constituency. Indeed, those who espouse regional approaches to governance are often vilified for their efforts. In one example, Myron Orfield was verbally attacked and received numerous threats for his efforts in promoting regional governance in the Twin Cities.[52]

Indeed, the need for political leader involvement in regional coalitions often extends beyond the local political leadership. Major development initiatives often require private sector leaders working with political leaders from the state and state-established special districts. In an analysis of three major economic development efforts in Chicago, Professor James Smith showed how critical public entities are to the success of each undertaking. Indeed, he found in his analysis of efforts to bring the 1992 World's Fair to Chicago, the construction of a new Chicago White Sox stadium and the redevelopment of Navy Pier, that it was not just the city political leadership that the private sector leaders worked with in building coalitions. The governor and other state government leaders and administrators and leaders of special purpose authorities played critical roles in the efforts.[53] The state and regional special authorities and in some cases the county (see Chapters 8 and 9) are increasingly becoming involved in regional governance coalitions. The effectiveness and duration of regional governance is improved when governments with regional authority are involved. These governments give political legitimacy, resources, and a continuing focus to regional governance initiatives, and they also make regionalism issues visible and important to the region. Finally, if the state established an umbrella government agency with a regional governing mandate, the agency would be able to develop and project a regional vision and identity as well as institutionalize the processes of regional problem solving.

Ultimately Government is necessary for effective regional governance. Regional coalitions of independent organizations are fleeting and are dependent on the willingness of the actors to collaboratively work together. Noted regionalists David Rusk and Neal Peirce maintain that some formal structure is ultimately necessary for effective regional governance. Rusk believes that there are a number of paths to regional government. Although in his view the most direct and efficient means in metropolitan areas is to fully empower county government and abolish municipalities, this is not the only route (and Rusk points out that this is not an option in the New England states without county government). Peirce stresses that it is necessary to draw all regional participants—business groups, nonprofit organizations, citizen organizations, universities, foundations, and so on–into region wide problem solving, and that collectively working with government, they become the governance structure of the region. But he also asks,

> Is there any middle way to get the benefits of regional governance without some form of overarching structure? . . . Again and again . . . we were driven to the conclusion that a region simply must have some form of umbrella regional governance structure.

For him there is no other way to bring a region to the point of "clear and shared governance, the ability to plan strategically and act cohesively."[54]

In summary, regional collaboration for effective regional governance is facilitated by the following elements:

- There must be opportunity or crisis. However, the opportunity or crisis will not by itself perpetuate or sustain continuing regionalism initiatives.
- Top business leadership must initiate the effort or be actively invested in the effort after it is initiated. Business leadership must give liberally of time and resources to make the effort successful.
- An active civic sector must be in place to promote networking and community.
- There must be a civic agency to spearhead the effort. The civic agency should have the full support of the business leadership, and the leaders of the agency must have a good working relationship with local and state political leaders. It should have adequate staff resources, facilitate and guide the process, be action oriented not just a report generator, and monitor the implementation of action plans. As facilitator of the process, the agency must remain objective and not be an advocate of a specific solution. The process cannot be perceived as business- or central-city-dominated.
- Broad involvement from other leaders and citizens in the region is important for successful regionalism. All geographic areas and sectors of the community affected by the issues should be involved in the deliberative process that arrives at a solution.
- Political leaders from throughout the region must be actively involved in the process to facilitate government support and action.

The Increase in Cooperation and Collaboration among Governments

Cooperation among governments and collaborative efforts with the private sector to solve regional problems are gaining ground in many metropolitan areas as the new direction in regional governance. Whereas local governments previously remained aloof from one another and only worked together when compelled by a crisis, a state mandate, or to obtain grants from federal or state governments, political and civic leaders are now initiating cooperative efforts and reaching out more to the nongovernmental community. Consultants advocating regional approaches to urban problems, such as David Rusk and Neal Peirce, writings by academics and others, and deteriorating conditions in central cities and suburbs (see Chapter 2) have been successful in focusing renewed interest in regional collaboration and cooperation.[55] Examples of successful collaboration in metropolitan areas have also been instrumental in focusing attention on this form of governance. A number of examples are presented below.

The spirit of cooperation is exhibited in metropolitan areas of the country where previously animosity or wariness existed. For example, in Boston the city's mayor successfully lobbied for the state to establish a Greater Boston Municipal Cooperation Commission to encourage cooperation among local governments. In the suburbs of St. Louis County a shared sales tax program was enacted into law. Charlotte, North Carolina, has experienced substantial success in combining city and county government functions.[56] The spirit of cooperation has led to unique experiments. For example, one city entered into an agreement with the YMCA whereby the city built a recreation facility with a pool and gymnasium that is managed and operated by the YMCA. Another city provides fire service to unincorporated areas and, in turn, has an animal control service agreement with the county.[57] Although these types of initiatives are not new, anecdotal evidence indicates that the frequency and extent of their occurrence across the country has significantly multiplied.

Despite the efforts of regionalists, there is still substantial resistance to cooperation. Old ways of providing services, historical barriers between municipalities, and concepts of municipal independence die slowly. In fact, in the fiercely independent suburbs of the Pittsburgh region, some distressed suburbs have gone without services rather than relinquish control. For instance, when the state of Pennsylvania suggested that several of the distressed communities in the Monongahela Valley consider merging police departments, one of the most costly services, they refused. The city of Clairton went without police protection for periods of time rather than give up local control of the function. The establishment of regional emergency 911 services in Allegheny County in the Pittsburgh region was recommended as a cost-effective way to bring electronic emergency dispatch services to the suburbs. This was successfully resisted by suburban political leaders who were more interested in maintaining local control of emergency dispatching than improving the quality of the service.[58] The role of civic organizations, as indicated above, is usually an essential element in new regionalism. The likelihood of regional cooperation among governments is often improved when it is facilitated through a neutral third party, such as civic organizations. These organizations transcend political boundaries and are in the most advantageous position to develop and nurture a network of private, nonprofit, and government organizations to address regional governance concerns. Civic agencies can also function as disinterested third parties in providing staff support and conducting research to keep issues on the public agenda.

Civic agencies can serve as a neutral third party to provide mediation between competing interests. An example of the advantages of third-party mediation was the development of a new water supply for the Denver region's growing population. There was substantial controversy on this issue involving the Denver Water Board, Suburban Water Suppliers, developers, and environmentalists. The issue was compounded by the fact that the water was to come from west of the Continental Divide. Diverting water to the Denver region was strongly opposed by west-slope interests. A nonprofit organization was designated to act as a neutral facilitator to work with the interested parties to mediate a solution. Through a process of meetings, small working groups, proposals, and counterproposals, basic agreements were reached in less than half the time required in a previous effort to increase the water supply to the region. Moreover, the bitter feelings felt for years by the last experience were not evident in this effort.[59]

Communities generally will only cooperate and work together to the extent that they have a self-interest or are required to by the state or federal government. Community self-interest is realized through substantial reduction in costs of the function or service improvement. Citizen pressure to provide or upgrade a service combined with pressure to keep taxes down could also prompt governments to seek to cooperate. In some metropolitan areas, central cities and suburbs that once were antagonistic competitors are starting to see benefits from working together on issues of mutual concern. Myron Orfield describes the coalition of the central cities and low-tax-capacity inner suburbs in the Twin Cities on tax-sharing schemes and other regional initiatives of common concern. Pitting the have-not communities against the have-communities worked in the Minnesota state legislature to bring advances in regional governance to the Twin Cities.[60] He feels that building coalitions of the central city with suburbs that share the same issues could be used in other metropolitan areas as an effective method to achieve tax-sharing and other regional governance policies. Tax-sharing schemes and other regional initiatives, could win support in the state legislature if more suburbs would benefit than be harmed. It is ironic that Orfield, an ardent regionalist, believes that conflict is necessary to bring about regional governance when others say such governance should be built on mutual cooperation, shared values, and trust.

The viability of Orfield's conflict model has not been demonstrated outside Minnesota. In fact, Orfield had only minimal success with this model in pushing a regional agenda in the Minnesota state legislature in the 1990s. There is evidence, however, that central cities and many suburbs are finding that they have many issues in common and are beginning to work together to obtain state support. This movement can be seen in recent events in

Chicago. In early 1997 the city hired a former executive director of a suburban council of governments to be the mayor's special assistant on suburban affairs. Besides advising the mayor on suburban issues, this position is a conduit for the city to reach out to the suburbs. As a result, the city is starting to include the suburbs in various activities. For example, the mayor invited suburban political leaders to participate in a meeting on transportation issues–thus giving the meeting a regional instead of a city focus.

These initiatives have progressed to the formation of a Metropolitan Area Mayors' Caucus comprised of some 30 mayors working together on issues to improve the quality of life and make the region more competitive in attracting and retaining business. Although there are still divisions between the city and the suburbs, such as suburban opposition to the expansion of Chicago's O'Hare airport, there are many issues that the city and the suburbs have in common. The purpose of the caucus is to present a united front to the state legislature and cooperate together on such issues as lowering property taxes, increasing state support for schools, improving workforce skills, and addressing common environmental and social issues.[61]

Case Studies of Cooperation and Functional Integration

Small successes of cooperation between independent governments on service delivery can lead to collaboration on regional governance issues. If small steps are successful, there can be a progression to greater and greater cooperation and integration of functions. Indeed, major functional consolidations among independent governments with a long history of autonomous, even competitive relationships usually begin with tentative steps at administrative cooperation with support and encouragement from the business sector. As urban areas embrace the collaborative approach to regional governance, a growing body of case studies is developing. This section covers only a few case studies of regional collaborative governance. These case studies of collaborative governance could serve as a model for other areas as they move toward greater interdependent relationships.

Collaborative Smart Growth in Salt Lake City: A Voluntary, Nonbinding Approach[62]

In the late 1980s and early 1990s, the Salt Lake metropolitan area real estate market started booming with much of the growth in sprawl development. The economy grew at twice the national average. There started to be public discussion about how the rapid growth threatened the region's quality of life and its outdoor recreation assets that were crucial to its tourism industry. A group of business leaders, working with elected government officials and nonprofit advocacy groups, established the Coalition for Utah's Future. A survey sponsored by this organization identified the strains of growth as the main public concern. The group approached the governor to encourage the state to establish a statewide land use planning effort. The governor declined but encouraged the group to try to build public support for regional growth planning. The Coalition's initiative was the establishment of Envision Utah with its first chairman, Robert Grow, who had substantial respect and stature among opinion leaders and the civic community. Grow recruited a broad-based group including developers, environmentalists, civic activists, and local government officials.

The first step was to stimulate public discussion about growth issues and smart growth plans. To this end, Envision Utah sponsored a survey of quality-of-life values that the public desired for the region. It then sponsored workshops and public discussion of planning scenarios to realize or preserve these values within a growth economy. Based on growth projections, Envision Utah developed and released four long-range development scenarios based on the current highly dispersed growth, a slightly less dispersed growth pattern, a moderate compact development pattern, and a more compact development plan. These scenarios received broad discussion and debate. The public was asked to vote on its preferred scenario. Of the approximately 3 percent of the public that responded, 56 percent preferred the moderate compact development plan. Envision Utah then started pushing for implementation of the plan. It developed planning tools for local governments and planners to use and pursued demonstration projects that included county-level growth plans and mixed-use housing, community, and commercial developments to promote walkable neighborhoods. It maintained public awareness campaigns and continued to host community workshops on various aspects of the growth plan.

Stimulated by the Envision Utah effort, the state legislature also got involved and passed the Quality Growth Strategy. This Strategy required the establishment of a commission to study growth in the state and make recommendations about providing state incentives to local governments willing to engage in more compact development plans. One success of the effort was the voter acceptance of the development of a light rail system of public transportation that previously had been voted down. As evidence that the regional planning concepts pushed by Envision Utah are taking hold, several Utah counties have incorporated core elements of the quality growth strategies including major land set-asides for conservation into their long-range plans. Transportation dollars have also been set aside to add three additional light rail lines and a commuter rail line. The compact growth concepts are still controversial, but the majority of the public has accepted the concept of smart growth.

Envision Utah has shown how effective a public–private collaborative can be in achieving regional governance in a decentralized local government system with a public that has traditionally been opposed to any form of regional planning. This organization has been in operation over 15 years, and the collaborative governing process that it pioneered in Utah against tremendous opposition appears to have become accepted as a way of life. It has even received glowing accolades from outside observers. For example, Janet Kavinoky, Executive Director of Transportation and Infrastructure for the U.S. Chamber of Commerce wrote that "collaboration–people getting together and working toward a common goal—seems to be a default way of doing business ... I think the secret sauce, the foundation of Utah Exceptionalism, is something I heard time and time again: a dedication to getting things done for the good of their community, their state and the future."[63]

Collaborative School Planning in Palm Beach County Florida: A Voluntary Binding Approach[64]

With the explosive growth in the urban areas of Florida, the state legislature overhauled the growth management laws. One part of the overhaul was to require the school districts in the state to establish county-wide collaborative school planning (CSP) to address the needs of the burgeoning school population. The intent of the CSP was to encourage local governments to enter into an interlocal agreement (ILA) with a financially feasible solution to ensure that the supply of school seats concurs with the demand generated by new residential development. Palm Beach County was the only county in the state to establish a CSP process that resulted in the desired ILA.

There were three solutions to the sprawl development in Florida in addressing the school crowding problem. One extreme was to limit new development with no action on developing new schools. This solution would not be supported by developers. At the other extreme was simply to embark on an ambitious school construction program to catch up and keep up with the growth. This solution would require substantial resources. The best solution was for CSP to put an aggressive school construction program in place while also integrating city and county planning processes with school facilities planning. This required bringing various stakeholders to the table in a collaborative process. The major support for the CSP was the school district and the county while cities and real-estate developers were generally opposed. Citizens did not have a specific position in regard to CSP. They simply wanted the school overcrowding solved and, as taxpayers, had to approve any bond issues of taxes to pay for schools. The pressure they exerted was to solve the problem and keep costs low.

There was substantial opposition to the CSP. The developers opposed because it implied another layer of bureaucracy that they would need to negotiate. The school district would have some enforceable level of influence over new development. The cities saw the process as diminishing their autonomy and authority over development. There was also an element of mistrust. The school district had a poor reputation among citizens and county and city officials. They were considered under qualified and not known for delivering schools on time. The county and the school district geographically served the entire county while the cities served only parts of the county. In addition, there was some difference in their constituencies. The communities with older populations or well established schools had less interest in supporting a school construction program than the sprawling communities.

The process took nine long years of consistent efforts to overcome resistance and keep stakeholders involved. The state supported the process, but the heavy lifting was at the local level. The critical elements in the success of the process were the leadership and perseverance of the chair of the school board and the chair of the county commission. The first attempt was from 1993 to 1995 and was not a success because of lack of funding for school construction. However, the committee kept meeting and sharing ideas once every two weeks. From 1996 to 1998 the state declared a moratorium on the process. After the moratorium was lifted in 1998, the county commenced the process again and by January 2001, the school board, the county, 32 municipalities, five special districts and one airport authority had signed the ILA. Overcoming the mistrust of the school district was a major factor in the success of the collaborative. The collaborative process was itself a factor in overcoming this mistrust through showing that the school district was capably led and able to carry out its commitments.

The stakeholders were also convinced that they would benefit from the CSP. The developers supported the CSP because the plan did not attempt to limit development, but to keep up with development. Cities benefitted because of the vigorous school construction and modernization program and were willing to give new residential development approval to the school district. There was a contractual agreement that if the school district did not meet its commitments on school construction and modernization, it would lose the authority to approve new residential permits. Residents supported a sales surtax dedicated to school modernization and construction that increased the value of their property.

Coalition Building in Pittsburgh

Regionalism has been an agenda item in the Pittsburgh region for much longer than in most other metropolitan areas. One reason is that the population of the region was substantially decentralized from the city by the early part of the twentieth century. As early as 1920, Pittsburgh contained only half the population of the county. By 2011 it had fallen to an estimated 25 percent. The economy of the region has also been decentralized from Pittsburgh since the middle of the twentieth century. The taxable valuation of the city was only 46 percent of the county in 1950 and, even with the redevelopment of the downtown area, had declined to 25 percent by 1990 and to 23 percent by 2010.[65]

During much of the twentieth century, the region had the third largest number of Fortune 500 headquarters in the United States. Its economy brought substantial wealth to the Pittsburgh area. Its strong and powerful business community is cohesive, is civic minded, and has substantial resources to invest in civic activities. Pittsburgh has a rich history of civic activism. The relationship between the city's political and business sectors has generally been positive. Pittsburgh's civic structure has been heavily involved in public policy issues, many with a regional focus. Government leaders generally looked to the civic sector for assistance in public policy issues.

The business community in Pittsburgh from the 1944 founding of the Allegheny Conference on Community Development (Conference), the elite business organization involved in public issues in Pittsburgh, claimed a regional as well as a city orientation. With its board composed of the top business and community leaders in the region, it coordinates all other major business-supported civic agencies. The Conference executives and most of the board members have access in both local and state governments. The Conference has historically played a catalytic role in bringing public and private leaders together to jointly solve policy issues. It formed a working relationship with the mayor of Pittsburgh, and jointly they brought about the famed Pittsburgh Renaissance after World War II. In the mid-1970s it embarked in partnership with the city political leaders on another revitalization of downtown.[66]

Although the Conference has historically promoted a regional government reform agenda, it never attempted to impose a formal metropolitan government on the area. Any attempt would have harmed its relationship with the political community. Instead, it developed a working relationship with political leaders and advocated a less threatening form of regionalism that included the transfer of functions from the city to the county and the expansion of county government authority. It also pushed home rule to improve county government structure and strengthen county authority to deal with municipal and regional issues.[67]

The Conference is a facilitator in building broad-based coalitions to study and generate support for public policies. It convenes task forces of leaders from all sectors of the community to study public issues and make recommendations and push for their acceptance. Although the Conference convenes the task force, it does not push a particular agenda on the task force. The task force operates with a high degree of independence. An

example is the task force the Conference established to make recommendations on county home rule. The chair was given full authority to select the
members of his committee, provided with staff support and operated
completely free from Conference constraints. He selected committee
members from a broad spectrum of the community, not just the business
community. The chair took ownership of the committee and was the lead
person in pushing home rule in the community. The Conference, as an
organization, stayed in the background. A united lobbying effort by county
political leaders and business leaders convinced the state legislature to pass
the desired legislation. After two previous failed attempts to obtain county
home rule, business and community leaders, mobilized by the civic sector,
played a prominent role in funding and generating support for the successful
home rule referendum.

If a task force or committee identifies a need for a new organization for
ongoing implementation, the Conference will create one. Examples of
organizations created by the Conference include ACTION-Housing in
1957 to work on improving housing and neighborhood revitalization, Penn's
Southwest Association in 1962 to market the region, and the Regional
Industrial Development Corporation in 1955 to develop and market
industrial and commercial properties.[68]

An example of public-private coalitions responding to opportunity or
crisis in Pittsburgh was the threat by the professional baseball team that it
would relocate from the region unless it was provided with a new stadium.
In addition, the convention center needed resources to renovate and expand
to remain competitive, and the cultural district had deteriorated and needed
funds to renovate. A Conference task force worked with political leaders in
an unsuccessful effort to gain voter approval for a regional sales tax to provide
the needed funding. Despite the setback, Conference leaders and city and
county political leaders continued working together and were able to obtain
additional funding from the state and other sources so that all the projects
were undertaken.[69]

Another example of how the partnership works in Pittsburgh was the
response by the Conference to an opportunity to improve regional governance. It acted on the suggestion of the chair of the Board of Commissioners
of Allegheny County to establish a regional development public–private
partnership involving all the counties in the Pittsburgh MSA. The Conference
took the lead in this effort because it had high visibility and the other counties perceived it as a neutral agency. The group has been successful in lobbying for favorable state legislation and funding for projects in the MSA.
They have also worked together to gain favorable interpretation of federal
environmental regulations.[70]

The Conference responded positively to yet another public policy crisis
involving the funding of cultural, recreational, and sports facilities located in
the city of Pittsburgh. Because there was substantial use of the facilities from

residents outside the city, Pittsburgh decided that it could no longer provide the major funding support. The Conference worked with county political leaders to convince the state legislature to allow the county to establish a regional asset district and increase the sales tax to fund regional assets throughout the county.[71]

Collaboration in the Denver Region[72]

The metropolitan Denver area has developed an approach to regional governance that unites this decentralized, sprawling region around economic development initiatives, but the collaboration extends beyond economic development into most public policy areas. It started with businesses coming together to form the Metro Denver Economic Development Corporation (Metro Denver EDC), an affiliate of the Denver Metro Chamber of Commerce. In 2003, still feeling the effects of the post 9/11 high-tech fallout, Metro Denver was in the economic doldrums.

Some of the region's business leaders decided to take matters into their own hands and work together to find ways to jump-start the economy. They reached out to other public, private and nonprofit organizations to form a regional economic development partnership that includes 70 cities, counties, and economic development organizations in the seven-county Metro Denver and two-county Northern Colorado region. Its collaborative approach to economic development includes support for the arts, bipartisan dialogue among the region's mayors, and proactive efforts to attract major sporting events. The organization has raised $13.3 million from the private sector to be used in an aggressive five-year plan to bring economic development to the region and brand the Metro Denver area as a sustainable hub for companies, entrepreneurs, and employees.

In 1993, area political leaders formed the Metro Mayors Caucus to create a neutral arena for the exchange of ideas on issues that affect the entire region. The Caucus is composed of 40 members from the region's local governments. This unique collaboration provides leadership and creative solutions for the region's most challenging issues. The Metro Mayors Caucus, with 11 other civic and government organizations, formed the Denver Living Streets initiative to support multimodal, sustainable transportation and to integrate with the use and form of adjacent development to achieve great destinations for people—not just the movement of people. The region's mayors also tackle growth management, water, housing, and health and wellness issues. The communities have agreed to work together on economic development and have signed an agreement not to offer companies incentives to relocate from one jurisdiction in the area to another.

The Denver metropolitan area provides strong regional support for sports, culture, and the arts. In 1988, voters approved a sales tax that earmarked one cent of every $10 to support art, historical, and scientific organizations in the seven-county Metro Denver region. The region established the Scientific and Cultural Facilities District (SCFD) to distribute the proceeds of the dedicated sales tax. It distributes some $40 million annually to more than 300 organizations throughout the metropolitan area. The Metro Denver Sports Commission (Denver Sports) is a regional group working to create economic and social opportunity through sports. The commission members include local businesses, area colleges and universities, local and state government entities, civic organizations, and professional sports teams. Through the commission's efforts, Denver has hosted events such as the NCAA Men's Basketball Tournament and the 2008 NCAA Frozen Four Hockey Tournament. In 2009, Denver was the first North American city to host Sport Accord, an international gathering of over 1,200 sports decision makers. In 2011, Denver hosted the Denver Big Air World Cup Snowboarding competition. The commission's efforts have also been instrumental in bringing the 2012 NCAA Basketball Women's Final Four and the 2014 FIL Men's Lacrosse World Championships to Denver.

Collaboration and Cooperation in Charlotte

There has been close functional cooperation between Charlotte and Mecklenburg County, North Carolina, for many years. This cooperation has led to consolidation of most functional departments. Although cooperation existed prior to 1971, a major impetus for consolidation of departments was the failed city–county consolidation effort in 1971. Consolidation was soundly defeated, despite support by the civic leadership and the two daily newspapers.[73] Two events followed the defeat. The town of Mint Hill incorporated to make it more difficult to be absorbed by Charlotte in any subsequent annexation or city–county merger, and the reformers turned to functional consolidation of services between the city and the county. Even though the city and the county started to cooperate and consolidate services, there were two other failed attempts in the 1990s to structurally consolidate the city and county governments.

With the incorporation of Mint Hill, there were six incorporated municipalities in the county besides Charlotte. To make further incorporations more difficult, the city and suburban municipalities divided the unincorporated area in the county into spheres of influence for future growth purposes. This meant that there would be no conflict between the governments in annexation of unincorporated territory. As unincorporated areas in the county develop, they are subject to annexation by the municipality over that area. This agreement and aggressive annexation by Charlotte have precluded further incorporations in the county.

The city has grown from 75 square miles in 1970 to 297.5 square miles. Its population has more than tripled from 1970 to an estimated 751,087 in 2012. The sphere of influence agreement limits Charlotte to a total land area in the county of 346 square miles, 66 percent of the total county. Charlotte also has 78 percent of the county population. Thus Charlotte, by a wide margin, dominates the suburbs.[74]

Functional consolidation has made substantial strides since 1971. In fact, most of the departments have been consolidated–some under the county and others under the city. Charlotte and its county are as administratively consolidated as some formal city–county consolidations. Very few services are offered by both the City of Charlotte and Mecklenburg County. The duplicate services include only storm water, computer services, licensing, communications, and the city–county government center. Mecklenburg County is solely responsible for parks and recreation, building inspection, elections, and tax administration. Charlotte provides the remaining services: planning and zoning, police, solid-waste disposal, public transit, water and sewer, animal control, community relations, historic landmarks and districts, cable television regulations, and purchasing.[75]

However, not all is well in the consolidated city and county functions. The parks and police functions were the largest and most controversial of the departmental consolidations. The merger was not accomplished according to original plans and it opened wounds that have yet to heal. Friction between top-level administrators is more evident now than before. There are different perceptions of how functions should be administered. There is the feeling that agreements made at the time of the parks and police consolidations are not being carried out. There is also a lack of continuing communication between city and county administrators. The city feels the county is not pro-development enough and announced the city's intention to take over building inspection, a function it consolidated with the county in 1983. The announcement of this intention, made before discussion with the county staff, has aroused negative feelings.

Further issues concern interpretation of the agreements. The county would like the city to police the parks as part of its police function. However, the city feels that the original agreement called for the county to police the parks and wants additional county funding before it is willing to comply. The county has forced the issue by reducing its park ranger staff, requiring the city to handle most of the police problems. Some county administrators also feel that the city park system, now under county jurisdiction, was extremely run-down, and required substantial county resources to bring it up to county standards. County staff feel that the functions it merged into the city were generally better managed and in better shape than the functions the city merged into the county. There is also a feeling by the county staff that the county is the appropriate level to consolidate services as it is accountable to all county residents.

It appears that the political calculus is moving toward less cooperation. There is some indication that there is starting to be a partisan divide between the city and the county. The politicians tend to support their administrations in any conflict that arises between the city and the county in the provision of services. The latest development is an effort by the city mayor to establish a task force to study total consolidation of the city and county. The mayor sought support from leaders in the nongovernmental community for this effort but did not solicit support from the county commissioners. The letter asked the nongovernmental leaders to sign a petition to the county commissioners in support of establishing a government study commission. To form a study commission, the county needs to add its approval. Members of the county commission felt that they had been blindsided by the mayor and that the mayor should have come directly to them. Such a move, according to some members of the commission, is driving a wedge to further cooperation and collaboration between the county and the city.[76]

Reasons for Functional Cooperation between Charlotte and Mecklenburg County

Possible reasons why Charlotte and Mecklenburg County have been able to cooperate and consolidate functions are the political and collaborative environment. The political leaders are not full-time politicians. Many political leaders are from the business community or have strong ties to the business community. There has not been a strong history of expansive government or excessive patronage. In a rapidly growing economy, providing government jobs has not been a major issue. Unionism is also not a strong factor in the community. People tend to be more independent and less concerned with job protection than in many other areas. There has also been a history and expectation of professional management at both the city and county. The politicians rely on professional staff for advice in policy-making, particularly in administrative areas. The business community is also extremely active in and supportive of improving government efficiency and effectiveness. There is extensive networking between political leaders and business leaders. Moreover, the area generally exhibits a pro-business climate which provides weight to business input in local government policy-making.

The Charlotte region provides an example of the benefits that can result from cooperation and collaboration with the private sector. The Carolinas Partnership, with public and private sector members from the 13 county metropolitan areas, markets the region for economic development. Those county governments also meet regularly as part of the Carolinas Coalition, while Charlotte and other cities have formed the Carolinas Urban Coalition of Cities. There is also a Metropolitan Transit Partnership. The collaborative economic development efforts have had some success. In one case a Japanese firm sought a new factory site in the area. The Charlotte Chamber of Commerce provided data on two sites in the region–both outside of Mecklenburg County. The firm chose one of the sites, which brought the area a $250 million construction project and about 700 jobs, many filled by Mecklenburg County residents.[77]

Despite the governmental cooperation and collaboration with the private sector, the Charlotte region is not without its problems. Neal Peirce, who did an assessment of the region, identified inadequate planning as the region's major problem. Land use decisions are made by private developers with little or no public planning. Some of the region's greatest pockets of congestion are in areas that are the most recently developed. According to Peirce's assessment, without overall regional planning, the overall result of individual developers' decisions will be deterioration in air quality, congestion, pollution, loss of community and formless sprawl.[78]

Takeaway

Collaborative regionalism is more advanced in some metropolitan areas than in others. The foregoing case studies provide an indication of the advantages that accrue from working together to advance the interests of the region. Building stable working relationships between leaders from the public and nongovernmental sectors is a long, difficult process, largely dependent for its success on the ability of the stakeholders to work together. It requires constant nurturing and successes for lasting governing coalitions to survive political and private leadership egos and changes. The case studies show a small but growing movement toward cooperation among independent governments and collaboration with the private sector in the provision of services. The case studies show the interrelationships between the two aspects of the new regionalism: collaboration with the private sector and cooperation among governments. The diversity of each case study shows that cooperation among governments can occur in any part of the country, in any size urban area, or at any stage in a region's development. There does not appear to be a certain type of metropolitan area that is more prone to become involved in cooperative and collaborative endeavors. There are, however, certain commonalities and elements that can be drawn from the case studies that were important in the development of these cooperative relationships.

One commonality is the importance of the civic infrastructure. Support and involvement in the endeavors from the civic and private sectors were evident in the case studies. The leadership of the civic or business community was heavily involved; often in initiating the process, providing or obtaining funding, and providing staff support to facilitate the development of collaborative efforts. The support and active involvement of the political leaders and top administrators of the city and county are essential for cooperation to be successful. Small successes in the effort usually lead to further collaboration on regional policy issues. For collaboration to endure beyond single projects or changes in leadership, it is important to develop a culture and expectation that governance will be a collaborative effort. This can be done by institutionalizing the process and holding regular meetings to discuss collaboration and policy issues. Collaborative governance is a long-term process and will develop in fits and starts.

It is undoubtedly easier for political leaders and administrators to not be involved in collaborative governance as it requires additional coordination and effort. Without political and business leadership support and active involvement, busy government administrators would not be inclined to cooperate. With the focus on process and inclusion rather than exclusion, the emphasis is on governance rather than government. It includes nongovernment stakeholders in public policy decisions and often involves nongovernment actors in implementing policy. Governments usually are not required to cooperate, but choose cooperation because they realize the advantages to their community from cooperation.

Critics of collaboration contend that it confers unfair advantage on large corporations, and it is focused largely on downtown development. They further argue that local governments are an unequal partner, contributing more than they receive in public benefits. However, the bottom line is that collaborative regional governance for fragmented metropolitan areas is growing as a way to achieve regional governance.

Notes

1. Floyd Hunter, *Community Power Structure* (Chapel Hill, NC: University of North Carolina Press, 1953).
2. Robert Dahl, *Who Governs?* (New Haven, CT: Yale University Press, 1961).
3. Ronald. K. Vogel, *Urban Political Economy* (Gainesville, FL: University Press of Florida, 1992).
4. Clarence. N. Stone, "Urban Regimes and the Capacity to Govern: A Political Economy Approach," *Journal of Urban Affairs*, 15 (1) (1993): 7.
5. Harvey Molotch, "The City as Growth Machine: Toward a Political Economy of Place," *American Journal of Sociology*, 82 (1976): 309–332; Harvey Molotch, "The Political Economy of Growth Machines," *Journal of Urban Affairs*, 15 (1) (1993): 29–53.
6. A. E. G. Jones, "Regulating Suburban Politics: Suburban-Defense Transition, Institutional Capacities, and Territorial Reorganization in Southern California," in M. Lauria, (ed.), *Reconstructing Urban Regime Theory* (Thousand Oaks, CA: Sage Publications, 1997), pp. 203–223.
7. Rosabeth Moss Kanter, "Business Coalitions as a Force for Regionalism," in Bruce Katz, (ed.), *Reflections on Regionalism* (Washington, DC: Brookings Institution, 2000), pp. 154–180.
8. R. Hanson, H. Wolman, D. Connolly, K. Pearson, and R. McMannon, "Corporate Citizenship and Urban Problem Solving: The Changing Civic Role of Business Leaders in American Cities," *Journal of Urban Affairs*, 32 (1) (2010): 1–23.
9. Keith G. Proven and Robin H. Lemaire, "Core Concepts and Key Ideas for Understanding Public Sector Organizational Networks: Using Research to Inform Scholarship and Practice," *Public Administration Review*, 72 (5) (2012): 639.

10. John D. Donahue, "The Race: Can Collaboration Outrun Rivalry between American Business and Government?" *Public Administration Review*, 70 (supplement) (2010): s151.
11. David Warm, "Local Government Collaboration for a New Decade: Risk, Trust, and Effectiveness," *State and Local Government Review*, 43 (1) (2011): 61.
12. Ibid.
13. Allan D. Wallis, "The Third Wave: Current Trends in Regional Governance," *National Civic Review*, 83 (Summer/Fall) (1994): 292–293.
14. David. K. Hamilton, "Organizing Government Structure and Governance Functions in Metropolitan Areas in Response to Growth and Change: A Critical Overview," *Journal of Urban Affairs*, 22 (1) (2000): 65–84.
15. Wallis, "The Third Wave: Current Trends in Regional Governance," p. 294.
16. Ed Council, "State-Local Partnership Policies: The Next Wave of Policy Making," *SIAM Intergovernmental News*, ASPA Section on Intergovernmental Administration and Management Newsletter 18 (Fall 1995): 3.
17. Howard J. Grossman, "The Future Is Now: The Case for a National Sub-State Regional Policy," *National Civic Review*, 83 (Winter/Spring) (1994): 86–89.
18. Allan D. Wallis, "Governance and the Civic Infrastructure of Metropolitan Regions," *National Civic Review*, 82 (Spring) (1993): 12.
19. Russell Matthew Linden, *Leading Across Boundaries: Creating Collaborative Agencies in a Networked World* (San Francisco, CA: Jossey-Bass, 2010), p. 56.
20. David D. Chrislip and Carl E. Larson, *Collaborative Leadership – How Citizens and Civic Leaders Can Make a Difference* (San Francisco, CA: Jossey-Bass Publishers, 1994), pp. 129–30.
21. Rosemary O'Leary, Yujin Choi, and Catherine M. Gerard, "The Skill Set of the Successful Collaborator," *Public Administration Review*, 72 (Special Issue) (2012): 570–582.
22. Russell Matthew Linden, *Leading Across Boundaries*, pp. 9–13. There are jurisdictional issues that will arise in any regional governance collaboration.
23. Ibid., p.140.
24. Dorothy Norris-Tirrell and Joy A. Clay, *Strategic Collaboration in Public Administration: A Practice-Based Approach to Solving Shared Problems* (Boca Raton, FL: CRC Press, 2010), pp. 5–6.
25. G. R. Teisman, and E. H. Klijn, "Partnership Arrangements: Government Rhetoric or Governance Scheme?" *Public Administration Review*, 62 (2) (2002): 197–206.
26. Bernard Ross and Myron A. Levine, *Urban Politics: Cities and Suburbs in a Global Age*, 8th ed. (Armonk, NY: M. E. Sharpe, 2012), p. 260.
27. Gregory D. Squires, "Public-Private Partnerships: Who Gets What and Why," in Gregory D. Squires, (ed.), *Unequal Partnerships: The Political Economy of Urban Redevelopment in Postwar America* (New Brunswick, NJ: Rutgers University Press, 1989), pp. 2–4; Marc Levine, "The Politics of Partnership: Urban Redevelopment Since 1945," in Gregory D. Squires, (ed.), *Unequal Partnerships: The Political Economy of Urban Redevelopment in Postwar America* (New Brunswick, NJ: Rutgers University Press, 1989), p. 25.
28. Levine, "The Politics of Partnership," pp. 19–26.
29. Alberta Sbragia, "The Pittsburgh Model of Economic Development: Partnership, Responsiveness, and Indifference," in Gregory D. Squires, (ed.), *Unequal Partnerships: The Political Economy of Urban Redevelopment in Postwar America* (New Brunswick, NJ: Rutgers University Press, 1989), p. 103.
30. W. Dennis Keating, Norman Krumholz, and John Metzger, "Postpopulist Public-Private Partnerships," in W. Dennis Keating, Norman Krumholz, and David C.

Perry, (eds.), *Cleveland: A Metropolitan Reader* (Kent, OH: Kent State University Press, 1995), p. 335.

31. Judith Welch Wegner, "Utopian Visions: Cooperation Without Conflicts in Public/Private Ventures," *Santa Clara Law Review*, 31 (2) (1991): 328–332.

32. Ross and Levine, *Urban Politics*, p. 260.

33. Jill M. Purdy, "A Framework for Assessing Power in Collaborative Governance Processes," *Public Administration Review*, 72 (3) (2012): 409.

34. Wegner, "Utopian Visions: Cooperation Without Conflicts in Public/Private Ventures," pp. 332–335.

35. For more on conflict of interest, see Richard Babcock, "The City as Entrepreneur: Fiscal Wisdom or Regulatory Folly?" *Santa Clara Law Review*, 29 (4) (1989): 931.

36. Michael Keating, *Comparative Urban Politics: Power and the City in the United States, Canada, Britain, and France* (Aldershot, England: Edward Elgar Publishing, 1991), pp. 167–168.

37. Ross and Levine, *Urban Politics*, p. 260.

38. R. Scott Fosler and Renee A. Berger, "Public-Private Partnership: An Overview," in R. Scott Fosler and Renee A. Berger, (eds.), *Public-Private Partnership in American Cities: Seven Case Studies* (Lexington, MA: D. C. Heath, 1982), pp. 9–10.

39. AnnaLee Saxenian, "Inside-Out: Regional Networks and Industrial Adaptation in Silicon Valley and Route 128," *Cityscape: A Journal of Policy Development and Research*, 2 (May) (1996): 41–45.

40. Clarence N. Stone, *Urban Regime Politics: Governing Atlanta* (Lawrence, KS: University Press of Kansas, 1989).

41. Robert D. Putnam, *Making Democracy Work: Civic Traditions in Modern Italy* (Princeton, NJ: Princeton University Press, 1993), pp. 91–99, 173–175. Other writers and researchers are starting to focus on civic regardingness and civic infrastructure. See, for example, Amitai Etzioni, *The Spirit of Community: Rights, Responsibilities, and the Communitarian Agenda* (New York: Crown Publishers, 1993); and William R. Dodge, *Regional Excellence: Governing Together to Compete Globally and Flourish Locally* (Washington, DC: National League of Cities, 1996).

42. D. Henton, J. Melville, and K. Walesh, *Grassroots Leaders for a New Economy: How Civic Entrepreneurs are Building Prosperous Communities* (San Francisco, CA: Jossey-Bass Publishers, 1997); M. Pastor Jr., P. Dreier, J. E. Grigsby III, and M. López-Garza, *Regions that Work: How Cities and Suburbs can Grow Together* (Minneapolis, MN: University of Minnesota Press, 2000).

43. See, for example, R. Scott Fosler and Renee A. Berger, "Public-Private Partnership: An Overview," in R. Scott Fosler and Renee A. Berger, (eds.), *Public-Private Partnership in American Cities: Seven Case Studies* (Lexington, MA: D. C. Heath, 1982) and Daniel Mazmanian and Michael Stanley-Jones, "Strategies II: Reconceiving LULUs: Changing the Nature and Scope of Locally Unwanted Land Uses," in Joseph F. DiMento and LeRoy Graymer, (eds.), *Confronting Regional Challenges: Approaches to LULUs, Growth, and Other Vexing Governance Problems* (Cambridge, MA: Lincoln Institute of Land Policy, 1991), pp. 63–66.

44. Katharine Lyall, "A Bicycle Built-for-Two: Public-Private Partnership in Baltimore," in R. Scott Fosler and Renee A. Berger, (eds.), *Public-Private Partnership in American Cities: Seven Case Studies* (Lexington, MA: D. C. Heath, 1982), pp. 18–25.

45. Kathryn A. Foster, "The Privatization of Regionalism," paper presented at the annual meeting of the Urban Affairs Association. New York, March 1996, and Henton, Melville, and Walesh, *Grassroots Leaders for a New Economy*.

46. Rosabeth Moss Kanter, "Business Coalitions as a Force for Regionalism," in Bruce Katz, (ed.), *Reflections on Regionalism* (Washington, DC: Brookings Institution Press, 2000), p. 160.
47. Henton Melville, and Walesh, *Grassroots Leaders for a New Economy*, and Keating; Krumholz, and Metzger, "Postpopulist Public-Private Partnerships."
48. C. James Owen and York Willbern, *Governing Metropolitan Indianapolis: The Politics of Unigov* (Berkeley and Los Angeles, CA: University of California Press, 1985), pp. 41–42.
49. John Brandl and Ronnie Brooks, "Public-Private Cooperation for Urban Revitalization: The Minneapolis and Saint Paul Experience," in R. Scott Fosler and Renee A. Berger, (eds.), *Public-Private Partnership in American Cities: Seven Case Studies* (Lexington, MA: D. C. Heath, 1982), pp. 193–194.
50. Sonya Klopfenstein, "Civic Leaders Team to Better the Peoria Area" *Journal Star*, May 16, 2002.
51. Hamilton, "Organizing Government Structure and Governance Functions in Metropolitan Areas in Response to Growth and Change," pp. 65–84.
52. Myron Orfield, *Metro Politics: A Regional Agenda for Community and Stability* (Washington, DC and Cambridge, MA: The Brookings Institution and Lincoln Institute of Land Policy, 1997).
53. James M. Smith, "Re-Stating Theories of Urban Development: The Politics of Authority Creation and Intergovernmental Triads in Postindustrial Chicago," *Journal of Urban Affairs*, 32 (4) (2010): 425–448.
54. Quoted in Worcester Municipal Research Bureau, *Considering Regional Government for Worcester–Part II: Proposals for Comprehensive Regional Governance*, Report No. 95–2 (Worcester, MA: Apr. 3, 1995), p. 17.
55. See, among others, the writings of the following: Henry G. Cisneros, (ed.), *Interwoven Destinies: Cities and the Nation* (New York: W. W. Norton, 1993); Anthony Downs, *New Visions for Metropolitan America* (Washington, DC: Brookings Institution, 1994); Neal R. Peirce, *Citistates: How Urban America Can Prosper in a Competitive World* (Washington, DC: Seven Locks Press, 1993); David Rusk, *Cities Without Suburbs* (Washington, DC: Woodrow Wilson Center Press, 1993); Larry C. Ledebur and William R. Barnes, *City Distress, Metropolitan Disparities, and Economic Growth* (Washington, DC: National League of Cities, 1992); H. V. Savitch, D. Collins, D. Sanders, J. P. Markham, "Ties That Bind: Central Cities, Suburbs, and the New Metropolitan Region," *Economic Development Quarterly*, 7 (November) (1993): 341–357.
56. Alan Ehrenhalt, "Cooperate or Die," *Governing: The Magazine of States and Localities*, September (1995): 29–30.
57. William J. Pammer Jr. and John L. Daly, "Reengineering in Counties and Cities: Truth and Consequences: Conversations with Managers and Department Heads," paper presented at the annual meeting of the Urban Affairs Association, Toronto, April 17–19, 1997.
58. Ehrenhalt, "Cooperate or Die," p. 32.
59. Daniel Mazmanian and Michael Stanley-Jones, "Strategies II: Reconceiving LULUs: Changing the Nature and Scope of Locally Unwanted Land Uses", in Joseph F. DiMento and LeRoy Graymer, (eds.), *Confronting Regional Challenges: Approaches to LULUs, Growth, and Other Vexing Governance Problems* (Cambridge, MA: Lincoln Institute of Land Policy, 1991), pp. 63–66.
60. See Chapter 3 for a discussion on the annexation battles that helped to create the antagonism between central cities and the inner suburbs. Myron Orfield, *Metro Politics: A Regional Agenda for Community and Stability* (Washington, DC and Cambridge, MA: The Brookings Institution and Lincoln Institute of Land Policy, 1997).

61. Gary Washburn, "Daley, Suburban Mayors to Form Caucus," *Chicago Tribune*, Dec. 3, 1997, sec. 2, p. 1.

62. Much of the following is taken from Xavier De Souza Briggs, *Democracy as Problem Solving: Civic Capacity in Communities across the Globe* (Cambridge, MA: The MIT Press, 2008), pp. 63–89.

63. Quoted in Ron Clegg, "My View: Utah's Secret Sauce is Cooperation," *Deseret News*, October 10, 2012, http://www.deseretnews.com/article/765610419/ Utahs-secret-sauce-is-cooperation.html [Accessed Jan 3, 2013].

64. Much of the following is taken from Esteban Dalehite, "Running Out of Classrooms! Solving Overcrowding through Collaborative School Planning," in Dorothy Norris-Tirrell and Joy A Clay, (eds.), *Strategic Collaboration in Public and Nonprofit Administration: A Practice-Based Approach to Solving Shared Problems* (Boca Raton, FL: CRC Press, 2010), pp. 123–148.

65. Allegheny Conference on Community Development, *The Greater Pittsburgh Region: Working Together to Compete Globally* (Pittsburgh: 1994); United States Census Bureau, *City, State and County Quickfacts*, http://quickfacts.census.gov/ qfd/states/42/42003.html [Accessed March 23, 2013].

66. Roy Lubove, (ed.), *Pittsburgh* (New York: New Viewpoints, 1976).

67. David W. Lonich, *Metropolitics in Allegheny County: The Evolution of a Regional Government,* unpublished PhD Dissertation, Carnegie Mellon University, 1991. See also David K. Hamilton, *Areawide Government Reform: A Case Study Emphasizing the Charter Writing Process,* unpublished Ph.D. Dissertation, University of Pittsburgh, 1978.

68. Lubove, *Pittsburgh.*

69. Pennsylvania Economy League, *Annual Report* (Pittsburgh, PA: 1999).

70. R. Stafford, Executive Director, Allegheny Conference on Community Development, personal communication, March 2001. See also Allegheny Conference on Community Development, Annual Report.

71. See Chapter 9 for a discussion of the Allegheny County Regional Asset District.

72. Most of this is taken from the website http://www.metrodenver.org/ [Accessed Jan. 26, 2013].

73. Timothy D. Mead, "The Daily Newspaper as Political Agenda Setter: The *Charlotte Observer* and Metropolitan Reform," *State and Local Government Review*, 26 (Winter) (1994): 30.

74. Henry G. Cisneros, *Regionalism: The New Geography of Opportunity* (Washington, DC: U.S. Department of Housing and Urban Development, March 1995), p. 6; U. S. Census Bureau. *City, State and County Quickfacts*, http://quickfacts.census. gov/qfd/states/37/37119.html [Accessed March 27, 2012].

75. Sammis White, *Cooperation not Consolidation: The Answer for Milwaukee Governance*, Wisconsin Policy Research Institute Report, November 2002, p. 12.

76. Linzi Shelton, "Mayor Foxx makes Pitch to Revamp City County," July 31, 2012, www.wsoltv.com/news [Accessed Aug. 2, 2012].

77. Harvey Lipman and Richard P. Nathan, "Working Together in the Capital Region," materials for Conference on Regionalization, Albany, New York, Oct. 26–28, 1992.

78. Neal Peirce and Curtis Johnson, "Shaping a Shared Future," *The Charlotte Observer*, Reprint, Sept. 17-Oct. 8, 1995, p. 4.

11 Regional Governance in Selected Metropolitan Areas in Other Countries

Governance of city regions is not just a concern in the United States. Growth of urban areas has created the same governance issues in other countries that are evident in America where the population and economic boundaries of metropolitan areas do not neatly fit into arbitrary political boundaries. This chapter briefly looks at how selected metropolitan areas outside the United States have responded or are responding to the governing issues faced by metropolitan areas. The major focus of this chapter is European countries as these countries during the colonial period had a major influence on local governance in other parts of the world. It is interesting to see how other countries adapted and changed the governing institutions to fit their own culture. Also, many countries had local governing institutions that go back thousands of years but had to adjust to the rapid urbanization of the twentieth century and the rise of citizen demands for more local government control. Moreover, in the global economy that is clearly evident in the twenty-first century, metropolitan areas across the world compete with each other for development. Available evidence indicates that those metropolitan areas whose governments are more united with the public and private sectors working together, all else being equal, appear to be more successful at attracting development.[1] By the study of other countries and their efforts to provide regional governing solutions, we can appreciate the global nature of regional governance problems and possibly gain new ideas and insights for metropolitan governance. Other countries in their efforts to provide regional governance solutions have tried many of the same approaches that have been described and analyzed in previous chapters.

Political and Cultural Traditions and Regional Governance

Local government structure and authority are highly dependent upon the culture of the country. In the United States, for example, the culture is to have strong, independent local governments. Centralization efforts will generally be resisted and any changes will only move incrementally unless they are mandated from the state. Even mandates from the state will only be marginally successful. Changes in the status quo will be resisted whether they are designed to centralize or decentralize local governance. For example, in Japan there is an effort to decentralize authority from the national government to the prefectures and the local governments. This is being strenuously resisted by the national bureaucracy and does not appear to have strong support among the national politicians. It is also resisted to some degree by the local officials because of the unknown. Change is always difficult.

Of course, no one metropolitan area is like another in terms of local and regional governing systems. Moreover, no one country is quite like another country in its orientation to regional government. There have, however, been attempts to identify a country's predisposition toward a strong centralized governance system that is supposedly oriented to professionalism and administrative efficiency or to a decentralized governance system that is more political and oriented toward local responsiveness. Cultural heritage and traditions are the basis for these groupings. Kübler and Heinelt,[2] looking at European countries and their colonial influences, categorized local governing systems as follows:

- The Franco group places a strong emphasis on democracy. These countries are especially resistant to centralization reforms. The essence of local government is political rather than functional. Office holders are expected to represent the interests of their community, especially in relation to higher levels of government. Countries in this group are found mainly in southern Europe. An example of this group with its emphasis on small democratic local government is France's large number of local governments and the unsuccessful attempts to reduce this number.

- The Anglo group comprises English-speaking countries including the USA with some caveats. This cultural heritage is focused on efficiency and envisions the first order of local government as the efficient and economical deliverer of local government services. In the search for efficient and effective delivery of services, these countries experiment with different forms of regional government that tend to centralize and consolidate local governments.

- The Germanic group includes Germany and northern European countries. This culture places equal emphasis on local democracy and the efficient delivery of public services. This group is the most formally decentralized of the three groups. Local governments in this group generally enjoy a strong constitutional status and a relatively high degree of policy-making autonomy and financial independence. An example is Germany with local governments recognized in the German constitution, which gives them substantial independence.

National traditions of local government thus play an important role in shaping the relationship between input (access) and output (service delivery). Political localism, as a reflection of community found in the Franco group, can be seen as placing a strong emphasis on access (democracy). The emphasis on functional capacity that is found in the Anglo group is oriented to service efficiency and effectiveness (outputs) as opposed to access (democracy). The Northern or Middle European model represents an attempt to emphasize access as well as efficient and effective service delivery. Based on this, the expectation is that the Franco group or tradition would be resistant to metropolitan governance. In contrast the Anglo-type environment, where the functional capacity of local government is central, can be expected to favor a shift from access to efficiency and effective delivery of services or from inputs to outputs. For the Northern and Middle European local government, they might lean either way. The impact of a new metropolitan governance structure on local governments in this group would unbalance the equilibrium between inputs and outputs, which would tend to be resisted by the local governments.[3]

According to these categorizations, the Anglo group is the only group that would appear to support more centralized government if it promised to improve services. The Germanic group might support a form of metropolitan government but would resist any diminution of local authority. The Franco group would strenuously resist any centralization effort.

Broad categorizations are fraught with problems as there are always exceptions to the categories. Over time countries and even urban areas develop their own local government traditions. For example, Barcelona and Madrid, supposedly within the Franco group, have followed an efficiency model more similar to the Germanic group instead of a political model. The most glaring outlier is the USA. Although it lies within the Anglo group and has a legally weak local government system characteristic of the Anglo model, it follows a highly decentralized political model. Indeed, most European countries appear to be more oriented to efficiency in service delivery than the USA and have added regional scale governments. Even within the USA, there are large differences among areas in their approach to regional governance as discussed in previous chapters. For example, the South is more open to centralized (efficient) regional governing systems than the Northeast and Midwest.

The point is that each country and, within each country, each metropolitan area develops its own traditions regarding local and regional governing systems. Moreover, each country has different ways to approach the restructuring of local government to meet regional governing pressures. Some nations mandate structural local government restructuring without a local vote. Other countries allow citizens to vote on proposed government reform. It is obviously easier to mandate changes than to obtain the approval of citizens on government reform. Heritage and cultural traditons do not determine the way countries approach the process of establishing regional government structure.[4]

With a few exceptions, foreign governments either at the state or national level are more involved with their local level governments than the United States. A number of foreign countries have a unitary government system with the power over local governments residing at the national level. In these countries, the national government dictates policy to the local government. Some countries like America have a form of federalism with sharing of powers between the national and state or provincial level. In most countries that share power, the federal system does not extend to local government. In other words, with some exceptions in the Germanic group, local governments are not recognized in the national constitution. They are thus not given independent status within the governing system and are under the control of a senior level government, usually the state or provincial government. Some countries are very involved in local government restructuring as the following case studies show. In others, the country or provincial government is more like the states in America, which reflects more of a laissez-faire approach to their local governments. It is my observation that the United States is the outlier in terms of giving maximum autonomy to local governments.

Examples of Approaches in Other Countries to Governance of Urban Areas

Other countries, in dealing with regional governing issues face the same policy issues that are faced by metropolitan areas in the United States. One issue is whether regional governance should be centralized or decentralized. Should the metropolitan area be covered by only one or a few governments or by a fragmented governing system? Is it more efficient to provide services and deal with regional policy issues through a centralized or decentralized governing structure? In the past the answer generally was some form of centralized system either combining governments or establishing an overarching tier with substantial authority over local governments. National or provincial governments instituted the structure despite the opposition of the local residents. (See the discussion on government structure changes in Chapter 1.) More recently, national and provincial governments seem to be less inclined to make structural changes that disrupt current local government structure or authority.

Political boundaries within metropolitan areas and even between countries are becoming less important in a globalizing world. Indeed, they are giving way to a globalizing economy. In Europe, for example, metropolitan regions are competing with each other across the world for development due to the rise of the global economy, the rise of the information society, new production and distribution concepts, and the increasing mobility of people, products, and companies. Government leaders in metropolitan areas are realizing that they need to work together to compete in this global market place. Government leaders also realize that they cannot change and restructure political boundaries to keep pace with the rapid economic changes that are happening. However, the growing economic inter-dependence centered on metropolitan areas, requires some form of metro-politan governance for regions to compete successfully with other city regions for development.

How do different countries with their cultural traditions approach metro-politan governance? There is no one-size-fits-all system. Other countries have tried and experimented with different approaches similar to those attempted in North America. Many countries have tried more than one approach and have often abandoned one approach to try another one. They have generally found that each approach has its advantages and disadvan-tages. Many large urban areas, particularly those in the Anglo group, have tried a tiered form of regional government, but most have abandoned this form in favor of a more consolidated or centralized form of government. Others, particularly in the Germanic group, have moved to a type of new regionalism or a collaborative form of governance. As urban regions grow and expand, they draw outlying communities with their own local govern-ments into their sphere of influence. A true consolidated system of govern-ment would continually require the annexation of these outlying areas into the central city, which creates political problems. As indicated, even within countries different approaches are evident. Spain is a good example of a country where its two major metropolitan areas have gone down different roads in their efforts to provide regional governance. Madrid has the tiered system of regional government that was instituted in 1983 at a time when most of the world was enamored with the solution of a tiered approach to regional government. Barcelona experimented with this approach before rejecting it and has instituted a collaborative or new regionalism approach.

Other countries have had similar experiences. Until about the last decade of the 1990s, the type of regionalism that was generally followed outside the United States was structural changes in the local government system to con-solidate governments or establish another tier of government over the myriad local governments. In most countries outside the United States the central or the provincial government mandated the change. The restructur-ing of local governments was generally not submitted to the voters for approval. The tiered system was the reform of choice because it provided a regional governing system without the local resistance and upheaval that attends the abolition of local governments. Many countries tried the metro-politan or tiered approach only to abandon it in favor of a more or less consolidated approach. Countries are also backing away from mandating structural changes. Regional governance is now taking many different forms and shapes.

Europe is a good example of the variety of regional governance directions that countries are taking. Some metropolitan areas in Europe have moved away from the structural reform system to a collaborative or new regionalism form involving a broad array of public and private actors. Helsinki and Barcelona are examples of this form of governance system. Some European metropolitan areas have moved to a hybrid form of regional governance. This form involves a tiered system of government, generally with a directly elected president and council and collaboration between the metropolitan government and private sector actors to foster the economic competitiveness of the region. This hybrid form is evident in the Hanover metropolitan area of Germany with a public–private partnership in which the regional tier and the city of Hanover as well as major companies located in the region are engaged in economic development activities. In addition to strong and viable networked or collaborative governing systems, there are some countries where little or no cooperation or collaboration exists. Metropolitan areas in France are the best example of this type of governing system with its strong local, decentralized traditions and non-involved private and civic sectors. This strong local autonomy, go-it-alone municipal tradition is also evident in some metropolitan areas in Germany.[5]

The experiences of the European countries in establishing regional government and governance clearly show that there is no one best way to provide regional governance, nor is there any one preferred approach. Much depends on urban growth patterns, culture, traditions, opportunity and leadership. The method of approaching regional governance policy and its implementation are also of extreme importance. When voting is allowed on regional governing changes, it allows those supporting the status quo to organize against any structural changes. If the senior level government mandates the change, it is difficult to obtain buy-in from the local leaders. Moreover, as the world becomes more enamored with democratic ideals, it is increasingly more difficult for a senior-level government to mandate changes to local or regional levels without participation and approval of the majority of the effected public and local leaders.

The following sections briefly review selected countries and metropolitan areas and their experiences and approaches to regional governance.

Regionalism in Germany

Germany has a federal system of government somewhat similar to the United States. One difference is that the local system of government is recognized in the national constitution, which gives local governments substantial authority. However, the states (*Länder*) exercise substantial control over the local governments. The German local government system consists of counties and municipalities. Large municipalities with more than 100,000 residents are usually independent cities, i.e. county free. There are

116 independent cities that provide all the local government services within their boundaries. Berlin, Hamburg, and Bremen have special status as city states. Cities less than 100,000 share service provision with their counties. In these cities some services are provided by the county and some by the city. Regional governance is voluntary and is formed by the cities and towns in the region coming together and agreeing to form a regional association. It is more a bottom-up approach than a top-down mandate. The *Länder* are generally not actively involved in regional governance. They might provide some incentives to establish regional governance approaches, but given the strong culture and constitutional status of local government autonomy, regional structures are not strong and often fleeting. Any permanent transfer of power from the municipal to the regional level is bitterly resisted by the local municipalities.[6]

According to the models developed and explicated above, Germany is a combination of a decentralized and centralized model resulting often in an uneasy equilibrium. Politicians and administrators think in terms of government structures instead of collaboration because networks do not lead to binding decisions. However, they are wary of regional structures because of the potential loss of autonomy and independence. German regional governance is beset with the same cooperation and collaboration issues and problems that are encountered in America's metropolitan areas. There is not strong state oversight or encouragement of regional governance. Land use planning is a function that local governments jealously guard. Any effort to move planning or any hint of loss over the planning function is strenuously resisted. This makes regional governance problematic. In addition, in many German cities the civic sector is either not well developed or not oriented to collaborating with governments on regional issues. Cooperation among governments and collaboration with NGOs is therefore precarious and flourishes only under special conditions. Moreover, the region is usually defined very broadly to encompass the economic area. These large areas often include a large number of municipal governments and major cities that in the past have often competed with one another.

Given the need to compete with other regions on a global basis and aware of the advantages of acting together for economic competitiveness, there is a propensity for local governments to think in regional terms. The major regional effort is to develop a sense of economic identity, to induce coopera-tion among governments, and form partnerships with the private and civic sectors to increase competitiveness with other regions within Europe and globally. Given this goal, one approach that has been developed by some metropolitan areas is to develop a regional tier or special district with limited functions and minimal authority or voluntary organizations that collaborate and cooperate for economic development purposes. The types of functions that are usually transferred to a regional body are some authority over the planning function, regional marketing, regional transportation, and solid and liquid waste disposal. The transfer is often piecemeal ·and occurs when the local governments realize that the particular function would be more cost-effectively provided on a collective basis at a larger, more inclusive level. In a few instances, the upper tier might be an elected metropolitan government with substantial authority over the municipal governments within its area.[7]

One example is the Frankfurt am Main region. This economic region is defined very broadly to include 445 local governments including counties, towns, urban counties, independent cities, and the major cities of Frankfurt, Wiesbaden, Mainz and Darmstadt. The region's cities have a long history of independence and autonomy. They have more often competed against each other than cooperated. Another barrier to working together as a region is that the economic boundaries of the region cover more than one *Land* (state). The political boundaries have nothing in common with the boundaries of the economic region. There is no sense of regional identity among the many local governments that are in the region and certainly not among the people living in the region. Given the many local governments in the region with their history of independence and the state governments involved, any attempt at regional governance is voluntary cooperation and collaboration and generally occurs in a bottom-up instead of top-down fashion. There have recently been some efforts by local government leaders to overcome this parochialism through voluntary associations to foster regional economic development. These efforts have not been successful at sustaining long-term economic development cooperation with the exception of a regional group that has had some success in developing a joint marketing approach.[8]

There is constant concern by the political leaders over loss of independence and autonomy. Since at least the 1970s reform proposals have been put forward to restructure government in the region. These have included establishing a two-tier government structure, some consolidation of governments or moving to an urban county form of government. The region is not just fragmented at the local government level but also at the *Land* level. This has contributed to the lack of regional identity and the competitive nature among the governments of the region. Actions by one *Land* have no authority in other *Länder*. Moreover, as indicated above, the local governments resist giving up authority to a regional body that would diminish their independence. In 1975, a planning agency was established by the *Land* to do regional planning for 43 municipalities in the region. It was a directly elected body with broad authority over planning including land use, transportation, and utilities. It had coordinating authority but no implementation authority. There was conflict among board members over regional versus parochial agendas, and the organization had difficulties in reaching agreements with the municipalities and service providers. It was abolished in 2000 and was replaced in 2001 with a regional association with no authority.[9]

Even though there are collaborative efforts to market the region for economic growth, the collaboration is voluntary and a number of cities including Frankfurt maintain their own marketing agencies. Despite some initial opposition to the regional marketing concept, cities are beginning to see the advantages of participating. Darmstadt recently indicated its intention to join the regional marketing effort. The difficulty in collaborative efforts in marketing the region is indicative of the competitiveness and lack of trust among governments. There are other collaborative efforts, some of which are more successful than others. There is a regional culture initiative to promote and market the region as a destination for culture and the arts. Again, this collaboration is voluntary. Nelles reports on her study of the area that it shows promise with 22 members, however Wiesbaden, a major city in the region, is not a member. Moreover, she reports that one of the best examples of regional cooperation in that area is transportation. This partnership involves not just local governments but the state and federal governments. Legislation passed by the European Union also dictates the governing structure for regional transportation systems. Because of all the parties involved, there has been very little political posturing and the collaborative effort is working acceptably well. The lack of conflict may be related to the role of the upper government levels and the regulations from these levels that must be followed.[10]

As was indicated in Chapter 10, civic capital is an important element in collaborative governance. Areas with low levels of civic capital will be less effective in regional governance initiatives. The Frankfurt region does not have a strong base of regionally oriented and well-connected leaders to bring partners together in collaborative efforts. Political leaders have been hesitant to push partnerships in which they are required to cede their authority to a regional entity. Almost all regional governance has been initiated by political leaders. That is one reason that divisive and sensitive issues have generally been avoided. The dearth of regionally oriented leaders from the private and nonprofit sectors advocating for collective action is a major reason for the lack of regional identity and weak regional governance. While there are a few civic organizations with a regional focus, most have failed to sustain themselves. One such organization, which so far has sustained itself, is an association composed of representatives from the business, cultural and educational communities that was established to market the region and build networks. While its meetings and actions have been sporadic, it has undertaken some initiatives to build a regional identity and focus including holding forums to discuss regional issues. The region still has a long way to go to develop a vibrant and involved civic sector actively engaged in regional governance issues.[11]

The Stuttgart and Hanover regions are presently the only two areas with directly elected regional councils. The Hanover council is instructive of this tiered system of government. It has substantial regional authority, which is unusual for Germany with its history of strong, independent local governments. The council replaced the regional planning association and covers the city of Hanover and the county surrounding Hanover. The chief executive officer is also elected and presides over the council, similar to a strong mayor council system. There is a division of power between the two tiers. Most of the functions related to economic development, environmental policy, large-scale infrastructure and social assistance funding are provided at the regional level while functions closely related to private households are assigned to the local level governments. The problems and issues accompanying an independently elected tiered system of government are evident in the Hanover region. There is potential rivalry between the regional president and the mayor of Hanover since both are directly elected and both represent the city and have a strong political role. In addition, the business community is not involved in collaborative efforts. This is due in part to a tradition of noninvolvement and also because they feel that their interests are being addressed without their active involvement. In addition, most of the major corporations in the region are branch offices, which further mitigate their commitment to the region. The local governments in the region do not trust the regional government to adequately represent their interests and still compete with each other for development. Finally, because of the tiered system of government, the decision processes are clumsier and more complicated.[12]

In summary, Germany exhibits mixed regional governing systems with some metropolitan areas more engaged in regionalism than others. Given the strong culture of local government autonomy, most regionalism initiatives are voluntary cooperation between governments with minimal involvement from the business sector. It should be noted that a number of services that are under the control of local government in the United States are outside the domain of German local government, such as health and education. Not providing these services might be a benefit for regional cooperation. In any event, most of the regional initiatives are oriented to economic development. Local governments are wary of regional efforts and the potential loss of local authority.

Regionalism in France

While Germany has a federal system of government with decentralized authority, the French have a unitary system of government with the national government intimately involved in local government. However, local autonomy is highly esteemed and the local level has substantial independence, which makes it nearly impossible to establish regional governance.[13] France has the largest number of local governments in Europe at almost 37,000 with the median commune (municipality) less than six square miles. Over 80 percent of the communes have less than 1,000 residents. The median local government territory is smaller than most other European countries. The median population in a commune was 380 in 1999, the lowest local government median population in Europe. This compares to Italy with a median population in 2001 of 2,348. This situation has led the government to encourage smaller communes to merge to form urban communities or group together in associations of several communes. In addition, a law passed by Parliament on February 6, 1992 suggested municipalities consider mergers and new forms of cooperation to rationalize municipal administration by taking common interests into consideration. This law has had minimal effect on the municipalities. There has been some pooling of services, but mergers are extremely rare as both residents and local government leaders maintain a strong sense of identity with their communes.[14]

The irony in France is that while the French have a strong sense of local autonomy, the unitary system has vested authority over local government in the national government. So there has been centralized authority over local government while at the same time there is pressure from the local level to maintain local autonomy. In 1982 the national government substantially decentralized authority to the local and regional levels. The regional level became a much more important element of governance. It was given authority, at local government option, over economic development, urban planning, and social housing equity issues, vocational training, and education. The decision-making organ is the regional council whose members are elected for six years. There is an advisory committee made up of representatives of businesses, the professions, trade unions and other employee organizations, regional voluntary organizations, etc.[15]

The decentralization allows an upper tier of government to take on a function at local government option. Agreement must either be from two-thirds of the municipalities or 50 percent of the municipalities, which represents two-thirds of the region's population. Although the political power still resides at the municipal level, the regional tier is becoming more of a political body as it takes on additional functions.[16] Even though the national government encourages mergers and regional governance and has established regional institutions and given them some authority, the governing system is highly decentralized due to the political and cultural traditions. The real authority, even in these regional institutions, still resides at the local level. This is in keeping with the Franco group's emphasis on local level democracy.

Regionalism in Spain

The Barcelona metropolitan area is composed of 32 municipalities, including the city of Barcelona. The area does not have its own specific metropolitan government. Since 1979, the autonomous communities have impeded the development of any regional government. The local governments jealously guard their autonomy. In fact, a form of metropolitan government that existed was eliminated in the Barcelona area in 1979. Two voluntary associations were established in 1987, one for transportation and one for water and sewage. A council of governments was also established to encourage cooperation. In 1997 another metropolitan-wide public transportation authority was set up. Although Barcelona has a fragmented system, the involvement of the civil society, including businesses, unions, the financial sector, and civic agencies, has fostered regional governance. The public and private actors have reached consensus on many regional policy issues because there have been events that have required the involvement of civic and private sectors, such as the 1992 Olympics. The civic and private involvement has had a stabilizing influence on the political leaders.[17]

As opposed to Barcelona, Madrid has a government tier that covers most of the region. Madrid's area-wide government has been in existence since 1983. There have been political disagreements between the regional level and the city of Madrid, but they have worked fairly well together because the same political party is in control at both levels. However, political disagreements resulting from different perspectives and constituents and institutional fragmentation have been obstacles to building an integrated vision of the metropolitan area.[18]

Although Spain is considered to be in the Franco group with emphasis on access rather than metropolitan governance, its two major metropolitan areas have embraced forms of regionalism. It is interesting that these two metropolitan areas have diverged in their forms of regionalism. They both started out with a tiered system of regional government, and then went separate ways. It might be that Barcelona was more fragmented than Madrid. The civic and business sectors appear to be more involved in governance in Barcelona than in Madrid. Again, it might be that the civic and business sectors in Barcelona realized that without their involvement, regional governance had little chance of being successful. In comparison, the business and civic communities in Madrid might have felt that their involvement was not needed or wanted because of the institutional structure that was in place.

Regionalism in Great Britain

In the unitary government system in Great Britain, the national government creates, abolishes and changes local governments. London introduced regional government with the creation of the London County Council in 1889. This second government tier was a multipurpose elected body that replaced a number of single purpose area-wide authorities. London and a number of local level governments retained their identity although a number of functions were transferred to the regional tier. In 1965 London's boundaries were significantly expanded to take in the growth in the urban area. New boroughs were created and a stronger upper tier was established with authority to provide regional services including housing and education, distribution of financial resources, and regional planning.[19]

Over the years since its creation, Britain significantly expanded the London County Council, renamed it the Greater London Council (GLC), and had established regional government over six other metropolitan areas. In 1985 these upper tiers that had been the system of choice by academics and practitioners supporting regional forms of government with a long history of use in Great Britain, were abolished by the Thatcher Government. The introduction and the abolition of regional government were made without a vote of affirmation by the residents. There were political considerations in the abolition of these tiers as none of the governments were controlled by the Thatcher Government, but there was also a desire to reduce the sphere and autonomy of local government and to further centralize power. There was little support for these metropolitan tiers and their passing was not contested by the constituent governments.[20]

The upper tier in the London area was replaced by the London Coordinating Committee. Functions formerly assigned to the upper tier were taken over on a joint basis by the local governments with one of the boroughs acting as the lead authority. Planning became the purview of the national government. Other coordinating functions and issues that were not devolved to the boroughs were elevated to the national level. In fact, the central government eventually appointed a minster to be responsible for London affairs. Between 1986 and 2000 there was only one tier of local government in London. In May 2000 the new Greater London Authority (GLA) was established on the same boundary as the former GLC. This change provided for the direct election of a weak mayor and a 25-member council. This was a first for London to have an elected mayor. The London boroughs maintain much of their independence. The mayor has limited power to coordinate action across London.[21]

The GLA acts like a parliamentary system of government with executive power vested in the mayor. The role of the council is to scrutinize the mayor's activity, make appointments to the permanent executive and some other appointments, endorse the budget and the mayor's proposals and conduct investigations on various topics. The mayor lacks the comprehensive powers and large staff of big city mayors in other countries. With the limited powers the mayor must rely on influence, persuasion and the support of partners. The GLA has added another layer of government to the complexity of governing the London region. London continues to be characterized by complex layers of public and public–private agencies operating at different scales. Business plays a significant role in governance at the regional, sub-regional and neighborhood scales. The central government retains the power to veto anything that is deemed to contradict national government interests and can ultimately control the city's budget. All of the changes had political overtones and proposals were adjusted to maximize the interests of the party in control of the central government. One scholar's assessment of regional government in London is that London still lacks effective government capacity.[22]

Future of Regional Governance in Europe

As in most countries, politics plays a major role in the makeup and the extent that metropolitan governance occurs. Moreover, some parts of Europe are more strongly influenced by politics than other areas. For example ideological differences are stronger in southern Europe than in northern and western Europe. This means that municipalities are more likely to cooperate in countries with fewer party and political divisions.[23]

One entity that is exerting substantial influence on integration and cooperation is the European Union (EU). The European Union is not allowed to interfere in the internal affairs of member states according to the political sovereignty of member states and the *principle of subsidiarity*. The subsidiary principle is a principle of decentralization, which states that decision making in governance should be handled at the lowest level of government that is capable of effectively addressing that issue. However, the European integration has fueled the growth of metropolitan areas and the resulting competition among metropolitan areas for economic development. Moreover, member states have transferred functions and policy covering those functions that promote economic integration to the European Commission and at the same time are generally decentralizing power to regional and local levels. As a consequence, the power and influence of national governments is being diminished as regions and the European Commission gain power. The EU encourages regional level governance with policies that promote and in certain areas, such as transportation, require a regional approach. The EU also subsidizes metropolitan areas that are economically backward. The support is designed for the region, not a specific city, which fosters cooperation among local governments to obtain the financial support.[24]

The conclusion drawn from one recent survey of eight urban areas in Europe was that major restructuring of local governments to consolidate municipalities or to establish an overarching tier of government with substantial authority was not likely to happen in present-day Europe as was the case in the 1960s and 1970s during the efficiency movement that swept Europe (see Chapter 1). Moreover, given the increasing size and complexity of urban areas, major restructuring would be bitterly resisted and probably not be effective if it was mandated by senior-level governments. The researchers found few examples of currently well-functioning administrative models of metropolitan governance. They indicated that the strong autonomy and identity of individual municipalities was a major reason for the resistance to structural reforms and lack of effectiveness of current regional governing systems. They concluded that metropolitan governance would only happen through cooperation and collaboration among willing local government actors. The researchers wrote,

> [I]t has become clear that the municipalities' willingness to work in unison toward metropolitan decisiveness is a necessary condition for a well-functioning metropolitan administration of any form. If the local governments involved do not recognize the need to form a metropolitan administration, they will be unwilling to help in establishing such an administration and to give substance and implementation to the policy such an administration wants to pursue.[25]

Regional Governance in East Asia

Most developed countries in East Asia have a unitary system of government so all authority flows from the central government. The central government in the major developed countries can structure cities and regions and assign functions without resort to approval by the local voters or local leaders. The central governments, however, have made some efforts to decentralize authority and decision making to the regional or local level. For example, in Japan the structure for regional governance varies depending on the size of the city. There is an effort to decentralize some authority from the national government to the prefectures and the local governments. This is being strenuously resisted by the national bureaucracy and does not appear to have strong support among the local politicians. However, there is some decentralization as cities with populations that are close to one million or more are able to take on some of the duties that would normally be performed by the state. For example, they have been given authority to control infrastructure development and transportation policy within their geographically designated region, not just within their city. In South Korea, decentralization has also taken place for large cities, providing them with much more autonomy from senior government oversight. The central cities of large metropolitan areas have also been given authority over the region and other municipalities in the region for planning and infrastructure development purposes.

In China large cities can become provinces, giving them much more authority in making decisions on development policies. One example of regional governance in China is Shanghai. It is the major city in the Yangtze River delta region. There are 16 cities in 3 different provinces in this region. With the central government's blessing and support, the region is working to cooperate in building a competitive region and integrate its efforts. The regional planning effort appears to be driven by Shanghai and the provinces. The municipal governments are involved in a regional cooperation forum, which was initiated by Shanghai. The cities in the region still compete with each other for development, but they are also cooperating with each other in other areas.[26]

Regional Governance in Canada

While the United States generally followed a decentralized decision-making process allowing local referendums to determine proposals on restructuring, Canada followed the Anglo model described above of efficiency in service delivery determined by centralized direction. Restructuring proposals were not submitted to the voters for approval but were mandated by the provincial governments. The decisions by the provincial governments on restructuring, however, were influenced to a significant degree by local politics. It was often the case that the party in power in the provincial government made local government restructuring decisions based on the wishes of influential party members of the ruling party.

Metropolitan government was established in Toronto in 1954 through action by the province of Ontario. A major reason for its establishment was to provide relief to suburban municipalities that were having difficulty providing essential services (most notably education, water supply, and sewage disposal) without prohibitive tax increases. Costs of the new government were allocated among the municipalities in proportion to each municipality's share of the assessed value of the total property within the boundaries of the area-wide government. Toronto had 62 percent of the total assessed valuation of the new government. The result of the tax base scheme was to use the city's resources to finance new infrastructure in the suburbs.

The federation plan adopted by the provincial legislature established a regional government (Metro) encompassing Toronto and its 12 contiguous municipalities. Toronto and the municipalities retained their separate identities, and the regional government was made responsible for functions of an area-wide nature, leaving the local functions to the municipalities. A representative from each of the 12 suburban municipalities and 12 officials from the city of Toronto constituted the governing body. The chair was appointed by the provincial government.[27]

The Toronto area experienced explosive suburban growth in the 1950s and 1960s. Growth was not only taking place in the suburbs within Metro's boundaries, but beyond the boundaries as well. In fact, the population in the fringe municipalities grew 96 percent between 1953 and 1963 compared to only 40 percent within Metro. By 1963, just nine years after the founding of Metro, the proportion of Toronto's population to that of Metro had declined from 57 percent to 38 percent, and its share of the assessed taxable property had declined to 44 percent. The seeds of the future problems for the Toronto region were sown by the decision in a 1966 restructuring not to extend Metro's boundaries to cover the additional development. Instead, these areas were reorganized on a two-tier principle similar to Metro. The result was the establishment of four regional governments in addition to the metropolitan Toronto government.[28]

As indicated in Table 11.1, similar growth patterns continued after 1981, except Toronto regained some population, but it never reached the peak

Table 11.1 Toronto Area Population (in Thousands)

	1951	1961	1971	1981	1991	1996	2001	2006
Toronto[a]	667.5	672.4	712.8	599.2	635.4	653.7	2,481.5	2,503.3
Metro	1,117.5	1,618.8	2,086.0	2,137.4	2,275.8	2,395.4		
Toronto CMA[b]	1,824.5	2,628.0	2,999.0	3,893.1	4,263.8	4,682.9	5,113.1
Percent Toronto to Metro	59.7	41.5	34.2	28.0	27.9	27.4		
Percent Metro to CMA[b]		88.7	79.4	71.3	58.5	56.0	53.0	
Percent Toronto to CMA[b]		36.9	27.1	20.0	16.3	15.3	49.0	

Source: Statistics Canada. General Review Bulletin, 71, 1963; Population Geographic Distribution 1974, Cat. 97: 101; Canada Yearbook various years. Ottawa: Minister of Industry.

Notes:
[a] The area changed at various times with population added. I give the population at the time the census was taken.

[b] CMA is census metropolitan area including metro and the suburbs outside of metro.

population of the 1971 census. The population growth in the other munici-palities in Metro also slowed down considerably, increasing by little more than 200,000 by 1996. However, explosive growth continued in the suburbs beyond Metro, growing by 250 percent during the 20-year period from 1981. Its percent of the Toronto metropolitan area (MA) population expanded from 29 percent in 1981 to 47 percent in 2001 and by the 2006 census constituted over half of the MA population. One of the purposes of the various restructurings that took place in the Toronto region was to capture the majority of the population within boundaries dominated by the city of Toronto. By 2006, Toronto no longer had the majority of the MA population.

In the years since its creation, the governing body and municipalities within the boundaries of Metro have changed, but there has been no exten-sion of the boundaries to absorb new development. In 1966 the 12 suburban municipalities were reorganized into 5 boroughs, and Toronto was enlarged. The governing body was enlarged to 32 or 33 members depending on whether the chair was chosen from outside the membership of the govern-ing body. Toronto retained 12 members, and each borough was allotted between two and six representatives based on population. Members of the body, except the chair, had to be elected members of the participating local units.[29] In 1988, another change provided for a directly elected council, with the mayors of Toronto and the five boroughs retaining their seats on the council as the last remaining vestiges of the original two-tier governing body concept.[30]

The financial arrangements continued to reflect an imbalance between Toronto and the other municipalities within Metro. Since Metro had no independent taxing power, each municipality contributed to Metro functions on the basis of its assessed valuation with the funds used where they were needed. Toronto, with the largest assessed valuation, contributed the most to Metro. For example, with less than 30 percent of the population, it still contributed over 40 percent of the revenues to Metro in 1986. Distribution of functions was established by the province. Most functions were shared between the region and the local level. Metro was responsible for major capital infrastructure such as trunk water and sewer lines, arterial roads, and waste disposal while municipalities were responsible for water distribution, local sewage collection, local streets, and garbage collection. Planning was also a shared responsibility. Most social services were administered regionally except Toronto operated its own housing program. Education, policing, and public transit were regional responsibilities administered by separate regional bodies.[31] Fire services and public health services remained the responsibility of the municipalities.

At the time, Toronto restructuring to a metropolitan tiered system was largely touted as a success story and as a model to emulate in other urban areas. It was a way to equalize services throughout the area and to distribute services to the appropriate government level based on scale economies. Through Metro, taxes could be redistributed from those communities with strong tax bases to those with weaker tax bases. The region was able to fund and benefit from development irrespective of the municipality in which it was located. All Metro communities benefitted from Toronto's highly developed commercial tax base for funding development in the other municipalities. However, this equalization came largely from Toronto sharing its tax base with the more affluent suburban residents living in municipalities with small industrial and commercial tax bases. Metro thus made it easier for the suburbs to develop and provide public services with the tax revenue provided by Toronto's tax base.

Although equalization is viewed as a positive development, it is ironic that Toronto, with its myriad central city problems, was a net contributor to the tax base pool. In addition to the tax revenue equalization, Metro created a regional identity for residents of the city and suburbs. This brought the city and suburbs together in a common bond that reduced the sharp divisions that one observes between city and suburbs in the United States. According to journalist Neal Peirce, it "fostered a lively, variegated downtown and neighborhoods, even while building a mass transit system that is the envy of most big cities."[32]

What was touted as the best solution to governing a metropolitan area had its problems. The tiered government brought together rich and poor, rural and urban communities with their different needs and wants. Conflict was inevitable over how resources were to be distributed. Toronto complained that its resources were being used to develop the suburbs. On the other hand, the more rural areas maintained that Metro was largely dominated by representatives from Toronto and their needs were not adequately addressed. Moreover, the more wealthy suburbs complained that they subsidized the social service needs of high-cost residents located largely in Toronto. The region was also not unified under Metro. The original two-tier government co-existed with four other two-tier regional governments that, in aggregate, dwarfed Metro with ten times the land area and about twice the population. Major growth was taking place in these other areas outside Metro.

There was increasing competition among the governments within Metro and in the region outside Metro for economic development. Toronto was the loser in this competition. One report stated that Toronto lost over 100,000 jobs to the suburbs between 1989 and 2004, 7 percent of its total employment. Most of this loss was to the suburban area (GTA) outside Metro. This area experienced an increase of approximately 800,000 jobs. One of the traditional economic advantages for a central city has been agglomeration economies evidenced by the concentration of multistory buildings in close proximity to each other. This traditional economic advantage has eroded in many American metropolitan areas as office space has dispersed from the central cities into suburban clusters. The same phenomenon is evidenced in Toronto. Although Toronto still has over 50 percent of the office space in the region, its dominance is eroding as it attracted only 21 percent of the new office construction in a ten-year period from 1995 to 2005.[33] With the competition between municipalities for development, Metro struggled to unify the other municipalities to obtain the advantages that come from working together for economic development. The other regional governments outside Metro were also not united but seemed to be united against Metro. With the conflict and competition among the governments within Metro, it was not able to provide a strong unified stance in its dealings with the other suburban and regional governments.

The conflict within Metro among the communities culminated in a non-binding referendum in Toronto in support of the abolition of the upper tier of government in 1994. Dissatisfaction with Toronto's two-tier government also existed in the municipalities surrounding Metro. They were critical of their required contributions to support funding of regional and social services within Metro. They felt that they were contributing more than their fair share. The more rural communities in the metropolitan region resented any contribution that supported any urban services. Thus, by the mid-1990s a growing body of opinion supported a change in the region's governance system. Critics of the upper tier stressed the existence of overlapping services and poor coordination with the lower tier. They further contended that the lower tier did not have mechanisms in place to produce cohesive development strategies.[34]

The major movement in Canada to change from a metropolitan system to a consolidated system commenced in 1993 with the merger of London, Ontario with its suburbs. This was followed by the province of Nova Scotia with the consolidation of eight governments to form the Cape Breton Regional Municipality in 1995. This was a small consolidation involving a population of approximately 120,000. This was followed quickly with the consolidation of three municipalities and a regional authority concerned primarily with public transit into the city of Halifax in 1996. This consolidation affected 354,000 people.[35]

On January 1, 1998, the new city of Toronto came into being through a merger of the former metropolitan level of government and its constituent lower-tier municipalities (Toronto, Etobicoke, North York, Scarborough, York, and East York). Although there had been criticism of Metro and a non-binding vote in Toronto in support of abolition of Metro, there was no support for a consolidation of the communities. In fact, there was substantial opposition from the residents and local political leaders. However, the majority of the local political leaders did not belong to the party controlling the reins of government at the provincial level. The province mandated the abolition of the upper tier and the merger of the constituent governments into the city of Toronto. Thus ended the metropolitan government of Toronto.

In addition to Toronto, other Canadian cities experimented with various local government reforms. Winnipeg, Manitoba, was restructured as a two-tier government in 1960 following the Toronto federation model, with 19 constituent municipalities and an area-wide government. Representation was by direct election from 10 wards, which combined city and suburban areas. Functions were divided between the regional government and municipalities. This system was strongly opposed by the mayor of Winnipeg. This resistance and the lack of clear responsibility for development between the city and the regional government created frictions that resulted in the regional government's dissolution in 1972. It was replaced by a consolidated city government in which the 19 constituent municipalities were merged into the city.[36] With the consolidation, suburban representation dominated the old city. The result was an emphasis on suburban development to the detriment of the old city. Andrew Sancton assessed the impact of the consolidated city after 20 years and concluded that the city's growth pattern is similar to that of other fragmented areas. Although the city still contains over 90 percent of the region's population, growth has spilled over the boundaries of the city. The population is growing much faster outside the city. This pattern of growth prompted the province to create a regional commission to deal with issues of a regional nature which, in effect, reestablished a tiered system of governance.[37]

Quebec also instituted a two-tier system in 1969 covering only Montreal and the 28 other municipalities on the Island of Montreal. The remainder of the metropolitan area was excluded. This area experienced governance issues similar to those of Toronto with major growth in the suburbs beyond the island and problems of cooperation and competition for development. With the focus on restructuring that was sweeping Canada in the 1990s, a number of proposals were put forward to deal with the more than 100 municipalities in the Montreal metropolitan area. One proposal was to create a metropolitan-wide government tier and four intermediate levels which would assume functions delegated by the member municipalities under the tier. This three-tiered structure was rejected along with other proposals during the 1990s.[38] Finally, in 2002, despite extensive opposition that was a factor in the defeat of the government in the ensuing election, the province eliminated the upper tier and combined the 29 municipalities with the city of Montreal.

There is a new twist to the consolidation that is being played out in Montreal. Because the amalgamation was so unpopular, the province allowed the amalgamated municipalities to vote on whether they wanted to remain in the amalgamated cities. To be able to vote on demerger, certain conditions had to be met. Twenty-two of the twenty-eight municipalities that had been merged into the city voted on demerger. The vote in favor was obtained in 15 of the 28 former municipalities, permitting them to leave the amalgamation. In the seven other former Montreal municipalities that voted, a majority voted to separate, but the required 35 percent of eligible voters did not vote. The de-annexation took place January 1, 2006.[39]

The tiered system of government in Canada during the course of its existence was not able to gain legitimacy or develop a supportive constituency to fight for its continued survival. No one was sad to see its demise. Indeed, there were many that had long advocated its elimination. James Lightbody, a keen observer of Canadian politics and government[40] gives three reasons for the demise of the metropolitan system in Canada:

- Inability to develop support from citizens, municipal governments, or provincial governments. Municipalities view them as a threat to their municipal powers. Provincial administrators view them as a potential and unnecessary rival. Representatives on the governing boards of the upper tiers usually were not directly elected but were mayors and councilors from the municipalities who viewed the regional government as a threat. Without direct election, the citizens did not develop an identity with the regional government, nor did the regional government develop a relationship with the citizens. Even where there was direct election, such as in Winnipeg, the metropolitan government was not able to function because of the battles over the divergent development agendas of the directly elected councilors and the mayors of the constituent municipalities. There was little public controversy in regional policies or politics. Because of lack of political interest in the regional government, power accrued to the bureaucracy. No constituency developed to support or fight for the survival of regional government.

- Regional government's original function was to provide infrastructure and services to property and coordinate the delivery of these maintenance-type services. Social services and equity issues were left to other levels of government. This original purpose did not materially change over the years. Public controversy or general interest group activity was not associated with this level of government. It operated out of the limelight with little or no interest from citizens or human services advocacy groups.

- Conflict between the constituent municipalities and the regional government was integral to the system because of the nature of the shared responsibilities. Municipalities could negatively affect most area-wide functions that require local participation. For example, regional traffic planning could be frustrated with neighborhood buffers and traffic restrictions; regional planning could be frustrated with zoning restrictions, and building regulations, or the issuance of building permits; efficient provision of sewer and water operations could be frustrated by the way the municipalities retail the water to their residents; and planning and developing arterial roadways could be frustrated through inadequate connectors and limited parking.

Government in metropolitan areas in British Columbia is more similar to that of the United States. It did not go through top-down restructuring. The Greater Vancouver Regional District in British Columbia is not a new level of government, but a mechanism to combine under one unit special districts providing regional services. It is also a vehicle to encourage future cooperation between municipalities. The district is governed by a board composed of elected municipal representatives. The number of votes each representative has is based on the population of the municipality he or she represents. Very few services are mandated by the province to be provided at the regional level. It is left to the municipal representatives to decide the services that should be provided at this level. Regional services provided by the Vancouver regional district include public transit, water and sewage services, garbage disposal and regional parks.[41]

Local governments are not forced to participate and can decide whether they want to join the programs of the district. The district operates by consensus. Governments in the Vancouver area have come to realize the advantages of working together on specific issues and willingly give up some autonomy for the benefits they receive from joint action. Harmony does not always exist and there is often contentious debate among members. Often decisions are excruciatingly slow, such as the ten-year process to gain acceptance of a regional development plan. But the system has proved to be resilient and capable of addressing regional policy issues and providing or coordinating regional services. The Vancouver area has been noted for its livability. (For a more detailed discussion on Vancouver, see Chapter 9.)

Takeaway

Countries outside the United States have a mixture of different types of regional governance. Governance of regions varies from country to country and even within countries. Overall, the most popular form initially was a tiered structure. This structure, with a number of exceptions, has been replaced by countries either going to a consolidated system or a cooperative and collaborative form of governance. This proves the contention that, given the political and cultural traditions of the country, there are many different ways to establish regional governance. One point from this brief overview is that regional governance of some form is occurring in most large cities outside the United States. Most regional governing systems also have their major focus on economic development. Finally there is generally a lack of regional identity and general resistance to any form of regional government among the populace.

Although countries will continue to experiment with structural changes, these will be less prevalent than in the past. Senior-level governments will still encourage and provide incentives for local government cooperation and consolidation, but they will be less inclined to mandate structural changes. Instead governments will establish special districts to provide regional services on an ad hoc basis as needed and encourage cooperation. With more freedom from state and national controls, regional governance will be a matter of local option.

With the increasing competition among regions within countries and across national borders for development, local governments in metropolitan areas are realizing the advantages of cooperating with each other and collaborating with the private and nonprofit sectors within the region. The approach to regional governance will be driven by the economic development imperative and will be more a bottom-up approach, instead of the top-down approach of the past. Regional governance in many other countries is increasingly becoming a matter of cooperation and collaboration similar to that of the United States.[42]

One observer claims that in an age of globalization the regions that will be able to compete best at the economic development game are those that are the most united. Those regions that are able to marshal governments, business, civic, labor and other nongovernmental organizations (NGOs) under a leadership able to bring the various disparate forces together to address regional governance issues and present a unified economic development agenda, will be most successful. These will not be the biggest city-regions, nor the ones that have a centralized government, but the ones that are able to present a united approach combining government and NGOs in a governing regime to address regional policy issues and pursue development policies. A polycentric local government system with its fragmented decision processes and tendency to compete rather than cooperate seems "quaintly out of step in a globally connected society."[43]

Notes

1. David Hamilton, David Miller, and Jerry Paytas, "Exploring the Horizontal and Vertical Dimensions of the Governing of Metropolitan regions," *Urban Affairs Review*, 40 (2) (2004): 147–182; Jen Nelles, *Comparative Metropolitan Policy: Governing Beyond Local Boundaries in the Imagined Metropolis* (London and New York: Routledge, 2012). Also, see Chapter 10 of this book.
2. Hubert Kübler and Daniel Heinelt, "Introduction," in Hubert Kübler and Daniel Heinelt, (eds.), *Metropolitan Governance: Capacity, Democracy and the Dynamics of Place* (London and New York: Routledge, 2005), pp. 1–9.
3. David Hamilton, *Measuring the Effectiveness of Regional Governing Systems* (New York: Springer, 2013), pp. 1–9; Heinelt and Kübler, "Introduction," in *Metropolitan Governance*, pp. 19–20.
4. Hamilton, *Measuring the Effectiveness of Regional Governing Systems*, pp. 1–9.
5. Heinelt and Kübler, "Conclusion," in *Metropolitan Governance,* pp. 189–190.

6. Martin Burgi, "Federal Republic of Germany," in Nico Steytler, (ed.), *Local Government and Metropolitan Regions in Federal Systems* (Montreal: McGill-Queens University Press, 2009), pp. 136–166.
7. Dietrich Fürst, "Metropolitan Governance in Germany," in Kübler and Heinelt, (eds.), *Metropolitan Governance: Capacity, Democracy and the Dynamics of Place*, pp. 155–156.
8. Jen Nelles, *Comparative Metropolitan Policy: Governing Beyond Local Boundaries in the Imagined Metropolis* (New York: Routledge, 2012), pp. 50–53.
9. Ibid.; Dietrich Fürst, "Metropolitan Governance in Germany," in Kübler and Heinelt (eds.), *Metropolitan Governance*, pp. 155–156.
10. Nelles, Comparative Metropolitan Policy, pp. 56–59.
11. Ibid., pp. 70–75.
12. Dietrich Fürst, "Metropolitan Governance in Germany," pp. 160–163.
13. Leo Van Den Berg, H. Arjen Van Klink, and Jan Van Der Meer, "A Survey of Metropolitan Government in Europe," in Donald Phares, (ed.), *Metropolitan Governance without Metropolitan Government?* (London: Ashgate Publishing Company, 2004), p. 83.
14. Nick Swift and Guy Kervella, *A Complex System Aims to Bring French Local Government Closer to the People*, http://www.citymayors.com/france/france_gov.html [Accessed April 22, 2013]; Heinelt and Kübler, "Conclusion," in *Metropolitan Governance*, pp.189–190.
15. Swift and Kervella. *A Complex System Aims to Bring French Local Government Closer to the People* [Accessed April, 22, 2013].
16. Heinelt and Kübler, *"Conclusion,"* in *Metropolitan Governance*, pp. 189–190.
17. Francisco Velasco Caballero, "Kingdom of Spain," in *Local Government and Metropolitan Regions in Federal Systems*, pp. 298–329.
18. Ibid., pp. 298–329; Heinelt and Kübler, *"Conclusion,"* in Steytler, (ed.), *Metropolitan Governance*, pp. 189–190.
19. Michael Goldsmith, "Metropolitan Government in England," in Kübler and Heinelt, (eds.), *Metropolitan Governance: Capacity, Democracy and the Dynamics of Place*, pp. 82–91.
20. Donald F. Norris, "Whither Metropolitan Governance?" *Urban Affairs Review*, 36 (4) (2001): 532–550.
21. Goldsmith, "Metropolitan Government in England," pp. 82–91; Peter Newman and Andy Thornley, "London: The Mayor, Partnership and World City Business," in Philip Booth and Bernard Jouve, (eds.), *Metropolitan Democracies: Transformations of the State and Urban Policy in Canada, France and Great Britain* (London: Ashgate Publishing Company, 2005), pp. 68–70.
22. Ibid.
23. Berg, Van Klink, and Van Der Meer, "A Survey of Metropolitan Government in Europe," p. 84.
24. Ibid.
25. Ibid., pp. 78–102.
26. Jiawen Yang, "Spatial Planning in Asia: Planning and Developing Megacities and Mega Regions," in Catherine Ross, (ed.), *Megaregions: Planning for Global Competitiveness* (Washington, DC: Island Press, 2009), pp. 35–49.
27. Andrew Sancton, *Governing Canada's City-Regions: Adapting Form to Function* (Montreal: Institute for Research on Public Policy, 1994), p. 77. See also, John J. Harrigan and Ronald K. Vogel, *Political Change in the Metropolis*, 7th ed. (New York: Longman, 2003) pp. 269–271; and Michael Keating, *Comparative Urban Politics: Power and the City in the United States, Canada, Britain, and France* (Aldershot, England: Edward Elgar Publishing, 1991), p. 125.

28. Sancton, *Governing Canada's City-Regions,* pp. 77–78.
29. John C. Bollens and Henry J. Schmandt, *The Metropolis: Its People, Politics, and Economic Life,* 3rd ed. (New York: Harper and Row, 1975), p. 285.
30. Michael Keating, *Comparative Urban Politics: Power and the City in the United States, Canada, Britain, and France* (Aldershot, England: Edward Elgar Publishing, 1991), p. 125; Harrison and Vogel, *Political Change in the Metropolis,* p. 270.
31. Francis Frisken, "Planning and Servicing the Greater Toronto Area: The Interplay of Provincial and Municipal Interests," in Donald. N. Rothblatt and Andrew Sancton (eds.), *Metropolitan governance: American and Canadian Intergovernmental Perspectives* (Berkeley, CA: Institute of Governmental Studies Press, University of California, 1993), p. 166.
32. Neal Peirce, "Cities Need to Update Formula for Success," *Arlington Heights (Ill.) Daily Herald,* November 25, 1996, sec. 1, p. 12.
33. City of Toronto, Report of the Governing Toronto Advisory Panel, *The City We Want—the Government We Need* (Toronto: November 2, 2005).
34. G. Williams, "Institutional Capacity and Metropolitan Governance: The Greater Toronto Area," *Cities,* 16 (3) (1999): 171–180.
35. Andrew Sancton, *Merger Mania* (Montreal: McGill-Queen's University Press, 2000).
36. Lionel D. Feldman and Katherine A. Graham, "Local Government Reform in Canada," in Arthur B. Gunlicks, (ed.), *Local Government Reform and Reorganization: An International Perspective* (Port Washington, NY: Kennikat Press, 1981), pp. 158–159.
37. Sancton, *Governing Canada's City-Regions,* pp. 24–27.
38. R. C. Tindal, and S. N. Tindal, *Local Government in Canada,* 6th ed. (Toronto: Nelson, 2004), pp. 122–124.
39. *Local Government Bulletin* No. 47, May 2004 and No. 48, June 2004, http://www.localgovernment.ca/show_libary.cfm?id=125 [Accessed April 10, 2006].
40. James Lightbody, *City Politics: Canada* (Peterborough, ON: Broadview Press, 2006), pp. 460–462.
41. Andrew Sancton, "Metropolitan Areas in Canada," *Public Administration and Development,* 25 (4) (2005): 317–329.
42. Steytler, "Comparative Conclusions" in Nico Steytler, (ed.), pp. 400–405.
43. Lightbody, *City Politics,* p. 520.

12 Future Directions for Regional Governance in a Global Society

And they shall build the old wastes, they shall raise up the former desolations, and they shall repair the waste cities, the desolations of many generations.

—Isaiah 61:4

As society becomes more global and as metropolitan areas become more complex, problems migrate to the regional level requiring a regional solution. Some form of regional governance is inevitable. In the previous chapters the various approaches to regional governance were presented and analyzed. This study proceeded in accordance with the framework explicated in Chapter 1, which included a process model, depicting responses to box growth and regional governance pressures (see Figure 1.2 and Table 1.11). The responses were categorized as either centralizing or decentralizing and either changes in government structure or changes in governance of regions. Centralizing responses involve either government structure changes or changes in governance, such as transfer of functions or authority to a regional level. Decentralization responses involve either the establishment of additional governments or governance responses that maintain the authority and independence of municipal governments. In other parts of the book, the various responses to, and the major influences on, governing regional areas were presented and analyzed.

As the United States was growing in the nineteenth century and becoming more urbanized, the urban growth surrounding the city usually became part of the city either willingly or unwillingly. The superior central city services were a major reason for the centralization responses in the nineteenth century. As services became more generally available in the latter part of the nineteenth century through special-purpose districts, suburban communities were able to obtain municipal services and still retain their independence. When given the choice, suburban residents generally chose to remain independent from the central city if their local government services could be provided.

During much of the nineteenth century, centralized government structural responses dominated. These responses were mainly annexations and consolidations. However, beginning in the later part of the nineteenth century and extending through the twentieth century, the resistance to centralized structural responses became intense to the point that decentralized responses became dominant. Initially, the focus was on structural government responses including new forms of general purpose government, easy incorporation laws and favorable local resident voting requirements. Decentralized structural responses enabling regional governance without loss of local identity with the advantages of economies of scale included regional single-purpose districts, privatization and interlocal agreements. Starting in the 1990s and into the twenty-first century, the focus has been on governance responses both centralizing and decentralizing, with decentralized responses dominating. The decentralized responses are more common because they are solutions to regional governance problems without requiring major changes in the authority or autonomy of the local governments in the metropolitan area.

Metropolitan areas exhibit various degrees of government fragmentation. Annexation of unincorporated territory has been the most successful form of government structure centralization (see Chapter 3). Growing areas of the South and some parts of the West have had the most success with this centralization response. Once the central city is surrounded by incorporated municipalities, annexation is generally foreclosed as an option. Other forms of centralized government responses, including city–county consolidations and federated government forms, have usually been rejected by the voters or, if adopted, have often only been partial consolidations. Even those areas that have succeeded in obtaining a form of centralized government, as they keep growing and expanding, exhibit a fragmented government pattern. As was discussed in Chapter 4, major government restructuring in large metropolitan areas is problematic and not likely to happen. Centralized government responses are still an option but more likely to occur in smaller, less diverse urban areas with adjacent unincorporated territory and be more likely to occur in the South and the West.

Advocates for centralized responses in the 1990s started moving away from advocating for a restructuring of government to advocating for centralized governance solutions. The type of regional governance that these advocates propose for large metropolitan areas is tax base sharing schemes and some form of overarching regional district with substantial authority. The Regional Plan Association's (RPA) 1996 recommendation for the New York region is illustrative of the recommendations that advocates of regional approaches started to make, and continue to make. The RPA modeled its recommendations on the Portland and Minneapolis-St. Paul systems. It recommended the establishment of a metropolitan service commission to assume some or all of the following responsibilities:

- Administer a regional urban growth boundary and oversee a regional land use planning system in which municipal plans would become consistent with regional goals.
- Consolidate transportation planning and capital budgeting through assuming responsibility for owning highways, bridges, and rail corridors, and contract for operation and maintenance of these systems with existing public authorities or private operators.
- Assume responsibility for funding land acquisition in the proposed regional reserves and assume control of state and regional parks, parkways, and greenways.
- Transfer from the states environmental, land use, and other regulatory responsibilities and taxing authorities.
- Assume responsibilities for environmental planning, regulation, and even operation of solid waste, wastewater treatment, and public water supply systems.[1]

Governing Decentralized Areas Going Forward

America's metropolitan areas continue to grow and change their form. As they grow, rather than maintain their form of a strong core, they are decentralizing into a dispersed network of cities and towns across a large urban region. Indeed, most of the growth of urban areas after the mid-twentieth century occurred outside the core area. As the center hollowed out, the growth was in "edge cities." As discussed in Chapter 2, many local policy issues and problems have migrated to the regional level and require regional approaches to address them. It is ironic that population and business have decentralized from the core city to the suburbs, while the solutions to governing issues more and more require a more centralized response.

The general direction that many metropolitan areas are taking to solve their regional problems is governance approaches. Centralized government approaches to the governing of large, diverse metropolitan areas appears to be impractical, if not impossible. Centralized governance approaches, such as establishing a form of an overarching regional district with some authority is difficult and in the United States has only been successful in the Portland and Twin Cities regions. There is no evidence that others will follow although this form of regional governance has had some success outside the United States (see Chapter 11). The development of urban counties is problematic and has been successful only in a few metropolitan areas. Tax-sharing is also resisted by those suburbs that are required to contribute although it has been instituted with success in a few areas. These and other centralizing governance responses will continue to be advocated and will be implemented in some areas. However, the decentralized governance responses or some combination of centralized and decentralized responses appear to be the most acceptable and will have the most application. The most recent decentralized governance trend that has some promise of acceptance is the collaborative approach described in Chapter 10.[2]

From Metropolitan Governance to Megapolitan Governance

As metropolitan areas grow, a major governing concern is attracting economic growth and development. Since economic development in metropolitan areas is not restricted to political boundaries, economic growth becomes a major regional issue. Policies that attract or restrict development become a regional problem. The advantages of a region's governments and private and nonprofit sectors working together for economic advantages were described in Chapter 10. It is becoming evident, as metropolitan areas grow, that there are advantages of linking neighboring metropolitan areas to take advantage of the strengths each area can contribute.

This concept of converging metropolitan areas cooperating and collaborating for mutual benefit can be applied to a number of areas. One example is the converging Orlando and Tampa regions. This combined region is highly tourist dependent, but combining the international airport in Orlando with the port facility and logistics that Tampa offers would be helpful in developing a more diversified economy. Another example is Phoenix and Tucson. These metropolitan areas share assets that can benefit each other in economic development. The two core city anchors have in the past not cooperated with each other, but they have assets that would provide synergies if they worked together to market and develop their region. Tucson has a research university with a strong capacity in space science and optics. It also has a medical school, while Phoenix has an international airport and professional sports that are attractive to companies.[3]

One of the problems of developing governing synergies in these megapolitan regions is the lack of sense of place. Very few urban regions have a unifying theme around which the public can identify. Developing a megapolitan identity can unify these metropolitan areas and make it possible to develop a culture of regional cooperation and collaboration. Developing this sense of place takes public and private sector collaboration in the first place. A megapolitan identity is an important element without which it will be difficult to develop continuing partnerships and collaborations. An example of a successful development of sense of place identity is the growing together of the Fort Worth and Dallas metropolitan areas. These two anchor cities had a long history of mutual animosity. When they had to work together to develop a regional airport, the name "metroplex" was born to refer to the combined metropolitan area. The public has embraced this name and has accepted the integration of the two core cities. The megapolitan area is unified around the airport, and the various cities in the region are cooperating and collaborating with the private sector on other regional initiatives.[4]

There is a disconnect between regional governing capacity and regional governing needs. The governing capacity is still focused within the jurisdictions of the myriad local governments while the governing needs are increasingly at a regional scale. As metropolitan areas continue to expand and economic activity spreads throughout the region, synergies can be developed with other neighboring regions. The core thus becomes less important as a centralizing focus. Governmental cooperation and collaboration with nongovernmental actors will become more critical for the economic growth of the region. Working together and across boundaries in networks and partnerships for the good of the whole will become more important. Responding effectively to governing issues of the megapolitan areas will require substantial amounts of trust building, deliberative processes, interlocal engagement, and networking on the part of local leaders.

William Barnes, retired after a long career with the National League of Cities, claims that jurisdictional boundary crossing will become essential for effective governance in metropolitan areas. Some networking will be at the regional level and some will be at a smaller scale, but engaging other municipal and nongovernmental leaders at various scales will be essential.[5] According to Barnes, the idea of a single central government over the entire metropolitan area is a notion that has run its course. The metropolitan areas are becoming too decentralized economically, politically and geographically to be governable from a central location. The argument is no longer which centralized governing system is best, but how to govern large, diverse regions with many local governments. Leaders, both governmental and nongovernmental, will need to collaborate and work together to effectively address regional policy issues and compete in an increasing global economy. For successful regional governing systems, the focus should not be inward on how to most effectively govern the region, but should be on how the region can effectively develop synergies with neighboring metropolitan areas to effectively compete in an increasing global economy.

Globalism and Regionalism

How will globalism affect regionalism? What will regional governance look like in an increasingly global society? As we become more interconnected as a society, local governments will be forced to become more interconnected. That means that regional governance will become even more critical. National borders will become less important as the economy continues to globalize. Markets will continue to have a strong influence on governance, and as markets become more regional and global in scope; metropolitan areas will become even more important as the level for organizing governance.

This will happen as metropolitan areas seek to compete for economic development nationally and internationally. In this competitive global society, local government leaders will need to become increasingly focused regionally in order to bring benefits to their individual municipalities. The traditional local government orientation of autonomy, isolation, and independence must be replaced by interdependence and partnerships for regions to successfully compete.

The traditional service delivery model of each local government producing all of its own services has been diminishing for some time as municipalities have resorted to privatization and interlocal agreements to provide a number of services. There will be continuing pressures to look for alternative service delivery methods. Professor Mildred Warner argues that the rush toward privatization in the 1990s sometimes resulted in replacing a local government monopoly on service delivery with a private monopoly because of the lack of competition in local government service markets. However, she claims that pressures to privatize will remain high, but governments will be more astute in arranging and managing service delivery.[6] The traditional in-house method of delivery will increasingly give way to alternative forms of delivery whether it is through privatization, interlocal agreements, or other arrangements.

There will also be increasing pressure to collaborate with the private and civic sectors. Those regions that are able to collaborate and work in public–private partnerships and coalitions will have the advantage in economic development. Regional collaborative governance is not in the future, it is here and is increasingly important in the competition for economic development. The old recommendations that reformers made to restructure government institutions have been replaced by new regionalism initiatives including cooperation and collaboration.

Government leaders are being forced to look at regional solutions because of the increased visibility of problems that cross government boundaries. Governments, under pressure to hold down costs of providing services, are exploring alternative ways and new approaches to meet the needs of their residents. It is not business as usual for local governments. While pressuring governments to be more innovative, residents continue to resist radical regional solutions that call for the extensive restructuring of political units. As indicated previously, changes in governance usually result from a crisis or an opportunity. Regionalism will only be accepted to the extent that there is a perceived crisis of governance or a major opportunity that can only be realized by some form of regional approach. The issues addressed by, and the authority granted to, a regional governing system will depend on the nature of the crisis or opportunity and how it is perceived by the public and the community leaders.

In the past local governments tended to respond to regional issues on a piecemeal basis. They would meet a regional challenge with a patchwork solution such as regional special districts to provide a service or a council of governments as a discussion and planning forum to meet a specific federal requirement. But these approaches and solutions have generally been ad hoc and from local government leaders with an inward-looking attitude. Their general orientation in cooperative ventures, at times mandated by some state or federal program, was not to give up any local prerogatives and only cooperate and work across boundaries when there was a clear benefit to the municipality, which it could not effectively and efficiently provide on its own. This thinking is changing of necessity in this increasingly global society.

William Dodge, a regional consultant, claims that there is an increasing number of government and civic leaders who think and act regionally. He calls these leaders regional citizens and argues that they will help build capacity for regional governance.[7] One example of a city leader who realized the advantages of a regional approach to governing is the former mayor of Grand Rapids, Michigan. He was willing to give up city control over the public transportation system and its jobs to a regional group to obtain improved service and a solid funding base. He was also the catalyst in the establishment of a regional partnership to take control of the city's water and sewer system that provided services to the city and most of the suburbs on a contract basis. One purpose of the partnership is to control sprawl development by requiring each community to establish a utility boundary. The mayor also worked to establish state legislation with incentives to encourage municipalities to consolidate services.[8]

In our globalizing world, traditional governance is giving way to new forms and methods. Public goods and services are increasingly being provided by a mix of governmental and nongovernmental entities. Market mechanisms are being increasingly favored in the delivery of public goods and services. Consortiums, often led by international organizations, are competing for and winning contracts to provide public services in metropolitan areas. One example of the internationalization of metropolitan services is the Chicago Skyway, a toll road connecting downtown Chicago to the Indiana toll road. This road, built and previously operated by Chicago, has been leased for 99 years to the Skyway Concession Company, a joint venture consisting of an Australian and Spanish firm. Chicago also leased its parking meters to a private international consortium led by the firm Morgan Stanley. Major investors in the newly formed company, Chicago Parking Meters LLC, are located in Luxembourg and Abu Dhabi.[9]

Toward Effective Regional Governance

An effective regional governance system should have some control over land use. Regionalist David Rusk in the latest edition of his book *Cities without Suburbs* states that for regionalism to succeed there must be regional control over land use for the orderly development of the region and to be able to integrate low-income housing throughout the region to diminish racial and economic segregation.[10] Regional land use plans should be comprehensive, and the area-wide governance system should have authority to compel municipalities to abide by its plans. Local government plans would be required to follow the regional land use plan, and the regional government should have final say in the event of differences between plans. Localities should be prevented from using their land use and other regulatory powers to secure competitive advantages over other metropolitan communities. Regional plans should ensure that the regulations of all governments in the metropolitan area make room for balanced and rational growth of their regions. Regionalist Peter Salins, forcefully stating the need for regional authority in land use controls, observed:

> When such communities reserve most of their residential districts for large houses on two-acre lots, when they ban multi-family housing or commercial activity, when they set impossible environmental standards, or prevent any new development, they go too far.[11]

As indicated in Chapter 9, Portland has been able to control sprawl and achieve favorable development patterns because of strong regional planning powers. Moving land use controls to the regional level is extremely controversial. In most areas where attempts have been made to locate strong land use planning powers in a regional government, they have been so strongly resisted that they were not successful, or their diminishing planning powers were either not enforced or later rescinded. However, this resistance is diminishing as the benefits of regional planning, especially transportation, infrastructure, and environmental problems, become more evident to both political leaders and citizens.

To be able to enforce its decisions and develop a regional identity among the residents, a regional governing system should have an independent political base. There needs to be a political body that can establish, build, and nurture a regional identity and constituency. The most appropriate way to develop a political base is to have a separately elected body that is responsible directly to the voters in the region. Through direct elections, voters participate in the regional governance process and can develop an identity with the regional level that would not be possible with an appointed governing body. With a political base, the regional governing body would be better able to address controversial regional issues. Building a regional constituency will only happen through an elective system, as political leaders' primary allegiance is to the constituency that elected them. Portland's elected regional body has been willing to tackle controversial land use decisions, while the Twin Cities' appointed regional body has not been as successful in addressing controversial problems.

As with the regional planning recommendation, an elected regional governing body is also a highly controversial recommendation. Advocates of regional government realize that the chances of obtaining voter approval for any form of regional governance system are remote. That is why they are turning to the state legislatures to pass legislation favorable to regionalism.[12] Through the deliberative process and appealing to the political self-interests of legislators, advocates of regional initiatives feel they have a much better chance of convincing the legislature of the merits of their arguments. This is particularly true if the local political leaders in the area support the regional initiatives. States generally reacted to regional crises in the past by mandating solutions to solve the specific crisis without addressing broader regional governance issues. However, as discussed in Chapter 5, states are becoming more involved in broader regional governing issues through growth management laws, boundary review commissions, affordable housing mandates, and more stringent incorporation procedures. Although local governments are cooperating and working more closely together, state government involvement is critical in bringing about effective regional governance.

The county's role in the new collaborative governance model is problematic. At one time regionalists saw the county as a strong candidate to provide regional governance. However, the county in most states has not acquired home rule powers and, thus, cannot provide the services or the leadership necessary to assume a regional governance function. Furthermore, governance has become more important than government. In addition, most urban regions contain more than one county. Regional governance needs to extend beyond the individual county to the entire urban area. Regionalism could still benefit with strong home rule counties; they could become the focal point of government involvement in collaborative regionalism as Allegheny County in the Pittsburgh area has become for that region.

The federal government's role in metropolitan areas is unlikely to grow in the future. In fact, it is likely to decrease as programs are turned back to the states and its financial involvement is reduced at the state and local level. However, the federal programs that remain will likely be designed to encourage regional coordination and integration. These programs will allow flexibility in addressing regional issues and require a more comprehensive perspective. The best examples that will likely be used as a model for other federal grant programs to induce regional cooperation and coordination are the federal transportation and homeland security programs.

Regionalism will continue to develop slowly and in the least controversial ways. Crises in local service delivery will lead to increased centralized responses. Centralization may occur almost imperceptibly or may come with much fanfare. Each metropolitan area is different and responds differently to regionalism pressures. As the number of experiments in cooperation and collaboration increase and private and nonprofit agencies become more involved in various collaborative projects, efforts will be made to build consensus on regional solutions and coordinate individual efforts.

To be successful regional initiatives must appeal to the mutual self-interests of governments and interest groups. Myron Orfield suggests that the central city and the suburbs with common interests form a coalition and work to obtain their agenda in the state legislature. He suggests that there are more suburbs that would benefit from regional governance strategies, such as tax-base sharing and growth management schemes, than would be disadvantaged. This coalition may obtain support from other legislators throughout the state who are concerned with reducing disparities in metropolitan areas. Working together, the coalition should be successful.[13] Christopher Leo maintains that the advances in regional governance in Portland were successful because they appealed to the self-interests of powerful interest groups, such as the farmers and environmentalists. These groups were able to convince suburban chambers of commerce, dominated by agricultural-oriented businesses, to support the movement. Developers were also convinced that more uniformity in building codes throughout the region was a reasonable trade-off to growth management controls.[14]

For regional governance to be successful, there must be strong political leadership. Cooperative and collaborative regionalism requires dedicated, aggressive leadership to bring municipalities together in support of regional initiatives. In some metropolitan areas it may be the central city mayor, and in other metropolitan areas it may be a county government political leader. Still in other areas, it may be a state legislator who is especially interested in problems of the region. It must be a political leader who is willing to transcend the cultural differences and animosities between the cities and the suburbs. He or she must be a catalyst in bringing political and community leaders together to address regional governance issues of mutual benefit. Major political leaders in some areas are initiating regionalism efforts. For example, the chairman of the Allegheny County Board of County Commissioners is providing political leadership to the regional governance efforts in the Pittsburgh MSA. The former mayor, Daley, in Chicago started a regional initiative by hiring a former executive director of a major and respected suburban council of governments to serve as his liaison to the suburbs.[15]

There appears to be a greater urgency than in the past to address regional problems by the business and civic communities. As discussed in Chapter 10, there is evidence that regionalism is receiving increased attention from the civic and business sectors leaders in these sectors are aggressively looking for ways to develop regionalism. They are working with government and other organizations to bring a regional focus to metropolitan areas. Studies and reports by business-supported civic associations are increasingly focused on regional governance approaches to solve issues that, at one time, were seen as central city, state, or federal government problems. For example, three different organizations are actively promoting regional cooperation in Chicago:

- The John D. and Catherine T. MacArthur Foundation is funding a number of projects to promote regionalism and cooperation among governments. It provided funding to establish a Cook County-Chicago task force on welfare reform. It provided funding to bring regionalist Myron Orfield to Chicago to conduct a study on disparities among local governments in the region. It funds a Regional Conversations Project, which includes studies and a newsletter focusing on regional issues.
- The Commercial Club has undertaken a project called *Preparing Metropolitan Chicago for the 21st Century*, which focuses on regional issues and solutions.
- The Metropolitan Planning Council has produced a number of recent reports, including *Creating a Regional Community: The Case for Regional Cooperation, Housing for a Competitive Region, and Removing Regulatory Barriers*, which deals with the availability of low-income housing throughout the region.[16]

Voluntary associations, such as councils of governments and regional planning councils, are seen by many as vestiges of past federal government efforts to force regionalism on the urban area. These councils can only have a role in the collaborative governance model if they reinvent themselves and remove the stigma of the past. Their ability to play a role seems to be limited because of the negative perceptions many community leaders have of them. However, in a few metropolitan areas, regional councils have played limited but important roles in regionalism (see Chapter 7). Councils must be aggressive in addressing regional issues or they will be left behind by other associations that act more quickly to bring government and private leaders together to find area-wide solutions. Regional districts have a major impact on service delivery and must be coordinated with other regional services. Without some form of regional service delivery coordination, it is not possible to provide effective overall regional governance.

A method to ensure some level of equity in local revenues is needed. Rusk claims that tax base sharing is an essential element of an effective regional governing system to reduce the fiscal inequities among municipalities that result from uneven growth and socioeconomic imbalances.[17] Although still only used in a handful of metropolitan areas, there is an increasing interest in using tax revenue sharing to support regional initiatives. Tax revenue sharing will likely grow in usage if the shared revenue is for a specific purpose and not for general government operations and does not reduce current revenue from contributor governments. Municipalities will not willingly give up tax resources unless they perceive a larger benefit in return. Sharing tax resources for economic development is one possible area of mutual benefit, particularly for jurisdictions that are too small to mount an economic development effort on their own. One inducement to tax revenue sharing is to allow local governments to institute a new tax or expand a current tax, with a portion of the increased tax revenue contributed to a shared tax pool. Seed money contributed by a larger government, such as the county or the state, could also be used as an inducement for municipalities to join.

Takeway

What is the takeway from this study? For one thing institutional arrangements have a major impact. Institutions matter and have a major influence on what can and cannot happen in regional governance. Institutional structures make regional governance either more difficult or easier to achieve. Autonomy and independence of local governments also matter. The diversity of the population and the number of municipalities are important elements. The cultural traditions and history of the metropolitan area make a difference in governance in the region of the development. It is also clear that in a decentralized metropolitan area with no overarching government and authority widely diffused, the nongovernment sector is a critical element in obtaining effective regional governance. Indeed, even in regions with some form of overarching governing system with authority over regional services, collaboration with nongovernmental actors and cooperation with other governments are important in effective regional governance. This is so because economic decisions by business have a major impact on the regional economy. If a major purpose of the region is to be able to compete economically with other regions and bring additional development to the region, it is critically important to involve leaders from that sector in the decision-making processes. It is also important to temper the influence of the economic sector with leaders of the nonprofit sector to allow for a balanced approach to regional governance.

As indicated above, collaboration and cooperation are increasingly important in regional governance. Indeed, a case can be made that decentralized regional governance responses will continue to dominate regionalism, particularly the use of voluntary partnerships and collaboration with nongovernmental organizations (NGOs) as an alternative to more formalized institutional adjustments. Cooperation and collaboration provide more flexibility for the governments involved and foster public–private partnerships and coalitions. Public–private partnerships and cooperation among governments are the middle ground between the economic imperatives that benefit from centralized public policy of the region and the reality of a politically decentralized governing system. This is an attractive approach to the regional governance problem. It might be the best response in some situations but not in others, or it might be useful in combination with other approaches as it brings public, private, and nonprofit stakeholders together in a common cause without the nearly impossible task of attempting to alter government structure.[18]

As was indicated in previous chapters, civic capital and involvement of the private sector is becoming more common and more important in regional governance. This is not just the case in highly decentralized areas like the United States, but in countries with unitary systems of government where senior level governments have established regional governing institutions. There are many different variations of regional governing systems. Each metropolitan area is unique with its own politics and cultural traditions. There is no one-size-fits-all regional governing solution. The best system will depend on the needs and traditions that are unique to that region. It is clear, however, that regardless of the institutional arrangements in the metropolitan area, some form of governmental cooperation and collaboration with the nongovernmental sector is an essential element for effective regional governance. Moreover, civic capital is an important element in fostering cooperation and collaboration. Nelles, from her case studies of four city regions in Canada and Germany, concluded that civic capital is a catalyst for more intense cooperation among governments and that it also facilitates the involvement of nongovernmental actors in the governing process. Those areas that have highly developed civic capital have greater levels of cooperation and collaboration.[19]

Elements that facilitate or serve as barriers to collaborative partnerships are the costs and benefits and how they are distributed across partners. If there is a fairly even distribution of benefits, there is a greater willingness to develop partnerships. Municipalities faced with high costs and vague benefits will not readily cooperate. Low costs and readily recognizable benefits, such as joint marketing, are more susceptible to the development of a cooperative effort. The size of the region also makes a difference in the intensity and extent of the involvement of nongovernmental actors in regional collaborative efforts. Nelles found in her studies that smaller regions result in fewer actors and networks. In smaller regions actors tend to be more familiar with each other and fewer actors and networks reduce barriers to coordination and communication. Thus, civic actors are able to more easily establish and facilitate cooperation and collaboration among governments and nongovernment actors.[20] It might be that size is less important as a barrier than the leadership and the organization of the civic sector. A strong leader committed to involvement in regional issues with substantial influence over major businesses in the region should be able to facilitate highly effective collaborative efforts. With strong civic leadership, size of the region would be an advantage as more resources in the civic community would be available in larger regions than in smaller regions.

Another barrier to cooperation among governments is the relative size of the dominant city in the region and the history of its relationships with the surrounding municipalities. Most metropolitan areas have a large center city that not only dominates the region but in the past has made efforts to annex or bully surrounding urban areas. As has been discussed in previous chapters, these are substantial barriers to overcome to form cooperative endeavors. Smaller suburban governments approach any cooperative endeavor with the central city as the junior partner. The central city and its dominance loom over any regional cooperative effort.

The bottom line from this study of regional approaches to governance is:

• Institutional arrangements have a major impact on regional governance. More decentralized regions require greater effort to address regional policy issues than centralized areas. When the region has a large number of independent local governments, obtaining consensus to pursue a particular regional policy is more difficult than with a smaller number of local governments. However, even one local government, regardless of the fragmentation in the area, can thwart a unified policy approach. The best case scenario for a unified regional approach is to have one government with authority over the area. However, the one regional government approach has its own problems of bureaucracy and remoteness. Moreover, it is not an option in most metropolitan areas.

• Along with institutional arrangements, the authority and independence of local government matter. A metropolitan area with independent, autonomous local governments that control the use of land within their borders, will make it much more difficult to engage in regional governance than an area where the local governments are less independent. Autonomous local governments with a history of independence are less likely to willingly give up any of their prerogatives to a regional governing arrangement than governments that are less independent.

• As indicated above, size and diversity of population make a difference in developing regional governance. Size and diversity introduce complexity and make it more difficult to come to consensus on regional governance issues. A more homogenous and smaller population will more readily agree on regional governing policies.

• It is an understatement that civic capital matters. Regions that have more developed civic capacity tend to be able to bring more resources to the table and surmount difficult issues. The stakeholders in an area with a strong civic capital environment will be more trusting of each other, because they will have generally worked together in other civic organizations. The civic sector is also a more neutral place where government and nongovernmental leaders can come together to discuss public policy issues that extend beyond political borders. With no overarching government, the civic organization can serve as the vehicle to bring the various stakeholders together where all participants can be treated as equals.

• Cultural traditions and history matter. Those areas with a culture and tradition of cooperation and collaboration that have been built up over the years will be able to capitalize on this culture and tradition in developing regional governance solutions. Areas without this culture will find it more difficult to develop collaborative governance. Moreover, areas with a history of cooperation and collaboration will be able to move into the more controversial social issues that plague regions.

• The role of the central city and the extent of its economic and population dominance over the area also make a difference. If the central city has a history of efforts to annex surrounding territory or bully and ignor the suburbs, the suburbs will be wary of the city and less likely to accept its leadership in any regional governance initiative. The central city and its dominance loom over any regional cooperative effort. It is also clear that effective regional governance cannot occur without the involvement of the central city.

• Leadership matters. There needs to be committed leadership to regional governance from the public and the private sectors. They need to be supportive of regional governance on a continuing basis. They need to be willing to lend their prestige and resources to facilitating and brokering regional governance solutions.

Finally, to reiterate what has been indicated a number of times in this study, there is clearly no one regional governance model that fits all situations. Each individual metropolitan area has its own regional policy issues that must addressed in its own way. However, there are a few imperatives metropolitan areas across the world are facing. One is increasing pressures for economic development. Another is the increased competition from other metropolitan areas in a global economy. In responding to these pressures, it is becoming clear that local governments in metropolitan areas, in order to compete, must move beyond their political boundaries which tend to isolate them and govern more from a regional scale.

Regionalists argue that the fragmented local government structure has not proven capable of rising to the challenge of effectively solving problems. These advocates maintain that if metropolitan areas are to be governable, providing opportunities for all to be economically independent and enjoy a minimally acceptable quality of life, there must be a realization that the region and its residents are interdependent. Regionalists contend that the rich communities can no longer continue to remain separated from the problems facing the metropolitan area as a whole. Residents can no longer isolate themselves from the problems of the region. Gated communities, a symbol of separation, will not solve the problems of the region. The residents of the region must come together in collective action. The region must present a united front to maximize its influence in obtaining resources, compete on the national and international stage for economic development, and obtain favorable legislation from federal and state governments. Competing for economic growth must become a regional collaborative and cooperative effort. The big cities can no longer ignore the suburbs, and the suburbs cannot continue to ignore the problems of the central cities. The problems of metropolitan areas today are not just problems in the central city but are problems that affect the entire area. Benign neglect is not the answer to metropolitan problems; mobilizing public and private resources through regional governance systems is.

Notes

1. Robert D. Yaro and Tony Hiss, *A Region at Risk: The Third Regional Plan for the New York-New Jersey-Connecticut Metropolitan Area* (Washington, DC: Island Press, 1996), p. 210.
2. This approach is also being advocated by a number of observers and researchers. See for example, Robert E. Lang and Arthur C. Nelson, "Megapolitan America. The Design Observer Group," http://places.designnobserver.com [Accessed Nov. 14, 2011].
3. Ibid.
4. Ibid
5. William R. Barnes, "Governing Cities in the Coming Decade: The Democratic and Regional Disconnects," *Public Administration Review*, 70, (special issue) (2010): s138–139.
6. Mildred E. Warner, "The Future of Local Government: Twenty-First Century Challenges," *Public Administration Review*, 70 (special issue) (2010): s145–147.
7. William R. Dodge, "Practitioner's Perspective–Regional Charters: The Future of Local Government," *Public Administration Review*, 70 (special issue) (2010): s148–150.
8. J. H. Logie, "Think Regionally, Act Locally," *Community News and Views* (Grand Rapids: Center For Urban Affairs Michigan State University, 2002), 14 (2).
9. Max Fisher, "Why Does Abu Dhabi Own all of Chicago's Parking Meters? *Atlantic Wire*, October 19, 2010, http://www.theatlanticwire.com/business/2010/10/why-does-abu-dhabi-own-all-of-chicago-s-parking-meters/18627 [Accessed Jan. 24, 2013].
10. David Rusk, *Cities without Suburbs: A Census 2010 Perspective,* 4th ed. (Washington, DC: Woodrow Wilson Center Press, 2013), particularly chap. 3. Most regionalists agree with Rusk that some form of area-wide land use powers is critical to the success of a regional governance system. See, for example, Anthony Downs, *New Visions for Metropolitan America* (Washington, DC: Brookings Institution, 1994); Neal R. Peirce, *Citistates: How Urban America Can Prosper in a Competitive World* (Washington, DC: Seven Locks Press, 1993), particularly pp. 308–310.
11. Peter Salins, "Metropolitan Areas: Cities, Suburbs, and the Ties That Bind," in Henry G. Cisneros, (ed.), *Interwoven Destinies* (New York: W. W. Norton, 1993), pp. 164–166.
12. One unsuccessful effort to create a multipurpose regional agency in the San Francisco area never made it through the state legislature because the bill's

sponsor would not accept a referendum requirement. Stanley Scott and Victor Jones, "Foreword," in C. James Owen and York Willbern, *Governing Metropolitan Indianapolis: The Politics of Unigov* (Berkeley and Los Angeles, CA: University of California Press, 1985), pp. xx-xv.

13. Myron Orfield, *Metro Politics: A Regional Agenda for Community and Stability* (Washington, DC and Cambridge, MA: Brookings Institution and Lincoln Institute of Land Policy, 1997), pp. 156–172.
14. Christopher Leo, "Regional Growth Management Regime: The Case of Portland, Oregon," paper in possession of the author, n. d.
15. "Regionalism the Right Way to Solve Problems," editorial, *Chicago Sun Times*, Jan. 13, 1997.
16. Edwin Eisendraft, "Voice of the People," *Chicago Tribune*, Sept. 20, 1997, sec. 1, p. 18. Eisendraft is regional director of the U.S. Department of Housing and Urban Development.
17. Rusk, *Cities without Suburbs*, p. 124.
18. Jen Nelles, *Comparative Metropolitan Policy: Governing Beyond Local Boundaries in the Imagined Metropolis* (New York: Routledge, 2012), p. 167.
19. Ibid., pp. 168–169.
20. Ibid., pp. 171–172.

Index

Page locators in **bold** refer to figures and tables.